Pelican Books
Political Change in Britain

David Butler is a Fellow of Nuffield College, Oxford.
He has been associated with all the Nuffield general
election studies and is the author or co-author of all
of them since 1951. His other books include
British Political Facts, 1900–1968 (with Jennie
Freeman), *The Electoral System in Britain Since 1918*,
and *The Study of Political Behaviour*. He is a frequent
contributor to the *Sunday Times* and to B.B.C.
television and sound programmes on political and
electoral subjects.

Donald Stokes is Chairman of the Department of
Science and Program Director in the Survey
Research Center, University of Michigan. He is
co-author of *The American Voter* and *Elections and
Political Order* and is engaged in a series of
comparative studies of electoral behaviour and
representative institutions in the English-speaking
world.

David Butler and Donald Stokes

Political Change in Britain

Forces Shaping Electoral Choice

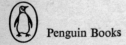 Penguin Books

Penguin Books Ltd, Harmondsworth,
Middlesex, England
Penguin Books Australia Ltd, Ringwood,
Victoria, Australia

First published by Macmillan 1969
Published in Pelican Books 1971

Copyright © David Butler and Donald Stokes, 1969

Made and printed in Great Britain by
Cox & Wyman Ltd,
London, Reading and Fakenham
Set in Monotype Times

Contents

Preface

Two authors appear on the title-page of this book and we bear sole responsibility for its contents. But we could not have begun to produce it without the assistance of many people and institutions. We are indebted first and foremost to the Warden and Fellows of Nuffield College, Oxford, and to the Survey Research Center and the Department of Political Science of the University of Michigan. Nuffield College not only found the bulk of the funds for the British field work but provided a home for the enterprise and encouragement throughout its long course. The University of Michigan forgave one author his protracted absence waiting for the 1964 British election to take place, and the Survey Research Center supplied the facilities for analysing the data as well as the roof under which the bulk of the book was written. Many other institutions contributed in different ways to our undertaking. In addition to Nuffield College, funds for our research came from the Nuffield Foundation, the Rockefeller Foundation, the John Simon Guggenheim Foundation and the National Science Foundation. We are very grateful to the British Market Research Bureau for the way in which they carried out our exacting fieldwork requirements, and in particular to Timothy Joyce and Charles Channon. We should also like to thank Mrs Wise of the Tabulating Research Center, and the staff of the Atlas Computing Laboratory, especially Paul Nelson. Our interviews were coded with great zeal and efficiency by various helpers in Oxford.

A devoted band of helpers worked at one period or another full-time on this enterprise and we must express our very deep gratitude to Don Aitkin, Ann Bishop, Martha Ion, Michael Kahan, Thomas Mann, Ron May, Virginia Nye, Douglas Scott, Margaret Squires,

Arthur Stevens, Margaret Thomas, Phyllis Thorburn and Robert Travis.

We want to make special mention of our obligation to Robert Putnam for his singular contribution to our trade union chapter and to Ralph Brookes, Angus Campbell, Philip Converse and Warren Miller for their intellectual stimulus and their penetrating and exact reading of our text. We must reserve a pantheon for Anthony King who laboured through four successive drafts of our manuscript, offering searching but always constructive criticisms.

We wish to thank Leslie Kish and Percy Gray for their kind advice on sample design and Irene Hess and Thomas Tharackan for organizing the computation of our sampling errors.

The Gallup Poll, National Opinion Polls and the Opinion Research Centre were most generous in allowing us to see and quote their findings, and Paul Duncan-Jones was indefatigable in helping us to analyse a vast body of N.O.P. data.

Others whom we should thank for their diverse and often very substantial help and criticism include:

Mark Abrams	Louis Moss
Paul Abramson	Stella Moyser
Michael Adler	Keith Ovenden
George Anderson	Michael Pinto-Duschinsky
George Bain	Peter Pulzer
Brian Barry	Graham Pyatt
Jay Blumler	Don Rawson
Susan Brooks	David Robertson
Ronald Butt	Garry Runciman
Richard Crossman	Patricia Ryan
David Deans	Michael Steed
James Douglas	Leigh Stelzer
Henry Durant	Humphrey Taylor
Sir Michael Fraser	Frank Teer
Peter Hyett	Nigel Walker
Gudmund Iversen	William Wallace
Austin Mitchell	Philip Williams

We should also thank those forbearing British citizens whose answers in thousands of hours of interviews made possible this book.

Our greatest debt, however, is to our wives and to our children for five years of long-suffering support as they endured the repeated separation and uprooting that transatlantic collaboration involves.

We have brought together in the Appendix a variety of materials that describe the technical details of the research. The reader may find there an account of the sample design, the rates of response achieved with our several samples, the sampling errors that are appropriate to our sample design and the texts of the questionnaires we used for our interviews in 1963, 1964 and 1966. We have interspersed in the texts of these questionnaires the percentage distributions of replies to almost all the questions which are of 'closed' form.

We have relied on the presence of these percentage distributions in the Appendix to simplify the empirical matter of the main text in one important respect. In many cases we have omitted a description of the sub-sample sizes from our tables when these can be reconstructed from a knowledge of the total sample and of the distribution of responses given in the texts of the questionnaires in the Appendix. We have also omitted frequencies from the tables for the sake of clarity of exposition whenever a frequency is approximately the same as the total sample size.

The authors of a book of this sort are faced by the problem of multiple audiences. We have written with a view to the interests of readers both inside the universities and out, both in Britain and elsewhere, both professionally concerned with politics and not. We have no illusions that we shall satisfy them all. Some readers will find the book needlessly abstract; others will wish that there could have been more theoretical modelling. Some will find the book too heavily quantitative; others will be impatient because we have reduced so much to prose or contingency tables, reserving to footnotes the more elaborate statistical models that underlie various of our findings. Some will find the book too remote from the day-to-day politics of Britain; others will sigh for a more general and comparative framework. From all these readers we invite a degree of sympathy for a dilemma that has been with us through all the successive drafts of these pages.

February 1969

DAVID BUTLER
DONALD STOKES

Preface to the Penguin Edition

The original text has been preserved virtually intact for this edition. There has been no attempt at up-dating and the only changes involve the correction of a small number of misprints in the original edition.

May 1971

Introduction

1 Approaches to Change

The possibility of rulers being constitutionally driven from office in a free election is relatively new in the history of government. The voters who now hold this power in the liberal democracies can, of course, exercise it only by selecting between alternatives that have been defined by competing leaders or groups. In Britain it is the political parties that provide the focus of choice. Indeed, in the longer historical view, parties antedate the mass electorate since it was they who enfranchised the voters and mobilized their support. But the public is not the creature of the parties, and the ebbs and flows of popular favour affect, often in quite unexpected ways, the whole conduct of British government.

The unpredictable quality of electoral change emphasizes the complexity of its sources. When the lives of governments were decided purely within the Houses of Parliament, those who sought power could well understand the motives and forces upon which its transfer depended. But when the ultimate decision moved outwards to thousands of polling stations across the country, these forces became vastly more complex and difficult to fathom. More than one government in recent years has felt its support in the country ebbing away without warning. Indeed, these rises and falls of party strength are often incomprehensible both to those whose fortunes most plainly depend upon them and to those whose profession it is to explain them.

This is a book about such changes. We shall look behind the fluctuations of party support in the early 1960s and the half-century before, exploring their sources in a systematic way. Since the sources are many, any systematic analysis must deal with a wide variety of phenomena; we have deliberately foregone the theoretical and empirical neatness that could be achieved by confining our view to the interplay of a few key factors. The full series of British election results reflects the overlay of a number of distinct processes of change, just as the single groove of a recording disc represents the overlay of the many instruments in a symphony orchestra. Any analysis of change must distinguish and treat separately its various components.

Types of Change

We shall find it convenient to think of the processes of change as being of three fundamental kinds. The first of these are changes which involve the physical replacement of the electorate. Even in a few short years, some millions of electors die and others come of age; the longer our historical view the greater the extent of the replacement. Of course immigration and emigration also yield some turnover in the electorate, as do many changes in the legal requirements for the franchise. But the effects of these in recent years have been small by contrast with the inexorable processes of birth and maturation on the one hand and of aging and death on the other.[1]

The importance of this sort of change is obvious. In any era the young will be unlike the old in many of their attitudes, and some of these differences will extend to politics. Therefore, replacing one with the other will alter the political complexion of the electorate a little every year; over time these effects will be cumulative. A man of seventy-five who died after voting in 1959 once had to choose between the competing claims of Asquith and Balfour. But a man who first became entitled to vote in 1964 was not born until the Second World War. The transition from the Macmillan triumph of 1959 to the Wilson victory of 1964 was in some part the result of the replacement of the first type of elector by the second. And if we consider the transition from Baldwin to Wilson the role played by the electorate's physical renewal must be far more extensive.

A second type of change is that which involves the electorate's

1. The coming of votes at 18 in 1970 is by far the largest change since 1928 when the franchise was finally granted to all women.

enduring party alignments. Support comes to any party for the most astonishing variety of reasons. But some of these will be general enough and enduring enough to be considered as bases of party alignment. Since the rise of the Labour Party the foremost of these in Britain has been social class. But other cleavages have cut across the electorate in modern times. During the years of Conservative–Liberal rivalry the issue of Home Rule produced one lasting realignment of party strength while the conflict of church and chapel provided another basis of enduring political cleavage. Furthermore, the role of social class itself has altered a good deal with the passage of time.

There is a very close connection between the renewal of the electorate and changes of party alignment. As we shall see, once an elector has acquired an allegiance to party he is unlikely again to be so open to political conversion. Therefore, he will be less responsive than a younger and previously unaligned elector when any new grounds of party cleavage develop. As a result the renewal of the electorate may have to proceed for many years before a changing alignment is fully reflected in party support. We shall in fact argue that such an evolutionary process has applied to the relationship between social class and party alignments.

The third type of change is that which involves the electors' response to the immediate issues and events of politics. Although, as we shall show, such stimuli have a greater effect on younger voters, the rise and fall of party strength between general elections – and even more the fluctuations expressed in local and by-elections and in the regular opinion polls – cannot mainly be due to the physical replacement of the electorate. These changes are due rather to the variability of behaviour among people who remain in the electorate. Most changes of this kind do not presage a lasting shift of party alignment. A hard budget, an unpopular prime minister, a severe winter, a sense that the Government has grown tired in power – influences such as these are overlaid on the more enduring bases of party strength and produce the fluctuations which are displayed in the many indicators of the state of the parties, including general elections. The ease with which these more ephemeral influences deflect the party balance depends on how deeply the more basic cleavages cut through the electorate. We shall develop this point as we interpret the increased volatility of the electorate in the 1960s. But these immediate and short-run influences must be clearly separated from changes in the country's lasting partisan alignments.

The distinctions among these types of change have helped to give structure to this book, as will be apparent shortly when we give a sketch of its contents. But these differences also call attention to other distinctions which are fundamental to our work. None of these is of greater importance than the difference between viewing change from the standpoint of the individual elector and from the standpoint of the full electorate or of the political system.

Elector and Electorate

A duality of focus between the individual elector on the one hand, and the full electorate of which he is part on the other runs throughout this book. We give sustained attention to the individual citizen, to the place of politics in his everyday world, to his changing political responses as he ages, to the imagery by which he interprets the link between politics and social class, to the conditions which make him accessible to the influence of political issues, and to his views of the political parties and their place in a party system. If we are to fathom the sources of electoral change we must learn a good deal about each of these things.

Yet the whole of electoral analysis must not be focused on the individual citizen. The reasons for his behaviour often lie in a wider political or social milieu. Moreover, the consequences of individual change can be known only by aggregating the behaviour of individual electors to see what is true of the electorate as a whole. Electoral analysis demands both the reduction or disaggregation of mass phenomena to individual terms and also the aggregation of individual phenomena to explore effects in the full electorate. Both of these intellectual processes are essential to almost every one of the chapters that follow.

The need for disaggregation or analytic reduction is heightened by the fact that so much of our electoral data comes in aggregated form. Public officials conscientiously count the votes to determine what constitutes the collective choice of the electorate. But in Britain the regulations governing the secret ballot prevent these results from being disaggregated in the official or unofficial returns. Because voting papers are shuffled together on a constituency-wide basis before they are counted, the smallest units for which general election figures are available contain on average 60,000 electors.

Constituency totals for turnout and party preference do hold many keys to understanding what is in the individual voter's mind. For example, the remarkable uniformity of swings in party support across all constituencies offer persuasive evidence of the importance of national political issues and events as opposed to more local influences on the choice of the individual elector.[2] Constituency figures also provide useful clues to the nature of regional variations, the effect of the presence of a third party and similar questions.

Yet there will always be barriers to our discerning individual changes from statistics of this kind. We may deduce from the uniformity of swings that voters respond more to national issues and leaders than to local factors. But their uniformity tells us nothing about which issues have been in the voter's mind and what their effect has been. This is of course the principal justification for the use of interview methods in electoral studies. The sample survey provides an additional tool for those who feel, with Namier, that they 'must search for such evidence as they can find of the roots of human behaviour'.

We have no illusions that our efforts at analytic reduction have met with full success. In many cases we shall at the most have clarified what needs to be known. Critics of voting studies, particularly those based on surveys, sometimes seem to assume that the investigators suppose that their methods are omnicompetent, offering a key to all mysteries. Nothing could be farther from our view.

2. For a discussion of the paradoxical sense in which the uniformity of party swings argues *against* a full nationalization of electoral forces the reader may, however, consult Chapter 13.

Perhaps we can help to make clear our position with a flight of fancy. Suppose there existed a body of information about the views and attitudes of the British electorate in the 1860s comparable to that which we have collected for the 1960s. Surely no one would question that such materials would be a priceless boon to any historian analysing electoral politics at the beginning of the Gladstone–Disraeli era. But equally no one would suggest that such data would explain all aspects of electoral change in the period. Indeed, if the survey's design had been limited by what could then have been known about the evolution of British society and politics, it would certainly have overlooked factors that have emerged as important only in the perspective of time. None the less, with all its limitations, such a cache of materials could not help but modify historical interpretations of the 1860s.

The Electorate and Political Leaders

We must equally avoid focusing the whole of electoral analysis on the electorate itself. The changes of party support that result from summing individual preferences at successive elections depend in the most immediate sense on attitudes and beliefs that the electorate has carried to the polling-station. We must give sustained attention to these social-psychological factors in individual preference if we are to understand electoral change. In view of the difficulty of knowing in detail the attitudes and beliefs of a mass citizenry, it is not surprising that electoral research should expend its major empirical effort in penetrating the voters' minds. But the sources of electoral change are to be found in the electorate itself only in the most proximate sense. If we are to develop a comprehensive account of change we must look beyond the electorate to its environment; beyond the immediate social-psychological factors in the electorate's 'response' to the changing 'stimuli' to which the electorate is successively exposed. For example, the economic motives that are so prominent in the electorate's behaviour are not free creations of the voters' minds. They depend on actual experiences of being out of work or on short time, of receiving a rise in wages, of having to pay more in the market place – factors which can often be summed up for the country as a whole by various macro-economic indicators, such as the unemployment rate or the cost of living index. To understand the relationship between these economic inputs and the outputs of party support we must examine individual perceptions and attitudes: does the voter think his condition has improved or worsened under the present Government? does he think it would change under a new Government? and so on. These introduce considerable slippage into the relationship of economic indicators to party support, as we shall see. But our account of economic influences would be limited indeed if we were to confine our attention solely to what is in the voters' minds and fail to consider the objective economic context of perceptions and behaviour, including the efforts of the Government to manipulate the economy for electoral reasons and to time elections for economic reasons.

An immensely important element of the environment in which the electorate behaves is of course provided by the parties and leaders who seek the public's support. So important are the parties in giving meaning to contests in the individual parliamentary constituencies in Britain that for many voters candidates have no identity other than their partisan one. Any developed analysis of electoral change must therefore take account of the behaviour of parties and leaders as well as of the electorate itself. Of course it is also true that the electorate is an exceedingly salient element of the environment in which political leaders behave; the past or the expected behaviour of voters is at the bottom of much of what governments and parties do or say, as they appeal for the public's support. Indeed, an interplay of élites and mass is so obviously at the heart of the electoral process that it must be central to any analysis of electoral change.

This is true not only of changes in response to immediate issues and events but also to those involving basic realignments of party strength. A modern example of the decisive importance that events at a level of *haute politique* can have for changes of mass alignments is the emergence of social class as the dominant line of electoral cleavage in Britain. As in many other countries of Western Europe, the enfranchisement of the industrial working class in Britain created circumstances favourable to the rise of a working class party and a greater polarization of electoral alignments along class lines. Yet it is impossible to account for this development in Britain without giving full weight to the events at an élite level which helped establish Labour as one of the leading parties. Were it not for the First World War and the resulting split between the Lloyd George and Asquithian Liberals, electoral alignments today might owe rather less to class, and rather more to those religious cleavages which had previously been so important in determining party support.

The interplay of élite and mass in electoral realignments is plain when there is a displacement of parties, but it may be of equal importance when the identity of the leading parties remains unchanged. This viewpoint is sometimes neglected in American commentaries which have sought to identify the 'critical elections' that have brought lasting shifts of Republican and Democratic strength. An election may of course be called 'critical' in the wholly descriptive sense of marking the appearance of a new pattern of support that persisted in subsequent elections.[3] But such elections have sometimes been seen as those in which there is an abrupt and profound change of the electorate's loyalties, establishing a new pattern of partisan dispositions sufficiently stable to endure irrespective of the changing conditions of future elections. Such a view almost certainly understates the importance of the choices and appeals subsequently presented to the electorate in deciding whether a new electoral pattern is to survive. If the issues and leaders that evoked the pattern persist in future elections, the pattern will tend to persist. If they do not, it may prove highly transient. One may at least imagine the Democratic Party, having suffered the disaster of 1896, retreating from Bryan's leadership and program as rapidly as the Republican Party, having suffered the disaster of 1964, retreated from Goldwater's leadership and program.[4] Under these circumstances the sectional

---

3. The late V. O. Key, who originated this term, used it almost wholly descriptively. See 'A Theory of Critical Elections', *Journal of Politics*, **17** (1955), pp. 3–18.

4. The election of 1964 indeed exhibited a sectional pattern of alignment

realignment of the 1890s might not have survived into the new century, and 1896 might not have come to be seen as a 'critical' election at all. Similarly, one may at least imagine the split among the British Liberals having been healed by the middle twenties and Labour having been overtaken by sufficient troubles for it to accept once again a subordinate role within a Lib–Lab coalition. Under these circumstances the trend towards the alignment of party support by class might have been retarded or even reversed.

To regard realignments of party strength as resulting from the survival of élite appeals does not involve any challenge to the importance of those processes within the electorate itself which conserve past displacements of party support. If the 'primary' issues that alter electoral alignments are allowed time to operate, their immediate effects will be conserved or even amplified by a number of 'secondary' processes within the electorate. Some of these are internal to the voter himself. The longer an individual holds to a new position, the more likely he is to develop a view of politics that makes it difficult to shift back; the working man who switches to the Conservatives as the party more likely to bring prosperity may well revise his hitherto unfavourable opinions of other aspects of the party. Some 'secondary' processes have to do with the formation of political attitudes in the family and other face-to-face groups. Indeed, the recruitment of children (and their children in turn) into their parents' party can maintain an electoral alignment long after its 'primary' issues have spent their force. In later chapters we shall speak of the 'age' of an existing alignment in terms of whether it rests more on 'primary' or such 'secondary' forces.

What we have said about transient displacements of the party balance implies that short-run changes of party strength must also be seen in terms of the interaction of parties and leaders with the electorate. This focus on interaction is explicit in much of the recent theorizing about competitive party systems. For example, the interactional models of Downs and others can equally be

hauntingly like that of 1896, although the roles of the parties had been completely reversed. See W. D. Burnham, 'American Voting Behavior and the 1964 Election', *Midwest Journal of Political Science*, **12** (1968), 1–40.

interpreted as theories of the behaviour of electors or as theories of the behaviour of the political leaders who seek their support.[5] Such a perspective will be an essential element of the treatment we give the issues and leader images that altered the strength of the Conservative and Labour Parties during the period of our studies. Although we have spent more effort on the behaviour of electors, our analysis deals at a number of points with the nature of the appeals and issues that confronted them.

The Context of Research

This is a book about the changing strength of British parties, and our work is bounded in a variety of ways by the politics of Britain. The class basis of party choice, the influence of trade unions, the role of the partisan national press, the place of the Liberal Party – all of these are given extensive treatment because of their import- ance in the British party system. In this book we are primarily concerned with features specific to one period in one country's political history.

Yet, in origin and intention, our work is not narrowly British. The analytic frameworks that we use draw heavily on earlier investigations in America and the continent of Europe. And, in the case of some of our findings, we have been helped in choosing between conflicting interpretations of British data by findings from other nations. This is true, for example, of the interpretation we give to the strengthening of party allegiance with age.

Moreover, our findings from Britain throw light on problems affecting other party systems – indeed on democratic politics as a whole. From classical times those seeking a systematic under- standing of politics have been obliged to sift the varieties of politi- cal experience found in the actual world. In this spirit the contrasts between electoral behaviour in Britain and elsewhere may be

5. See, for example, A. Downs, *An Economic Theory of Democracy*, New York, 1957, pp. 114–41; G. Tullock, *Toward a Mathematics of Politics*, Ann Arbor, 1967, 50–61; and O. Davis and M. Hinich, 'A Mathematical Model of Policy Formation in a Democratic Society', in J. L. Bernd, ed., *Mathe-matical Applications in Political Science, II*, Dallas, 1966, pp. 175–208.

searched for clues to the effects of specific features of the institutional or cultural context of mass behaviour. One of our later chapters will, for example, test whether the familiar ideological framework of left and right has any reality in popular thought about politics in Britain; one element of this test depends on the presence of a third British party, in contrast to the relatively pure two-party system of America: both countries have broadly-based major parties whose ideological differences are certainly less than those of left and right in European multi-party systems. Yet Britain's mild departure from a strict two-party condition extends our ability to prove the nature and sources of ideological patterns of thought.

The area of our research has limits in time as well as space. The fact that the primary data on which this book is based were collected between 1963 and 1966 inevitably gives our work a temporal context. We have consulted election returns and other evidence pertaining to a much longer interval of time, indeed the whole of this century. And we have relied on our respondents' memories to recall information about the past, as, for example, the class, partisan and religious identifications of their parents when they themselves were young. Moreover, from what we know of the present we shall offer some conditional judgements as to the future, such as the likely effects of selective mortality on the relative strength of the parties as the cohorts making up the present electorate continue to age. But our investigations are inevitably anchored in the detailed evidence from a specific three-year period.

It is not a simple matter to say what limitations these temporal bounds have imposed on our findings. We feel most keenly the constraints due to one of the parties having held a preponderant lead during most of three years; although party fortunes fluctuated, the period was one of exceptional Labour strength. The difficulty this puts in the way of analysis is not exactly that of a Labour 'bias', although allowances must certainly be made for the very pro-Labour readings of many of our measures of the country's mood and allegiance. The difficulty lies more in the limited extent of the changes we are able to analyse. There was more change in this period than might at first be evident. Party support was astonishingly fluid at an individual level, as we shall see. And the party tide changed direction at least twice during our studies. But our findings would be clearer on a number of points if this work could be extended over a period in which the balance of party strength swung sharply against Labour.

The need to observe variation applies to causes as well as consequences. We can assess the importance of potential factors in electoral change only if they exhibit variation. For example, the importance of rising standards of living for class and political identifications can be assessed only if some fraction of electors experiences such a change of living style while others do not. The fraction that will have done so in a brief interval will be small. Our own findings in this area, although suggestive, are necessarily limited by the negligible incidence of fairly fundamental changes of standards of living among the electors whose attitudes and behaviour we observed.

As the temporal context of such research widens these difficulties become less troublesome. The varied circumstances of succeeding periods can give a surer understanding of the importance of various factors in electoral change. The number of elections and of distinct periods of change must always remain small, and the limits of the evidence received from the unfolding of political history sets bounds to the discovery and testing of hypotheses. But these bounds will be less severe as the temporal span of our observations lengthens.

Traditions of Electoral Research

Consideration of what goes on in the voter's mind is as old as democracy – did not Aristides learn that electors can be repelled by those whom they see as upright in excess? In Britain the traditional wisdom of candidates and agents has been passed down from election to election, leaving a remarkable accumulation of folklore on what makes effective campaigning. But the systematic study of elections and electioneering has a relatively brief history.

André Siegfried in 1913 began a pioneer exploration of the correlations between voting returns and census data in various parts of France. Were it not for the requirement in Britain that votes be counted on a constituency-wide basis, a legacy of the electoral reforms of the late nineteenth century, we might have looked forward to a number of studies which examined election returns by ward or polling station or other electoral unit. The requirement that ballots be brought to a central place within a constituency and physically shuffled has necessarily limited any such approach, at least at the parliamentary level.[6]

The coming of opinion polls from America in the late 1930s opened up new horizons. All students of politics are indebted to the Gallup organization and its rivals for a large body of data on the way in which sexes, classes and age groups have divided their support between the parties. By their repeated surveys, they provide time series of political soundings which make it possible to pinpoint the moments of substantial political change. The polls have also, with gradually increasing sophistication, reported on public attitudes to the most salient political issues and on the extent of mass exposure to the various means of information and persuasion; they have provided the political parties with the tools of market research – although, in Britain at least, these have been used only slowly and tentatively.[7]

The polls in Britain may now have assumed a political importance greater than in their country of origin – largely because British elections have no fixed dates. The Government is able, with these improved barometers of party strength, to exploit the country's mood to party advantage; a prime minister's power to choose when to go to the country has become an increasingly important asset to the incumbent party thanks to Keynesian management of the economy, or at least to improved forecasting of economic trends. As opinion polls built up a record of accuracy

6. See A. J. Allen, *The English Voter*, London, 1964, for the most ambitious attempt in this direction. Local elections offer a promising field for applying such techniques since wards are often small enough to offer real scope for correlations between census and voting data.

7. See R. Rose, *Influencing Voters*, London, 1967; see also D. E. Butler and A. King, *The British General Election of 1964*, London, 1965, pp. 66–71, 91, 98, and *The British General Election of 1966*, pp. 33, 66–9.

in predicting election results during the 1950s, their influence on the political community grew. They now play a predominant part in all speculation about the date and outcome of the next election, and they contribute greatly to the morale and authority of both Government and Opposition.

A number of academic studies have made use of and refined the pollsters' techniques. Professor Lazarsfeld's 1940 work in Erie County, Ohio,[8] has served as a model for three of the leading British explorations of voting behaviour;[9] each of these attempted to trace the influence of the various efforts at persuasion and to isolate the types of people who wavered or switched by interviewing a cross-section of electors more than once during and after the campaign. Although these studies offered many valuable insights into what happens in an election, they were not as rewarding as might have been hoped, simply because so few people appear to have been influenced by the campaign.[10]

But there is another limitation to these initial British voting studies, important though they were. Their approach, like that of the pollsters, tended to be confined by established sociological categories; they sought to find relationships between voting behaviour and class or sex or age or newspaper readership. But they did not go very far in exploring the reasons for these relationships or for the exceptions to them. Why have a preponderance of young

8. P. F. Lazarsfeld, B. Berelson and H. Gaudet, *The People's Choice*, New York, 1944. See also its sequel, B. Berelson, P. F. Lazarsfeld and W. McPhee, *Voting*, Chicago, 1954.

9. M. Benney, R. H. Pear and A. P. Gray, *How People Vote*, London, 1956, a study of the Greenwich constituency in 1950; R. S. Milne and H. C. Mackenzie, *Straight Fight*, London, 1954, and R. S. Milne and H. C. Mackenzie, *Marginal Seat*, London, 1958, studies of the North-East Bristol constituency in 1951 and 1955.

10. See J. Trenaman and D. McQuail, *Television and the Political Image*, London, 1961. This followed in the series of constituency studies using a panel approach. It is based on 1959 surveys in two constituencies in the Leeds area. It failed to find any marked switches in vote or attitude during the weeks of the campaign, whether or not the electors were watching television. However, a sequel, J. Blumler and D. McQuail, *Television in Politics*, London, 1968, did find that in the same constituencies in 1964 exposure to television was associated with a marked rise in Liberal support.

people voted Labour? Why have women been more Conservative than men? What has been the basis of working class Conservatism? In the pioneer studies, the intellectual and emotional processes that link attributes to attitudes were not pursued very far.[11] The literature has been particularly unsatisfying on the question of class, the characteristic most often cited in explanations of partisanship: social class has been variously and loosely defined, while its adequacy as an explanatory formula has been left unquestioned.

Furthermore, localized election studies – perhaps more clearly in Britain than in America – have tended to get divorced from the mainstream of politics; they can too easily become exercises in sociological measurement, neglecting both the relationship between local and national behaviour and the place of the election in a historical context, as well as the working of the political system.

The distinctively British contribution to election studies was pioneered by R. B. McCallum in 1945. As a historian he sought to gather together all available information about one election campaign as it occurred and to present a record that would help future historians. He and his successors in the Nuffield series of general election studies have tried to describe and analyse the issues of each contest; the way in which these were presented by the party leaders and by the mass media; the organizational efforts of the parties, nationally and locally; and the outcome, in all its statistical detail.[12]

But the authors of the Nuffield studies have become increasingly aware of the limits of their approach. Although the formal election

11. Some new trends are developing. In general terms R. Rose, *Politics in England*, London, 1965, and in a specific field R. T. McKenzie and A. Silver, *Angels in Marble*, London, 1968, represent a new approach to the underlying explanations of electoral behaviour. See also G. Runciman, *Relative Deprivation and Social Justice*, London and Berkeley, 1966.

12. R. B. McCallum and A. Readman, *The British General Election of 1945*, Oxford, 1947; H. G. Nicholas, *The British General Election of 1950*, London, 1951; D. E. Butler, *The British General Election of 1951*, London, 1952; D. E. Butler, *The British General Election of 1955*, London, 1955; D. E. Butler and R. Rose, *The British General Election of 1959*, London, 1960; D. E. Butler and A. King, *The British General Election of 1964*, London, 1965; and D. E. Butler and A. King, *The British General Election of 1966*, London, 1966.

campaign has a dramatic unity, compressing into a few weeks a debate over the past and future of British politics, it makes only a limited contribution to deciding the outcome of the contest. A national history of an election, like a constituency voter study, will offer very meagre explanations of the electorate's behaviour if it concentrates on the events of a mere three weeks. Each successive Nuffield study has therefore devoted more and more space to the events of the previous Parliament and to broad economic and social changes.

But it is not only in a temporal way that the Nuffield studies have needed expansion. They have, as the authors fully recognized, suffered from two great gaps – at the level of *haute politique* and at the level of mass behaviour. The authors have not had the opportunity to see private papers or diaries to document their explanations of what happened at the top level (although, to an increasing extent, they have interviewed the leading figures in the campaign and thereby, perhaps, diminished the gap between what they could write immediately on the rationale of campaign decisions and what subsequent historians or autobiographers will reveal.)[13]

At the level of mass behaviour the Nuffield studies have been able to draw on three sources: the impressions of politicians and the press about the electorate's mood, the evidence of the opinion polls and the evidence of the election results about both the general verdict and the detailed deviations from it. All of these sources are valuable but all have important limitations when one comes to the difficult task of analytic reduction, of drawing conclusions about the individual voter. These limitations of sources, keenly felt by the authors of the Nuffield series, have been an important stimulus to the writing of this book.

Our research also reflects the evolving concerns of those who have carried forward the series of studies associated with the Survey Research Center of the University of Michigan. Unlike the earlier constituency studies, the Center's work was from the beginning national in scope. Interview surveys of the American electorate have in fact been undertaken in each presidential elec-

13. See D. E. Butler, 'Instant History', *New Zealand Journal of History*, **2** (1968), pp. 107–14.

tion since 1948 and congressional election since the early 1950s. The initial focus of this work was the individual elector and the motives of his behaviour. By the mid-1950s, however, this focus was combined with a strong interest in aggregation of individual behaviour to explain the electorate's collective decision and the place of the mass public within the total political system.[14]

This trend prompted additional studies that explored the relationship between the mass electorate and the legislative institutions in which it was represented. Such work was first undertaken on the American Congress in the late 1950s. Interviews with Members of Congress and opposing congressional candidates, matched with interviews with the constituents whose support they sought, have provided an interesting portrait of the nature of legislative representation in the context of American politics.[15] Aspects of this work have been repeated in Britain through interviews with Members of Parliament and defeated parliamentary candidates as well as with the complementary samples of electors whose replies comprise the main data of this book. The results of this work form the subject of a separate report.

Interest in the electorate's role within a wider order also led to comparative electoral studies. Many of the historical, legal and social factors that are immensely important in conditioning electoral attitudes can be appraised only by examining the experience of several nations, since these factors will differ so little in the experience of any one of them. The interest in comparisons of this kind has been a further important stimulus to the writing of this book. Our focus here is upon Britain; but at many points our treatment of the British experience has relevance for comparative studies.

14. This trend is apparent in the closing chapters of A. Campbell, P. E. Converse, W. E. Miller and D. E. Stokes, *The American Voter*, New York, 1960, and even more clearly in *Elections and the Political Order*, New York, 1966, by the same authors.

15. See W. E. Miller and D. E. Stokes, 'Constituency Influence in Congress', *American Political Science Review*, 57 (1963), 45–56. Reprinted in *Elections and the Political Order*, pp. 351–72.

Elements of Design

We felt from the beginning that the objectives of this research would require a large-scale survey of British electors, nationwide in scope, and involving two or more contacts with our sample of electors at widely separated points of time. The fact that at least one of these approaches was to follow directly after a general election introduced a degree of uncertainty into our plans, given the prime minister's freedom to choose a date. We were clear, however, that one of the contacts with our sample should be outside the context of an election, and we went ahead in the summer of 1963 with an interview survey of 2009 randomly selected electors in 80 randomly selected constituencies of England, Scotland and Wales. The exclusion of Northern Ireland was due solely to the prohibitive outlay of resources that would have been required to enlarge our Ulster sample so as to do justice to the special political circumstances of the area.

In the event, almost a year and a half separated this first round of interviews and the dissolution of Parliament. Following the General Election of 1964, however, we re-interviewed as many of those contacted in the summer of 1963 as could be found, as well as a number of additional respondents selected to enhance the sample's representativeness in the autumn of 1964.[16] The result of the 1964 election suddenly posed a fresh problem. After an unexpectedly long wait for one election, it was now clear that we were likely to have another sooner than anyone had thought. Therefore, we laid plans to contact our panel of electors a third time whenever Mr Wilson might dissolve Parliament, and immediately after the election in March 1966 we re-interviewed as many of these people as we could, in addition to a number of new respondents drawn to enhance the representativeness of the sample.

Those who were interviewed on all three occasions gave on average more than three hours of conversation over this thirty-four-month period. This afforded an opportunity to explore a very wide range of questions, as well as to observe the evolution of

16. Full details of panel mortality and the complementing of our original sample are given in the Appendix.

thought and behaviour over a lengthening interval in the lives of these individuals. By the end of the third interview we had, for example, gathered more than two dozen distinct items of information about the present and former party preferences of each respondent. These interviews differed from the more familiar newspaper opinion survey not only in their length but also in their emphasis on letting the respondent express his attitudes or perceptions or recollections in terms of his own choosing. Many of the questions we put to our sample invited one of several alternative responses, fixed in advance. But many were 'open-ended' or 'free-answer' questions which gave the respondent full latitude to express his ideas in terms which had meaning for him, and some of our most important findings – for example, as to the links that are thought to connect class and party – come from seeing what these terms were.

Although our interview surveys furnish much of the evidence used in this book, we have not intended to provide a conventional survey report. On the one hand, we have raised issues not covered by our questionnaire and have drawn extensively on many other sources of evidence. On the other hand, we have set forth very much less than an exhaustive report of the replies given by our respondents.[17]

Plan of the Book

Two interlocking dualisms give structure to this book. First, the book divides into halves on the basis of the broad distinction between the construction and the application of analytic frameworks. In the first ten chapters we set forth a series of frameworks or perspectives for the analysis of changing political attitudes. In the second ten chapters we apply these to the electoral history of the early 1960s and to the half century which preceded it. But this separation is not at all rigidly enforced; there is much in the book's first half that has to do with application and there are a number of points in the second half where it is convenient to extend our

17. Some further data are available in the percentages which are presented together with our questions in the Appendix.

frameworks of analysis. None the less the broad distinction between construction and application is what divides the book in two.

But each half divides again into two parts on the basis of the distinctions we have drawn between long-term and short-term electoral change. This cross-cutting division too has blurred edges; there is a good deal in Part One and Part Three that has to do with short term variations of party strength and there are many things in Part Two and Part Four that bear on changes of more enduring partisan alignments. None the less we have broadly ordered our argument on the basis of these two distinctions, rendered diagrammatically thus:

	Changes of alignment	Transient variations
Construction	Part One	Part Two
Application	Part Three	Part Four

Part One begins with several fundamental aspects of the individual elector's orientation to politics. It deals first (Chapter 2) with the place that perceptions of the parties have in the motives for participating in politics and with the generality of party allegiances and then turns (Chapter 3) to the way these allegiances take root and change over the individual's lifetime. This perspective provides the basis for a model of political change based on generations. We next examine (Chapter 4) the strength and nature of the most pervasive cleavage line of party support, that of class, and (Chapter 5) the way in which this cleavage has been modified over time. Indeed, in the longer historical view the alignment by class can be set (Chapter 6) against the evidence of several earlier bases of alignment and several bases which may come to have increasing importance with the 'aging' of the alignment by class. At the end of Part One we turn to the political role of a class-related organization, the trade union (Chapter 7).

Part Two sets forth several frameworks for the analysis of

current influences on the electorate. We consider (Chapter 8) the nature of political issues, examining the interaction of leaders and electorate in terms of issues and the conditions which must be satisfied if an issue is to alter the party balance in the country as a whole. Attention is given (Chapter 9) to the relationship of attitudes towards several issues at once and to the adequacy of a model of the interaction of parties and electorate in terms of a more embracing dimension of left and right. We consider in some detail (Chapter 10) the means and extent of the flow of political information to the electorate, giving special attention to the role of the highly partisan national press.

Part Three develops a broad description of the evolution of party strength over the present century. The treatment of earlier decades (Chapter 11) applies our developmental model to study the effects of the movement of successive generations through the electorate; it suggests the role of the fertility and mortality differentials found in modern Britain, and also offers some observations on the likely future effects of selective mortality. The treatment of the early 1960s (Chapter 12) gives a more intensive account of the movements of individual support of recent years, distinguishing the different components underlying the net change of party support over each of several intervals. By considering (Chapter 13) these movements over several intervals together we are able to detect persistent tendencies in the behaviour of those who change, gaining insight into the reasons for an exceedingly paradoxical aspect of the swings of party support that have been observed since the Second World War. Consideration of the movements of party strength involving the Liberals (Chapter 14) shows how extensive have been the exchanges of mass support between the Liberals and the major parties during the period of our work.

Part Four applies the frameworks of Part Two to assess the forces acting on the electorate in the early 1960s. We explore a number of the issues which were current in this period (Chapter 15), as well as several properties of the images of the parties as they were formed in the minds of the voters (Chapter 16). Detailed attention is given to the electoral impact of the party leaders (Chapter 17) and the economic context of the contest of the parties (Chapter 18). We consider (Chapter 19) the influence of the campaign on the electorate's behaviour and the impact of generalized beliefs as to the desirability of transfers of power and of perceptions of the readiness of the parties for such a transfer to take place. We conclude (Chapter 20) by surveying what has been done and left undone and placing our work in a broader stream of political inquiry.

Part One

	CHANGES OF ALIGNMENT	TRANSIENT VARIATIONS
CONSTRUCTION	▨	
APPLICATION		

2 Parties in the Voter's Mind

The role played by the parties in giving shape and direction to the behaviour of voters is so taken for granted that its importance is easily missed. Without it, however, the mass of the people could scarcely participate in regular transfers of power. The individual elector accepts the parties as leading actors on the political stage and sees in partisan terms the meaning of the choices which the universal franchise puts before him. British government would be fundamentally changed if parties were absent from the voter's mind.

The service performed by the parties in giving meaning to politics for a remote electorate may indeed be one main explanation for the flourishing of party systems in the modern world. Since Britain so obviously has a one-party Cabinet and a Parliament operating strictly on party lines, it might seem natural for the British elector to accept parties as leading actors and accord them support simply because they are there. But it might equally be argued that the parties are there because they have been able to win support from electors who accept their role as leading actors. In the evolution of British democracy the parties were fostered as élite cadres by their ability to become objects of universal awareness. Party government is partially a tribute to the politicians' success in appealing for mass support in their parties' names.

Indeed, the factors which induce the voter to see the parties as the main figures of politics probably lead him to see them as more unitary objects than in fact they are. An inside observer, knowing the actual tensions within the parties over policies and personalities, might wonder that the elector can give the parties so definite an identity. The public indulges in a similar sort of gentle reification in regard to churches and firms and other organizations. But in few of these are the heterogeneous elements in what is perceived so open to view. The seeing of parties as single entities is the more remarkable in places where parties are still more fissiparous; for example, the electorate sees the parties as leading actors in the United States in spite of the frequent cross-voting in both houses of Congress and in spite of the fragmented nature of the parties' national and local structure.

The sources of this simplification in the public's mind have fascinated writers on political psychology. Graham Wallas, that pioneer exponent of so many political concepts, suggested half a century ago that the parties loomed large in popular perceptions of politics because the electorate required 'something simpler and more permanent, something that can be loved and trusted, and which can be recognized at successive elections as being the same thing that was loved and trusted before; and party is such a thing'.[1]

Why should the parties have such a definite identity in the public's mind? Part of the answer lies in the remoteness of the citizen from the affairs of government. Whatever may once have been possible in Athens or Venice, nations of the size and social complexity of Britain have all developed a political division of labour that reserves most governmental decisions to a relatively small élite. As we look for the sources of the hold of party on popular thinking about politics, it is well to begin with the remote and marginal nature of politics for the British voter.

The Remoteness of Politics

Individual responses to politics are wonderfully varied. There is no single elector, no archetypal citizen who epitomizes the British voter's condition. The Welsh miner with a political tradition based on pit and chapel, the London shop assistant who glances occasionally at a political headline after gutting the sports pages, the Manchester businessman who sees his interest as affected by day-to-day decisions in Westminster and Whitehall, the widow in Bournemouth who is cut off from any contact with the outer

1. G. Wallas, *Human Nature in Politics*, London, 1910, p. 83.

world – each would differ fundamentally in the degree and kind of his interest in politics. Yet we could hardly overlook the limited extent of political involvement across the whole electorate.

Certainly playing the role of voter is unlikely to inspire any deep involvement in political affairs. Voting for Parliament ordinarily requires only a few minutes of time every fourth or fifth year. If the elector also uses his franchise at the annual local elections, the visits which he pays to the polling booth will still be a negligible part of his life. The behaviour demanded of those who play this role is hardly sufficient to bring politics to the centre of the voter's consciousness.

Few voters, moreover, engage themselves in any deeper involvement in the party system. A profile of the electorate's participation in several types of activity is drawn in Figure 2.1. Our detailed evidence suggests that these forms of political behaviour comprise a cumulative hierarchy; those in the small minorities most involved in politics, the active campaigners or the meeting-goers, tended also to be part of the larger groups performing less demanding acts such as voting in local elections. But what is most notable here is the small number who do anything at all beyond voting in General Elections. Only one in two voted in local elections and only one in ten went to an election meeting. Only one in fifty took an active part in the campaign, and the number engaged in party activities between campaigns was altogether negligible.

Nor are the mass of people engaged in political behaviour outside the party system. The networks of interest groups linked to Westminster and Whitehall are operated by élites that are as restricted in size as those that play continuously active roles in the party system. The survey undertaken in Britain by Almond and Verba, looking beyond the closed circle of interest group politics, found only one elector in twenty who recalled ever having sought to influence any matter before Parliament.[2] In rare moments of social and political upheaval, such as the General Strike of 1926

2. G. A. Almond and S. Verba, *The Civic Culture*, Princeton, 1963. The question 'Have you ever done anything to try to influence an act of Parliament?' elicited these replies: 'often' (0·8 per cent); 'once or twice' or 'a few times' (5 per cent); 'never' (92 per cent); and 'don't know' (2 per cent).

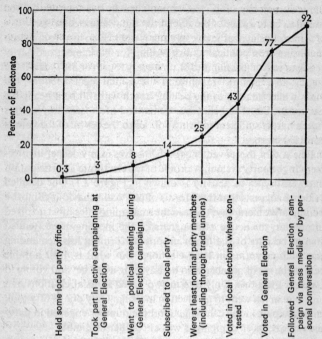

2.1 Frequency of Forms of Mass Partisan Activity, 1964

or the Chartist demonstrations of a century before, larger numbers engaged in political acts outside the party system. By contrast the numbers taking part in demonstrations against nuclear arms or the Vietnam war have been relatively small.

The limits of the public's overt political activity are matched by the limits of its political information. Over the past thirty years survey studies in various countries have demonstrated how limited is the mass electorate's information about policy issues, or the structure and processes of government, or the identity of leading political figures. Such findings are surprising only against a naïve or idealized conception of political democracy. Large portions of the electorate may indeed be ignorant of things which are taken completely for granted by knowledgeable observers. For example, the vast majority of West German electors has repeatedly been found to be unaware of the role of the Bundesrat, while two-thirds of Americans do not know that members of the House of Representatives are elected every two years.[3]

Glimpses of similar political innocence have been given by surveys in Britain. The Gallup Poll indicated in 1963 that several million electors thought that Britain already belonged to the European Common Market. National Opinion Polls found a sizeable fraction of the electorate in 1964 supporting the idea that it would be right to nationalize the mines and the railways. The majority of a sample interviewed for the *Sunday Times* in 1962 could not name any political figure in either party other than the party leaders themselves. We shall see in Chapters 8 and 9 evidence of how little our own sample had formed stable opinions on major policy issues confronting the Government and how few of them placed any such opinions within a more embracing ideological framework, such as that of left and right. Indeed, in 1963 we encountered respondents who were unable to identify Harold Macmillan after he had been Prime Minister seven years; one even believed that Mr Attlee was still at the head of government.

Yet the electorate's response to politics in modern democracies is far from one of blank incomprehension. However complex and distant the realm of government may seem, voters are capable of behaving in a purposive way and of seeking goals they value. Indeed, the parties would never have succeeded in harnessing the allegiance of the electorate if they had not been seen as a partial means to such ends. The parties have achieved their prominence as political actors in the public's mind by linking themselves to goals that matter to the electorate whose support they seek.

3. An excellent summary of studies disclosing the limits of the public's information about politics and government appears in John Wahlke's paper, 'Public Policy and Representative Government: the Role of the Represented', Department of Political Science, University of Iowa, 1967, pp. 6–10.

Parties and the Voter's Goals

The ends to which the parties have sought to link themselves have to do with the things that governments are thought to have an influence upon – in a word, the 'outputs' of government, a term that we shall use very broadly. There is of course nothing distinctively modern about the belief that governments affect the world in ways that their peoples, whether enfranchised or not, care deeply about. The Tudors won support by ending the disorders of the Wars of the Roses, just as the Roman imperium was widely accepted for the improved conditions of life that it brought. Although traditional societies can still be found in which the mass of people remains largely unaware of the role of central political authority, this has not been true of western communities for a very long time.

What is quite new is the immense scope of governmental activity and the ever wider range of outputs of which the public may be aware. Asked in the early 1960s what problems they thought the Government should do something about, our sample of the British electorate unleashed a flood of replies which spread over a remarkably wide terrain.[4] Many of the matters touched by these replies were economic – reducing unemployment, creating jobs in depressed areas, increasing exports, containing the cost of living, fostering economic growth; many dealt with welfare and the social services – raising pensions, altering family allowances, providing free medicine and other health services, building more houses, keeping rents down, improving schools; others dealt with transport, with crime and punishment, with industrial peace, with immigration and race, with defence and Britain's place in the world, and with an astonishing number of other matters ranging from the lifeboat service to the control of Bingo.

The increase in government outputs gives considerable importance to the ability of political leaders to form links between what the government does and what the public values. Indeed, the party battle is often fought in essentially these terms, and big rewards

4. The series of questions asked about problems government might affect is numbered 16 in the text of the 1963 questionnaire given in the Appendix.

have gone to the leaders who managed to persuade large numbers of electors to see these links in a particular way. A striking example of this was provided by Lloyd George with his insight in 1918 that the public could be made to see that housing should be a major goal of government policy. What bonds the public will accept are, of course, not entirely in the province of political élites to determine. Indeed, in some cases the correspondence between what the Government is thought to affect and what it actually can affect is remarkably weak. We shall have reason to note that governments were generally held to account for the country's prosperity long before the advance of economic science had put into the hands of governments the tools required for the pursuance of rational economic policies.

The enlargement in the role of government has also greatly complicated the public's problem in connecting effect with cause. The technical difficulties of assigning responsibility for past government action or inaction, and of calculating probabilities of future action has increased far more rapidly than the political sophistication of the general public, despite the spread of education and of mass communications. Probably it was easier for the country in the sixteenth century to know how order had been restored than in the 1960s to know why Britain's balance of payments had gone wrong.

Modern electorates tend to 'solve' the problem of causal reasoning by assuming that certain causal relationships must exist rather than by discerning what they are. The elector focuses his attention primarily on certain conditions which he values positively or negatively and simply assumes that past or future governments affect them. The public can call for a government's dismissal in economic hard times just as it calls for a team manager's dismissal in a losing season, in each case concluding that causal relationships must exist without knowing in detail what they are.

The goals or the conditions that governments are thought to affect may be quite specific and concrete – raising pensions, abolishing the 11-plus examination and the like. But they are often defined in terms that are diffuse or general. Indeed, goals of overwhelming importance in modern British politics have been the interests or welfare of the middle and working classes. The elector looking back on a government's performance may be quite unsure how in practice it has affected these ends and he may be even less clear how future governments might affect them. But the belief that government action influences the welfare of different social classes is none the less enormously important in the behaviour of many voters. Similarly the belief that actions of government affect peace or economic prosperity or national prestige or other diffuse goals may enter the voter's calculations without his having undertaken more than the most rudimentary reasoning as to how they do so. The country's satisfaction or dissatisfaction with the achievement of general and even semi-conscious goals probably lies behind many of those changes of electoral 'mood' which seem so evident to the political observer. The generality of the goals that matter to the electorate is a theme we shall often touch on in later chapters.

The perceived link between government and the fulfilment of conditions which the public values is only one part of the chain that links goals to electoral choices in the voter's mind. The distinctive place of party in forging this chain involves two main additional links.

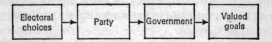

The three arrows in this sketch offer a key to much that follows later in the book. We have commented already on the last of these arrows, a link that is very real in the public's mind even if the electorate rarely has a very developed understanding of the causal relationships that lie beneath it. There can equally be no doubt that the middle of these arrows is real to the public. The electorate accepts the partisan nature of British government, and the identity of the party 'in power' is one of the few facts that are almost universally known. Indeed the true extent of knowledge of something so taken for granted is not easily checked in a survey without putting respondents off. None the less in mid-1964 we did put to a pilot sample a question designed to ascertain whether they knew the identity of the governing party. In this little test every respondent knew that the Conservatives were in office and almost all had a reasonably accurate view of how long they had been there.[5]

The partisan character of governments tends to associate the parties in the public's mind with the effects that government is thought to have. With the machinery of the state in party hands the outputs of government become the responsibility of the ruling party, and the elector can hold the party in office to account for the conditions which the Government has permitted to exist. He can also try to get a party into office in the belief that it will be able to use the power of government to change these conditions in a given way. Once again, the voter's perception of the causal relationships between government actions and changing conditions may be remarkably unformed. The fact that a party is in power when what he wants actually happens may serve well enough; he may indeed have extraordinarily little understanding of how long an output of government has normally been in the making. In this sense, party government serves to institutionalize *post hoc ergo propter hoc* reasoning on a grand scale.

With more than one party seeking his support, the voter's judgements about values and party control will often be comparative ones. He may contrast the performance of the party that has held office with what he thinks its rivals would have done, just as he may contrast the probable performance in the future of the rival claimants on power. But these judgements need not be comparative. Given the fundamental asymmetry between being in and out of power, it is inevitable that the ruling party should receive the closer scrutiny. There is for example evidence that the public tends to reward the party in power for good times and punish it for bad without attempting to say whether times might have been better, or worse, under an alternative government. In politics, too, the team manager may be sacked even though he has done better than his potential successors in keeping setbacks from turning into utter disaster.

5. Our pilot survey was with fifty-two randomly selected respondents from four constituencies, two urban and two rural. To each respondent we put the question 'Can you tell me which party is in power and how long it has held office?'

Illustrations of the degree to which the electorate associates the parties with the putative outputs of government that it values positively or negatively appear in many chapters of this book. Some of these links have to do with the bases of enduring party alignments, especially the values represented by the interest of the social classes. But these connections are also formed in terms of goals or conditions to which the public gives more varied and individual valuations or concerning which it sees the parties as more sharply set apart at some times than at others. We shall develop each of these points when we set out a framework for the analysis of political issues.

The partisan character of governments is not an immutable feature of the British constitution. There have been periods of coalition rule and the opinion polls periodically report wide support for its return – suggesting that awareness of party government is more widespread than acceptance of its desirability. The plainly visible tenure of power by single parties sets Britain apart from countries where coalition rule is the norm and where constitutional arrangements make the question of control more complex. It would be interesting to know more about the perceptions of the electorate in these contrasting situations. Survey evidence suggests that the American public has a much fuzzier sense of party control in national government.[6] Beliefs about the partisan identity of coalition government would justify comparative study; how for example do the electorates of Holland or Finland see their Governments in party terms?

The leftmost arrow of our sketch on p. 46 suggests the final contribution of party in linking the electoral act to outputs of government in the voter's mind. The parties being thought capable of affecting the world in ways that matter, in effect organize the voter's choice at the polling station. The only candidates with a

6. The proportion of the American public that can reliably say which party is in control of the Congress has at times been less than half. See D. E. Stokes and W. E. Miller, 'Party Government and the Saliency of Congress', *Public Opinion Quarterly*, **26** (1962), 531–46. Plainly one of the factors that has affected the size of this fraction is whether the Presidency and the houses of Congress are in the hands of the same party.

hope of succeeding are those who carry a party's designation. We shall see in Chapter 19 that, without party labels on the ballot paper, virtually every voter was able to make the link between candidate and party, even though many knew nothing else about him: they perceived that to vote for a candidate was to vote for a government of his party, one which he would sustain in power throughout the life of a Parliament.

Moreover, the electorate's response to the partisan choices it faces in the constituencies can be expected to produce a single-party government. In all elections since the war, the sum of individual choices has, through the electoral system, given possession of the government machine to one party. Even the closest of contests has produced a decisive result. No process of bargaining between parties has been interposed between the voter's act and the formation of an administration; the electorate has been able to see a clear and immediate relation between its collective judgement and party control.

It would be wrong to suppose that this full chain is sharply defined in the elector's mind. We have drawn it for analytical purposes and not as a literal description of his categories of thought; we have tried to be clear about the crudeness of several links, especially the limits to many voters' understanding of how the parties guide the actions of government and of how the actions of government may affect the conditions they value. Moreover, there can be little doubt that the electorate feels at times that the chain is a frail one and that the choices at the polls, as defined by the parties, are fairly irrelevant to the problems facing the country. But there is equally little doubt that, whatever the degree of its ignorance or confusion, the electorate attempts to use the ballot to achieve things it cares about.

There is no reason to expect the mass of people to be particularly introspective about this process. None the less we did probe the extent of the public's awareness of the relation of its behaviour to the actions taken by government. In the summer of 1963 we put to our sample this series of questions:

Over the years how much do you feel the Government pays attention to what the people think when it decides what to do?

Why is that?

How much do you feel that having political parties makes the Government pay attention to what the people think?

Why is that?

And how much do you think that having elections makes the Government pay attention to what the people think?

Why is that?

By any test this sequence of questions proved extraordinarily difficult for the ordinary respondent to cope with; it was clear, whatever the defects of our question wording, that we were on difficult ground. It was also clear that many voters felt that the Government did most things without any reference to the public's views. Fully half our sample replied to the first of these questions by saying that they didn't think the Government paid much attention to what the people thought, and less than one in ten felt that the Government paid a great deal of attention. The replies to the succeeding questions gave, however, a somewhat different balance of views, as Table 2.2 shows. The influence attributed to elections

2.2 Perceptions of Popular Influence on Actions of Government

	Good deal	Some	Not Much	Don't Know	Total
Over the years how much do you feel the Government pays attention to what the people think when it decides what to do?	8%	20	50	22	100%
How much do you feel that having political parties makes the Government pay attention to what the people think?	21%	29	16	34	100%
And how much do you think that having elections makes the Government pay attention to what the people think?	46%	26	9	19	100%

is the more impressive in view of the fact that these conversations were held outside the context of an election campaign.

Of equal interest is the insight into the public's image of party government offered by our respondents in amplification of their answers to the three root questions. Many of our respondents had a clear, if weakly developed, sense of the importance of parties and elections in linking the people to actions of government. A housewife in Uxbridge explained the Government's attention to the people by observing 'They would never get into power otherwise'; an estate agent in Blackpool, 'If they wish to remain in power it is very necessary'. A painter in Bridgwater explained his answers this way:

(Why Government pays attention?) They've got to take notice of the people.

(Why parties help Government pay attention?) They've got to have a party to get the views of the people.

(Why elections help Government pay attention?) The people feel they have a chance of altering things.

A widow in Leek said:

(Why Government pays attention?) I think they try their best to run the country properly, so they have to pay attention.

(Why parties help Government pay attention?) Because they need the people's votes and having several parties keeps them on their toes.

(Why elections help Government pay attention?) For the same reason. Support is needed to keep them in power.

And a clerical officer in Bermondsey said:

(Why parties help Government pay attention?) The whole parliamentary system ensures that they take notice through the Opposition.

(Why elections help Government pay attention?) It's obvious that if they want power they must show interest.

From a full reading of these replies, we attempted to classify our respondents into three general groups. The first of these was made up of those who showed a relatively developed sense of popular control through a competitive party and election system, mentioning especially the dependence of parties on electoral support even before being prompted by the third of our questions. The second group was made up of those who voiced some belief in the public's influence on government but did not mention control through competitive elections until prompted. The third group was made up of those who showed no sort of belief in popular influence. Some of them indeed expressed a contrary view, saying that governments dupe the people and make election promises only to break them. 'It's too easy to talk and promise things – they don't have to carry them out' was the view of a machinist in Hexham. But the largest element in this third group were those who simply failed to express any generalized belief in the influence of the people over the actions of government.

Such a classification gives an interesting profile of the extent to which the idea of influence has crystallized in the electorate's mind. We have no illusion that this categorizing of belief is more than suggestive, but the figures set out in Table 2.3 do indicate, however roughly, the existence in the minds of many voters of a generalized

2.3 Beliefs about Popular Influence

Respondent held well-developed understanding of popular control through a competitive party and election system, to which he felt British politics conformed	13%
Respondent held at least a partial understanding of popular control through a competitive party and election system and saw elements of such a system in British politics	47
Respondent had not crystallized a general belief in popular control through a competitive party and election system	40
	100%

belief in the role of parties and elections in linking the electorate to government outputs. What we are tapping here is primarily the degree to which the voter has formed *generalized* beliefs about popular influence. In addition many voters who perceive a more specific focus of influence have fallen into the last category of Table 2.3; this was true, for example, of a number of respondents who see the parties as drawing electoral strength by representing class interests.[7]

The Intrinsic Values of Party

All great realignments of party strength have involved values that the electorate attaches to the outputs of government, and the same may usually be said of the larger short-run fluctuations in party strength. But it is inevitable that the parties should develop values of their own in the elector's mind. As long-established actors on the political stage it is natural that they should have become objects of mass loyalty or identification. As a result, the success of a given party and the confounding of its enemies have a value in their own right for many electors, quite apart from the uses which the party might make of power. The dramatic idiom is not misplaced. A protagonist in the political drama can evoke from the electoral audience a response at the polling station which has mainly to do with the values of having one's heroes prevail. The same point is suggested by other idioms that are often applied to the electoral contest, especially those of games. Commentaries on politics are rich with sporting metaphors, and the values of partisan loyalty may be as intrinsic to the contest as the values of loyalty to a team.

The intrinsic appeal of a party may indeed rest on inclinations that lie deep within the personality of the individual elector. We shall not probe very far into the realms of personality in this book, but we have no doubt that such factors supply part of the motives

7. It should also be noted that we had focused on the respondent's sensitivity to the influence that electors may achieve from the Government's anticipating the electoral consequences of its acts. But electors may also have influence by choosing between rival governments on the basis of policies to which they are committed to give effect in office. The distinction between influence that involves governments anticipating the behaviour of the electorate and influence that involves the electorate anticipating the behaviour of governments is of course not a clear one in the public's own mind. But by placing a heavier accent on the first of the two processes of influence we may have understated somewhat the extent of the public's generalized beliefs about the links between their electoral choices and the outputs of government.

of electors who find intrinsic values in supporting a given party.[8] Of course it is also true that personality factors can be part of the reason why an elector values certain outputs of government and hence the party that seems likely to achieve them; a voter's desire for Britain to brandish nuclear weapons may be a projection on to government of aggressive tendencies that go back deep into childhood. But it seems likely that such factors are more often involved in the intrinsic values that the elector finds satisfied in party allegiance.

Our view of the 'intrinsic' values of party should be broad enough to include a number of psychic or social utilities that party may have for the voter that are distinct from the values government may supply. The intrinsic values of partisanship may, for example, be those of preserving harmony in the friendship group or the home or the nuptial bed. Or they may be those of reducing the costs to the individual of obtaining the information he needs to discharge his civic duty as elector, as we shall note later. We shall indeed speak of a variety of such personal and social uses of party allegiance as 'intrinsic' values to set them off from the utilities which may flow from the actions of government. There is no doubt that these residual values are often in the voter's mind.

This aspect of party support is more easily understood when it is seen how early in life partisan inclinations may appear. The child who knows nothing of the uses of power may still absorb a party preference from his home, as we shall see in the next chapter. This early role of the family has its counterpart in the influence of a succession of associations in adolescence or adulthood. Many of the groups found at work or church or public house may foster a common political inclination among their members, perhaps through reinforcing values associated with specific governments' outputs, but still more through reinforcing the intrinsic values of party.

There is indeed an important interplay between these two kinds of values in the shaping of long-term party strength. The great

8. Exceedingly suggestive studies of factors of this kind are H. J. Eysenck, *The Psychology of Politics*, London, 1954; R. E. Lane, *Political Ideology*, New York, 1962; and A. F. Davies, *Private Politics*, Melbourne, 1955.

changes of alignment – in the 1840s, the 1880s, the 1920s and the early 1940s – were plainly linked to things that large sectors of the public wanted of government. But the 'primary' changes induced by forces of this kind will subsequently be amplified by 'secondary' changes that have relatively more to do with intrinsic values of party support that the individual discovers within his family and small group, or within his own mind, after supporting the same party for some while. We shall see evidence in Chapter 5 that the class realignment of modern politics took a generation and more to complete and also that this realignment, as time has passed, has depended less and less on the primary forces that first created it – with the probable consequence that preferences have come to move more fluidly across class lines.

Electoral history suggests that strong new primary forces can sweep away political attachments that depend mainly on the intrinsic values of party. Yet it would be unwise to discount the importance of accustomed loyalties. Among other things, they enter in at least two ways into the motives that induce citizens to go to the polling station. Despite the limited demands on time and energy made by voting, the act is not costless to the individual, as various commentators have noted, and the problem of explaining why people take the trouble to vote, when a single vote can make so little difference, is a real one.[9] Much of the answer is supplied by the several kinds of value we have been discussing. The elector has the *instrumental* motive of voting: the casting of his ballot may contribute to the election of a government whose outputs he values. He may also have the *expressive* motive of voting: the casting of his ballot shows support for the party he identifies himself with, and has an intrinsic value of its own.

Yet we must also allow for the *normative* motive of voting; the casting of the voters' ballot may reflect primarily a sense of civic obligation. Indeed, the democratic ethos creates a strong presump-

9. An influential statement of the costs, indeed of the 'irrationality' of voting, appears in A. Downs, *An Economic Theory of Democracy*, New York, 1957, pp. 260–76. For an interesting alternative theoretical argument, see W. H. Riker and P. C. Ordeshook, 'A Theory of the Calculus of Voting', *American Political Science Review*, 62 (1968), 25–42.

tion that the elector will use his franchise, and this idea is heavily reinforced by the mass media as well as by everyday conversation as polling day approaches. Blurred ideas of popular sovereignty and universal suffrage are so interwoven in the prevailing conceptions of British government that the obligation to vote becomes almost an aspect of the citizen's national identity. As a result, a number of people are drawn to the polling place who would be unlikely to get there otherwise.

But those who are drawn to the polling station in this way must support some party when they are there. The democratic ethos has obliged them to take action about a distant and complex realm of affairs, one that is not clearly enough defined to give them a motive for voting but for their sense of civic obligation. The result is to create yet another intrinsic value in having a tie to party. The elector who possesses a firm attachment has a basis for preferring one party programme, one set of political leaders, and indeed one interpretation of current political reality to its rivals. The psychological convenience of such a habitual tie adds to the values that are intrinsic to being a party supporter.

Partisan Self-images and Electoral Choices

The values which the individual sees in supporting a party usually extend to more than one general election. There may be strong continuity in the outputs of government, such as the welfare of a class, which provide the individual with the same basis for his choice over successive contests. Moreover, the values involved in party support of the intrinsic sort tend by their very nature to be enduring ones. As a result, most electors think of themselves as supporters of a given party in a lasting sense, developing what may be called a 'partisan self-image'.

This phenomenon is a familiar one in many party systems. Writing of 'party identification' in their book on Norwegian parties Valen and Katz ask:

Why is such a concept necessary? Why not simply use voters' reports on their voting behaviour with which party identification is of course correlated? The reason is that we need a more generalized measure of the individual's orientation to take account of a variety of behaviours.[10]

The United States has produced the most intensive studies of such dispositions towards party; these have demonstrated that there is a remarkable degree of independence between the elector's generalized identification with party and his behaviour in particular elections, especially in the choice of a President.[11] From the time when comparable measurements of these identifications began to be taken on a nationwide scale in the early 1950s, the distributions of party loyalty have fluctuated only negligibly from sample to sample despite massive swings in the presidential vote.

There is no doubt that the partisan dispositions of British voters tend to be generalized ones. Looking back over their own past voting in general elections, well over four-fifths of our respondents said that they had always supported the same party. These recollections probably exaggerate the true extent of continuity, but the report is none the less impressive. Moreover, our repeated measurements of the preferences of our panel showed the majority holding fast to the same party from 1963 to 1966, although, as we shall show, the minority whose partisanship fluctuated was of a size that some will find surprising.

To study more closely the nature of our respondents' partisan self-images, we asked them at each interview, quite separately from questions about their voting, to describe their partisan inclinations in a more general way and we were able to divide the sample into those who described themselves as Conservative, Labour or Liberal in this more general sense.[12] Roughly 90 per cent of the sample accepted such a generalized partisan designation without hesitation at each interview, and of those who did not, about half were willing, on being pressed, to say that they generally thought of themselves as closer to one of the parties.

10. H. Valen and D. Katz, *Political Parties in Norway*, Oslo, 1964, p. 187.

11. The most extended discussions of the concept of party identification appear in *The American Voter*, pp. 120–67 and in *Elections and the Political Order*, pp. 9–157.

12. The wording of this question varied slightly between the first and the second and third interviews. See Appendix, questions 37a of the 1963, 49a of the 1964 and 48a of the 1966 questionnaires.

One of the clearest evidences for the generalized nature of partisan dispositions in Britain comes from local government elections. In 1963, for example, those who went to the polls in local elections that were fought on a party basis voted to an overwhelming degree in line with their expressed party self-image, as Table 2.4 shows.[13] Some small deviations are apparent. Almost certainly the lesser solidarity of Conservatives shown here reflects the disillusion which affected the party's supporters in the spring of 1963. But the most central fact is that well over 90 per cent of our respondents stayed with their generalized tie to the national parties, though local elections might be thought to be fought on entirely special local issues. This dominant role of a more general partisan

2.4 Local Election Vote in May 1963 by Partisan Self-Image[a]

| | Partisan Self-Image | | |
	Conservative	Labour	Liberal
Local election vote			
Conservative	85%	1%	2%
Labour	3	95	4
Liberal	6	2	88
Independent[b]	4	1	6
Other[b]	2	1	0
	100%	100%	100%

[a] This analysis is limited to people identifying themselves with one of the three main parties who were also qualified electors in wards where candidates of their 'own' parties contested the local council elections in May of 1963.
[b] A candidate whose ties to one of the main parties were a matter of general knowledge was classified as partisan rather than as 'independent' or 'other'.

tie is entirely consistent with the evidence our sample gave of their lack of involvement in local issues. When we asked those who voted in the May 1963 elections whether there were any issues that had

13. Many local elections were not fought on a party basis and in many more one or more of the national parties were not represented. We checked from external sources the pattern of candidatures in each ward where we conducted interviews. An interesting proof of the veracity of our respondents is that none claimed to have voted for a party which had not in fact put up candidates in their ward.

especially concerned them, four out of five said 'no' without hesitation; the remainder mentioned matters that were in fact more often the concern of Westminster than of the Town Hall.

The significance of generalized party ties is further illustrated by their link with participation in local elections. We asked each of those who expressed a generalized partisan self-image how strong the tie was.[14] Table 2.5 shows that the chance that an elector would vote increased sharply with the strength of his

2.5 Local Election Turnout by Strength of Partisan Self-Image, 1963

| | Strength of Partisan Self-Image[a] | | |
	Very Strong	Fairly Strong	Not very Strong
Proportion voting in local council elections[b]	64%	54%	39%

[a] Classification based on Question 37b of the 1963 questionnaire.
[b] This tabulation is based on respondents identified from external sources as living in wards which had partisan local government contests in May of 1963.

general attitude to the parties. These findings are wholly consistent with the growing tendency to interpret local government elections as referenda on the national parties.

In view of the generality and continuity of partisan dispositions it is natural to wonder whether a partisan self-image may not survive in the elector's mind during a temporary defection to nonvoting or even to support of another party. This sort of tenacity of generalized partisan identifications is one of the most central findings in American studies. Large numbers of voters have defected to the presidential candidate of the opposite party in every recent election. But their proclaimed party allegiance has remained remarkably undisturbed during such defections; in fact, it continues to be a better predictor of what the voter will do in future elections than is his current presidential vote. In the Eisenhower elections of 1952 and 1956 millions of traditional Democrats voted Republican for President, just as millions of traditional

14. See Appendix, questions 37b of the 1963, 49b of the 1964 and 48b of the 1966 questionnaires.

Republicans voted Democratic in the Johnson–Goldwater contest of 1964. But many of these defectors maintained their normal loyalties in voting for other offices in the same year and the great majority of them returned to the fold in subsequent presidential elections.

Has this pattern any parallel in Britain? The answer is that, in the main, partisan self-images and electoral preferences travel together in Britain far more than in America. We can draw this contrast in terms of comparable assessments of self-image and electoral choice at three points of time on each side of the Atlantic. On the British side we have the evidence provided by our respondents in 1963, 1964 and 1966. On the American side we have comparable reports of partisan self-image and votes cast for Congress in 1956, 1958 and 1960 from a panel study conducted in those years by the Survey Research Center.[15]

The essence of this Anglo-American difference can be seen by comparing in each country the stability of self-image and voting

2.6 Stability of Partisan Self-Image and Voting for Congress
1956–58–60

		Party Preference in Voting for Congress		
		Stable	Variable	
Partisan Self-Image	Stable	76	16	92
	Variable	2	6	8
		78	22	100%

15. We deal here with voting for the national House of Representatives rather than for President in order to have measurements from each of three elections, including that in 1958 when no President was chosen. This necessarily limits us to a smaller fraction of the American panel than of the British panel, since the proportion that voted in the mid-term congressional election as well as in the congressional elections accompanying the presidential contests in 1956 and 1960 was smaller than the proportion of the British panel voting or expressing a party preference for Parliament at each of our interviews in Britain.

behaviour. Table 2.6 sets out the American findings. It shows first of all that more than threequarters of this group of panel respondents held steady in both their self-image and their party choice for Congress.[16] The table shows too that a measurable element varied in both their self-image and party choice. The great majority, though not all, of these movements were in concert: something like one elector in twenty altered his self-image in harmony with his vote, and it would therefore be wrong to present party identification in America as completely steadfast in the face of changing electoral preferences.

But the most notable pattern that emerges from the American findings turns on the entries in the other diagonal, the upper right-hand and lower left-hand cells. Roughly eight times as many American voters in this panel changed their electoral choice while keeping the same partisan self-image as changed their partisan self-image while keeping the same electoral choice. We may conclude that party identification was more stable than voting for Congress in this period.

The British findings diverge from the American at several points. Table 2.7 compares the stability of self-image and electoral choice

2.7 Stability of Partisan Self-Image and Voting Preference for Parliament, 1963–64–66

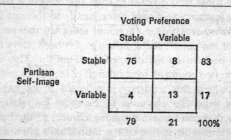

		Voting Preference		
		Stable	Variable	
Partisan Self-Image	Stable	75	8	83
	Variable	4	13	17
		79	21	100%

16. They were not only steady but consistent, for other analyses show that only a trifling fraction held throughout to a self-image and a party choice that did not agree.

in our British panel. We start with an apparent similarity: in both the British and American panels the proportion holding fast to the same self-image and the same electoral choice over three moments of time is virtually identical; but this actually indicates a somewhat greater stability among British electors, since we had to remove from the American panel those (almost half) who failed to vote at the mid-term congressional election of 1958.[17]

Table 2.7 also shows that self-images are more stable than vote preferences too; the number in our panel who changed their electoral choice while keeping the same self-image was roughly twice the number who changed their self-image while keeping the same electoral choice. In America the inequality was eight-to-one. Lastly, more than twice as many British electors varied both their electoral choice and their partisan self-image; although not all were cases of tandem movements, something like one British elector in eight moved in concert on self-image and electoral choice in this period, as compared with one in twenty in the American panel. Among Americans who changed their vote only 30 per cent changed their self-image; among Britons 61 per cent did so.

We shall wait until Chapter 13 to explore a further subtlety in these findings. The fraction of the electorate which changes its partisan self-image seems greater in Britain than in the United States. Yet those who do change from one interview to the next have some tendency to return subsequently to the earlier image. There is, in other words, a 'homing' tendency representing the influence of the voter's social milieu and other factors that may draw him back to an accustomed partisanship. The difference between the two countries seems therefore mainly to reside in the extent to which this tendency is reflected in an explicit and generalized belief that the voter forms about his relationship to party, one that can survive deviating choices at the ballot box.

The more durable nature of the individual's party self-image when he is voting for the opposite party in America must largely

17. In the British panel, as in the American, only a trifling fraction of those who held the same self-image and electoral preference throughout this period failed to agree on both.

be due to the different challenges faced by the elector in the two countries. On polling day the British electors vote only for a single office at a single level of government. The American has to cope simultaneously with a vast collection of partisan candidates seeking a variety of offices at federal, state and local levels: it is small wonder that he becomes conscious of a generalized belief about his ties to party, although some of his individual choices are not guided by it. He will tend to develop a generalized conception of his ties to party even if he comes to feel that he is an 'Independent' voter free of such ties. It is indeed revealing that in the American political vernacular the term 'Independent' is used by a substantial section of the electorate to assert their freedom from a party. There is no real British equivalent. British political commentators use 'floating voter' as a term of art for electors who change their preferences, while candidates who stand for office without party backing call themselves 'Independents'. But there is no term by which the ordinary voter is accustomed to declare his party irregularity. The electoral system has not provoked him to find one.[18]

Without this prompting from the electoral system, the British voter is less likely than the American to make a distinction between his current electoral choice and a more general partisan disposition. The majority of voters do in fact have general dispositions towards party which give continuity to their behaviour in a succession of specific choices. But in transferring their vote from one party to another they are less likely to retain a conscious identification with a party other than the one they currently support.

Yet some electors in our sample did keep a fixed partisan self-image while altering their vote, as Table 2.7 demonstrated. This pattern is partly to be understood in terms of the interplay of the values a voter associates with the outputs of government and

18. When in August 1966 the Gallup Poll asked British electors the question 'In politics as of today, do you consider yourself as Conservative, Labour, Liberal or Independent?' only 3 per cent, given this explicit prompting, chose Independent. An equivalent question in the U.S. consistently draws an 'Independent' response from around 25 per cent of the sample.

those which are more intrinsic to his support of a given party. Although a voter who is traditionally aligned with his party will tend to value his party's success for its own sake, there can be political issues that lead him to see values in leaving his party in the short run. Indeed, as we shall see in Chapter 19, the tradition of alternating governments is strong enough to make a voter whose party has been long in power more ready to make such a change.

3 The Political Life Cycle

There has been a natural inclination in electoral studies to consider single elections. While the focus is a useful one, it is important to see that one election with all its preliminaries is but a moment in the life of the nation or the individual citizen and that much is to be gained by taking a longer view. The processes of change are hardly to be understood without doing so. We begin here with the development of political attitudes during the lifetime of the individual voter, identifying several phases of the political 'life cycle'. We then consider some frameworks needed to analyse political change with the advance of generations in the electorate as a whole.

The concept of a political life cycle involves a certain licence. Against the background of the twentieth century's political changes it may seem absurd to discuss a systematic pattern of individual development that can be likened to the biological life cycle. Why should the evolution of attitudes in a man born in 1884, who grew up in the gentlemanly world of the Conservative–Liberal struggle, resemble that in a man born in 1924, who grew up under the conditions that culminated in the Labour landslide of 1945? Why should either resemble that of a member of the age cohort first voting in the 1960s? We shall argue that there are, in fact, common aspects to the way in which each of these political generations absorbed its political ideas. Indeed, the very concept of a 'political generation' – of there being a common pattern in the behaviour of those entering the electorate in the same period – implies that the young show a common susceptibility to political ideas during their years of growing awareness.

Taking some liberties, we may distinguish four ages of political man – his infant innocence of the existence of politics (the likelihood of his having been born at all has significance for political change, as we shall see); his childhood, adolescent, or early adult years when he first becomes aware of politics; his later adult years in which political interest increases and party attitudes harden; and his old age when, though his partisan allegiance probably remains unchanged, his attention to politics declines towards relative indifference (once again, the timing of his ultimate demise is politically significant). Of these, the second and third provide our main concern. We shall consider first the formative years, the period of what is often called the individual's 'socialization' into politics, and then the years in which political attitudes are less susceptible to change.

The Impressionable Years

W. S. Gilbert's quatrain about everyone's being born 'either a little Liberal or else a little Conservative' is often cited in acknowledgement of the deep childhood roots of partisanship in Britain, amounting to the inheritance of party allegiance. But inheritance in this case is social rather than biological and Lamarckian rather than Darwinian: it is acquired political characteristics that are transmitted, however imperfectly, from parent to child.[1]

1. Interest in political socialization has spread so rapidly that the political development of the young is by now almost a standard subject of empirical studies in a number of countries. In Britain the most systematic attention has been given the subject by Richard Rose. See his *Politics in England*, London, 1965. See also Paul Abramson, 'The Differential Political Socialization of English Secondary School Students', *Sociology of Education*, **40** (1967), 246–74 and Jack Dennis and others, 'Political Socialization to Democratic Orientations in Four Western Systems', *Comparative Political Studies*, **1** (1968), 71–101. See also R. P. Kelvin, 'The Non-Conforming Voter', *New Society*, 25 November 1965, 8–12. In America works such as Herbert H. Hyman's *Political Socialization*, Glencoe, Illinois, 1959, and Fred I. Greenstein's *Children and Politics*, New Haven, 1965, have become classics, and extensive empirical studies have been done on the influence of the family, peer groups, the school and other socializing agencies. See, for example, Robert Hess and Judith Horney, *The Development of Political Attitudes in Children*, Chicago, 1967, and M. Kent Jennings and Richard G. Niemi, 'The Transmission of Political Values from Parent to Child', *American Political Science Review*, **62** (1968), 169–84. Political socialization

In most human societies the impressions made on the young are first of all the work of parents and the immediate family. But we should be clear about the complexities of the link between the political outlook of the family and the outlook developed in the young. Parental influence may indeed be direct, if uncoercing: the child may accept the political norms of his family group, which will be pre-eminently those of his parents. But parental influence may work in less direct ways and the child may accept from his parents modes of outlook which, although not immediately political, must inevitably colour his later political judgements. For example, a family pessimism about human nature may lead both father and son to shun reformist parties.

Moreover, the family must be the carrier of the beliefs and values of a wider culture. Obviously this is true in terms of the whole nation; to have been brought up as an Englishman (or Welshman or Scot) must have immense consequences for a man's approach to politics. Equally clear, and more important for our present theme, are the consequences of being part of one of the sub-cultures of the nation, particularly those defined by class. The child's place in the social structure, acquired from family, would have a profound influence on his political attitudes even if the family itself did little to socialize him into the norms of his sub-culture. This influence stands revealed when the norms of family and social milieu conflict; the son of a Conservative working man, as we shall see, may put aside his inherited partisanship for that of his working-class friends. But equally these instances of conflict reveal the deep impress of the childhood home; the survival of the parents' norms in a class environment whose norms are different testifies to the family's influence on the young.

The family may help form the child's impression of other aspects of politics than the virtues of the parties. There is, for example,

has also been a fundamental process in the influential conceptual frameworks authored by Gabriel Almond and David Easton and their associates. See Gabriel A. Almond and James S. Coleman, *The Politics of Developing Areas*, Princeton, 1960, Chapter 1; Gabriel A. Almond and Sidney Verba, *The Civic Culture*, Princeton, 1963; and David Easton, *A Framework for Political Analysis*, New York, 1965.

evidence that the interest which politics holds for the adult elector is influenced by the degree of interest it held for his parents. Only one in three of our respondents who remembered both parents as interested in politics said that politics was of 'not much' interest to themselves, whereas nearly 60 per cent of respondents who said that neither parent was interested in politics said that they too were not interested.[2] The same traces are to be seen in the respondent's memory of how early in life he first became aware of politics. Of those still in their twenties and therefore least removed from their childhood years, the number remembering themselves as politically interested by the age of ten is twice as large among those who recall both parents as interested in politics as it is among those who recall neither parent as interested.

But it is the direction of the child's partisanship that is the foremost legacy of the early years. A child is very likely indeed to share his parent's party preference. Partisanship over the individual's lifetime has some of the quality of a photographic reproduction that deteriorates with time: it is a fairly sharp copy of the parents' original at the beginning of political awareness, but over the years it becomes somewhat blurred, although remaining easily recognizable. The sharpness of the first reproduction is shown by Table 3.1, which examines the early preferences of those who remembered each of their parents as either Conservative or Labour partisans. Children of parents who were united in their party preference were overwhelmingly likely to have absorbed the preference at the

2. Our dependence on the child's recall introduces obvious problems of interpretation which should be borne in mind at many places in this chapter. Cautionary evidence as to the frailties of recall is supplied by studies of the young which have also obtained data on the political attitudes of parents. See, for example, Richard H. Niemi, *A Methodological Study of Political Socialization in the Family* (unpublished doctoral dissertation, University of Michigan, 1967). It is far from obvious, however, whether these errors of recall will in a particular case inflate or diminish the correlation observed between parent and child. The tendency to remember one's parents as having one's own beliefs will of course magnify the relationship falsely. But more random errors of memory will tend to understate the real strength of these ties. There is indeed evidence that in some cases these opposite effects are substantially offsetting, but any of our findings that involve the child's recall should be read with a degree of caution.

3.1 Earliest Party Preference by Parents' Conservative or Labour Preference

Respondent's Own First Preference	Parents' Partisanship		
	Both Parents Conservative	Parents Divided Con/Lab	Both Parents Labour
Conservative	89%	48%	6%
Labour	9	52	92
Liberal	2	—	2
	100%	100%	100%

beginning of their political experience. We shall shortly return to the legacy of parents whose preferences were divided.

The progressive blurring of this first reproduction can be seen by examining the current preferences of the same respondents (those who remembered each of their parents as Conservative or Labour). The preferences of these respondents as adults in the mid-1960s are shown in Table 3.2. The imprint of the family's partisanship is still clear but it is more blurred than it was in Table 3.1. The greater erosion of Conservative preferences among those of divided parentage reminds us that the forces which have

3.2 Present Party Preference by Parents' Conservative or Labour Preference

Respondent's Own Present Preference	Parents' Partisanship		
	Both Parents Conservative	Parents Divided	Both Parents Labour
Conservative	75%	37%	10%
Labour	14	49	81
Liberal	8	10	6
Other	—	—	—
None	3	4	3
	100%	100%	100%

intervened in the adult years may not favour the parties in equal measure.

When the direction of mother's preference is distinguished from father's it is plain that each parent, and not the father only, helps to form the nascent partisanship of their children. Table 3.3 shows the proportions of our adult respondents whose first preferences were Conservative according to the various patterns of their parents' preference. This array is a remarkable testament to the

3.3 Proportion of Earliest Preferences Conservative by Pattern of Parents' Preference[a]

| | | Father was | | |
		Conservative	Neither[b]	Labour
Mother was	Conservative	89%	46%	50%
	Neither[b]	68%	27%	16%
	Labour	41%	8%	6%

[a] Each entry of the table gives the proportion of respondents within a given pattern of parental preferences whose own first preference was Conservative.

[b] The 'Neither' category includes those whose parents were of Liberal or changing preference or of no remembered preference.

joint influence of mothers and fathers. Nor would the figures differ in any substantial way if they were presented separately for men and women. Apparently both sons and daughters were equally susceptible to this joint influence and not only sons to fathers or daughters to mothers.

Fathers, however, have had much more to do with the partisanship of their children since their own partisanship was so much more likely to have been visible in the family. Table 3.3 indicates that when the mother was partisan, and agreed with the father, she strongly reinforced his influence on the child, and that when the mother was partisan, and disagreed with the father, she was, if anything, a little more likely to carry the child with her.[3] But the case of the partisan father and the neutral or non-political mother was a far commoner one in the childhood experience of the present electorate. Indeed, all but a quarter of our respondents recalled a clear partisanship for their fathers, but nearly half were unable to attribute a partisanship to their mothers.

Table 3.4 shows how, largely as a result of this, there is a greater

3.4 Agreement of Elector's Party with Party of Father and Mother[a]

		Whether Elector's Party Is Same as Father's		
		Yes	No	
Whether Elector's Party Is Same as Mother's	Yes	39	9	48
	No	21	31	52
		60	40	100%

[a] This tabulation is limited to respondents who were themselves self-described Labour or Conservative supporters and who remembered at least one of their parents as being Labour or Conservative.

tendency for an elector's partisanship to agree with his father's. The table, which classifies all respondents who were themselves Conservative or Labour and who remember at least one of their parents as being Conservative or Labour, shows more than twice as many fathers having supplied a lead independent of mother as the other way round. But we can see from the prior table that this is entirely the result of the greater likelihood that fathers had a party allegiance that was known to their children.

3. A recent nationwide study of American high school seniors and their parents showed these adolescents as more likely to be influenced by their mothers than their fathers when the two parents disagreed as to party. See M. Kent Jennings and Kenneth P. Langton, 'Mothers *versus* Fathers: the Formation of Political Orientations among Young Americans', *Journal of Politics*, **31** (1969), 329–58.

This difference reflects the greater politicization of men in British society. Involvement in political affairs was by no means equalized at a stroke (or two strokes) with the coming of a fully equal franchise in the 1920s.[4] Even in the 1960s the interest which the men in our sample took in politics was greater: three-fifths of our women respondents said they had 'not much' interest in politics, as against only one-third of our men. An interesting additional characterization of the relative political weight of mothers and fathers as remembered by the present electorate is found in our respondents' account of the main reasons why their parents held the party allegiance they did. Fewer than a fifth mentioned the influence of some other member of the family on their fathers. But nearly three-fifths attributed their mother's party allegiance to the influence of her husband or someone else in the household.

The increasing politicization of women is reflected in the ability of the men and women of our four age-cohorts to associate a

3.5 Recall of Parents' Party Allegiance Within cohorts by Sex of Parent and Child

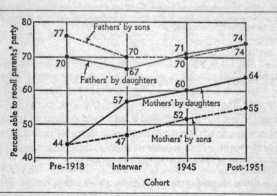

4. Most women over 30 were given the vote in 1918, but it was not until 1928 that the age of women's voting was reduced to 21 and the franchise became effectively equal for men and women.

partisan self-image with their mothers.[5] This evidence is contained in Figure 3.5, which shows as well the extent to which sons and daughters could associate a party allegiance with their fathers. The figure makes plain that for men and women of all cohorts the father's partisan image is the sharper of the two. But the strongest trend in these data is the growing awareness among daughters of a partisan attitude in their mothers. In view of the mother's importance in defining for her daughters the woman's role, this trend has evident relevance to the deepening political involvement of women as the century advanced.

In politics as in so much else the family's influence is large because the child's opinions are unformed. But the family is not the sole influence in the impressionable years, especially those of adolescence and early adulthood. The plasticity which renders the young open to so deep an impress from their parents also renders them more open to influences from other quarters than they will be later, when set in their adult ways. Many of these influences are lodged in a wider social milieu of school or work. In particular, the widening contacts of the young must often bring them the values and norms which connect party to class.

Such a process is reflected in the entries of Table 3.6 overleaf, which have been built up by comparing the first remembered party preferences of children from Conservative and Labour homes with those of their parents and comparing their parents' party preferences with the dominant political tendencies of their class – Conservative in the case of middle class families, Labour in the

5. Since we shall often use these cohorts in the course of our analysis, it is well to set out their definition in some detail. The oldest group, the 'Pre-1918' cohort, is comprised of those who came of age soon enough to have qualified to vote in the General Election of 1918. We include in this group women who were by then of age, despite the fact that they had yet to receive the vote. The next oldest group, the 'Interwar' cohort, is comprised of those who came of age between the General Elections of 1918 and 1935. Once again, we shall overlook the fact that women between the ages of twenty-one and thirty were not enfranchised until the General Election of 1929. The third group, the '1945' cohort, is comprised of those who came of age between the General Elections of 1935 and 1950. The youngest group, the 'Post-1951' cohort, is comprised of those who did not come of age until after the General Election of 1950.

3.6 Agreement of Earliest Preferences with Parents' Partisanship Among Children from Conservative or Labour Families by Whether Parents' Partisanship was Aligned with Class

Respondent's earliest party preference[a]	Parents Supported[b] Party	
	Dominant in Class	Opposite Party
Agreed with parents' preference	91%	70%
Differed from parents' preference[c]	9	30
	100%	100%

[a] See Question 43b in the 1963 questionnaire.

[b] Includes cases in which one parent was remembered as favouring the party dominant in the class (or the opposite party) and the other as having no preference.

[c] Includes all cases in which the earliest preference of the child was remembered as differing from that of the parents.

case of working class families. The table shows a greater erosion of family political traditions where they are inconsistent with those of class. But the table shows equally the strong continuity of these traditions even when dissonant with a class milieu. The first preferences of fully 70 per cent of respondents whose families were not aligned with the majority of their class agreed with their parents' preference.

Indeed, the survival value of these minority political views was still very evident at the point of our respondents' adult lives when we interviewed them. The evidence of this is set out in Table 3.7, which has the same structure as the prior table but substitutes the respondent's current preference for the one he remembers holding when he first became aware of politics. It is seen that the present allegiance of fully 58 per cent of respondents whose families were not aligned with the majority of their class continued to coincide with the preference to which they were exposed in the home as children.

We would expect the individual's class milieu to play a greater role in forming the allegiance of the young in cases where the parents were of mixed political views or held no clear views as to party. The evidence of this showing the proportions of earliest and

3.7 Agreement of Present Preference with Parents' Partisanship Among Children from Conservative or Labour Families by Whether Parents' Partisanship was Aligned with Class

	Parents' Supported[b] Party	
Respondent's present party preference[a]	Dominant in Class	Opposite Party
Agrees with parents' preference	85%	58%
Differs from parents' preference[c]	15	42
	100%	100%

[a] See Questions 37a and 37f in the 1963 questionnaire.
[b] Includes cases in which one parent was remembered as favouring the party dominant in the class (or the opposite party) and the other as having no preference.
[c] Includes all cases of respondents who did not hold their parents' party preference.

present party preferences consistent with those dominant in the child's class among children of parents who were of mixed allegiance or held no clear party allegiance is set out in Table 3.8. Indeed, evidence from other countries indicates how extraordinary a role is played in Britain by the individual's class milieu in forming

3.8 Agreement of Earliest and Present Party Preferences with Partisanship Dominant in Respondent's Class Among Children of Parents with Mixed or No Party Allegiance[a]

	Among Children of Parents	
	Of mixed party allegiance	Of no party allegiance
Proportion of respondents whose earliest preferences agreed with those dominant in their class	65%	70%
Proportion of respondents whose present preference agrees with those dominant in their class	74%	73%

[a] This analysis is limited to children who have remained in their parents' social class.

a partisan allegiance in those who have not experienced a clear partisan influence from their parents. Table 3.9 contrasts the British findings with those from comparable interview studies in

3.9 Extent of Partisanship in Adults Not Associating a Party Preference with Their Father, in Four Nations

	Great Britain	France[a]	United States[b]	Japan[c]
Percent holding a party preference among adults who do not associate a party preference with their fathers	89·5	47·7	50·7	61·1

[a] From a nationwide survey undertaken in France in 1958 and reported in P. E. Converse and G. Dupeux, 'Politicization of the Electorate in France and the United States', *Public Opinion Quarterly*, 26 (1962), pp. 578–99.
[b] From the nationwide surveys undertaken in the United States by the Survey Research Center. Reported in P. E. Converse and G. Dupeux, ibid.
[c] From a nationwide survey undertaken in Japan in 1967. Data kindly furnished by Professor R. E. Ward and Dr A. Kubota.

France, the United States and Japan. The data available from these other studies make it necessary that we confine our attention to the influence of the father. It is clear from the table that a very sharp contrast indeed is found between the incidence of adult partisanship among those from relatively non-political homes in Britain and these other lands. We do not suggest that influences related to class are wholly responsible for the allegiances formed by electors from such homes. But the formative role of class is strongly implied by the preceding table, 3.7. The individual who begins life without a partisan lead from his parents tends to accept the lead that is so clearly given in Britain by a class milieu, with the consequence that the British electorate is far more politicized in a partisan sense than are most democratic electorates.

The relative impressionability of the young also means that they will be unusually open to the influence of issues and events which dominate national politics at the time of their entry into the electorate. If strong forces move the country towards one of the parties we can expect these forces to be most clearly evident in the behaviour of the youngest electors, on whom the weight of prior loyalties sits more lightly. The effects of such forces are vividly illustrated in our own sample by the reported first votes of those who entered the electorate in the Labour years after the Second World War. But the profile of the main parties' support among new voters over a generation suggests in a remarkable way the ebbs and flows of party fortune. These proportions are reconstructed from the reported first votes of our sample in Figure 3.10, which plots the Labour Party's share of new votes for the two main parties in

3.10 Labour's Share of Support for the Two Main Parties from New Electors, 1935–66

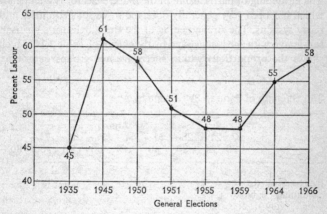

each election from 1935 to 1966. This profile of the behaviour of the youngest electors indicates clearly the surge in Labour's strength during the Second World War and its aftermath, the decay of its strength during the Conservative years of the 1950s, and the fresh Labour surge in the early and middle 1960s.[6]

6. We may indeed speculate that the reduction of the voting age to 18 in 1970 could mean a long term boost to the party that is uppermost at the time this large new bloc of young people become voters.

These formative influences have carried over into later voting. The greater Labour feeling of the Second World War and its aftermath could still be seen in the support for the two leading parties in the mid-sixties. Among those who first voted in the Labour years of 1945 and 1950 the proportion voting Labour in the General Election of 1964 stood at 60 per cent; among those who first voted in the Conservative years of 1951, 1955 and 1959, at only 53 per cent. With the aging of the voter the relatively plastic attitudes of youth tend to harden and the acquired habits of the early voting years begin to become more deeply fixed.

The Later Years

The hardening of partisanship in the mature elector is a tendency which has been very generally observed in various countries and party systems. The strengthening of the British elector's partisan self-image with age is suggested by the entries of Table 3.11, which shows the proportions within successive age groups describing

3.11 Strength of Partisan Self-Image by Age

| | Age | | | | | | | | |
	21— 20 24	25— 30	31— 40	41— 50	51— 60	61— 70	71— 80	80+
Percent de- scribing selves as 'very' or 'fairly strongly' attached to party[a]	47 58	62	65	73	74	73	76	88

[a] See question 37b in the 1963 questionnaire.

themselves as very or fairly strongly attached to a party.[7] The

7. A survey undertaken by the Opinion Research Centre in 1968 tended to confirm this finding as to the strengthening of party allegiance with age.

increase seen here is too regular to be explained in terms of a greater politicization among those who grew up in an earlier era, and we shall see additional evidence in a moment that the period in which the elector first became politically aware is less important in this connection than the length of time the voter has held to the same partisan belief.

A comparable pattern is found in actual behaviour. Since strongly felt ties are less likely to be displaced, the strengthening of partisanship in the aging voter implies that older electors will be less changeable in their voting. Such a trend is shown by Table 3.12 in terms of the constancy of party choice between the General

3.12 Constancy of Party Choice 1959–64 by Cohort

	Pre-1918	Interwar	1945	Post-1951
Proportion supporting same party in the 1959 and 1964 elections	86%	81%	79%	58%

Elections of 1959 and 1964 within the four age cohorts that we have previously defined. The strong political tides during the 1959 Parliament affected the several cohorts very unequally; the young were much more prone to desert a prior party choice.

There is evidence that what determines the strength and un-

The replies to the question 'How strongly Conservative, Labour or Liberal do you feel?' within three age groups were these:

	21–34	35–54	55+
Very strongly	21%	36%	49%
Fairly strongly	40	34	30
Not very strongly	24	19	14
Don't know	1	1	—
Without party allegiance	15	10	7
	101%	100%	100%

changeability of partisan ties is not so much the voter's age in years as the duration of his attachment to one party. Younger voters tend to be more plastic because their party preferences tend to be more recent. But older voters who have supported a party for as brief a time prove to be just as weak and changeable in their partisanship. When the strength and duration of partisanship are examined within age-levels, it is quite clear that what counts is the duration of the party tie and not the age of the elector himself. This finding is reflected in Table 3.13, where each of three age levels are divided into people who have supported the same party for 13 or more

3.13 Proportion Strongly Partisan by Age and by Duration of Present Party Tie[a]

		Age		
		25–39	40–59	60+
Duration of Present Party Tie	13 years or more	81%	80%	82%
	Less than 13 years	64%	70%	54%

[a] Each entry of the table shows the proportion describing themselves as very or fairly strongly attached to party within a group jointly defined by age and duration of present partisanship.

years and those who have not. It is plain from the table that it is duration of party support rather than age itself which strengthens party loyalty. Among those with long-established partisanship, age made no difference to its strength. Among those with a more fickle voting record, the old were, if anything, more weakly attached to their current party than the young. The same pattern is found if these data are examined by comparing changeableness in voting with age and duration of partisanship.

That psychological attachments become stronger the longer they are held is a fairly general finding in the social sciences,[8] as we have

8. Comparable American evidence of the deepening of partisanship with time is given by *The American Voter*, pp. 161–4.

noted; furthermore it is easy to sense how the recurrence of election campaigns can progressively deepen the partisanship of the committed voter. We observed in the previous chapter that each general election confronts the voter once again with the necessity of acting on distant and complex matters about which he is very imperfectly informed. In this situation an established partisanship provides the voter with a simple means of sorting political leaders into the worthy and less worthy, and of making judgements on the merits of conflicting party claims whose full evaluation could require a lifetime of study. Moreover, a partisan commitment simplifies his choice between rival candidates for Parliament whose party label may be for him their salient or their sole characteristic. Every time a partisan tie functions in this way it is likely to become stronger. The voter's experience over a series of campaigns can indeed be regarded as a kind of 'learning', in which the rewards of increased clarity and simplicity reinforce the party ties that supply them.

The psychological processes that underlie the strengthening of partisanship with time must be fairly complex. Some writers have found the concept of 'immunization' a useful one; electors whose partisanship is new, as the youngest electors' will always be, are more susceptible to the contagion of political change, whereas those of a longer partisan history have been immunized by their repeated experience of party politics.[9] Our view is that these processes must involve the increasing experience that the partisan voter gains over time in accommodating new political information within his existing partisan frameworks. The longer a given tie with party is held and the more experience the elector has in coding new messages consistently with it, the less likely is it that information about new issues and events will lead him to revalue the parties. We might indeed think of the committed voter as a kind of information processing device whose circuitry for receiving and inter-

9. Those who first gave currency to this image asserted that 'we mean not a metaphor, but the literal logic of the immunity idea: resistance to disturbances is built up by disturbances; lack of resistance to disturbances is due to lack of disturbances'. See W. N. McPhee and J. Ferguson, 'Political Immunization', in W. N. McPhee and W. A. Glaser, eds., *Public Opinion and Congressional Elections*, New York, 1962, pp. 155–79.

preting messages in a given way becomes increasingly effective as additional information is received and stored. But the elector whose partisan circuitry is still undeveloped has a higher probability that messages about new political issues or events or leaders will cause him to revalue the parties. We shall return to this phenomenon in Chapter 10 when we consider the flow of political information to the individual voter.

Certainly it is plain that committed voters are likely to interpret many political events in a partisan fashion. Those who study the political effects of the mass media report frequent examples of such party bias. One of the nicest is the tendency for the television viewer to score highly on the 'appreciation index' measuring response to a party political broadcast if he already sympathizes with the party.[10] An equally clear example from our own interviews is the tendency of the committed voter to see the personal qualities of his own party leader in a particularly favourable light. The Labour stalwarts in our sample were especially prone to discover purely personal deficiencies in Harold Macmillan, Sir Alec Douglas-Home and Edward Heath alike, just as steadfast Tories remained disenchanted with Harold Wilson through three interviews. There were of course differences in the degree of esteem felt for the different party leaders by these voters, and we shall consider these in some detail in Chapter 17. But the biasing effects of party allegiance were evident in perceptions of every leader in these years.

It is worth while mentioning a process which is often attributed to the aging elector but for which there is in fact little evidence. Both academics and journalists have thought that many voters begin their political lives on the left and move rightward as they grow older. A theory of political 'senescence', as it is sometimes called, fits comfortably the more general belief that the attitudes of youth are naturally liberal or radical, while those of age are naturally conservative. Empirical support for such a theory is thought to be supplied by the fact that Conservative strength is

10. Evidence on this point from two recent elections may be found in *The British General Election of* 1964, p. 162 and p. 182 and *The British General Election of* 1966, p. 144.

greater among older electors than it is among younger. The profile of party support by age seems at first glance to lend the theory a good deal of credence.

Such a process evidently contributes to political change in some party systems but its importance in Britain seems limited. One indication of this can be seen in some further irregularities of party strength by age. When the age profile of party support is examined more closely, it is seen that in the 1960s Conservative strength tended to be weakest among those in early middle age, i.e. those born in the 1920s and just before. Electors younger than this tended actually to be a little *more* Conservative than those who lay within the precincts of early middle age.

This irregularity, although an embarrassment to any simple theory of conservatism increasing with age, can readily be reconciled with the concept that the *conservation* of established political tendencies is what increases with age. The profile of age support in the mid-1960s can be accounted for in terms of the impress of early political forces on the young and the preservation of these forces in the hardening allegiances of later years. We must ask not how old the elector is but when it was that he was young. Voters who were of early middle age in this period, among whom Conservative support is weakest, were too young to have voted before the Second World War but entered the electorate in the postwar Labour flood. Electors who were older than this came of age when Labour was far weaker; indeed, many reached maturity before the Labour Party could establish any serious claim to power. We would expect electors who were younger than the 1945 cohort to be most variable in their party support, since they were still, in the 1960s, in their impressionable years.

More detailed empirical evidence on these points is supplied by profiles of party support by age drawn from the data of National Opinion Polls. In each of several periods in the mid-1960s N.O.P. massed the evidence of several successive samples, permitting unusually reliable estimates to be made of the division of party support within successive age groups. Figure 3.14 on the next page shows the profile of party strength by ten-year age groups during the election campaign of 1964. This curve confirms the slight

3.14 Labour's Lead Over Conservatives by Age, 1964 Election[a]

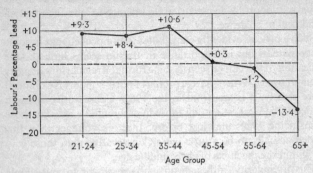

[a] Source: National Opinion Polls; per cents based on total sample.

peaking of Labour support among the 35–44 group, which came of age in the years from 1941 to 1950. A fairly sharp decline of Labour strength is seen in the older age groups, while a somewhat lower level of Labour support is seen among the younger.

Additional insight into the elector's differing susceptibility to change at different ages is gained by comparing this profile for the autumn of 1964 with one from the prior winter of 1963–4, when the country's mood was a good deal more Labour. This comparison is given by Figure 3.15. The pattern that stands out is the relationship between age and extent of change. The movement towards the Conservatives in fact diminishes monotonically in successive age groups.

The pattern of Figure 3.15, although far from a conclusive test, is not very kind to the senescence hypothesis. If we were to suppose that the political movements of this period were the result, first, of a general weakening of Labour's strength for reasons which were likely to affect any elector and, second, of a movement of aging voters towards a Conservative position, we should expect a stronger rightward movement at higher ages or at the very least a more uniform shift to the Conservatives at all ages. The pattern that is in fact observed is more consistent with the alternative

3.15 Labour's Lead Over Conservatives by Age, Winter 1963–4 and 1964 Election[a]

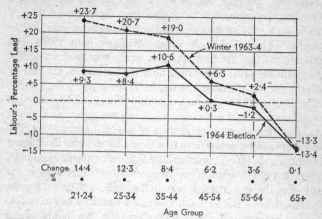

[a] Source: National Opinion Polls ; per cents based on total sample.

concept that the conservation of established tendencies, rather than Conservatism as such, is what increases with age. There is about these data more of immunization than of senescence.[11]

The descriptions given by our respondents of their own partisan histories were no kinder to the view that senescence has been a major element of political change in Britain. The proportion of early Labour sympathizers who had gone over to the Conservatives was no larger than the proportion of early Conservatives who had turned to Labour. And the proportion of Conservatives who had become Liberals was a good deal larger than the

11. Similar comparisons over the period of Labour's spectacular slump of 1966–8 show a similar profile of volatility. Change was less marked in each successive age group. But the period from 1964–6 yields conflicting evidence: while our own sample shows the same pattern as the N.O.P. figures for the other periods, N.O.P. suggests a fairly massive swing to Labour among older voters, supposedly won over by the substantial pension increase of 1965. It is beyond our present scope to reconcile this difference, although it may be partly attributable to the universal survey problem of getting a representative sample of older people. Certainly this deviant case does not vitiate our general contention that the changeableness of electors tends to diminish with age.

proportion of Labour supporters who had become Liberals.

Moreover, the great majority of those who had changed in a given direction remembered doing so when the dominant tides of politics were moving that way. Shifts from Labour were mainly linked to the period of Conservative ascendancy in the 1950s. And shifts away from the Conservatives were in most cases linked either with the great Labour era after the Second World War or with the years of Conservative decline in the early 1960s.

The fact that those who are young in a given period are exposed to common political influences, which are conserved as a cohort ages, gives rise to the phenomenon of political generations. The differences among generations that have been exposed to different influences and different problems are a recurring theme of political commentary. The importance of generational differences at the level of political leadership was indeed one of Bagehot's most eloquent themes. But such differences are equally a key to understanding changes at the level of the electorate. We should extend our discussion of the individual's life cycle and consider the framework that might be needed to analyse in these terms changes in the electorate as a whole.

Generational Models of Electoral Change

Political immunization is only one of the processes we must take into account in viewing the sources of change in terms of political generations. We may suggest several others by setting out a grossly simplified model of political equilibrium, one that would leave the party balance wholly unchanged as successive generations moved through the electorate. The model is one under which all parents have an identical number of children who unfailingly inherit a party allegiance from which they never deviate throughout lifetimes of uniform length. Such a model is false to British experience in all of its particulars, but each of its errors – the assumptions of uniform fertility, of full inheritance of partisanship, of undeviating allegiance throughout life, and of uniform mortality – calls attention to a potential source of electoral change.

Let us examine first of all the assumption of uniform fertility.

The fact that birth rates and party preference both differ by class should be enough to suggest the importance of differential fertility for the strength of the parties. We shall refer in Chapter 11 to the census estimates that seven children were born to wives of manual workers for every five children born to wives of non-manual workers during most of the period in which the present electorate was born (although the effect of this was partially offset by greater infant mortality in the working class). Moreover, we shall set out evidence from several interview studies, including our own, that disclose differences of fertility between Conservative and Labour families *within* the working class. Indeed, our evidence suggests that beliefs as to family size tend in an interesting way to be tied to a wider pattern of values and beliefs, of which political allegiance and aspirations of social mobility are also part. The political consequences of varied fertility rates are transparently evident.

The second of our assumptions, that of unfailing political inheritance, is false to the empirical evidence that we have already examined. Much can be learned, however, by studying the nature of the influences that intervene between parent and child. Not all displacements of the parents' allegiance will alter the party balance in the offspring's generation. Failures of political inheritance can be mutually offsetting and disturb neither the partisanship of generations nor the party balance as a whole; the model of unfailing inheritance is only one of a number of possible equilibrium models. But the likelihood that changes of this sort will shift the party balance is of course high.

This will be true even if these changes are largely random or idiosyncratic. Let us suppose, for example, that one of the parties has twice the adherents of another in the parents' generation and that there is a one-third chance that the child will support the opposite party, whichever that is. These assumptions imply that the ratio of support will be reduced from 67:33 in the parents' generation to only 57:43 in the children's – and to only 53:47 in the grandchildren's. The multiplicity of transient issues that act on the elector in his adult years may have an important role in keeping the partisan difference between the generations from being more extreme.

But the main source of change lies in political forces which move large parts of the electorate in a common way. In Chapter 5 we shall examine in some detail the process by which the conversion of the children of working class parents has continued the realignment of partisanship by class which began much earlier in the century. And we shall see evidence at a number of points of the effects on successive cohorts of the issues and events that dominated politics when they were young.

The manner in which the last of our assumptions, that of a uniform span of life, is false to British experience also holds a good deal of significance for political change. The political importance of selective death is implied by the fact that the Conservatives in the modern period have held a greater share of the political allegiances of women and of the middle class, groups which are marked by longer life. Indeed, the differences of survival between men and women and between the middle and working class offer additional reasons why the oldest electors are the most Conservative: Conservatives have tended to live longer.[12]

But the inferences to be drawn from the facts of differential mortality are both subtle and mixed. The likelihood of dying varies more by age than by anything else, including class and sex, and if the oldest age-cohorts favour one of the parties more strongly than the accumulated effects of the selective mortality would lead one to expect, then that party stands to suffer unequal losses due to current deaths. We shall give evidence that this was the situation of the Conservatives at the end of the 1950s: since the party enjoyed an advantage among the oldest electors quite apart from that which the difference in death rates by sex and class would have built up over time, it stood to lose as this age-cohort moved out of the electorate.

Taking account of these several processes, we can, by aggregat-

12. Let us suppose on purely hypothetical grounds that the difference in life expectancy favoured the Conservatives by four years (i.e. the life of a normal Parliament). On present life expectancies the average Conservative would have the chance to vote in thirteen elections before he died and the average Labour elector in only twelve. Thus, for a party equilibrium to be maintained, all other things being equal, the Conservatives would need to recruit only 92 per cent of the number of new voters required by Labour.

ing our data on the life cycle of single electors, describe the evolution of partisanship within an entire age-cohort. And by tracing over the years the progress through the electorate of cohorts of differing party composition we may study the evolution of party strength in the electorate as a whole. In Chapter 11 we shall pursue this type of aggregate analysis over a period of half a century.

We have mentioned the importance of the individual's social milieu for political conversions. In Britain this milieu is defined pre-eminently in terms of social class. As the differential mortality rates by class remind us, social factors lurk behind many of the processes we have considered. The direction of parental partisanship, the factors reinforcing or weakening the family's influence in the early years, and the continuity of party allegiance in the adult are all deeply affected by the individual's class location. We turn to the impact of class in the chapters which follow.

4 Class and Party

In contemporary interpretations of British voting behaviour class is accorded the leading role. Pulzer was entirely in the academic main stream when he wrote, 'class is the basis of British party politics; all else is embellishment and detail'.[1] The same view is echoed among party activists. The Labour canvasser is warned away from the surburban villas lest he 'stir them up', while some Conservative agents can be heard dismissing council housing estates as '90 per cent socialist'. There is, in fact, evidence that party allegiance has followed class lines more strongly in Britain than anywhere else in the English-speaking world.[2]

But, in view of the large amount of attention focused on the correlation between class and party in Britain, the evidence about the nature of this link remains oddly limited. The analysis of class alignments is incomplete in two main respects. First, too little attention has been paid to the beliefs that link class to party in the voter's mind. The fact of partisan differences between classes is documented in a wealth of statistical evidence; the system of ideas, the attitudes, motives and beliefs which lie behind the observed differences have been largely neglected. Second, treatments of class alignment have tended to be static in their approach. Class has supplied the dominant basis of party allegiance in the recent past; but within living memory the alignments were less clear and

1. P. G. J. Pulzer, *Political Representation and Elections*, London, 1967, p. 98.

2. An excellent comparative survey of Britain, Canada, Australia and the United States appears in R. R. Alford, *Party and Society*, Chicago, 1963. Alford's examination did not extend to New Zealand where class differences in party support approach British levels. See A. Robinson in S. Lipset and S. Rokkan, ed., *Party Cleavages and Voter Alignments*, New York, 1967, pp. 95–112.

even in recent years they have shifted noticeably. This chapter considers some problems in the measurement of class and explores the links between class and party, including the beliefs that give meaning to politics in terms of class. The chapters that follow consider the changing nature of this relationship.

The Bases of Class

The literature on class is voluminous. Apart from providing the most obsessive theme in English novels for the last two centuries, class has been at the centre of sociological studies for more than a generation. No one who has read Hoggart's brilliant essay, for example, or Bott's enlightening study, or who has followed the refinement of the concepts of class and status in the writings of Runciman and of Goldthorpe and Lockwood can fail to appreciate how varied and subtle are class phenomena.[3] The identity and number of classes, the attributes characterizing classes, the relationship between classes, the openness of classes to individual movements up and down between generations or within one adult lifetime – these are all matters that are seen very differently in different parts of society.

We, therefore, sought to interpret the class system in the light of our respondents' own perceptions of it. In view of the wide currency of 'class' we kept the term while allowing our respondents to define the class categories in their own words.[4] We began by asking whether the respondent thought of himself as belonging to a class. Those, about half the sample, who said that they did

3. See A. M. Carr-Saunders and D. Caradog Jones, *A Survey of the Social Structure of England and Wales*, 2nd ed., Oxford, 1937; D. V. Glass, ed., *Social Mobility in Britain*, London, 1954; W. G. Runciman, *Relative Deprivation and Social Justice*, London, 1966; Margaret Stacey, *Tradition and Change, A Study of Banbury*, London, 1960; R. Hoggart, *The Uses of Literacy*, London, 1957; E. Bott, *Family and Social Network*, London, 1957; and J. H. Goldthorpe and D. Lockwood, 'Affluence and the British Class Structure', *Sociological Review*, n.s. **11** (1963), 133–63.

4. The series of questions we describe here was put to a random half of the sample interviewed in the autumn of 1964. The questions are those numbered 69a to 69g in the text of the 1964 questionnaire given in the Appendix.

were then asked in a completely unprompted way to name their class. The replies offer remarkable evidence of the primacy of the 'middle' and 'working' class designations; only one in five of such respondents failed to make use of one or other of the two. Those who did offer something else were mainly scattered among the 'upper' class, the 'lower middle' class, the 'upper working' class categories with only a small residue.[5]

Those who had replied to the initial question by saying that they did not think of themselves as belonging to a class were then asked whether they would place themselves in the middle or working class if pressed to do so. The overwhelming majority said that they would; indeed, we were left with only one respondent in twelve who neither volunteered nor accepted a middle or working class identification. The hold of these two broad categories on popular thought was underlined by the fact that less than a quarter of those who had described themselves as middle or working class chose, under probing, to qualify their answer by saying that they were in the upper or lower rather than the average part of their class. The way in which the eleven-twelfths of our sample who had volunteered or accepted an upper, middle or working class designation distributed themselves across this wider set of categories is shown in Table 4.1. Although society is stratified in many subtle ways

4.1 Extended Upper, Middle and Working Class Self-Images, 1963

Upper Class	Upper Middle	Middle Class	Lower Middle	Upper Working	Working Class	Lower Working	Total
1%	3%	25%	4%	10%	53%	4%	100%

and multiple, conflicting images are associated with each social category, it is difficult not to read the figures of Table 4.1 as evi-

5. Some of this residue – which amounted to less than 4 per cent of those questioned – in effect offered a synonym for the more frequent categories. Several described themselves as being of the 'professional class', one said he was of the 'labour class' and one placed himself in the 'miners' class'. One cheerful eccentric, a very fat publican, said he belonged to the 'sporting class'.

dence of the acceptance of the view that British society is divided
into two primary classes. This is much more than a sociologist's
simplification; it seems to be deeply rooted in the mind of the
ordinary British citizen.[6]

In view of the extraordinary hold of this dichotomy we sought
to explore the characteristics that people attributed to members of
the middle and working class. Once again we found wide agreement. As Table 4.2 on the next page shows, occupation provided
the main basis for characterizing the classes. When our respondents
described the kind of people who belong to the middle class,
references to occupation outnumbered references to wealth or
income by three to one and references to education or manners or
shared attitudes by twelve to one. When they described the kinds
of people who belong to the working class the primacy of occupation was even more striking.[7]

The role of occupation in perceptions of class is matched by its
primacy as a predictor of the class with which a man identifies
himself. There is overwhelming evidence that occupational status
is the best guide to whether an individual places himself in the
middle or working class. There is, of course, a circular element in
such observations; 'occupational status' is measured by sorting
a very large number of individual occupations into a hierarchy
that is based on judgements about their relative status made by
census officials or academics, or even by the public itself. Yet a

6. F. M. Martin found that four out of five respondents chose 'middle'
or 'working' as class designations. See his chapter 'Some Subjective Aspects
of Social Stratification', in D. V. Glass, ed., *Social Mobility in Britain*,
London, 1954, p. 55. The results of a number of other surveys show that a
greater dispersion of answers can be produced by presenting a sample
initially with a more elaborate set of categories, but this does not qualify
our inferences from the replies to a less structured series of questions.

7. The presence of the term 'working' in the designation of the class may
well raise the suspicion that the frequency of occupational replies has been
inflated by nominal answers which do not really distinguish the working
from middle class in occupational terms. Detailed inspection of the evidence, however, showed this not to be the case. Those who characterized the
working class in terms such as 'people who work for a living' were found
in almost every case to have in mind the manual/non-manual distinction or
comparable occupational criteria.

4.2 Descriptions of Class Characteristics

	% of responses
What sort of people would you say belong to the middle class?	
Occupation — non-manual, white collar, skilled, professional, self-employed	61%
Income and level of living — rich, wealthy, comfortably off	21
Attitudes and hierarchical location — snobbish, superior, aristocratic	5
Manners and morals — social graces, moral standards, attitudes towards work	5
Educational level or intelligence — well educated, intelligent, public school, university	5
Family background, breeding	1
Political — supporters of Conservatives, of right wing, of centre	1
Other	1
	100%
What sort of people would you say belong to the working class?	
Occupation — manual, semi-skilled and unskilled, people who work for a living, employees	74%
Income and level of living — poor, low income, people who live in poor housing, in slums	10
Manners and morals — social graces, moral standards, behaviour, attitudes towards work	7
Attitudes and hierarchical location — humble, subservient, people without airs, lower classes	5
Educational level or intelligence — poorly educated, left school early, unintelligent	3
Other	1
	100%

subjective element is involved in treating almost any 'objective' social characteristics in hierarchical terms. This is true, for example, of education; whether people of more education are to be accorded higher status than those of less, other things being equal, depends ultimately on the values that the society in question happens to hold at the time.[8]

The measurement of occupational grade necessarily involves the investigator in some intricate problems of assessment.[9] We

8. This subjective element in the relationship of education and social status is plain enough at the top of the educational range on both sides of the Atlantic. Anyone who has observed the matter at close hand knows, for example, how irrelevant the earning of a doctorate is in raising the class position of an Oxbridge graduate beyond where it was when he received his first degree, not to mention where it had been when he left Eton.

9. The complexities of occupational status are faithfully recorded in the evolution of measures of social grade in Britain. Stevenson's original index, prepared in 1911, consisted of five hierarchical grades – professional, intermediate, skilled, partly skilled and unskilled – to which he assigned occupations on the basis of his own and others' estimates of relative prestige. See the *Annual Report of the Registrar-General for England and Wales, 1911* and the *Proceedings of the Royal Statistical Society*, 1928, pp. 207–30. This ranking was incorporated in the decennial Census Classification of Occupations and has persisted with some modifications up to the 1961 census.

Later investigators became increasingly dissatisfied with the large and exceedingly heterogeneous Class III of the census grades. Until the 1961 census this middle group contained actors, aircraft pilots and laboratory assistants, among others, as well as skilled manual tradesmen. Hall and Jones improved the discrimination between middle-range occupations by introducing seven hierarchical grades, basing their classification in part on judgements of occupational prestige elicited from a sample of the general population. See J. Hall and D. Caradog Jones, 'Social Grading of Occupations', *British Journal of Sociology*, **1** (1950), 21–49. The Government Social Survey uses seven grades, distinguishing clerical workers from skilled operatives. By the later 1950s most market research organizations had come to use a sixfold classification (with the widely known designations A, B, C1, C2, D and E) which was first employed by Research Services Limited when that firm had responsibility for the national readership survey of the Institute of Practitioners in Advertising (I.P.A.). The distinction between C1 and C2 was intended to separate lower non-manual from skilled workers. Classification of respondents was normally done by interviewers on the basis of the occupation of the head of the household, supplemented at times by data on income or on the physical condition of the dwelling. The problems of comparing doorstep classifications made by interviewers of very different training and practices led to a desire within the market research agencies for the existing categories, A to E, to be explicitly defined in terms of the Registrar General's Classification of Occupations and for the coding of occupational grade to be done by central office staffs on the basis of these definitions. This is the approach we have adopted here.

have relied in our own coding of occupational level on a detailed classification of occupations into social grades proposed by a working committee of the Market Research Society, using the occupational categories of the 1961 Census Classification of Occupations. We have, however, modified these definitions to divide the lowest group of non-manual workers, those designated as C1 in conventional market-research terms, between those who have some skilled or supervisory role and those who do not.[10] Thus the categories we have used are these:

Our Designation	Market Research Designation	
I	A	Higher managerial or professional
II	B	Lower managerial or administrative
III⎫ IV⎭	C1	⎧ Skilled or supervisory non-manual ⎩ Lower non-manual
V	C2	Skilled manual
VI	D	Unskilled manual
VII	E	Residual, on pension or other state benefit

How do self-placements into the middle and working class differ across these occupational categories? Table 4.3 shows the relationship between the respondent's subjective class identification and the occupational level of the head of the respondent's household.[11] The proportion of respondents identifying themselves

10. Examples of our assignment of occupations to social grades and a discussion of the reliability of our measurement of social grades appear in M. J. Kahan, D. E. Butler and D. E. Stokes, 'On the Analytical Division of Social Class', *British Journal of Sociology*, **17** (1966), 127. We should make special acknowledgement of our great debt to Michael Kahan for his contribution here and throughout this chapter.

11. We have followed the practice of categorizing respondents on the basis of the breadwinner's occupation even where the respondent is working, on grounds that the occupation of the major figure in the family group tends to give the family as a whole its position in the class system. In this and what follows we have excluded group VII, a residual category comprised mainly of state pensioners without other means of support, on

4.3 Class Self-Image by Occupational Status of Head of
Household, 1963

	Higher Mana-gerial I	Lower Mana-gerial II	Super-visory Non-manual III	Lower Non-manual IV	Skilled Manual V	Un-skilled Manual VI
Middle Class	78%	65%	60%	32%	17%	9%
Working Class	22	35	40	68	83	91
	100%	100%	100%	100%	100%	100%
	(90)	(133)	(256)	(177)	(673)	(428)

with the middle class falls continuously from 78 per cent in group I
to 9 per cent in group VI. The very sharp cleft between group III
and group IV underlines the psychological validity of treating
social stratification in terms of two main classes. But this cleft
occurs not between manual and non-manual but between skilled
or supervisory non-manual (III) and other lower non-manual (IV).
There is a further sharp drop in middle-class identification between
groups IV and V, but the self-placement of the lower non-manual
group (IV) shows them to be more like the skilled manual stratum
(V) than they are like the next higher non-manual grouping (III).
It is plain that the combination of group IV and group III within
the market research category C1 involves lumping together people
who diverge markedly in their subjective class identifications.[12]

grounds that these people lie somewhat outside the occupational stratification order. Less than 3 per cent of our respondents fell into this category.
   12. Groups III and IV in fact differ not just in their reaction to the abstract
question 'Which class would you say you belonged to?' but in more concrete patterns of conduct. For example, 20 per cent of group III were found
to read a journal of record – *The Times*, the *Guardian* or the *Daily Telegraph* – a proportion not very different from the 22 per cent of group II
respondents who did so. But the proportion of group IV who were found to
read a journal of record was not more than 5 per cent. *Daily Mirror* readers,
on the other hand, amounted to 11 per cent in group III but to 28 per cent
in group IV.

The close alignment of occupational level and class self-image accords well with our evidence that occupation is the most important of the elements that characterize the classes in the public's mind. There are other elements, of course – education, income, style of living and the like. These are not independent of occupation – income and occupation are, for example, closely linked – but they are not wholly dependent on it; we would therefore expect them to make some distinct contribution to the individual's image of his own class. Table 4.4 shows an example of this by

4.4 Proportion Identifying with Middle Class by Income Level and Occupational Grade 1963[a]

| | | Occupational Grade | | | |
		I–II	III	IV–V	VI
	£1200+	72%	71%	54%	—
Annual	£750—1199	63%	64%	24%	15%
Income	£350—749	66%	51%	15%	8%
	£349 or less	62%	42%	16%	7%

[a] Occupation and income are those of the head of household.

recording the extent to which middle-class identification varies by income within four levels of occupation. At every level the higher the income the more people feel middle class, but this is especially apparent in the intermediate levels, III, IV and V, where the cues lent by occupational status are presumably less clear.[13]

A similar pattern emerges when we consider the respondent's housing, the aspect of his style of living which is probably most important to his image of his class location. Table 4.5 shows the extent of middle class identification within three occupational levels for those who are house-owners, for those who rent their homes from a private landlord and for those who live in council

13. Indeed, in the highest and lowest grades, where these cues are sharper, the rise is only slight, although the absence of unskilled workers who are very highly paid makes it impossible to trace this relationship for grade VI over the full income range.

4.5 Proportion Identifying with Middle Class by Type of Housing and Occupational Grade

		Occupational Grade		
		I–II	III–IV	V–VI
Type of Housing	Owns or is buying home	73%	58%	18%
	Rents non-council housing	60%	37%	13%
	Rents council housing	60%	29%	10%

housing.[14] Once again the proportion feeling middle class varies with the level of housing within each occupational grade, although the influence of housing appears to be strong only in the intermediate occupational range.

The images which people have of themselves as middle or working class therefore depend on a variety of life circumstances and are much more than an empty verbal response to a survey question. Tracing the full set of 'objective' influences on these 'subjective' images would draw us beyond the political concerns of this book.[15] Because of the pre-eminent importance of occupa-

14. Our ordering of levels of housing may in some instances be wrong, especially where privately rented accommodation falls below the quality of council housing. Nevertheless, the findings in this table and Table 5.6 below offer a general indication for our ordering.

15. If we rest our judgement on the techniques for estimating a linear model developed by Sewall Wright and others the sketch of these influences that is most consistent with our evidence would be on these lines.

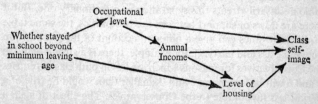

Owing to departures from strict linearity, the arbitrary scaling of several of the variates, and the presence of inevitable errors of measurement, the results of such an analysis should be treated with caution. None the less, they are quite consistent with the emphasis we have placed on occupational level as a formative influence on the individual's image of his class.

tion we shall use it in most cases as a measure of class location, although we shall often consult the individual's image of his own class and occasionally turn to other 'objective' influences. Although such simplifications are unavoidable, the complexities of the underlying relationships must be kept in mind throughout our analysis of the ties of class to party.

Appraising the Relationship of Class and Party

Even the most straightforward description of the alignment of class and party holds subtleties to trap the unwary. Let us set out the relationship in the simplest form, allowing for the two classes and the two parties which dominate British life and politics; the electorate can be classified thus within a four-fold table.

	Middle class	Working class
Conservative	a	b
Labour	c	d

This sort of table is thoroughly familiar in the literature on social class, but its simplicity is deceptive. First, a caution must be offered about the separation of Conservative from Labour.[16] The table necessarily treats this separation as a stationary one. But if there are flows of support between the two parties, the same table at different times can give a different account of the relationship between class and party. If, for example, there is a strong swing to the Conservatives for reasons which are felt in both classes, entries *a* and *b* will be larger and *c* and *d* smaller than would be true of a period less favourable to the Conservatives. The effect of such a contrast may be illustrated in this way:

16. Of course, the table also simplifies the situation by ignoring Liberals and minor party supporters, as well as those without a current preference.

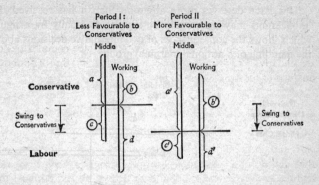

We may think of the change between the first and second period as
having the effect of moving downwards the dividing line between
Conservative and Labour in both columns of our four-fold table,
that is, within both the middle and the working class. As our figure
suggests, *b* and *c*, which were equal in period I, become markedly
unequal in period II; the Conservatives' share of the working class
vote has become much larger than Labour's share of the middle
class vote for reasons which may have little to do with class *per se* –
as we shall do well to remember when we contrast the data from
1959 with that from 1963–6.

A second, albeit similar, caution is necessary about the way in
which the separation of the middle and working class can alter the
description of the relationship of class and party given by our
four-fold table. Although the division of the population into two
social classes has ample warrant, the actual point at which the
division should be made is far from certain. We have been particularly aware of this in our own use of occupation as a distinguishing
attribute. The orthodox view has been that the occupational
distinction between middle and working class should follow the
distinction between manual and non-manual. But, as we showed
above, a sharper cleft in class self-images occurs before the lowest
level of non-manual occupations is reached. We have therefore
preferred to group these lowest white collar people with the working class when we divide the hierarchy of occupations into two.

This issue deserves more attention than it has received. Its implications may once again be suggested visually by a figure which shows the consequences of two alternative decisions about the handling of a notional marginal group:

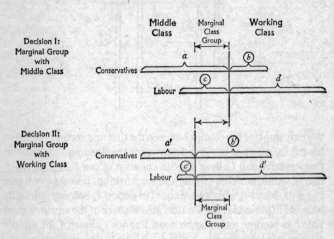

Under the first of these decisions the proportions supporting the Conservatives in the middle class and Labour in the working class are nearly equal. But under the second decision the proportions are notably different. When one considers the pattern of past discussions of class voting, it becomes plain how much the argument must have depended on the conscious or implicit coding decisions by which voters were divided between classes.

A third caution about descriptions of the relationship of class and party can be illustrated by our four-fold table. It is essential to distinguish between the class *source* of each party's support and the party *destination* of each class's support. Answering the questions whence each party's vote has come and where each class's support has gone requires quite different operations with the four entries in our table. To say how much each class has contributed to a given party's support we would want to express a and b as proportions of all Conservative voters $(a + b)$ or c and d as propor-

	Middle class	Working class	Totals
Conservative	a	b	$a + b$
Labour	c	d	$c + d$
Totals	$a + c$	$b + d$	

tions of all Labour voters ($c + d$). But to say how much of a given class has supported each of the parties we would want to express a and c as proportions of all middle class voters ($a + c$) or b and d as proportions of all working class voters ($b + d$). Each of these calculations has its uses but they are not the same. Indeed, the failure to distinguish the question of the class source of party support from the question of the party destination of class support has led to serious misinterpretation of poll findings, as we shall see in the next chapter when we consider the basis of working class Conservatism.

Class Cleavages in Party Support

Our findings on the strength of links between class and partisanship in Britain echo broadly those of every other opinion poll or voting study.[17] The ebbs and flows of party strength over the period made for some variation in the entries of our four-fold table, but the difference between the parties' share of votes in each class remained enormous. Here, for example, are the figures from our interviews in the summer of 1963. Table 4.6 makes plain that there were strong enough cross-currents in each class for partisanship not to have been determined entirely by class. Yet its pre-eminent role can hardly be questioned.

The tie of party to class is in fact still more impressive if we

17. The full Gallup figures on this from 1945 to 1964 are set out in an article by Dr Henry Durant in R. Rose, *Studies in British Politics*, London, 1966, pp. 122–8. The National Opinion Poll figures for 1964 are set out in *The British General Election of 1964*, p. 296, and for 1966 in *The British General Election of 1966*, p. 260.

4.6 Party Support by Class Self-Image, 1963

| | | Class self-image | |
		Middle	Working
Partisan Self-Image	Conservative	79%	28%
	Labour	21	72
		100%	100%

distinguish in these data the preferences of electors who qualified their middle or working class identification. The support for the two parties across the full range of class self-placements is shown in Table 4.7. Apart from the Conservative unanimity of the tiny

4.7 Party Self-Image by Extended Class Self-Image, 1963

| | | Class Self-Image | | | | | | |
		Upper Class	Upper Middle	Middle Class	Lower Middle	Upper Working	Working Class	Lower Working
Partisan Self-Image	Conservative	100%	84%	79%	76%	48%	28%	23%
	Labour	0	16	21	24	52	72	77
		100%	100%	100%	100%	100%	100%	100%

minority who described themselves as upper class, the greatest departure here from the percentages of Table 4.6 is the 48 per cent supporting the Conservatives among those who described themselves as 'upper working class'.

It is not surprising to find that the profile across our six occupational grades is very similar. Table 4.8 shows the continuous fall of Conservative strength down the occupational scale. Once again the figure which seems most discrepant from the strong pattern of the array is that for lower non-manual (IV), the highest occupational group which still tends to identify itself with the working class (as Table 4.3 showed); the Conservatives gathered in much more than half the support of this group.

The intermediate partisanship of the 'highest' working class

4.8 Party Self-Image by Occupational Status, 1963

	Higher Mana-gerial I	Lower Mana-gerial II	Super-visory Non-manual III	Lower Non-manual IV	Skilled Manual V	Un-skilled Manual VI
Conservative	86%	81%	77%	61%	29%	25%
Labour	14	19	23	39	71	75
	100%	100%	100%	100%	100%	100%

group in both the self-rated and the occupational profile suggests that it constitutes an intermediate social group occupying a somewhat ambiguous position in a class system of two primary groupings. There is indeed a great overlap between those who are in the lowest non-manual occupations and those who describe themselves as 'upper' working class, even though the correspondence is far from complete. A full discussion of the class position and party inclinations of these people would draw us fairly deeply into questions of industrial organization, social mobility and perceived status that lie beyond our scope.[18] These electors, drawn in conflicting directions by their ambiguous location in the social hierarchy, stand out from those solidly on one side or the other. Table 4.9 shows the Labour proportion at each occupational level among those who saw themselves as middle class and those who saw themselves as working class. This table has three main regions. The four left-hand cells in the upper row constitute a firmly Conservative region: among non-manual workers who identified themselves with the middle class, the Conservatives attracted on average nine out of ten of those who supported a major party. The two right-hand cells in the lower row constitute a firmly Labour

18. See D. Lockwood, *The Black-Coated Worker*, London, 1958, J. Goldthorpe, D. Lockwood, F. Bechhofer and J. Platt, *The Affluent Worker: Political Attitudes and Behaviour*, London, 1968, and W. G. Runciman, *Relative Deprivation and Social Justice*, London and Berkeley, 1966.

4.9 Proportion Labour Among Major Party Supporters by
Occupational Level and Class Self-Image, 1963

		Higher Mana-gerial I	Lower Mana-gerial II	Super-visory Non-Manual III	Lower Non-Manual IV	Skilled Manual V	Un-skilled Manual VI
Class Self-Image	Middle	10%	11%	9%	17%	46%	55%
	Working	43%	42%	43%	48%	76%	79%

region: among the great body of skilled and unskilled manual
workers who identified themselves with the working class nearly
eight out of ten supported Labour in preference to the Conservatives. The other six cells in the table form a middle region in which
party support was fairly evenly divided: among non-manual
workers who called themselves working class and among manual
workers who called themselves middle class the balance of partisanship was remarkably equal. It is interesting that lower non-
manual workers, whether they identified themselves with the
middle or the working class, differed little in their level of Labour
support from those of similar identification among supervisory or
higher occupations. In other words the higher Labour preference
of the lowest non-manual group, as shown in the earlier table, 4.8,
can be seen as overwhelmingly linked to their greater tendency to
identify themselves with the working class.

In marked contrast to the intimate ties between class and
Conservative and Labour support, support for the Liberals was
remarkably unrelated to class self-image and to occupational
grade. The Liberals indeed constitute a standing challenge to any
over-simple account of class and party. The level plateau of Liberal
strength, shown for 1963 in Table 4.10, is very unlike the ridges
and valleys of major party support that we saw in Table 4.9. The

4.10 Proportion Liberal by Occupation Level and Class Self-Image, 1963

		Higher Mana- gerial I	Lower Mana- gerial II	Super- visory Non- Manual III	Lower Non- Manual IV	Skilled Manual V	Un- skilled Manual VI
Class Self- Image	Middle	12%	20%	16%	24%	12%	10%
	Working	22%	14%	13%	14%	10%	5%

middle class element, so dominant in Liberal leadership, is just evident in their mass support, the party faring least well in the lower region of the working class. But the main impression conveyed by these figures is of the breadth and evenness, in class terms, of the Liberals' appeal.

These varying patterns of class support for the main parties draw us back to the question of the basis of the ties between class and party. This is a question that may scarcely seem to need an answer. One of the most perceptive students of class in Britain has remarked,

There is nothing, in a sense, that needs to be explained about a South Wales miner voting Labour or an executive of General Motors voting Republican. The simplest model of rational self-interest is enough to explain these cases . . . [19]

Although such a view catches an important aspect of the truth, it can easily lead to the neglect of worthwhile questions. At the very least, we may wonder whether 'rational self-interest' should be construed in wholly individual terms, or whether some who belong

19. W. G. Runciman, *Social Science and Political Theory*, Cambridge, 1963, p. 94.

to a common class may not perceive a more general class interest even when they would have difficulty particularizing it in terms of their own individual interest. We may also wonder whether some class voting may not have less to do with perceived interests, either individual or general, than the influence of distinctive class norms. Some who vote Conservative in the stockbroker belt, like some who vote Republican among General Motors executives, may simply be complying with the norms of their subculture; they may mark their ballots with no more thought of governmental consequences than they have when they mow their lawns or go to church. Here we begin to touch on questions which, to a peculiar degree, elude definitive answers: yet we feel it is worthwhile to outline three distinct models of the nature of class partisanship and to set out evidence for their validity and their relative importance.

Politics as Class Conflict

The first of these models involves the conception of politics as a conflict of *opposed* class interests, with the parties attracting their support by representing those interests. It is easy to associate such an intellectual view with Marx, although conceptions of class conflict go back as far as Aristotle and the playing out of this conflict in the parliamentary arena involves a thoroughly non-Marxist acceptance of the rules of the constitutional game.

Seen in terms of class conflict, the game of politics will benefit one class at the expense of the other. In the language of game theory, we might indeed say that the distinguishing feature of the class conflict model is that politics is seen as a 'zero-sum' game, in which the gains of one class are matched by the losses of the other. More is involved than a simple belief that the parties 'look after' class interests: these interests are seen as opposed and their opposition is what the party battle is thought to be about.

The voter who holds strongly to such a view will tend to sort his perceptions of various social and political relationships into a distinctive pattern. Let us consider first his probable view of the triad comprised by himself, his own class and the opposite class.

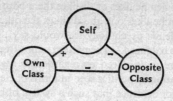

The individual whose party support is rooted in beliefs about class conflict will tend to form a strong positive identification with his own class and a negative identification with the opposite class – and will tend to see the relationship between the classes as one of necessary conflict. When we extend this approach to include the parties as well as the classes it is not difficult to assign to each of the relationships within it a positive or negative value, on the basis of a class-conflict view of politics:

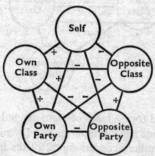

The bond between the voter's class and his party is seen as one of positive representation of interests, and so too is the bond between the opposite class and its party. The distinctive aspects of this intellectual view are, however, the negative 'cross-relationships' perceived between the classes and the parties. The projection of class conflict into the political arena arrays each party against the 'other' class.

This ideology of conflict consists therefore of a complex of 'balanced' triads of attitude and belief – 'balanced' in the sense that the individual will perceive a supporting relationship between any two objects when he likes or dislikes them both and a hostile relationship when he likes one and dislikes the other. To use the language of academic psychology we would say that the entire configuration was balanced.[20] The pattern of positive and negative bonds shown here may indeed be regarded as a social-psychological representation of politics seen in terms of class conflict.

In our search for evidence that such a system of beliefs does in fact underlie at least some class voting, we have focused on the most distinctive elements of the configuration: the negative cross-relationships between the voter's own class and the opposite class and between his own class and the opposite party and his response to the perceived positive relationship between the opposite class and party.

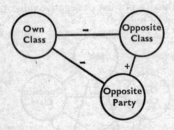

We have looked for evidence of these psychological ties in the extended replies our panel sample gave in several interviews to a very free set of questions concerning their likes and dislikes about the parties.[21]

20. The property of balance was first given systematic attention by Fritz Heider in 'Attitudes and Cognitive Organization', *Journal of Psychology*, **21** (1946), 107–12, but Festinger, Osgood, and many other writers have since considered this aspect of cognitive organization. An admirable statement of the relevance of theories of cognitive balance or dissonance to political analysis is given by R. E. Lane and D. O. Sears in *Public Opinion*, Englewood Cliffs, New Jersey, 1964, pp. 44–53. The formal property which gives 'balance' to our configuration representing a class conflict belief system is the fact that it is impossible to find within it a triad including an odd number of negative bonds.

21. The questions are numbered 6a to 7b in the 1963 questionnaire, 9 to

A well-developed example of beliefs in which conflict plays an important part was given by the replies of a retired porter in South Shields. Asked in the summer of 1963 what he disliked about the Conservatives, he said,

Their representation of unearned capital. Their disregard for the working classes. They are solely a money class representing high finance, which is detrimental to the prosperity of the country and people.

Asked what he liked about the Labour Party he said,

They represent my standard of living and are endeavouring to achieve many things that are more essential to the working people.

In the autumn of 1964 this respondent's answers to the same questions were as follows:

(Dislikes about Conservatives) They are absolutely class biased. They have no room for the working class, and their whole attitude is in support of the capitalists.

(Likes about Labour) They are seventy-five per cent for the uplifting of the working classes.

And in the spring of 1966:

(Dislikes about Conservatives) They are controlled by national and international capital. I hold them responsible for every war Great Britain has been in. I blame them for subjecting the working class to a mean, bare living. Their whole interest is self-interest.

(Likes about Labour) They are the proper party to look after the working classes in respect of the social services and education and the welfare state generally. I like their guidance of the trade union movement.

Evidence that the negative cross-relationships shown in our

---

12 in the 1964 questionnaire, and 7 to 10 in the 1966 questionnaire in the Appendix. We have in addition searched for beliefs linking class to party in the replies to this series of questions: 'Do you think that [middle/working] class people vote mainly for one party or are they fairly evenly divided between the parties?' (If mainly for one) 'Which party is that? Why do you think they vote mainly for that party?'

diagram of a conflict belief system do exist appeared in the replies of a number of less articulate respondents. For example, a Barnsley housewife whose husband was a repairman for the National Coal Board said:

(Dislikes about Conservatives, 1963) They don't help the working class. They're out to make money on anything.

(Likes about Labour, 1963) More for the working class. They believe in helping those who need it – like old people and people with large families.

(Likes about Labour, 1964) More realistic. More for everybody. A lot of them are from the working class and have a better idea of things and what people need.

(Dislikes about Conservatives, 1966) I don't like them at all; they are more for the money people than the working class.

(Likes about Labour, 1966) They are better for the working class. They do more for us. They have a better idea of what does us most good and they understand our problems better.

Some respondents had a developed sense of the way a zero-sum game between classes is played in the political or governmental arena, particularly the significance of the Budget. For example, a middle-aged Glasgow hosiery knitter, a crane-driver's wife, said this in the summer of 1963:

(Dislikes about Conservatives) Well, I think when they are in power and there is any Budget it is usually the better class people who come off the best; like income tax benefits.

(Likes about Labour) As far as the working class families are concerned, they are more liberal with income tax reliefs. I have always believed that Labour is for the working class.

But the bulk of respondents who expressed ideas about class conflict in the political arena used more general or diffuse images. For example, a domestic servant in Stoke-on-Trent spoke in these terms:

(Dislikes about Conservatives, 1963) They are not good to the workers. They would squash you down if they could; would have you work for nothing if they could.

(Likes about Labour, 1963) They are more for the workers. They would be good for the workers. They are giving you a fair deal.

(Dislikes about Conservatives, 1966) They would squash you if they had the chance. They wouldn't give you any help.

Beliefs in the existence of conflict were more often expressed in working class responses, as we shall see in a moment. But a number of middle-class respondents also voiced the sense of opposed class interest distinctive to such a system of ideas. The wife of a textile technician in Paisley, for example, gave clear evidence that she perceived the Labour Party as representing an opposed class interest:

(Dislikes about Labour, 1963) This attitude towards money. They seem to think they can rob the rich to save the poor.

(Dislikes about Labour, 1966) I don't like their attitude towards the richer people – that they are the ones who should pay for all the extras and help that the poor people get.

It would, however, be wrong to assume that anything like a majority of electors saw the tie of class to party in terms of conflict between classes. When laid against a fully developed model of such a belief system, the beliefs actually expressed by most of those in our sample who voted in 'accord' with their class were fragmentary and incomplete. If we are to account for the bulk of class voting we must take account of other belief systems as well.

The Simple Representation of Class Interest

One alternative conception of the ties between class and party is a variant of the conflict model. Politics may be seen as an arena in which the parties do indeed represent class interests – but interests which are not necessarily seen as opposed. The absence of a sense of conflicting interests may reflect a belief that, in the language of game theory, politics is a *positive-sum* rather than a *zero-sum* game; such a belief is strongly embedded in the theory of representation which, nearly two centuries ago, Burke applied to the interests of his day. Alternatively, it may simply reflect the fragmentary nature of the perceptions of electors able to see clearly enough that their party looks after the interest of their class, but not much beyond that.

Such a relatively unadorned conception of a party as representing the interest of a class was apparent in the comments of many of our respondents. For example, a miner's wife in Don Valley, who spoke of the main parties in these terms in the summer of 1963:

(Likes about Conservatives) No, I don't take much notice.
(Dislikes about Conservatives) No, I tell you I'm not interested in them.
(Likes about Labour) Well, I think we'd be better off if they got in. They would do more for the working classes.

A belief that one of the parties looks after the interest of a particular class is not in this case coupled with hostility towards, or even any very developed ideas about, the opposite party or class. The same fairly unelaborated belief in Labour's role as representative of working class interest was expressed by the same woman three years later:

(Likes about Conservatives, 1966) Nothing.
(Dislikes about Conservatives, 1966) They promise all sorts of things; but they don't carry them out.
(Likes about Labour, 1966) They haven't had much chance yet, but I think now they will really get down to things. They are for the working people.

Asked why working class people vote mainly for Labour, she replied simply, 'It's their party.'

A belief in the simple representation of class interest, unaccompanied by a strong sense of class conflict, is similarly evident in the replies given over three interviews by a bricklayer's wife in Central Ayrshire:

(Likes about Conservatives, 1963) I wouldn't really know how to answer this question. I wouldn't know what to say.
(Dislikes about Conservatives, 1963) Nothing.
(Likes about Labour, 1963) I like them because they're for the working class people. That's the only real point there is about them.
(Dislikes about Labour, 1963) There's nothing I don't like about them.

(Why do working class people mainly vote Labour?) Because they think Labour will do things for them and get them things to suit their income.

(Likes about Conservatives, 1964) Nothing.

(Dislikes about Conservatives, 1964) They seem to go back on what they say sometimes.

(Likes about Labour, 1964) I think they try their best to keep what they promise for working class people and the old folks; that is the main thing, the old folks.

(Dislikes about Labour, 1964) Nothing.

(Main reason she voted Labour, 1964) To me Labour is for the working class. It is only right to vote for people who will try to help you.

(Likes about Conservatives, 1966) No, nothing.

(Dislikes about Conservatives, 1966) I don't like their attitude towards the Labour Party. (Didn't like their attitude?) I didn't like some of Mr Heath's remarks about them.

(Likes about Labour, 1966) Mr Wilson is a man who will stand by his word. They are really out to help the working class.

(Main reason she voted Labour, 1966) It is for the working class.

For such a respondent the element of the larger system that is overwhelmingly important is the simple triad between the elector, his own class and his class's party:

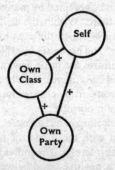

The individual, identifying with a particular class, forms a positive bond to the party which looks after the interest of the class, without necessarily forming any of the negative bonds that are distinctive of the conflict model of the relationship of class to party.

It would, however, be remarkable if perceptions of class interest were involved in all cases of individual behaviour consonant with the dominant partisan tendencies of the middle and working class. Many who vote 'with' their class do so for reasons that do not directly involve class interest. Many middle class voters, for example, believe that the education and business experience of Conservative leaders give them greater general skill in governing, especially in handling the country's finances. Although this belief is shared by a number of working class voters as well, its greater incidence in the middle class adds to the distinctiveness of middle class voting without directly involving class interest.

Partisanship in the Class Culture

The individual's response to the political norms of his class milieu can also help to keep the classes politically distinct without perceptions of class interest necessarily being involved. However important the perception of interests may have been in creating the political divergence of classes in the first place or in sustaining them in the longer run, anything so pervasive as the norm of Labour voting in the working class or Conservative voting in the middle class is likely to be accepted by many members of the class simply because it is there. Within the British nation there are distinct class sub-cultures which differ as to dress, speech, child rearing and much else. The processes by which individuals accept the norms of these cultures are quite general, and it would be as absurd to see perceived class interests in all class voting as it would be to infer such interests from class differences in the time of dinner or the rituals of mourning.

Party choice as a reflection of a class norm involves a triad similar to that associated with the model of politics as the simple representation of class interests. The individual supports a party because he perceives a positive bond between the party and his own class. But in this case the bond may be formed of nothing more than the individual's perception that the party is positively valued by his class. There can be no doubt that the bonds between the classes and the parties are widely perceived in the electorate. A belief in such a normative bond ran through a number of our respondents' free descriptions of the parties and the reasons for their own allegiance. A labourer's wife in Stirling, for example, explained her support of Labour by saying simply that 'I always vote for them; it's the working man's place to vote Labour.' A clerical officer in Bermondsey said he voted for the Conservatives because 'I feel they are more in keeping with my station in life.' The wife of a Durham miner explained working class support for Labour in these terms: 'The area itself has a lot to do with it; it's a lot of working class together, like around here.' The influence of

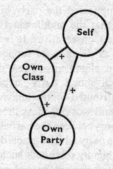

class in determining the partisanship of a local environment is a theme to which we return in Chapter 6.

The closeness of the association of class and party in the public's mind is attested to by two other kinds of evidence in our studies. The first is the way our respondents placed the parties on a simple scale extending from middle class to working class. As part of a wider assessment of party 'images' we asked a random half of our sample at each interview to place the Conservative and Labour parties on twelve scales, of which this was one.[22] Fully 90 per cent of our respondents placed the Conservatives towards the middle

22. The format of these scales followed the lines of the 'semantic differential' technique due to Charles Osgood and his associates. See C. E. Osgood, G. J. Suci and P. H. Tannenbaum, *The Measurement of Meaning*, Urbana, 1957.

class end of the scale, and 83 per cent put Labour towards the working class end. Indeed, the separation of the parties in class terms exceeded their distinctness on all the other scales by a very wide margin.[23]

The diffusion of political norms, especially in the working class, is also reflected in the proportion of our respondents who perceived their own class as giving its preponderant support to a particular party. Among our middle class respondents a third said that most of the middle class voted Conservative; among working class respondents fully three-fifths maintained that their class mainly supported Labour. Despite the fact that many of these people themselves supported the party of the 'opposite' class, almost no one said that the middle class supported Labour or the working class the Conservatives. It is noteworthy that those who saw their class as dividing its support were less one-sided in their own partisan alignments. These differences are set out in Table 4.11, which shows party support according to the political tendency attributed by the individual to his own class. Both in the middle and working class those who said that their class divided its support between the parties were less likely themselves to adhere to the party which attracts dominant support from their class. Some ambiguity surrounds such a difference, since the observed pattern may also reflect the tendency of those who deviate from their class to lessen any psychological tension or dissonance by failing to acknowledge the class norm. Yet such an alternative interpretation would also assume that the norm has a motive power for the individual, a power which in other cases has aligned the voter with the perceived norm.

This simple normative quality of party allegiance within class groupings, especially in the working class, had its origin for many electors in the childhood home. The importance of class location

23. By treating each party's ratings as a separate group of observations we may formalize the distinctness of the parties' placements on these scales in terms of ω^2, the proportion of the total variances of these ratings that is attributable to the difference of the mean party placements. For the middle class/working class scale ω^2 achieved a value of $0\cdot71$. On none of the other eleven scales (see question 64 of the 1963 questionnaire) did it achieve a value exceeding $0\cdot37$; indeed, the average value for the eleven was $0\cdot12$.

4.11 Party Preference by Class Self-Image and Perception of
Class Political Norms

	Individual identifies with			
	Middle class and perceives Middle Class as		Working class and perceives Working Class as	
	Mainly Conservative	Evenly divided	Evenly divided	Mainly Labour
Respondent's preference:				
Conservative	75%	65%	33%	21%
Labour	12	18	54	72
Liberal	13	17	13	7
	100%	100%	100%	100%
	(n = 159)	(n = 308)	(n = 431)	(n = 731)

to the child's understanding of his parents' party allegiance, especially his father's, emerges very strongly from what our adult respondents recalled from their childhood about the reasons for their fathers' preference. Indeed, the summary of reasons given for the partisanship of Conservative middle class fathers and of Labour working class fathers in Table 4.12 suggests that the appropriateness of a particular party to a particular class was for many

4.12 Reasons Recalled for Party Preference of Fathers Who
Voted With Majority of Their Class

Main reason recalled for party reference	Of Conservative Middle-Class fathers	Of Labour Working-Class fathers
Class-related	32%	69%
Traditional feeling	19	6
Influence of others in family	16	7
General approval of party	33	18
	100%	100%
	(n = 107)	(n = 419)

children the main explanation as to why their parents voted as they did, especially in the working class. The significance of this for a sub-cultural interpretation of class voting is plain enough. An elector who absorbed in childhood a belief about a normative bond of class and party, and who finds this bond reinforced by many of the face-to-face associations in his adult life, may easily accept party allegiance as a natural element of his class culture, quite apart from any well-defined understanding of the benefits that his party may confer upon his class or himself.

A Profile of Beliefs about Class and Party

Although the difficulties are formidable, it is worth attempting some tentative estimate of the extent to which the approaches to class and party described in our three models are manifest in the electorate. We base our judgement on the evidence furnished by respondents whom we interviewed three times from 1963 to 1966 and who held throughout the period consistent class and party allegiances – either Conservative and middle class or Labour and working class. The questions were those which yielded the quotations earlier in the chapter. First, we inspected our respondents' verbatim comments on their likes and dislikes about the parties at each of the interviews. Second, we examined their descriptions of the reason for their party preference at each of the interviews. Third, we looked at the reasons given by respondents in the first interview to explain why their class accorded preponderant support to a given party.

Respondents who gave evidence in any interview of perceiving class interests as opposed fell into our first category. Respondents who referred only to class benefits were classified as believing in a simpler representation of class interests. Among those who did not speak of class interests at all, we sorted into a separate category those who gave some indication of seeing support for a particular party as a norm appropriate to their class.

Such a categorization is far from including every elector whose vote conforms to the dominant political tendency of his class. Many happen to vote 'with' the majority of their class for reasons that have nothing to do with class interests or norms. The differing net effect of such influences in the middle and working classes helps to keep the classes politically distinct without any explicit belief in class interests or norms having to be present in the voter's mind. And the traditional character of voting means that some electors vote 'with' their class to reward or punish a party which they value positively or negatively for reasons having little to do with contemporary interests of any kind.

Our classification of beliefs yields a very different profile for the middle and working classes, as Table 4.13 shows. This table makes clear how very much more salient to the working class are the ideas

4.13 Beliefs About the Relation of Class and Party Held by Middle Class Conservatives and Working Class Labour Voters

Nature of Beliefs	Conservative Middle Class	Labour Working Class
Politics as the representation of opposing class interests	13%	39%
Politics as the representation of simple class interests	12	47
Politics as an expression of class political norms	10	5
No interest-related or normative content	65	9
	100% ($n = 96$)	100% ($n = 301$)

of class interest and class conflict. Seven in eight of our working class Labour supporters gave evidence of seeing politics as the representation of class interests, and almost half of these regarded such interests as opposed. Among middle class Conservatives fewer than one in three gave evidence of seeing politics in terms of the representation of class interests.

The meaning of this profile of working class beliefs depends a good deal on one's expectations. The theme of class conflict is a muted one, affecting less than half the working class Labour electors – yet, in terms of numbers, they are a formidable body. In later chapters we shall examine in greater detail the identity of those who do think readily in terms of class conflict, especially when we consider in Chapter 7 the consequences of trade union membership.

What is mainly notable in Table 4.13, however, is the contrast between the middle and working classes. This contrast fits what a number of writers have said about the images of the social order held by those in different class locations. In particular, Dahrendorf, after reviewing the empirical work of Centers, Popitz, Willener and Hoggart in a variety of national settings, noted the 'strange and important fact' that

those 'above' visualize society as a comparatively ordered continuous hierarchy of positions; those 'below' are, above all, struck by the gap between them and 'the others'.[24]

He associates with this divergence a markedly different tendency to see society in terms of conflict:

It would seem that the dominant groups of society express their comparative gratification with existing conditions *inter alia* by visualizing and describing these conditions as ordered and reasonable; subjected groups, on the other hand, tend to emphasize the cleavages that in their opinion account for the deprivations they feel. . . . The integration model, the hierarchical image, lends itself as an ideology of satisfaction and conservation; the coercion model, the dichotomous image, provides an expression for dissatisfaction and the wish to change the *status quo*. Even at a time at which the revolutionary ideologies of the Marxist type have lost their grip on workers everywhere, there remains an image of society which, in its political consequences, is incompatible with the more harmonious image of those 'above', whether they be called 'capitalists', 'ruling class', or even 'middle class'.[25]

Our evidence certainly shows that the working class is much more prone than the middle class to see politics in class terms,

24. R. Dahrendorf, *Class and Class Conflict in Industrial Society*, rev. ed., Stanford, 1959, p. 284.
25. ibid., p. 284.

whether including conflict or not. The words of a factory bench worker in Nuneaton – 'it's a case of us and them and they're them' – rarely had a counterpart in the comments of our middle class respondents. This difference of outlook between middle and working class accords well with differences of party ideology. The Conservatives can style themselves as the representatives of a more national interest, one that includes the interest of all classes within a hierarchical social order. The middle class elector can therefore identify his party with an existing social order which preserves the interest of the upper and middle classes without relying on concepts of class interest and conflict that are so evident in working class thought.[26]

The Conservatives' appeal as a 'national' party, the governing agent of an integrated if stratified social order, has helped keep the middle class strongly Conservative since the rise of the Labour Party. This image is indeed one that holds considerable appeal for working class voters as well, as a number of Labour politicians ruefully note; the Conservatives' ability to see their party as above politics – indeed, as above class interest in any narrow sense – is often mentioned wryly by their opponents. But in the main the working class held to a more dichotomous view of the social order, and Labour's image in the period of our work still reflected the party's explicitly working class origins and trade union connections.

26. Some observers have wanted to see the values associated with the Conservatives, aligned with the most prestigious institutions of British society, as a dominant national pattern, from which all Labour support ought to be seen as 'deviant'. Parkin, for example, has written, 'In other words, the values and symbols which have historically attached to the Labour Party and other parties of the Left, are in a sense deviant from those which emanate from the dominant institutional orders of this society. Examples of such institutions would include the Established Church, the public schools and ancient universities, the élites of the military establishment, the press and the mass media, the monarchy and the aristocracy, and finally and most importantly, the institutional complex of private property and capitalist enterprise which dominates the economic sector – the postwar innovations in public ownership notwithstanding.' F. Parkin, 'Working Class Conservatives: A Theory of Political Deviance', *British Journal of Sociology*, **18** (1967), 280.

The relation of class to party is not, however, a static one. Conceptions of the social order have changed in an age of relative affluence, and the balance of beliefs about class and party has inevitably been modified as older electors have died and younger ones have come of age. These processes are continuing ones. We should therefore examine several aspects of change that involve class, tracing the historical evolution of the class alignment.

5 Class and Change

There is nothing immutable in the relation of class to party. A glance at earlier periods or a comparison with the experience of other countries both suggest how variable this relationship can be. Several types of very broad social and economic trends may alter the ties of class to party. They can certainly be changed, on the one hand, by sustained economic growth. The postwar affluence of Britain, if it has failed to achieve the mass *embourgeoisement* of British workers, may none the less have weakened the intensity of party allegiances which have their basis in class. On the other hand, the changing composition of the labour force must alter the class source of party support, and probably the pattern of party allegiance within classes as well. Between 1950 and 1965 there was, in fact, a fall of about 5 per cent in the proportion of the work force engaged in manual occupations, a mass alteration of status that could hardly fail to have a political impact.[1]

Moreover, quite apart from occupational changes and economic growth, the turnover of the electorate introduces a dynamic element to the relationship between class and party. The labour force is constantly transformed by deaths and comings of age. Not every son succeeds to the occupation of his father, and those whose occupations are at a social level conspicuously above – or below – that of their fathers' may also differ in their politics. Social

1. See G. S. Bain, 'The Growth of White Collar Unionism in Great Britain', *British Journal of Industrial Relations*, **4** (1966), 304–35. For a comprehensive account of changes in the composition of the work force in the period 1931–61, based upon the Registrar-General's social classifications, see R. Knight, 'Changes in the Occupational Structure of the Working Population', *Journal of the Royal Statistical Society*, Part 3 (1967), 408–22.

mobility and economic change are linked of course by the fact that the rising proportion of non-manual occupations is a principal reason for changes of social level between father and son.

Social Mobility and Political Mobility

In order to analyse social change between generations it is necessary to recapture from respondents the social condition of their parents. There are frailties in this kind of recall – and genuine complexities introduced when fathers have a varied occupational career – but we have relied on more than one measure of social change. We have sought to compare the respondent's present class identification with the identification he attributes to his family when he was young. We have also gathered detailed information about the nature of the respondent's father's work so that we could compare the respondent's present occupational grade with that of

---

2. The turnover of occupational grade between the father of each respondent and the current head of household is set out in this table.

Father's Occupation

	I	II	III	IV	V	VI		(n)
I	1·1	1·0	1·2	0·4	1·4	0·5	5·6	(93)
II	0·8	2·0	1·0	0·4	2·6	1·6	8·4	(139)
III	1·3	1·7	3·1	1·2	4·5	3·1	14·9	(243)
IV	0·5	0·7	1·9	0·4	2·9	2·2	8·6	(139)
V	0·8	2·0	2·3	2·3	16·0	14·8	38·2	(604)
VI	0·1	0·8	1·0	1·5	8·3	12·6	24·3	(385)
	4·6	8·2	10·5	6·2	35·7	34·8	100%	
(n)	(75)	(133)	(172)	(103)	(574)	(546)		

Head of Household's Occupation (row labels I–VI)

his childhood home, the occupation of both father and son being coded on the basis set out in the previous chapter.

The class movements between generations perceived by our respondents are consistent with the upward bias of the British occupational structure. Eighty-four per cent of electors, as is shown by Table 5.1, placed themselves in the same class as their families when they were young – 18 per cent in the middle class, 66 per cent in the working class. Of the remaining 16 per cent who see their present class status as differing from their parents', more than two-thirds perceived the movement to be upward; between generations there was a net gain of 6 per cent for the middle class. A similar upward bias is disclosed by the comparison of occupational grades of our sample with those of their fathers in childhood.[2]

If we summarize the entries in this table to show the movement for two alternative definitions of middle and working class the following patterns emerge.

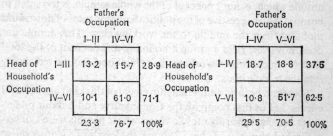

	Father's Occupation				Father's Occupation		
	I–III	IV–VI			I–IV	V–VI	
Head of Household's Occupation I–III	13·2	15·7	28·9	Head of Household's Occupation I–IV	18·7	18·8	37·5
IV–VI	10·1	61·0	71·1	V–VI	10·8	51·7	62·5
	23·3	76·7	100%		29·5	70·5	100%

By the definition of the middle class we have normally used (I–III) 25·8 per cent of people have moved across the occupational barrier that divides middle from working class; the net balance of upward movement is 5·6 per cent. If we take a non-manual/manual division (I–IV and V–VI) the gross movement between middle and working class is 29·6 per cent and the net upward movement is 8·0 per cent. By either measure the gross movements between class in occupational terms are considerably greater than the subjective movements shown in Table 5.1. But the net upward movement, whether 5·6 per cent or 8·0 per cent compares very closely with the 6 per cent upward movement that emerged from our respondents' rating report of their father's class and their own.

5.1 Perception of Present and Childhood Class

		Perceived Class of Childhood Family		
		Middle	Working	
Present Class Self-Image	Middle	18	11	29
	Working	5	66	71
		23	77	100%

In view of the dependence of these indicators on human memory, we have sought to identify purer groups of the socially mobile by separating out those whose upward or downward movement is confirmed both by their perceptions of their own and their fathers' class and by a comparison of their own and their fathers' occupational grade. Such a combined test leaves a group of downwardly mobile which, being 2 per cent of the whole sample, is too small to be more than suggestive of the political consequences of downward mobility from the middle to the working class. This double test does, however, yield a group amounting to 7 per cent of the total sample which, from a working class childhood, has moved clearly into the middle class.

There can be little doubt that movement of this kind has political effects. Let us first compare the Conservative and Labour preferences among upwardly mobile voters whose parents were Conservative or Labour. As Table 5.2 shows, the legacy of a Conservative parentage is clearly apparent in the preferences of upwardly mobile children, whereas the legacy of a Labour parentage is substantially eroded, though not blotted out. The fact that among those who come from a working class Labour background 57 per cent are Labour – a proportion vastly greater than the Labour percentage among the middle class as a whole – is a tribute to the influence of early socialization in the family. But the difference of 37 per cent between the proportion of Labour supporters among children of Conservative parents and the proportion of Conserva-

5.2 Conservative and Labour Preferences among Middle Class Electors with Conservative or Labour Working Class Parents

Upwardly mobile Offspring are	Parents were: Conservative	Labour
Conservative	94%	43%
Labour	6	57
	100%	100%

tives among children of Labour parents can be regarded as a measure of the conversion rate associated with moving from working to middle class.

This tendency can also be seen among middle class people with working class parents whose political sympathies were Liberal or divided or non-existent. In these cases, as the disparities in Table 5.3 show, the Conservatives gained far more than Labour; those lacking a clear party background tended to be assimilated into the middle class party.

Too simple a view of the nature of social and political change should not be read into Tables 5.2 and 5.3. Undoubtedly the pro-

5.3 Conservative and Labour Preferences among Middle Class Electors with Liberal or Non-political Working Class Parents

Upwardly mobile Offspring are	Parents were: Liberal or mixed	Non-political
Conservative	60%	72%
Labour	40	28
	100%	100%

cesses underlying these figures are very diverse. We presume that in many cases political conversion *follows* a change of class location, as the individual is exposed to different class-related beliefs about politics. In other cases changes of party may be an early, anticipatory, response to a change of social location which is far from complete. The office boy may not take long to adopt the political views that will suit him for the board room.

There must also be cases where Conservative partisanship is one of a cluster of ideas and values within the childhood family that predispose an individual to move upwards. It is not only that children rising into the middle class are liable to switch away from their parents' partisanship to Conservatism. It also appears that those who rise into the middle class are drawn to a disproportionate extent from children of working class Conservatives. When we compare the rate of upward mobility among those born into the working class according to the party of their parents, we find more than twice as many children from Conservative as from Labour homes moving into the middle class.

The key to this difference probably lies in the family's aspirations for the child's success in education and in other pathways to higher status such as marriage. It is plausible to suppose that working class parents who are Conservative are less likely to view the social order as a conflict between 'us' and 'them' and more likely to believe in a functional division of labour which values the higher social strata positively, or at least in neutral terms. Such parents would also be more likely to encourage, or at least not to oppose, their children's moving into the middle class, through education, marriage or choice of job. In view of the extent to which a child's educational attainment is determined by motives absorbed from his family, it may well be that the additional opportunities provided for working class children by the reform of the educational system have benefited to a disproportionate extent those from Conservative homes. Evidence of a higher rate of upward mobility in children from such homes is given by Table 5.4.

The advantage to the Conservatives of the long-term rise of non-manual occupations is therefore partly diminished by the fact that some upward mobility between generations simply makes

5.4 Rate of Inter-Occupational Movement from Working Class
to Middle Class by Party of Parents

| | Parents were: | | |
	Conservative	Labour	Other[a]
Proportion of offspring now middle class	29%	12%	23%

[a] Includes Liberals, mixed Conservative and Labour, and non-political parents.

middle class adults out of working class children who were already
disposed to be Conservative. However, this diminution may in
turn be partly offset by the lower rate of downward mobility and
by the weaker tendency of those who do slip down the social scale
to be converted to the working class party. The contrasting effects
of upward and downward social mobility have been widely commented on in Britain and elsewhere.[3]

The reluctance of the downwardly mobile to accept working
class norms can be seen in the fact that even among those who
admit to becoming working class only a minority support Labour.
The contrast in conversion rates among those who see themselves
as above their parents' class and those who see themselves as below
it is shown in Table 5.5. In order to remove the effect of the relationship between mobility and parents' party, this comparison is
given only for parents who had supported the party of their class.
Whereas 43 per cent of middle class children of working class
Labour parents had become Conservatives, only 32 per cent of
working class children of middle class Conservative parents had
become Labour.

The data on changes between generations presented here suggest
that in the longer run an expanding economy may appreciably
affect the proportions voting with their class by altering the occupational composition of the labour force. Yet changes of this kind

3. See, for example, B. G. Stacey, 'Inter Generation Mobility and Voting',
Public Opinion Quarterly, **30** (1966), 33–9, for a presentation of British
evidence. For a general and comparative survey of this question see S. M.
Lipset and R. Bendix, *Social Mobility in Industrial Society*, Berkeley, 1959.

5.5 Party Preference of Upward and Downward Mobile Electors

Present Party Preference	Middle Class Electors with Working Class Labour Parents	Working Class Electors with Middle Class Conservative Parents
Conservative	43%	68%
Labour	57	32
	100%	100%

will be very gradual. By contrast, it is sometimes thought that an expanding economy has a much more dramatic short-run influence on class self-images and party preference simply by raising working class people to middle class levels of affluence. Indeed, during the 1950s, when a rising curve of prosperity coincided with a rising curve of Conservative strength, the *embourgeoisement* of the British worker became a favourite theme of electoral commentary.

Affluence and Political Embourgeoisement

Although the *embourgeoisement* hypothesis has been presented in several ways, we shall treat it as referring to a process of conversion whereby the prosperous working class acquires the social and political self-images of the middle class as it acquires middle class consumption patterns. This process is quite distinct both from the sort of upward occupational mobility we have just been considering and from any direct political responses to prosperity which leave class self-images unchanged.

Our interpretation of the hypothesis is at least faithful to popular usage. What mainly provoked the discussions of political *embourgeoisement* following the Conservatives' third successive victory in 1959 was the suspicion that middle class consumption levels were eroding the industrial worker's identification with the working class and, with it, his commitment to the Labour Party.[4] During the 1950s real incomes had risen on average by almost 3 per cent per annum. The number of private cars had jumped from two million in 1950 to five million in 1959. Refrigerators, washing machines and television sets all ceased to be middle class luxuries and appeared on the mass market. Even before the 1920s, when Neville Chamberlain launched his housing programme, the Conservatives had espoused the dream that a property-owning democracy would be a Conservative democracy. Was that dream now being realized?

The collapse of Conservative strength in the early 1960s dealt a rude blow to the embourgeoisement hypothesis. If the Conservative gains of the 1950s were really the result of prosperous workers coming to think of themselves as middle class, these gains should surely not have been so abruptly swept away. The reversal of party fortunes suggested that economic expansion had benefited the Conservatives more as the governing party during a prosperous period than as the party of an expanding middle class. Since the early 1960s the embourgeoisement idea has come under increasingly sharp attack from those who are sceptical whether anything so deeply rooted as identifications with class will be transformed merely by changes in consumption.[5]

We share this scepticism. Indeed it deterred us from investigating the influence of washing machines, refrigerators and the like on social and political identifications. Yet one kind of consumption pattern – that relating to housing – seemed to us sufficiently important to warrant attention. In our 1963 and 1964 interviews we ascertained whether our respondents lived in council houses rented from their local authority, in privately rented accommodation, or in houses which they owned themselves or were buying on mortgage.

4. See M. Abrams and others, *Must Labour Lose?*, London, 1960 and C. A. R. Crosland's lecture 'Can Labour Win?' reprinted in his *The Conservative Enemy*, London, 1962, pp. 143–63.

5. See in particular, J. H. Goldthorpe and David Lockwood, 'Affluence and the British Class Structure', *Sociological Review*, 11 (1963), 133–63, and J. H. Goldthorpe, D. Lockwood, F. Bechhofer and J. Platt, *The Affluent Worker: Political Attitudes and Behaviour*, London, 1968.

In view of the numbers that had moved, we were able to identify only a small sub-sample whose housing level changed during the seventeen months between interviews. Overall there was, of course, an upward movement: the number of house owners increased; roughly equal numbers of families moved in either direction between council and non-council rented housing; and twice as many families (though only 2 per cent of the total sample) moved from being council tenants to being owner-occupiers as moved the opposite way.

Changes of housing level and, with it, of neighbourhood milieu, did not produce dramatic shifts of class identification. None the less, a marginal upward bias of class identity could be detected among those whose housing level had risen. Table 5.6 shows this bias in its display of the joint distribution of middle and working class identifications in 1963 and 1964 among those whose level of housing was higher in the autumn of 1964 than it had been in the summer of 1963. In none of these groups did as many as one-fifth alter their self-description in class terms, but in each case the trend of change was upward. Among those who moved from council tenancies to home-ownership almost one-fifth changed their identification from working to middle class. So far as we can tell from the very small samples involved, a lowering of housing level did not yield a comparable trend from middle to working class identification. But we should emphasize that the total numbers whose class identifications changed when their housing-level changed were so limited that the net effect in the electorate as a whole must have been negligible.

What is more, when a rise of class identification accompanied a rise in housing, there is no evidence that there was also an increase in propensity to support the Conservatives. If anything, those who improved their housing between 1963 and 1964 became somewhat more Labour in their partisanship, despite the trend to the Conservatives in the country as a whole during this period. If such a finding were based on a larger sample, we might be tempted to turn the embourgeoisement theory upside down and to envisage the possibility that the 'new' middle class identified its interests with the policies of the 'new' Labour party, including perhaps its

5.6 Changes of Class Self-Images Among Electors Whose Level of Housing Rose from 1963 to 1964

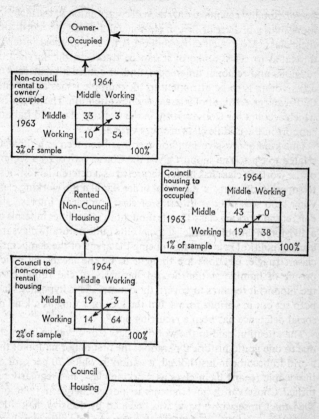

promises of easier mortgages. At the very least our data do not support the view that the style of life associated with a higher level of housing led to the political embourgeoisement of those who ascended to it.

The Decline of Working Class Conservatism

Social mobility can make only a small contribution to the fact that more than a quarter of British electors fail to vote in accord with their class. Most such cross-support is to be explained in terms unrelated to class. Some of it can be traced to the survival of religious and regional differences, and of course a great deal of cross-voting is to be attributed to the multiple issues and events that at any given time hold the electorate's attention. The influences which account for Conservatism in the working class and Labour support in the middle class are very varied.

One kind of cross-voting, however, has been seen as intimately related to class. The support given the Conservatives by a section of the working class has been interpreted as a deferential response to superior elements in the social order. Unlike the working class voter who sees politics in terms of class conflict or interest, the deferential working class Tory is thought to see politics in terms of a division of labour in which a social élite quite naturally plays the leading political role. Far from being the arena of the democratic class struggle, elections are thought to be the means by which people of humble station accord the party of the ruling class the support it requires to govern the country. This hypothesis has been set out in various forms, but the idea of voting as a kind of social deference has been a recurring one.[6]

The attention paid to the working class Conservative is largely due to one grand historical paradox: the first major nation of the world to become industrialized, a nation in which 70 per cent of the people regard themselves as working class, has regularly re-turned Conservative governments to power. Between 1886 and 1964 the Conservative party was defeated by decisive majorities only twice – in 1906 and 1945. Such a record could only have been

6. See R. T. McKenzie and A. Silver, *Angels in Marble*, London, 1968, for the most comprehensive discussion of this theme. See also E. A. Nord-linger, *The Working Class Tories*, London, 1967; R. Samuel, 'The Defer-ence Voter', *New Left Review*, January–February 1960; and W. G. Runci-man, *Relative Deprivation and Social Justice*, London and Berkeley, 1967. For an earlier discussion not without a modern ring, see W. Bagehot, *The English Constitution*, London, 1867.

achieved through heavy 'defection' to the Conservatives among the industrial working class. In recent years polling data on class and party have amply confirmed the hypothesis that the working class elector was likelier than the middle class elector to support the party of the opposite class.

In one respect, however, polling data have exaggerated this difference between classes. Reports of poll findings often divide a sample into its party groups, whose composition is then compared by sex, age, class and other characteristics. Such a procedure is right for describing the class origin of party support. But, because the working class so heavily outnumbers the middle class, this presentation seriously distorts the party destination of class voting. The distortion can be simply illustrated by presenting our evidence on the relationship of class and party in two contrasting ways. Table 5.7 shows the class origin of party support in 1963 by calculating the proportions of people within each party who

5.7 Occupational Grade by Party Self-Image, 1963

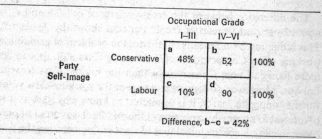

		Occupational Grade		
		I–III	IV–VI	
Party Self-Image	Conservative	a 48%	b 52	100%
	Labour	c 10%	d 90	100%

Difference, b−c = 42%

fall in each of the two main occupational levels. The difference of 42 per cent between the cross-preference cells, *b* and *c* of this table is enormous. Even in this period of Labour ascendancy the Conservatives drew more than half their total support from the working class, whereas Labour drew only a tenth part of its support from the middle class.

It requires only a short additional step to conclude from this that the working class is vastly more disposed to support the

Conservatives than the middle class to support Labour. But such a conclusion would be seriously misleading. The evidence takes on a very different appearance when we calculate the percentages within classes, instead of within parties, to show the party destination of class voting. The startling result of such a rearrangement is shown by Table 5.8.

5.8 Party Self-Image by Occupational Grade, 1963

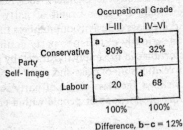

The difference between the cross-preference cells, b and c, is now 12 per cent instead of the 42 per cent shown by Table 5.7. This reduction by no means eliminates the problem of explaining working class Conservatism. The working class still appears as more likely to vote Conservative than the middle class to vote Labour. Moreover, so long as any part of the working class votes for the 'opposite' party, it is of interest to know why, just as it is of interest to know why a portion of the middle class votes Labour. None the less, since the imbalance of class voting between the two classes is one of the prime causes for the attention given to working class Conservatism, it is important to stress how easily this imbalance can be exaggerated.

Our view of Conservative support in the working class can also be fundamentally transformed by a further redeployment of the evidence. When we looked at the behaviour of successive cohorts, the greater cross-voting of the working class is found to occur very largely in the older age-groups. The decay of working class Conservatism in younger voters is evident in Table 5.9, which shows

5.9 Cross-Support by Cohort, 1963

	Age-cohort			
	Pre-1918	Inter-war	1945	Post-1951
Difference between percent of Working Class supporting Conservatives and percent of Middle Class supporting Labour	33	16	2	6

for each of our four age-cohorts the benefit to the Conservatives from the crossing of class lines, i.e. the magnitude of b minus c which we saw in Table 5.8 to be 12 per cent for the electorate as a whole. In the younger age-cohorts middle class electors were very nearly as prone to support Labour as working class electors were to support the Conservatives. Indeed, when we examined this trend separately for men and women in our sample, we found that among men of the 1945 cohort, who were peculiarly susceptible to the mood evoked by the Second World War, middle class electors were more likely to be Labour than working class electors were to be Conservative. These additional findings are set out in Figure 5.10 on the next page.

If we look at these patterns in the light of the ideas of political inheritance and change set out in Chapter 3, we are led to adopt a fundamentally revisionist view of the phenomenon of working class Conservatism. The Labour Party is relatively very new in the evolution of British politics. It is only since the First World War that it has been a serious contender for power. By that time our oldest cohort had already come of age, and the parents of the next cohort had been socialized into a party system in which Labour had no major part.[7] Given the extent to which party loyalties are transmitted in the childhood home, time was needed for historic attachments to the 'bourgeois' parties to weaken and for 'second-

7. Six constituencies out of seven had never had a Labour candidate before 1918.

5.10 Cross-Support Among Men and Women by Age-cohort, 1963

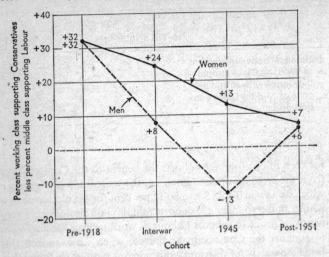

ary' processes to complete the realignment by class. With the collapse of their party, Liberals had of course to go elsewhere – and the destination of their support is a question we shall discuss in Chapter 11. But Conservative loyalties would continue to be transmitted to the working class children of Conservative parents long after the rise of a working class party.

Moreover, the Conservatives in Britain fought a brilliant delaying action in contrast to many conservative parties on the continent. The rate at which the new voters of the working class were recruited to the working class party was not a constant of nature but depended on the appeals of the parties themselves. Disraeli and Lord Randolph Churchill recognized that their party's success depended upon the wooing of the working man. On the Liberal side Joseph Chamberlain did the same and, when he changed camps in 1886, he brought over to the Conservatives a solid new body of working class support, particularly in the industrial Midlands. The receptivity of the Conservatives to new social policies after their debacle in 1945 reflected their desire not to be cut off from support in the working class.

It is only with the 1945 and post-1950 cohorts that we come to a group of electors whose partisan attachments were less strongly affected by an earlier electoral history and by Labour's late start as a national party. Among these cohorts, the Labour Party has come much closer to a full seizure of its 'natural' class base. Of course, substantial cross-voting continued to occur within each class, but the rate of such cross-voting was much more nearly equal.

This characterization of change is supported by the differing pattern of change within the two classes. When we compare over our four age-cohorts the trend of the two cross-voting rates which make up our index of relative cross-voting, it becomes clear that the lessening of the gap has been due more to the decline of Conservative support in the working class than to a rise of Labour strength in the middle class. Figure 5.11 suggests the contribution

5.11 Cross-Support in the Middle and Working Class by Age-cohort, 1963

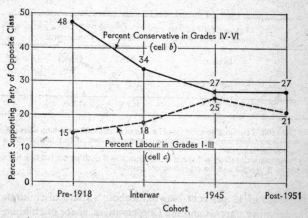

of these two trends to lessening the unequal cross-support of the two classes. Such figures lend credence to the hypothesis that in successive age-cohorts Labour has come to occupy more and more of its 'natural' ground. Despite the insights of Birch,[8] commentaries on Tory voting in the working class have tended to look for factors which might *de novo* deflect a working class voter to the opposite party rather than to see the unequal strength of the two parties in the opposite classes as at least partially due to an evolutionary process by which the bars to Labour strength in its own class have been successively removed.

The progressive conversion of the working class to the Labour Party is confirmed by our data on the changes of party from parent to child. The attenuation of family traditions that held sway before the emergence of Labour can be shown first by examining Labour and Conservative preferences among children of Labour and Conservative working class parents at the beginning of their political life cycle. These preferences, as shown in Table 5.12, indicate once again the profound influence of the family. But the

5.12 Labour and Conservative Earliest Preferences among Working Class Children of Labour and Conservative Working Class Parents[a]

Respondent's Earliest Party Preference was:	Parents were:[b]	
	Labour	Conservative
Labour	94%	19%
Conservative	6	81
	100%	100%

[a] This table is confined to children of Labour or Conservative working class parents who are themselves working class and whose own earliest political preferences were Labour or Conservative.
[b] Parents are classified as Labour or Conservative if both supported one of these parties or if one did and the other was not partisan.

difference of 13 per cent between Labour's share of children of Conservative parents and the Conservatives' share of children of Labour parents suggests that at the beginning of political aware-

8. See A. H. Birch, *Small Town Politics*, Oxford, 1959, pp. 110–11.

ness there already had been some drift of preference towards the working class party.

This drift is even more evident in the main parties' share of the current adult preferences of the same group, as Table 5.13 shows.

5.13 Labour and Conservative Current Preferences among Working Class Children of Labour and Conservative Working Class Parents[a]

Respondent's Current Party Preference was:	Parents were:	
	Labour	Conservative
Labour	91%	32%
Conservative	9	68
	100%	100%

[a] The definitions of this table conform to those of Table 5.12, except that current party preference replaces earliest preference.

The difference between Labour's share of children of Conservative parents and the Conservatives' share of children of Labour parents has now risen to 23 per cent, although the influence of early background is impressive among the 68 per cent of children from the Tory working class who still support the Conservatives.

The drift of working class children towards the Labour Party is also seen in the first preferences and in the present partisanship of working class people from Liberal or from politically divided homes. This evidence is given in Table 5.14, which measures the tendency to move towards the working class party by the extent to which the upper proportion of either column exceeds the lower. On this basis there was a drift of 22 per cent towards the Labour Party in the earliest and current preferences of this group.

We would, however, expect the earliest and the strongest drift towards the working class party among the children of families in which no contrary partisan commitment had to be swept away. Evidence that this is the case is given in Table 5.15 on the next page, where the drift may be gauged once again in terms of how much the upper entry in each column exceeds the lower. The table shows

5.14 Labour and Conservative Preferences among Working Class
Children of Liberal or Mixed Working Class Parents[a]

	First Preferences	Current Preferences
Labour	61%	61%
Conservative	39	39
	100%	100%

[a] This table is confined to children of Liberal or divided working class parents who are themselves working class and whose earliest or current preferences are Labour or Conservative.

that Labour has captured nearly three-quarters of the major
party preferences of this group and that this mobilization of support among children of uncommitted working class families
occurred quite early in the child's political experience. Indeed, the
proportion of our working class sample who could not attribute
a party allegiance to their parents was sufficiently large for the
crystallization of Labour preferences in this group to account for

5.15 Labour and Conservative Preferences among Children of
Working Class Parents of No Clear Partisanship[a]

	First Preferences	Current Preferences
Labour	71%	73%
Conservative	29	27
	100%	100%

[a] This table is confined to children whose working class parents are not remembered
as having had a clear partisanship, who are themselves working class and whose
earliest or current preferences are Labour or Conservative.

somewhat more than half the net increment of Labour strength between generations.

An evolutionary view of Conservative strength in the working class gives further insight into its sources. If these ties are partly a legacy of the past, the Conservative allegiances of many working class electors will have been formed long ago; indeed, in some cases they will have come down in family or local tradition from a time well before the intrusion of class into British politics in the twentieth-century sense. The intrinsic values of party ties are quite enough to have sustained the voter in his traditional allegiance for many years.

We would expect the political norms or interests of the working class to have dissolved conflicting political allegiances more fully among working class electors to whom class is relatively salient. Evidence for this emerges when we divide our sample into those who associated themselves spontaneously with a class and those who did not. At each interview we began our questions about class with one asking whether or not the respondent thought of himself as belonging to a class. The replies allowed us to separate respondents into those for whom the salience of class was relatively strong and those for whom its salience was less.

The relationship of class to party in the two groups shows an interesting contrast, which is set out in Table 5.16 on the next page. It is clear that cross-support in the middle and working classes is much more nearly equal among those for whom class is more salient. But substantial defections in the working class make it quite unequal among those for whom class is less salient; indeed, among the working class in this latter group, the proportion supporting the Conservative Party is fully 43 per cent. Working class electors who are strongly aware of class are more likely to see politics in terms of the norms and interests of their class and to accord Labour their support. Those to whom class is less evident are more likely to see politics in terms of other values, including those received from the past.

In this sense, it is the failure of Labour's distinctive class appeal to make an impact on a particular segment of the working class that is the key to Conservative support there. Without the restraint

5.16 Relationship of Class to Party by Salience of Class[a]

	Salience of Class High			Salience of Class Low	
	Grades I–III	Grades IV–VI		Grades I–III	Grades IV–VI
Conservative	80%	[b] 28%	Conservative	79%	[b] 43%
Labour	[c] 20	72	Labour	[c] 21	57
	100%	100%		100%	100%
	Difference, b − c = 8%			Difference, b − c = 22%	

[a] The salience of class was measured in the 1963 interview by the question numbered 65a in the text of the questionnaire.

of this appeal, many working class electors are able to give their support to the Conservatives – and to the Liberals too – for reasons that need not be distinctive to the working class. It certainly needs no especial deference by the socially humble to the party of the ruling class to account for the Conservatives' success in drawing support. We had in our sample a number of respondents who could be described as pure specimens of the socially deferential. But we were much more impressed by the fact that the Conservatives attracted working class support for many of the same reasons they attracted support generally in the country.

The difficulties in limiting one's view to the working class may be illustrated in terms of attitudes towards one of the main traditional symbols of British society, the monarchy. When our working class respondents were asked how important they felt that the Queen and Royal Family were to Britain, a clear difference emerged between Conservative and Labour supporters. As Table 5.17 shows, almost three-quarters of the Conservative working class felt that the monarchy was very important, whereas the comparable proportion among the Labour working class was not much more than half.

5.17 Belief in Importance of Monarchy by Party within the Working Class

	Conservative working class	Labour working class
Proportion feeling Queen and Royal Family are very important to Britain[a]	72%	54%

[a] See question 24 of the 1963 questionnaire.

This cleavage helps us to understand the value patterns which separate Conservatives and supporters of Labour in the working class. Indeed, this difference has not escaped the eyes of those who have argued the importance of the deference motive. It is not difficult to suppose that attitudes towards the monarchy fit into a much more general structure of beliefs, one that includes the obligation on those of inferior social status to accord their betters the support they need to rule. Yet a note of caution is introduced into such an interpretation by extending this comparison to the middle class as well, as we do in Table 5.18.

5.18 Belief in Importance of Monarchy by Party and Class[a]

		Partisan Self-Image	
		Conservative	Labour
Class Self-Image	Working Class	72%	54%
	Middle Class	70%	32%

[a] Entries of table are proportions believing that the Queen and Royal Family are very important to Britain in response to question 24 of the 1963 questionnaire.

This table makes clear that the stronger association of the Conservatives with this traditional symbol is a general one and is by no means confined to the working class. Indeed, it turns out that the difference is rather muted in the working class. The party groups among working class electors are much more agreed on the monarchy than are those in the middle class; Labour's working class supporters are positively royalist by contrast with those of the middle class. The same point can be extended to other grounds of the Conservatives' appeal. If our view is confined to the working class it is, for example, easy to interpret support for the Conservatives because they are educated men as evidence of the deference motive. But when we see that this aspect of the party's image also reaps an advantage among middle class electors, many of whom have completed university or secondary education, we may wonder whether support on this ground need be seen as a mark of social deference.

It is clear that a great deal turns on the meaning given to the concept of deference. It is possible to see much of the Conservatives' support in the middle class as well as the working class in terms of social deference. Such a formulation would presumably be consistent with the argument advanced by Parkin and others that the Conservatives are the beneficiaries throughout British society of their alignment with the dominant religious, educational and economic institutions and that only where residential or occupational concentration allows the working class to build defences against a 'dominant' value pattern will it be able to assert its own 'deviant' values, including support of the working class party.[9] Such an argument draws attention to the importance of the structure of industry and the pattern of residential concentration for the maintenance of party allegiance, although it can too easily assume a dominant national value pattern as a first explanatory principle; we shall see in later chapters that persuasion within local residential areas erodes middle class Conservative support in areas of low middle class concentration as well as building Conservative support in the working class in areas of low working-class concentration. But if the Conservatives' appeal as a 'national' party aligned with national institutions is to be styled in terms of deference, it is at least clear that this is not a deference that is

9. F. Parkin, 'Working-Class Conservatives: a Theory of Political Deviance', *British Journal of Sociology*, **18** (1967), 278–90.

peculiarly likely to be evoked among people within the lower social strata by reason of their humble station.

The Aging of the Class Alignment

Since we have argued that Labour has with time occupied more and more of its class ground and indeed that the process is still continuing, it may seem paradoxical to suggest that the class basis of party allegiance is becoming weaker. On a purely statistical basis, this suggestion flies against the evidence: middle and working class electors were as far, or farther, apart politically in the youngest age group as among the older cohorts. But statistical appearances can deceive and, even beneath more polarized behaviour, the strength of the class basis for party support may have softened in recent times. The intensity of the class tie may have declined at the same time as its extent became more universal. It seems worthwhile to pursue these speculations further, even though we lack the evidence to come to any clear verdict.

The first ground for our supposition lies in factors that broadly condition the electorate's view of class and politics, especially the visible change in British conditions of life. The affluence of the postwar world is much more than an illusion of the party propagandists. Real incomes have risen steadily to levels far above those of the prewar world. Although British economic growth has not kept pace with that of some other advanced countries, it has still sufficed to bring within the reach of the mass market entirely new categories of goods and services. Even those pockets of poverty untouched by a high-wage and high-employment economy have been substantially reduced by a diversity of state welfare services. The concentration of wealth in the hands of a few may have been as great as ever, but the great bulk of wage earners were far above the poverty standards of the 1930s.

This revolution in economic conditions may not have brought about the embourgeoisement of the British worker in the sense of social identification with the middle class. None the less it is very apparent that the gap in living standards and social habits between the bulk of the middle class and the bulk of the working class has diminished with the rise of disposable income and the levelling influence of the educational system and the mass media, notably television. In Britain, as in other countries, growing affluence tended to undermine the idea of politics as a zero-sum game in which the gains for one class are seen as losses for the other. It was harder to sustain embittered class attitudes when the national wealth was visibly increasing to the benefit of the great mass of the people. The bitter recital of incidents or events with which a number of our respondents expressed their feeling about party or class were related almost without exception to pre-war conditions. No one who culls the references of this sort from a sample of several thousand could miss the sense of the remembrance of things past.[10]

A clearer suggestion that the class alignment may have weakened comes, however, from a comparison of the beliefs about class and party that are held by successive age-cohorts. When the classification of beliefs set out in Chapter 4 is applied to working class Labour voters who entered the electorate in successive periods, we find that the image of politics as the representation of opposing class interests is increasingly accepted as we move from the pre-1918 to the inter-war cohort and reaches a peak in the cohort which entered the electorate over the Second World War and its aftermath. But such an image is accepted less frequently among Labour's working class supporters who entered the electorate more recently. This profile is shown by Figure 5.19, which also gives the proportions of working class Labour electors in each cohort who said, in response to a more general question about the extent of difference between the parties, that there was a 'good deal' of difference between them. This evidence suggests that the 1945 cohort entered the electorate at a time when party support was most clearly connected with perceived class differences and that

---

10. The content of such responses is illustrated by the reasons for hating the Conservatives given by a woman of seventy-seven, who had herself been widowed at seventeen: 'I always remember when my father was killed down the pit. And later, when my mother tried to get some assistance, they threatened her with the workhouse. That's all they cared for us.'

5.19 Frequency of Belief in Politics as Conflict of Opposed Class Interests and Belief in Wide Differences Between Parties Among Working Class Labour Electors in Successive Age-cohorts[a]

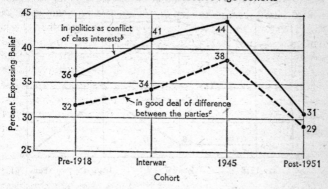

[a] See definition of age-cohorts in Chapter 3, p. 73.
[b] Proportion of consistently working class Labour element of each age-cohort of three-interview panel which was coded as seeing politics in terms of a conflict of opposing class interests. See classification of beliefs, Chapter 4, pp. 108–24.
[c] Proportion of working class Labour respondents in each cohort who said in 1963 that they saw a 'good deal' of difference between the parties. See question 9 of the 1963 questionnaire in the Appendix.

his connection has been attenuated in the years that followed.[11]

A similar, though not identical, picture is given by the corresponding profiles of belief among middle class Conservatives in successive age-cohorts. As Figure 5.20 shows, the parties are more likely to be seen as widely differing by middle class Conservatives in the interwar and 1945 cohorts. More important, a relatively strong peaking of belief in politics as a conflict of opposing class interests is seen in the cohort which entered the electorate with Labour's accession to power in the aftermath of the Second World War. In accord with the generally lower incidence of such beliefs among middle class electors, the proportion holding this view does

11. Indeed, if we consider the relative proportions of each cohort who held stable and consistent class and partisan self-image over three interviews and held a conflict view of the relation of class and party, the decline of the strength of the beliefs underlying the class alignment is still more striking.

5.20 Frequency of Belief in Politics as Conflict of Opposed Class Interests and Belief in Wide Differences Between Parties Among Middle Class Conservative Electors in Successive Cohorts[a]

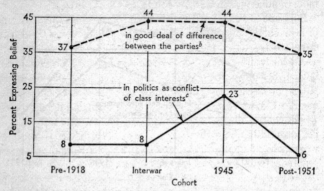

[a] See definition of cohorts in Chapter 3, p. 73.
[b] Proportion of middle class Conservative respondents in each cohort who said in 1963 that they saw a 'good deal' of difference between the parties. See question 9 of the 1963 questionnaire in the Appendix.
[c] Proportion of consistently middle class Conservative element of each age-cohort of three-interview panel which was coded as seeing politics in terms of a conflict of opposing class interests. See classification of beliefs, Chapter 4, pp. 108–124.

not approach the corresponding proportion in the working class. But the hold of a conflict image on the minds of middle class voters seems also to have declined between the 1945 and post-1951 cohorts.

A trend of this kind must be due in some part to the profound transformation of the electorate's condition, especially the rising affluence which has affected all classes in recent years. But there should be a word of caution against too readily explaining any weakening of the class alignment, when or if it occurs, in terms of the electorate's disposition to respond to politics on the basis of class interests. Our view is that such a weakening depends too on the behaviour of the parties themselves, especially Labour's convergence towards the Conservative position in terms of composition and outlook. The Conservatives have themselves been sensitive to the need for appealing fairly broadly across the class spectrum, as we have noted. The approaches invoked by Lord Randolph Churchill and Joseph Chamberlain have had their modern adherents in Lord Woolton and R. A. Butler.

But Labour's transformation has been the more striking, in terms of both social composition and policy. The party was conceived out of a belief in the 'social composition' theory of representation, and its early efforts were focused on increasing the representation – indeed, the physical presence – of working class people in the House of Commons. The working class origins of the Parliamentary Labour Party were still very apparent in the interwar years: 72 per cent of the MPs were rank-and-file workers and only 15 per cent university-educated. But by 1966 the proportion of workers had fallen to 30 per cent and the proportion of university graduates had risen to 51 per cent.[12]

Greater significance, however, should probably be attached to the transformation of the party's social identity at the highest level, especially when Labour has been the governing party. Figure 5.21

5.21 University Educated Proportion of Labour Cabinet Ministers, 1924–69[a]

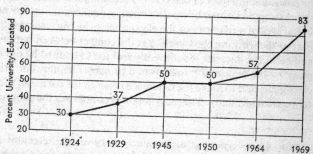

[a] This figure is based on a table in R. Rose, *Class and Party Divisions*, University of Strathclyde, 1968, p. 28.

shows the per cent university educated in Labour cabinets from 1924 to 1969. The rise over a generation is indeed striking. From

12. See W. L. Guttsman, *The British Political Elite*, London, 1963, p. 105; see also *The British General Election of 1966*, pp. 208–11.

roughly a third in the 1920s and never more than half during Labour's tenure after the Second World War, the fraction of ministers educated at a university rose during the 1966 Parliament to something like seven in eight. In fact, only one member of the Labour Cabinet at the beginning of 1969 had an occupational past that could be described as manual. Of course, many leading Labour figures are of working class background. But there is no doubt that the social origins of Labour politicians have become increasingly middle class as local selection committees have preferred more educated candidates and as party leaders have sought out the administrative aptitudes demanded by ministerial office.[13]

This social transformation has been matched by Labour's dilemma of policy. The party's historic justification for existence was the improvement of the lot of the working class, and this motive has underlain Labour's social programmes, especially the successive extensions of the welfare state. But Labour in power, or near it, has also had to face problems and formulate policies touching national goals and not simply the more sectional or parochial interests of class. It is indeed arguable that only by doing so could Labour have established its qualifications to govern in the eyes of a majority of the electorate, including a substantial part of the working class itself. Yet the conflict between national and sectional interests is sufficiently real for Labour to be drawn away by the tenure of power from a primary identification with class goals and to make the difference between the parties in these terms seem less sharp. The most notable example was the adoption

---

13. It is noteworthy that despite our sample's stronger sense that the working class is united in support of Labour (62 per cent thought it was) than the middle class is in support of the Conservatives (only 35 per cent thought it was), the sample placed Labour farther from the working class end of a scale running from working to middle class than it placed the Conservatives from the middle class end (see question 64 of the 1963 questionnaire). Our interpretation of this at first puzzling finding is that the terms 'Labour Party' and 'Conservative Party' evoked an image more of party leadership than of the mass following and that in these terms Labour's image was more mixed than the Conservatives'.

by Labour Chancellors in the middle 1960s of economic policies that would heighten unemployment and lower the real incomes of working people in order to right the country's international balance of payments and defend the pound.[14]

Several aspects of the electorate's behaviour are consistent with the weakening of a dominant class alignment. The first of these is the greater volatility of electoral behaviour that has been manifest as the postwar period has advanced. After the cataclysm of 1945 there was a period of notable electoral stability. The swings between general elections were small and few by-elections showed exceptional swings. The Rochdale and Torrington contests in 1958 perhaps suggested the magnitude of the electorate's susceptibility to change. But in 1962 and 1963 anti-Conservative swings outside all precedent began to occur. And these were as nothing compared to the swings against Labour that began at the end of 1967. If we take as a simple measure the proportion of by-elections in which the Government's share of the total vote fell by 20 per cent or more, we derive a picture of increasing volatility as shown in Table 5.22.

5.22 Proportion of By-elections Showing Falls in the Government Vote amounting to 20 Percent or More of the Total Poll

1945–51	3%
1951–55	2%
1955–59	10%
1959–64	18%
1964–66	—
1966–68	48%

The weakening of Labour's identification with distinctively working class goals is also consistent with the notable fall of electoral turnout in traditional working class strongholds. Indeed,

14. The Gallup Poll's repeated sampling of opinion on the questions of whether 'there is any really important difference between the parties' gives evidence of a long-term decline of differences perceived between the parties over the postwar period. Replies to this question are susceptible to short-run change, especially with the onset of election campaigns, but the trend seems none the less evident.

a lessening of the perceived difference between the parties in class terms may have a good deal to do with the general fall of turnout in the country, down from 84 per cent in the election of 1950 to 75 per cent in 1966. But it probably played a much more important role in the far deeper reductions of turnout in solid working class areas, especially the mining seats. Participation has also reached exceedingly low levels in recent elections within urban working class areas, notably London's East End.[15] But the fall in the mining seats is the more notable because participation there has been so high since the rise of the Labour Party and the realignment of electoral support on a class basis. For voters deeply imbued with a belief in working class interests, a movement by Labour away from these goals does not increase the reasons for supporting the opposite party so much as it removes the motive to vote at all, since the parties are thought to differ less and less in class terms.

The weakening of the class alignment is also consistent with the emergence of rival bases of enduring party support. Those who have written of the primacy of class have argued that the class alignment has been sufficiently strong to overwhelm other cleavages, especially religious or sectional ones. The direction of influence may actually have been partly the reverse, with the removal of the Irish question preparing the way for the pre-eminent role that class was to play. But a weakening of the class alignment might lead us to expect alternative grounds of cleavage to become more evident. This may indeed be the background to the spectacular weakening of traditional ties in two traditionally partisan areas, Scotland and Wales. Nationalist candidates in these countries had never made much headway until the middle 1960s; the great bulk of them had lost their deposits. But a Welsh Nationalist won a by-election in July 1966 and a Scottish Nationalist in November 1967. By the summer of 1968 the opinion polls and the local elections were showing the Scottish Nationalists, who had won but 5 per cent of the vote in 1966, with the support of 30 to 40 per cent of Scottish electors.

15. Between 1955 and 1966 turnout fell by 3·8 per cent in mining areas and by 3·6 per cent in large cities. In almost every other type of constituency it rose slightly. See *The British General Election of 1966*, p. 279.

The bearing of the strength of the class alignment on this sectional or nationalist development calls our attention to the role of class in regional differences in the recent past. And the appearance of rival grounds of political cleavage also turns our view to the bases of party support which were of greater importance before British politics entered its modern phase. In particular, today's political allegiance still bear marks of the religious cleavage that cut across British politics at the beginning of the century.

6   Variations of Alignment

The pre-eminence of class in electoral alignments is not a universal fact of modern politics, as we have said. There are many countries and party systems where race, or religion, or region, or other lines of potential cleavage are more important than class in defining electoral support. We can indeed imagine a very different electoral history for modern Britain. The Irish question in particular might have influenced the pattern of party politics even more radically than it did. This issue, which so clearly cut across class lines, led to a drastic realignment of parties in the 1880s, with Joseph Chamberlain leading a large body of the industrial working class over to the Conservatives. To this day it leaves a major mark on the politics of Clydeside and Merseyside. It is not beyond possibility that if Europe had escaped a general war in August 1914 the United Kingdom would have slipped into civil war over the position of Ulster under Dublin Home Rule. The resulting conflict might have left scars on the British body politic comparable to those imposed on the United States for a hundred years by its own civil war. In such a politics the place of class would have been very different.

Certainly there are variations in British electoral behaviour which cannot be attributed to class in any simple way. Some of these variations reflect traditions and interests which reach far into the past, well before the present manifestations of the class or party system, and some reflect current particularities, such as the differing economic make-up of different parts of the country. This chapter is concerned with such variations. We start with the evolution of the religious alignment before turning to differences between regions and to the related question of more local political traditions. In some cases the discussion will not lead us away from class so much as towards an understanding of additional ways in which social structure is reflected in electoral behaviour.

The Political Legacy of Religion

Religious issues have not been at the heart of British politics since early in this century. But they once were a focus of party cleavage; the battles over the position of Church Schools under the Balfour Education Act of 1902 and over Welsh Disestablishment a decade later are still remembered. Indeed, going farther back, it is hardly too strong to say that British politics, which had revolved so over-whelmingly around religion in the seventeenth century, were still largely rooted in religion in the nineteenth century. The Conservatives were accepted as the Anglican and High Church Party, while the Liberals were the spokesmen of disestablishment and dissent. The Conservatives were, moreover, the party of Ulster and the Protestant ascendancy in Ireland, and the sectarian element in the Irish struggle reinforced the imprint of religion on British politics.[1]

The legacy of past religious cleavage is still very evident in the political allegiances of today. Moreover, the patterns of present allegiances show with great clarity the way in which the impact of religion has declined. These patterns must be examined with an eye to the influence of class, since religious preference and, still more, religious attendance differ between classes; failure to allow for this can lead to the political significance of the marked differences of party support evident in the several denominations being vastly exaggerated. Because of the dominant numerical position of the Church of England, satisfactory statistics about the links between religion and partisanship have seldom been offered. The numbers in our sample preclude us from speaking with any confidence about the strength of the parties within the smaller

---

1. The natural way in which these religious identifications were reflected in party allegiance is suggested by the explanations given by two of our respondents of the reasons for their fathers' partisanship: a Glasgow chargehand said 'He was an Orangeman and a Freemason, so of course he was a royalist and voted Tory'; a London butcher's wife said, 'Dad was an Irish Catholic, so of course he was against the Conservatives.'

denominations.[2] None the less, Table 6.1 makes it plain that the differences between denominations are very marked. Methodists, and Roman Catholics, as well as those of no religious preference, showed large Labour majorities. But those who adhered to the two established churches, especially the Church of England, were more nearly equally divided in a period when Labour was comfortably in the lead over the country as a whole. The links between Anglicanism and Conservative preference are still clearer if we take account of active religious observance. A very large fraction

6.1 Partisan Self-Image by Religious Identification, 1963

	Conservative	Labour	Liberal	Others, None		
Anglican	41%	44	10	5	100%	(n = 1273)
Church of Scotland	39%	48	6	7	100%	(n = 187)
Methodist	23%	55	19	3	100%	(n = 140)
Other non-conformist	37%	36	20	7	100%	(n = 127)
Roman Catholic	24%	62	8	6	100%	(n = 169)
No religious preference	31%	52	8	9	100%	(n = 64)

within all denominations, but above all within the Church of England, treats its church membership as entirely nominal.[3] Indeed, the proportion of Anglicans claiming to attend church at

2. Despite the decline in religious observance almost half the marriages in Britain take place in an Anglican church and almost half the babies are christened in an Anglican font. When our sample were asked their religious preference, the replies were as follows:

Church of England	64%	Other non-conformist	4%
Church of Scotland, Presbyterian	9%	Jewish	1%
Methodist	7%	Other	1%
Catholic	9%	No preference	3%
Baptist	2%		

If we consider England only, the Church of England proportion rises to 71 per cent.

3. One of our interviewers recorded a colloquy with a respondent who said 'none' in answer to her initial question about religious affiliation. She then inquired, on her own initiative, whether she ought to put him down as 'atheist' or 'agnostic'. The respondent thereupon asked to be told the difference between the two, and our interviewer, more deeply involved than she cared to be, undertook to do so. After hearing her account, the respondent said, 'You had better put me down as Church of England.'

least once a month is not more than 16 per cent, as compared with 39 per cent of Church of Scotland members, 45 per cent of non-conformists, and 73 per cent of Roman Catholics.[4] Figure 6.2 shows the link between attendance and Conservative preference among Anglicans. The Conservatives' share of allegiances to the

6.2 Partisan Self-Image Among Anglicans by Frequency of Church Attendance

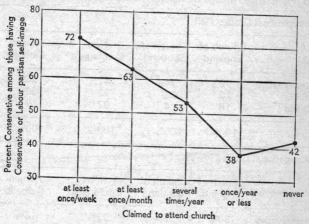

two main parties fell from 72 per cent among Anglicans who said they go to church at least once a week to 38 per cent among those who said they attend once a year or less (and 42 per cent among those who said they never attend). The regular attender at Church

4. The frequency of church attendance claimed by members of the major religious groupings were these:

	At least once a month	At least once a year	Less than once a year	
Church of England	16%	40	44	100%
Church of Scotland	39%	27	34	100%
Non-conformist	45%	32	23	100%
Roman Catholic	73%	11	16	100%

Among Anglicans the proportion claiming to attend church at least once a week was less than a tenth; among Roman Catholics, fully two-thirds.

of England services was overwhelmingly likely to be Conservative; the purely nominal Anglican was in most cases Labour.

Yet the patterns shown in 6.1 and 6.2 can be deceptive, since denomination and churchgoing differ between classes, as party preference itself does. Table 6.3 repeats the profile of party allegiance within each of the main church groupings separately for

6.3 Partisan Self-Image by Religion and Social Class

Occupational Grades I–III

	Church of England	Church of Scotland	Non-Comformist[a]	Roman Catholic
Conservative	72%	74%	41%	55%
Labour	10	22	22	26
Liberal	18	4	37	19
	100%	100%	100%	100%

Occupational Grades IV–VI

	Church of England	Church of Scotland	Non-Conformist[a]	Roman Catholic
Conservative	30%	25%	22%	18%
Labour	55%	59	62	69
Liberal	15	16	16	14
	100%	100%	100%	100%

[a] Includes Methodists, Baptists and other non-conformist denominations.

those in middle class and those in working class occupations. The picture that had been drawn by Table 6.1 is substantially transformed. Within all of the church groupings class is shown to be strongly linked to party. Indeed, the difference between classes within the Churches of England and Scotland is very nearly as great as in the country as a whole. But the significance of the religious groupings does not vanish altogether. There is still a discernible difference of Conservative strength between Anglicans on the one hand and non-conformists on the other in both the middle and working classes. The remarkable strength of the Liberals among middle class non-conformists is a point to which we shall return.

With allowance for class, the relationship between Conservative preference and the frequency with which Anglicans go to church is further transformed. Figure 6.4 shows this relationship separately for middle class and working class Anglicans, and makes it plain that the major political cleavage within the Church of England is by class and not by frequency of church attendance. The two

6.4 Partisan Self-Image of Middle Class and Working Class Anglicans by Frequency of Church Attendance

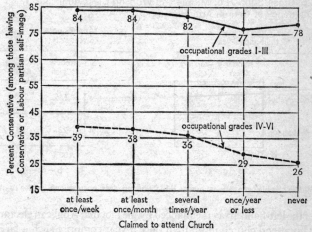

slopes of Figure 6.4 are far gentler than the single slope of Figure 6.2. Indeed, the tendency of Conservative support to rise much more rapidly with attendance in the earlier figure is a reflection of the fact that middle class Anglicans are more often found in church. But Conservatism does still increase with attendance, in both classes. Among middle and working class Anglicans alike, involvement in religious observance and commitment to the Conservative Party go together, although at very different overall levels of Conservative strength.

This pattern bears strongly on the questions of 'cross-voting' and working class Conservatism which we have discussed in Chapter 5. We can see that the tendency of working class Anglicans to support the party of the 'opposite' class (and the solidarity of middle class Anglicans in support of their 'own' party) is substantially greater among those who attend church. The contrast in cross-support tendencies between those who attend more than once a year and those who attend less emerges clearly from Table 6.5 which sets out four-fold arrays of party support by class for these two groups of Church of England electors. The importance of the much greater imbalance of the b and c cells

6.5 Cross-Support of Middle and Working Class Anglicans by Frequency of Church Attendance

	Attends more than once a year			Attends once a year or less	
	Middle Class	Working Class		Middle Class	Working Class
Conservative	83%	b 37%	Conservative	77%	b 27%
Labour	c 17	63	Labour	c 23	73
	100%	100%		100%	100%
	b − c = 20%			b − c = 4%	

Middle class is occupational grades I–III; working class, occupational grades IV–IV.

of the left-hand array is enhanced by the fact that Anglican electors who attend church more than once a year comprise such a large fraction of the English electorate. We see here in fact a primary source of working class support for the Conservative Party.[5]

5. We have here as well a partial explanation of the greater Conservatism of women, who tend also to be more faithful in religious observance. Twenty per cent of our women respondents but only 13 per cent of our men said they go to church once a week; 47 per cent of men but only 32 per cent of women said they go to church never or less than once a year. But this explanation is not more than a partial one: even among men and women with comparable habits of church attendance, the women are somewhat more Conservative.

These variations of party support within the Church of England give added significance to the differences of party strength that are observed between Anglican and non-conformist electors. If not 'the Tory party at prayer', the Church of England is nevertheless something that millions of Conservative electors identify themselves with.

Seen in this way the greater tendency of middle class electors to call themselves Church of England and, if they do, to attend church takes on new meaning. Certainly the religious differences of the middle and working class ought not to be seen simply as the source of a 'spurious' correlation between party and religion. They are rather among the ties that bind the middle class more strongly to the Conservative Party. The traditional symbols of the Church of England and Conservative Party have an appeal for many working class electors too, as we have seen. But their appeal for the middle class is peculiarly strong. The British establishment has traditionally been Church of England, while non-conformity has tended to carry lower social status. The strong Anglican traditions maintained in the most prestigious parts of the educational system and the constant association of the Church with Royal ceremonies may have helped, during this period of religious decline, to preserve the social primacy of the official national religion.

Yet there is evidence that the ties of religion and party in the modern electorate are distinctly a legacy of the past. The religious differences we have found are weak compared with those which an earlier era would have yielded. Some of the most interesting evidence in the whole of our research is that describing the gradual decay of this basis of party support. The extent of this decay is at once apparent if we set out the party allegiances of Anglicans and non-conformists by class in the several age-cohorts that make up the present electorate. Table 6.6 on the next page examines the relationship of class to party within the Anglican and non-conformist groups in the oldest of the age groups, the pre-1918 cohort. Among those growing up before the First World War, the difference between Anglicans and non-conformists was enormous. Half the working class Anglicans and the overwhelming bulk of the middle class ones were Conservative. With the non-conformists

6.6 Partisan Self-Image by Class and Religion Within Pre-1918 Cohort[a]

	Church of England			Non-Conformist	
	Middle Class	Working Class		Middle Class	Working Class
Conservative	82%	b 50%	Conservative	46%	b 19%
Other	c 18	50	Other	c 54	81
	100%	100%		100%	100%
	b − c = 32%			**b − c = −35%**	

difference of balance of cross-support in two religious groups: 67%

[a] Middle class is comprised of occupational grades I–III, working class of grades IV–VI. The definitions of age-cohorts here and in subsequent tables are those set out in Chapter 3. We have grouped Labour and Liberal partisan self-images as 'other'.

the picture was almost exactly reversed; even among the middle class the Conservatives were in a minority. These differences are reflected in the diverging 'cross-support' tendencies in the two religious groupings. Among Anglicans cross-support in class terms (cell *b* less cell *c*) is 32 per cent in the Conservatives' favour. But among non-conformists it is 35 per cent *against* the Conservatives. The total divergence of 67 per cent between these two figures is shown at the bottom of the table.

When we turn to those who grew up during and after the Second World War these contrasts had largely disappeared. There was little difference in party support among Anglicans and non-conformists in the working class, and even in the middle class the gap was very much less than in the oldest cohort. This marked attenuation of religious differences is shown by Table 6.7. The entries of the two parts of this table make clear that the difference of the cross-support by class within the two religious groups is not nearly so large in the post-1951 cohort as it is in the pre-1918 cohort. Indeed, the divergence of the two measures of cross-support is not more than 12 per cent (as shown at the bottom of the table), whereas in the oldest cohort it is a full 67 per cent.

6.7 Partisan Self-Image by Class and Religion Within Post-1951 Cohort[a]

	Church of England				Non-Conformist	
	Middle Class	Working Class			Middle Class	Working Class
Conservative	68%	b 27%		Conservative	53%	b 30%
Other	c 32	73		Other	c 47	70
	100%	100%			100%	100%
	b − c = −5%				b − c = −17%	

difference of balance of cross-support in two religious groups: 12%

[a] See definitions in footnote to Table 6.6.

We can moreover show that this change has been a continuous one, extending over the four cohorts comprising the present electorate. Indeed we can stretch our analysis back into generations that have passed the possibility of voting by asking our respondents about their fathers' religious and party preferences when they were growing up. On the assumption of an average gap of thirty years in the ages of father and child, such a procedure yields two additional cohorts which have passed out of the electorate: the fathers of the interwar cohort and the fathers of the pre-1918 cohort.[6]

Figure 6.8 on the next page shows, for six cohorts, the balance

6. We include these figures on the fathers of our two oldest cohorts to suggest the extension into the past of the greater religious cleavage found in the pre-1918 and interwar cohorts themselves. But several considerations preclude our regarding these data as comparable to those we have from our living respondents. The data on fathers pertain to partisanship at time past, those on respondents to partisanship at the time of our studies. Our data on past cohorts pertain only to fathers, those from our living cohorts to everyone. Some fathers have reproduced themselves less than others or not at all, and therefore are under-represented in the memories of living cohorts. We shall return to the problems which these considerations pose for analysis when we examine in Chapter 11 the evolution of party strength over half a century.

6.8 Balance of Cross-Support Among Anglican and
Non-Conformist Electors by Cohort

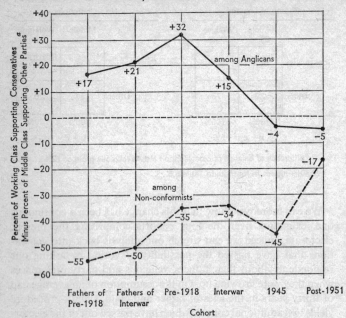

[a] Each of the plotted values represents the difference, within a given religious group of a given cohort, of the proportion of working class whose partisan self-image (or remembered partisanship, in the case of fathers) is Conservative and the proportion of middle class whose partisanship is Liberal or Labour.

of cross-support for the parties by class within the Anglican and non-conformist groups; in other words the figure plots for each religious group the difference between the proportion of working class electors supporting the Conservatives (entry *b* of Tables 6.6 or 6.7) and the proportion of middle class electors failing to support the Conservatives (entry *c*). The parallel swings of the two curves suggest the broad historical rises and falls of Conservative strength, especially the decline of Conservative support over the Second World War. But the dominant trend of the figure is the steady attenuation of the difference of the cross-support patterns in the two religious groups. The gap between church and chapel declines without interruption from 72 per cent among those who came of age in the 1880s to 12 per cent among those who came of age after 1950.[7]

The erosion of the religious cleavage as the class alignment became more predominant has carried farthest in the working class. Figure 6.9 shows the progressive release of working class cohorts from the religious motives which influenced party allegiance so deeply in an earlier day. In our youngest two cohorts no significant religious difference is associated with the incidence of working class Conservatism. But among our oldest respondents, religion makes a vast difference to the likelihood of a working class voter's being a Conservative.

6.9 Conservative Strength Among Working Class Anglicans and Non-Conformists by Cohort

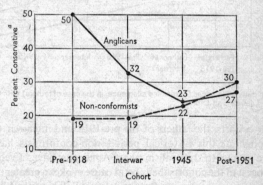

[a] Of partisan self-images aligned with the Conservative, Labour and Liberal parties.

The weakening of the religious alignment has involved a weakening of the Liberal–non-conformist axis. In much of our discussion

7. The religious feelings of an earlier day were captured by the remarks of a sixty-six-year-old Carmarthen painter, an elector of the pre-1918 cohort, who recalled the basis of his father's partisanship: 'If you are chapel you are Liberal. If you are church you are Conservative. My father was church.'

we have grouped the Liberals and Labour as opponents of the Conservative Party. But Figure 6.10 charts Liberal strength in successive Anglican and non-conformist cohorts. Here again, we have extended our historical reach by adding two

6.10 Liberal Strength Among Anglicans and Non-Conformists by Cohort

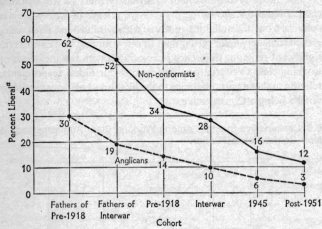

[a] Of party allegiances (or recalled allegiance, in the case of fathers) with Conservatives, Liberals and Labour.

prior cohorts, the fathers of the pre-1918 and inter-war cohorts. Throughout this historical period non-conformists have been more prone to Liberalism than Anglicans have. Even in the youngest of the cohorts the Liberal cause evokes a greater response among non-conformists. But the original link between Liberalism and non-conformity was so strong that its decline inevitably appears spectacular.

The displacement of the Liberals as the Conservatives' main opponent is one of the keys to the displacement of religion by class as the main grounds of party support in the recent past. Once the Liberals had fallen behind an explicitly class-based party, for reasons which owed as much to the splits between Liberals' leaders as to Labour's electoral appeal, it was natural that electoral support should more nearly follow class lines and that the electorate's attention should turn from the issues of church schools and disestablishment towards the class-related issues that were the basis of Labour's challenge. If Ireland had remained in the United Kingdom following a protracted struggle, a quite different religious dimension might have shaped British politics. As it was, the minority religions were left to go their own way, and the ties of religion to party steadily weakened, although they are still plainly visible in the older segments of the electorate.

The legacy of religion is partly to be seen in regional terms. Indeed, the cleavage of church and chapel was nowhere deeper than in Wales, which is today the most anti-Conservative area in all of Britain. The Labour Party inherited from the Liberals a tradition of non-conformity and alienation from the establishment which is to be understood partly in religious terms, especially in Wales and the North, away from London. The interlocking of religious and regional differences is indeed sufficiently important to lead us to a more general consideration of regional variations of the central class theme of recent politics.

National Uniformity and Regional Variations

Behind a good deal of contemporary comment on British electoral behaviour lies an exceedingly simple image of political alignment and change. It is often assumed that enduring allegiance to party is based on class and that changeability is a response to the transient issues of national politics. In its crudest form this image is a simple model with two factors; the first factor, class, explaining the continuities of electoral support and the second factor, the national issues of the moment, explaining the short-term fluctuations of party strength which are seen in all parts of the country. The model envisages two quite different kinds of homogeneity of electoral behaviour between areas. On the one hand, the class basis of enduring allegiance is everywhere the same; on the other hand, electoral change, being a response to common national issues, is also everywhere the same.

Such a model has at least the virtue of highlighting the irregular way in which different parts of the country actually behave. Of course, the generally uniform pattern of swings between the parties has always been broken by regional and local variations; we shall moreover argue in Chapter 13 that even very uniform swings may conceal a paradoxical lack of uniformity. But, by any measure, swing is far more uniform across the regions than is class support for the parties. Any idea that class provides a universal ground for party allegiance is difficult to reconcile with the extraordinarily uneven spread of party support between regions, continuing decade after decade. These differences are sometimes neglected because of the attention focused on the impressive evenness of swing.[8] But the scale and endurance of the basic regional differences can be shown by comparing the results in two evenly balanced elections thirteen years apart. Figure 6.11 shows the relative strength of the two main parties in 1951 and 1964 in twenty-five regions.

Two points stand out from this figure. First, the electoral tides

8. The relative uniformity of British swings emerges when we look at comparable American figures. The standard deviation of swings from the national average is almost three times as great in the United States as in Britain.

	Britain				United States		
Year	Seats included	Mean Swing	Standard Deviation of swing	Year	Seats included	Mean Swing	Standard Deviation of swing
1950–51	224	0·7	1·4	1952–54	318	4·3	5·2
1951–55	349	1·8	1·4	1954–56	333	2·2	5·1
1955–59	455	1·1	2·2	1956–58	324	6·9	5·5
1959–64	370	3·5	2·4	1958–60	227	2·7	5·6
1964–66	429	3·2	1·7				

The constituencies included in this table are those whose boundaries were not significantly altered and whose patterns of major party candidature were the same at both elections.

The congressional districts included in this table are those which had major party candidates at both elections.

For an extended discussion of this difference between the two countries see D. E. Stokes, 'Parties and the Nationalization of Electoral Forces', in *The American Party Systems*, W. N. Chambers and W. D. Burnham, eds., New York, 1968, pp. 182–202.

6.11 Regional Differences in Conservative Percentage Lead over Labour in 1951 and 1964

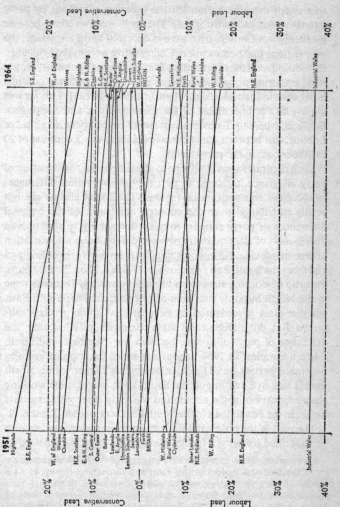

The Figure is based on the tables given in *The British General Election of 1951* pp. 249–63 and *The British General Election of 1964* pp. 301–16.

that swept over the nation left the ordering of regions by party strength almost undisturbed. The only regions that became markedly less Conservative were in Scotland and Lancashire; the only regions that became more Conservative were in the Midlands. But second, and more important for our present argument, are the wide, enduring disparities between regions. The extreme contrast is between industrial Wales, where in 1964 as in 1951, Labour was almost 40 per cent ahead of the Conservatives, and South East England, where the Conservatives stayed over 20 per cent ahead of Labour. But between many other areas there was a contrast of 20 to 30 per cent in the party lead.[9]

Such contrasts are a challenge to any simple class explanation of party allegiance, although in part they merely reflect differences in the class composition of regions. The social classes are not evenly distributed over the country, and some of the regional differences of party support may be due simply to this uneven distribution of class make-up between different regions. Variation of this sort is evident in our own samples from the North of England and from the South East. As shown by Table 6.12 on the next page, the ratio of working class to middle class was roughly three to one in the North but only two to one in London and the South East, whether class is measured by occupational grade or class self-image. But this difference of class composition is less than the difference of party allegiance between our Northern and South Eastern samples. In 1964 Labour's share of the support given to two main parties was 11 percentage points higher in the North than it was in London and the South East, whereas the working class proportion of the population was only 8 percentage points higher in the North than in the South East, as we see in Table 6.12.

The part of the political difference between regions that cannot be explained in terms of class composition must be reflected in

9. In one important respect we have exaggerated the political homogeneity of the United Kingdom in this chart and throughout the book. As a matter of research strategy we confined our sampling to the 618 constituencies of England, Scotland and Wales, excluding twelve seats in Northern Ireland; these are therefore omitted from Figure 6.11 as well. But we recognize that by doing so we have excluded the most outstanding element of diversity within the nation.

6.12 Class Composition of North and South East England[a]

	North	London and South East
Occupational Grades		
I–III	24%	32%
IV–VI	76	68
	100%	100%
Class Self-Image		
Middle	26%	34%
Working	74	66
	100%	100%

[a] In 6.12 and Table 6.13 we have defined the North as including Cheshire, Cumberland, Durham, Lancashire, Northumberland, Westmoreland and Yorkshire; and London and the South East as including Berkshire, Buckinghamshire, Dorset, Essex, Hampshire, Hertfordshire, Isle of Wight, Kent, London, Middlesex, Surrey and Sussex.

differences of party support by class between regions. The different rates at which the middle and working class give their support to the parties in the North and South East is shown in Table 6.13. In the North the proportion of the middle class supporting the Conservatives is no greater than the proportion of the

6.13 Party Support by Class Self-Image in the North and South East, 1964[a]

North of England				South East		
		Class Self-Image				Class Self-Image	
		Middle	Working			Middle	Working
Partisan Self-Image	Con.	74%	b 26%	Partisan Self-Image	Con.	80%	b 33%
	Lab.	c 26	74		Lab	c 20	67
		100%	100%			100%	100%
		b − c = 0%				b − c = 13%	

[a] For definitions of regions see footnote to Table 6.12.

working class supporting Labour. But in the South East the Conservatives' strength in the middle class exceeds Labour's strength in the working class by 13 percentage points, as reflected by our measure of 'cross-support'. Plainly the electoral differences between these large areas involve more than the simplest facts of their class composition. Indeed, when we examine the relative contribution of both kinds of differences we find that the overall difference of party strength between the North and South East is due more to variations of party support by class than it is to the differing class makeup of the regions.[10]

10. To make clear the basis of this comparison let us denote by P the proportion Labour among middle class major-party supporters in the South East (hence $1 - P$ is the proportion Conservative among such electors in this region), by Q the proportion Labour among working class electors in the South East (hence $1 - Q$ is the proportion Conservative among working class electors in this region), by W the proportion working class among electors supporting one of the two main parties in the South East (hence $1 - W$ is the proportion middle class among major-party supporters in the South East), by δ the difference between P and the proportion Labour among middle class electors in the North, by ϵ the difference between Q and the proportion Labour among working class electors in the North, and by α the difference between W and the proportion working class among major-party supporters in the north. It follows from these definitions that Labour's proportion of major-party supporters in the South East is

Lab (S.E.) $= P(1 - W) + QW$

and in the North is

Lab (N) $= (P + \delta)(1 - W - \alpha) + (Q + \epsilon)(W + \alpha)$.

It is easily shown that the overall difference of Labour's proportion of major-party support in the two regions can be represented as a linear combination

$$\text{Lab(N)} - \text{Lab (S.E.)} = \underbrace{\alpha(Q - P)}_{\substack{\text{class} \\ \text{composition} \\ \text{effect}}} + \underbrace{(\epsilon - \delta)W}_{\substack{\text{class} \\ \text{support} \\ \text{effect}}} + \underbrace{\delta + (\epsilon - \delta)\alpha}_{\substack{\text{interaction} \\ \text{effect}}}$$

whose components can be associated with differences of class composition and of the pattern of party support by class by seeing how each of the components depends on the values of δ, ϵ and α. The left-hand component is seen to involve only α and may therefore be interpreted as the portion

The size of our sample precluded us from pursuing this analysis to smaller sub-regions of the country. For this purpose we aggregated a great many nationwide samples interviewed by National Opinion Polls over a three-year period. By this means we were able to assemble enough cases to speak with some confidence about the varying relation of class to party in eleven regions into which the country has often been divided for statistical purposes.[11] We set out in Table 6.14 the results of this detailed regional analysis.

The uniformity in the relationship of class and party is far greater across the regions of Britain than it is in many countries.

---

of Labour's greater strength in the North which is due to the difference of class composition between North and South East. Of course the value of this component depends also on P and Q, but not on the *difference* between P and Q and the values of the corresponding rates of party support in the North. The middle component is seen to involve only δ and ϵ and may therefore be interpreted as the portion of Labour's greater strength in the North which is due to differences of the pattern of party support by class between the two regions. The right-hand component is seen to involve both types of differences between the regions and may therefore be regarded as an 'interaction' term. Since δ and ϵ are of roughly equal magnitude, however, their difference almost vanishes and this interaction term is in this case negligible. Indeed, since δ and ϵ tend to vary together, we have found this to be true in most applications we have made of this method, and we have been able to decompose an overall political difference between regions into a term that reflects the difference of class composition and a term that reflects variations of the pattern of class support. In the case of our comparison of the North and South East, an overall difference of 10·5 per cent decomposes into 3·8 per cent due to differences of class composition, 6·6 per cent due to differences of class support, and 0·1 per cent due to the interaction of the two.

11. National Opinion Polls allowed us access to all the data on voting intention, social grade, age, sex and marital status, union membership and certain other items collected by them between October 1963 and December 1966. This cumulatively amounted to a probability sample of 120,000 interviews. We have drawn on this vast body of data in our analyses of age-cohorts and of union voting, as well as in the regional analysis presented here. N.O.P. used the Registrar General's (Old) Standard Regions in classifying respondents from these surveys. They also used the normal market research coding of social grade based on occupation and interviewers' assessment. For these reasons it is not possible to match their findings comprehensively with our own.

6.14 Regional Patterns of Party Support by Social Class, 1963–6

South and Midlands

	West Midlands						East Midlands				
	All	AB	C1	C2	DE		All	AB	C1	C2	DE
Con	43·3	77·7	61·5	36·1	32·6	Con	40·4	83·2	60·4	33·5	28·7
Lab	49·7	13·8	29·6	57·1	61·4	Lab	51·9	8·9	30·3	59·0	64·3
Lib	6·9	8·0	8·8	6·7	5·9	Lib	7·6	7·7	9·0	7·5	6·9
Other	0·1	0·5	0·1	0·1	0·1	Other	0·1	0·2	0·3	—	0·1
	100 %	100 %	100 %	100 %	100 %		100 %	100 %	100 %	100 %	100 %
n =	10,611	914	2,007	5,061	2,629	n =	8,529	560	1,631	3,838	2,500
	100 %	8·6	18·9	47·7	24·8		100 %	6·6	19·1	45·0	29·3

	South Central						East Anglia				
	All	AB	C1	C2	DE		All	AB	C1	C2	DE
Con	50·1	78·3	62·2	42·5	36·6	Con	44·2	75·1	59·1	35·1	28·9
Lab	39·5	10·5	25·3	46·8	55·8	Lab	44·4	13·0	27·2	53·9	61·5
Lib	10·3	10·9	12·5	10·6	7·3	Lib	11·2	11·7	13·5	10·7	9·6
Other	0·1	0·3	—	0·1	0·3	Other	0·2	0·2	0·2	0·3	—
	100 %	100 %	100 %	100 %	100 %		100 %	100 %	100 %	100 %	100 %
n =	6,284	779	1,495	2,495	1,551	n =	8,603	1,144	1,984	3,095	2,380
	100 %	12·4	23·2	39·7	24·7		100 %	13·3	23·0	36·0	27·7

	South-West						London and South-East				
	All	AB	C1	C2	DE		All	AB	C1	C2	DE
Con	47·0	77·4	63·8	38·2	28·2	Con	45·1	74·1	58·5	33·6	28·5
Lab	38·2	9·9	21·6	46·9	56·1	Lab	44·1	13·0	28·8	56·0	63·8
Lib	14·6	12·6	14·5	14·6	15·6	Lib	10·6	12·7	12·5	10·1	7·4
Other	0·2	0·1	0·1	0·3	0·1	Other	0·2	0·2	0·2	0·3	0·3
	100 %	100 %	100 %	100 %	100 %		100 %	100 %	100 %	100 %	100 %
n =	8,738	1,141	2,115	3,315	2,167	n =	20,939	3,115	5,609	7,488	4,727
	100 %	13·1	24·2	37·9	24·8		100 %	14·9	26·8	35·8	22·5

Source: National Opinion Polls

Yet Table 6.14 shows substantial variation both of class composition and class support for the parties in these eleven regions. The distributions of social grade appearing at the foot of each table show how much the social composition of regions varies. In London and the South East 41·7 per cent had non-manual occupations (A, B or C1). In Wales the proportion was only 26·4 per cent; in the North East only 23·6 per cent. But the political differences between regions involve also marked variations of party support

6.14 Regional Patterns of Party Support by Social Class
(continued)

Scotland, Weles and North of England

	Scotland							North East				
	All	AB	C1	C2	DE			All	AB	C1	C2	DE
Con	40·7	79·8	61·6	30·5	28·9		Con	35·0	72·7	60·6	26·5	25·2
Lab	50·8	10·8	29·4	60·6	63·6		Lab	59·4	18·6	31·0	69·2	69·5
Lib	6·0	7·2	6·7	5·7	5·3		Lib	5·5	8·5	8·2	4·2	5·2
Other	2·5	2·2	2·3	3·2	2·2		Other	0·1	0·2	0·2	0·1	0·1
	100%	100%	100%	100%	100%			100%	100%	100%	100%	100%
$n =$	12,803	1,354	2,329	3,901	5,219		$n =$	8,385	590	1,392	3,758	2,645
	100%	10·6	18·2	30·5	40·7			100%	7·0	44·8	44·8	31·6

	Lancashire and Cheshire							Yorkshire				
	All	AB	C1	C2	DE			All	AB	C1	C2	DE
Co	41.1	74·1	57·3	34·6	29·6		Con	38·6	78·9	56·9	28·0	26·3
Lab	50·1	14·8	30·6	57·3	63·2		Lab	52·0	10·0	30·7	63·6	65·9
Lib	8·5	10·8	11·9	7·7	6·9		Lib	9·2	11·0	12·2	8·3	7·7
Other	0·3	0·3	0·2	0·4	0·2		Other	0·2	0·1	0·2	0·1	0·1
	100%	100%	100%	100%	100%			100%	100%	100%	100%	100%
$n =$	18,932	1,853	3,584	7,186	6,309		$n =$	9,159	966	1,814	3,936	2,443
	100%	9·8	18·9	38·0	33·3			100%	10·5	19·8	43·0	26·7

	Wales				
	All	AB	C1	C2	DE
Con	22·2	58·0	41·9	15·2	13·5
Lab	71·7	30·8	46·0	79·9	82·9
Lib	5·0	9·5	10·1	4·0	2·9
Other	1·1	1·7	2·0	0·9	0·7
	100%	100%	100%	100%	100%
$n =$	7,565	715	1,278	3,126	2,446
	100%	9·5	16·9	41·3	32·3

Source: National Opinion Polls

by class. In the South Central region 42·5 per cent of skilled
manual workers (C2) gave their support to the Conservatives; in
Wales 15·2 per cent did so. Labour's share of the lower white
collar group (C1) ranged from 21·6 per cent in the South West to
46·0 per cent in Wales.

We may indeed see how much more than simple differences of
class composition is involved in the partisan differences of regions

by grouping these data roughly into the 'two nations', the depressed North and the expanding South, that gave rise to so much political comment in the early 1960s. The figures of Table 6.14, which arrange the regions into these two broad groupings, reveal marked differences of party strength: Labour's proportion of the support for the two leading parties was on the average ten per cent higher in the massed samples of Scotland, the North East, Lancashire and Cheshire, Yorkshire and Wales than it was in the samples of the West and East Midlands, the South Central region, East Anglia, the South West, and London and the South East.

Some part of this difference is due to the varied class composition of these 'two nations'. Among those supporting the two main parties, the working class proportion voting Labour was 7·5 percentage points higher in the North and Wales than it was in the Midlands and South. But this difference would not by itself account for the partisan difference separating these two halves of the country even if every manual worker were Labour and every non-manual worker Conservative, which is by no means the case. The political cleavage between the two nations is also due to their differing patterns of party allegiance within the classes, as Table 6.15 makes clear. In the North of England, Scotland and Wales

6.15 Party Support by Class in Two Regional Groupings, 1963–6[a]

	North of England, Scotland and Wales			South and Midlands	
	Middle Class	Working Class		Middle Class	Working Class
Conservative	70·3%	b 29·5%	Conservative	74·7%	b 37·0%
Labour	c 29·7	70·5	Labour	c 25·3	63·0
	100·0%	100·0%		100·0%	100·0%
	b − c = −0·2%			b − c = 11·7%	

[a] This table is formed by recombining the National Opinion Polls data given by Table 6.14. Liberal and 'other' preferences have been excluded. 'Middle class' is formed of occupational grades A, B and C1, 'Working class' of occupational grades C2, D and E.

Labour's strength among working class electors in this period was as high as the Conservatives' strength among middle class electors; the level of 'cross-support' in the two class groupings was virtually identical. But in the Midlands and South, Labour's share of the working class vote was decidedly less than the Conservatives' share of the middle class vote; the balance of cross-support was 11·7 per cent in the Conservatives' favour.

We can in fact estimate what proportion of the difference in behaviour between the two areas is the result of basic differences in the way the classes allocated their support and what proportion is the result simply of differences in the relative size of the classes. Such an analysis shows that the first kind of difference is more than twice as important as the second; more than two thirds of the overall difference of 9·3 percentage points in Labour's strength in the two areas was due to the contrasting patterns of party support within class while less than a third was due to the simple difference on the relative size of the classes.[12] The key to the two nations politically lies largely in factors that have produced the contrast of party strength within classes.

The quest for such factors would cover a very broad terrain of social and political history. Certainly the scale and type of industrialization and the experience of economic distress – in the 1960s, the interwar period, and before – have been very different in the two nations. And there are historical patterns of alienation from established authority in the peripheral regions, most notably in the case of Wales. In one respect, however, we should see class as an explanatory factor in a slightly more complicated way than is involved in simple differences of class composition.

A good deal of empirical support can be found for the principle that once a partisan tendency becomes dominant in a local area processes of opinion formation will draw additional support to the

12. The basis of these calculations is set out in the footnotes to page 176 above. The overall difference of 9·3 per cent in Labour's proportion of support for the two main parties in North and South divides into a component of 2·8 per cent representing the 'class composition' effect, a component of 6·4 per cent representing the 'class support' effect, and a component of 0·1 per cent representing the 'interaction' effect (which is once again altogether negligible).

party that is dominant. If this is true, perceptions of class interest may impart to an area a political tendency that is exaggerated still further by the processes that form and sustain a local political culture, thereby altering the pattern of party support within classes. The effects of a local political environment are plainly relevant to the regional variations we have examined, as well as being of interest in their own right.

The Influence of a Local Political Environment

The tendency of local areas to become homogeneous in their political opinions has attracted the attention of many observers and been described in many ways.[13] We may see evidence of this tendency in Britain by examining two contrasting types of local areas, each of which is likely to have a strong social and political ethos. On the one hand, the mining areas are traditionally seen as the archetypal strongholds of solidary working class support for Labour. On the other, the seaside resorts, even more than the suburbs, seem to stand out as communities permeated by the Conservatism of the middle class. We have several areas of each kind in our sample, and we have examined our samples of each for evidence of the influence on the local political environment.

These two kinds of areas differ immensely in their class com-

13. The earliest statement of this phenomenon is Herbert Tingsten's enunciation of the 'theory of the centre of political gravity'. See his *Political Behaviour*, London, 1937. Several American authors have used the term 'breakage effect' to describe the tendency of a locally dominant party to get more support than it might expect to receive on the basis of class or other factors, on the analogy of the way those who organize horse-race betting keep the odd pennies when winnings are rounded off. See B. R. Berelson, P. F. Lazarsfeld and W. N. McPhee, *Voting*, Chicago, 1954, pp. 98–101; P. Cutright and P. Rossi, 'Grassroots Politics and the Vote', *American Sociological Review*, 23 (1958), 171–9, and D. Katz and S. J. Eldersveld, 'The Impact of Local Party Activity Upon the Electorate', *Public Opinion Quarterly*, 25 (1961), 1–24. For comparable evidence in Britain see F. M. Martin in 'Social Status and Electoral Choice in Two Constituencies', *British Journal of Sociology*, 2 (1952), 231–41, and F. M. Bealey, J. Blondel and W. McCann, *Constituency Politics*, London, 1965, pp. 154–65.

position. Table 6.16 shows that only 14 per cent of our sample in mining seats called themselves middle class and only 11 per cent performed occupational tasks within our categories I, II or III. But the comparable proportions of our sample in the resort areas

6.16 Class Composition of Mining and Resort Areas

	Mining	Resorts
Occupational Grade		
Grades I–III	11%	44%
Grades IV–VI	89	56
	100%	100%
Class Self-Image		
Middle Class	14%	43%
Working Class	86	57
	100%	100%

were 43 and 44 per cent. These facts of class composition would be enough to assure a marked divergence of party support in the two kinds of areas. But the much more spectacular difference has to do with the behaviour of the classes, as Table 6.17 shows. The

6.17 Partisan Self-Image by Class in Mining Seats and Resorts

	Mining Seats			Resorts	
	Class Self-Image			Class Self-Image	
	Middle Class	Working Class		Middle Class	Working Class
Conservative	64%	b 9%	Conservative	93%	b 52%
Labour	c 36	91	Labour	c 7	48
	100%	100%		100%	100%
	b − c = −27%			b − c = +45%	

Conservatives actually outran Labour among the working class of resort areas. In fact, if we were to take account of Liberal support as well, Labour would be found to have attracted the support of only a third of the working class in the seaside resorts.[14] The Conservative advantage in the cross-support proportions was a staggering 45 per cent. In the mining seats, however, the picture is almost reversed. The Labour Party received fully 36 per cent of the middle class vote and lost less than a tenth of the vote of the working class. Indeed, the balance of cross-support in the mining areas was 27 per cent in favour of Labour. The difference of this balance in the two types of areas is as large as any we have seen.

These differences ought not to be assigned too readily to any single explanatory principle. Several processes can have helped to exaggerate a partisan tendency that had already been imparted to the mining and resort areas by perceptions of class interest. Some writers have argued that a local electorate will perceive and conform to local political norms.[15] Others have suggested that this tendency reflects the persuasive influence of informal contacts on the shop floor, in the public house and other face to face groups of the elector's world.[16] These processes will draw those who hold a minority opinion towards the view that is dominant in their local milieu, exaggerating the strength of a leading party and altering the pattern of party support by class. In Chapter 13 we offer evidence of these persuasive effects when we consider the remarkable uniformity of partisan change throughout widely differing constituencies.

Evidence that these processes are much more extensively at work emerged when we divided our cumulated file of National

14. We are indeed reminded of the ancient story still told in Labour circles of the Bournemouth elector who entered the polling station and timidly inquired where servants voted for Brigadier Page-Croft.

15. A Yorkshire miner's daughter among our respondents explained her vote simply, 'We lived in a Labour district.'

16. Excellent reviews of alternative explanations of this phenomenon are given in R. Putnam, 'Political Attitudes and the Local Community', *American Political Science Review*, **50** (1966), 640–54, and K. R. Cox, 'The Voting Decision in a Spatial Context', in R. J. Chorley and P. Haggett, eds, *Progress in Geography*, London, 1969.

Opinion Polls into distinct constituencies. The 120,000 interviews taken by the N.O.P. organization over the period from 1963 to 1966 were conducted in 184 constituencies, giving an average of more than 600 respondents in each, a sample that is quite large enough for reliable estimates to be formed of the class composition of each constituency and of the Conservative and Labour proportions within each of the classes. Figure 6.18 exhibits, first, the

6.18 Conservative Proportion of Middle Class Support for Two Main Parties by Proportion of Constituency That is Middle Class[a]

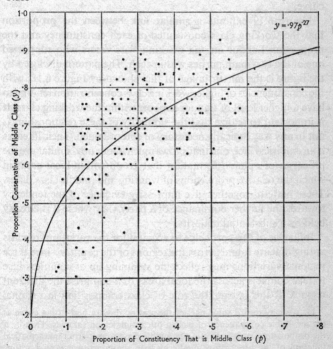

$$y = \cdot 97 p^{\cdot 27}$$

Proportion Conservative of Middle Class (y)

Proportion of Constituency That is Middle Class (p)

[a] This figure is based on data from 184 constituencies in which the National Opinion Polls interviewed more than 120,000 respondents from 1963 to 1966. The analysis shown here is limited to electors who supported the Conservatives or Labour. 'Middle class' is defined as occupational grades A, B or C1.

relationship between the proportion that the middle class constituted in each constituency and the proportion Conservative among
middle class voters who supported one of the two main parties in
each constituency. It can be seen at once that the constituencies of
higher middle class concentration tended to have a higher level of
Conservative support within the middle class. This relationship is
not a linear one; the underlying processes of opinion formation do
not aggregate in this simplest way. We have drawn on the figure a
curve which seems to fit the observed relationship well, although it
is of course true that there are substantial variations about such a
curve.[17]

Figure 6.19 exhibits a similar link between the proportion
that the working class constituted of each constituency and the
proportion Labour among working class voters who supported
one of the two main parties within each. The pattern disclosed by
the figure is the mirror image of that shown by Figure 6.18, with
the constituencies of higher working class concentration tending to
have a higher level of Labour support within the working class. It
is important to realize that the similarity of these relationships is
not in any way logically necessary or foreordained. Their likeness
is an empirical fact, one that shows much about how similar are the
processes of opinion formation that go on within local areas in
which the relative proportions of working and middle class differ.
These patterns together give impressive evidence of the tendency
towards the further dominance of a party view where it is already
held by a substantial majority.

Influence of this sort helps to account for the variations of class
voting that are found across the regions of the country, since these
regional variations may reflect the summing up of countless face
to face contacts across the local areas that comprise the different
regions. If this is true, the role of class composition in regional

17. We may regard some part of the scatter about a best-fitting curve as
the inevitable consequence of basing our estimates on samples. That is, if
the proportion Conservative in the middle class were a strict mathematical
function of the proportion middle class in the constituency as a whole,
some blur would be introduced into their observed relationship in our
sample data because of the error inherent in estimating these proportions
from samples even as large as those used.

6.19 Labour Proportion of Working Class Support for Two Main
Parties by Proportion of Constituency That is Working Class[a]

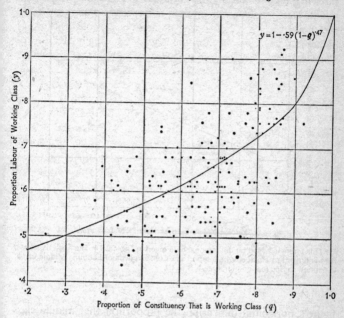

Proportion Labour of Working Class (y)

Proportion of Constituency That is Working Class (q)

$$y = 1 - \cdot59(1-q)^{47}$$

[a] This figure is based on data from 184 constituencies in which the National
Opinion Polls interviewed more than 120,000 respondents from 1963 to 1966. The
analysis shown here is limited to electors who supported the Conservatives or
Labour. 'Working class' is defined as occupational grades C2, D and E.

variations may be larger than is at first apparent. We have seen
that if the chances of a middle or working class elector supporting
a given party were the same in all regions, differences between
regions in the relative proportions of middle and working class
could explain only a small part of regional variation of party
strength. But differences of class composition may have a subtler
and less direct influence on party strength via the processes of
opinion formation in the local environment. Evidence consistent
with such a view is given by Figure 6.20. We have plotted on this

6.20 Conservative Proportion of Middle Class Vote by Proportion of Region Middle Class in Nine Regions of England[a]

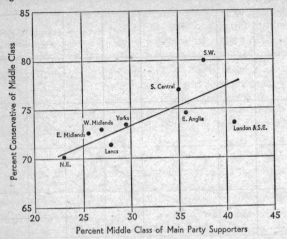

[a] This figure is based on the regional data given in Table 6.14. The analysis shown here is limited to electors who support the Conservatives or Labour. 'Middle class' is defined as occupational grades A, B or Cl.

figure's horizontal dimension the proportion that middle class electors comprise of those who support one of the two main parties in each of the nine regions of England for which we have detailed data from the National Opinion Polls. And we have plotted on the vertical dimension the proportion of these middle class electors in each region who are Conservative. The chart shows a clear tendency for the Conservatives' share of the middle class vote to be greater where the concentration of the middle class is on average greater. A similar tendency is found for Labour's share of the working class vote to be higher in regions where the average concentration of the working class is greater.[18]

But no one would suggest that all regional differences have their

18. The product moment correlation associated with the regional plot given by Figure 6.20 is +0·74.

roots, directly or indirectly, in class. The degree of scatter to the plotted points of Figure 6.20 must reflect the limits of class as a sole explanation of enduring regional differences of party strength. Part of the remaining variation is a legacy of the religious alignment; there is also a tendency for Conservative strength to be less in regions where the concentration of non-conformists is greater. If we had included a point for Wales in Figure 6.20 it would have exaggerated the trend found in the regions of England. Wales had a lower proportion of middle class electors than any other region save the North East. But the Conservatives' share of middle class support in Wales was 15 percentage points lower than in any other region of Britain.

The explanation of regional differences therefore involves a number of variations on the theme of class. Thus far we have, however, skirted an influence, closely related to class, that is often thought to have a profound effect in disposing millions of electors towards Labour. The experience of membership of a trade union is seen as shaping the political attitudes of workers and their families in ways that go beyond the influence of their working class location. It is therefore right that we include in our consideration of the grounds of lasting alignment the influence that may be exerted by the trade unions.

7 Trade Union Influence

The electoral weight of the trade unions is a recurring theme of political commentary in Britain. Some have seen in the division between trade union families and the rest of the electorate a pre-eminent basis of party allegiance. Anderson calls trade unionism 'the one decisive phenomenon which appears to determine a worker's political allegiance far more than anything else',[1] while Blondel states that the solid core of the Labour vote is based on the membership of trade unions and speaks of such membership as 'perhaps the most satisfactory single element of "explanation"' of party ties that cut across class lines.[2]

It is obvious that the influence of unions is closely aligned with the influence of class. We must indeed be careful not to attribute to the unions' persuasiveness political allegiances which are actually formed from perceptions of the norms and interests of a class. But we must be equally careful not to miss the role which unions may play in linking class to party. The unionized worker who experiences class conflict in an industrial setting may be readier to see such conflict in a political setting, approving Labour's role as a champion of working class interests. In the same way the presence of unions and the threat of strikes may inspire a conflict image of society and politics in many who lie outside the unions' ranks.

The Background of Trade Union Influence

Trade unions are woven into the fabric of British politics. The Labour Party came into being in 1900 in order to increase the

1. P. Anderson, in P. Anderson and R. Blackburn (ed.), *Towards Socialism*, London, 1965, pp. 262–3.
2. J. Blondel, *Voters, Parties, and Leaders*, London, 1963, pp. 67–8.

representation of organized workers at Westminster; the party is still a federation of trade unions and constituency parties and nine-tenths of its central income is provided by the unions. About one-third of Labour M.P.s are directly sponsored by trade unions, with union subventions playing a vital role in their constituency party's finances; many unsponsored M.P.s are active trade unionists. At the annual conferences of the Labour Party the block votes of the four or five largest unions, provided that they are united, can decide any issue; on the National Executive Committee of the Labour Party, twelve of the twenty-eight members are direct representatives of the unions while six more are, effectively, chosen by union votes.

But in practice the unions are not nearly so dominant in the Labour Party as this would suggest. The unions are not a monolithic block, but have deep divisions on political as well as industrial matters. Union leaders, although not without power when politically roused, are much more concerned with union than with party affairs. Despite some notable exceptions the ablest union officials tend not to go into Parliament or to take party posts. The sponsored M.P.s in the Parliamentary Labour Party and the National Executive Committee supply a loyal ballast to each body; but they provide few of the men whose drive and ideas shape the party's course.[3] As far as the Labour Party is concerned, the unions possess at the most a limited power of veto, unlikely to be exercised except on matters bearing very directly on union concerns.

Yet the whole political scene is still coloured by the massive size of the trade unions' membership. Out of a total electorate of 36 million, some 8 million are members of trade unions and 7 million

3. No one serves both on the N.E.C. and on the General Council of the T.U.C. The union representation on the N.E.C. is weak because, given a choice, almost all union leaders would prefer to sit on the General Council. The parliamentary representation of the unions is limited by the fact that most union officials are barred, by both the hours of work and their union rules, from combining a full time union post with membership of Parliament. For a full discussion of the nature of union involvement in politics, see M. Harrison, *Trade Unions and the Labour Party Since 1945*, London, 1960.

of these are members of unions affiliated to the Labour Party.
Many millions more are wives or husbands or near relatives of
union members. Of our total sample in the summer of 1963, 26 per
cent reported that they themselves were union members, 9 per cent
that they were married to union members and 2 per cent that they
were otherwise related to union members in their immediate
households. The total of these proportions – 37 per cent – is a
quantity of commanding importance for the strength of British
parties.[4]

Union membership can, of course, mean many things. To one
man the fact of belonging to a trade union may be the most central
concern of his existence, while to another it may be a trivial fact of
which he is barely conscious. Moreover, membership can require
very different degrees of deliberate choice. 'Closed shop' agree-
ments exist formally in only a minority of work places, although in
many more it may be difficult to resist informal pressures to join.
Mining and printing are almost the only major industries where
the closed shop is, for practical purposes, universal, but segments
of engineering and transport (notably shipyard workers and
seamen) are in fact almost 100 per cent unionized.[5]

4. Some members, particularly of white collar unions, do not see their
organization as a union. While the numbers in our sample claiming membership of unions affiliated to the Labour Party and the T.U.C. or just to
the T.U.C. came reasonably close to the numbers that the official returns
would have led us to expect, the numbers reporting membership of unions
and associations which, although outside the T.U.C., are listed by the
Registrar of Friendly Societies, were low. In fact 93 per cent of the claimed
union members in our sample were in T.U.C. unions although on the
Registrar's figures, the proportion should be 88 per cent. Since we are here
concerned with union membership as an attitude of mind, the failure of
some white collar trade unionists or their wives to be conscious of union
membership as such means that those trade unionists who are omitted from
consideration in this chapter are those whose omission is for our purposes
least serious. For a discussion of white collar union membership see G. S.
Bain, 'The Growth of White-Collar Unionism in Great Britain', *British
Journal of Industrial Relations*, **4** (1966), 304–35.

5. The nature of our evidence and the focus of our book do not allow us
to explore in detail the circumstances that conduce to joining a union.
There are of course enormous variations between different occupations,
industries and regions. The predominant structural forces that determine

For the purposes of our own analysis we have been less interested in the objective facts than in the individual's perception of whether his membership is voluntary. In fact 44 per cent of union members in our sample said that membership was a condition of their job, 56 per cent that it was not.[6] But, of course, those who perceived their membership as voluntary may, in joining a union, have demonstrated very different strengths of disposition. To assess these differences we asked each voluntary member what fraction of his workmates who were performing jobs comparable to his own were union members, and we divided this group into three, those whose workmates were entirely, mostly, or only partially unionized. The distribution of our sample of union members across these degrees of voluntarism is shown by Table 7.1

7.1 Voluntarism of Trade Union Membership, 1964

Membership compulsory at place of work	44%
Membership voluntary and	
'Some' workmates are members	11
'Most' workmates are members	26
'All' workmates are members	19
Total of union members	100%
	($n = 405$)

Non-members too may exhibit wide differences of disposition in their failure to join a union. Some will actually have refused to join. Of those who have never been asked, some will feel disposed to join if encouraged, some will be uncertain as to what they would do, and some will be clear that they would refuse. Table 7.2 considers the distribution of non-members across these categories

whether or not a man joins a union seem to be the extent to which his employment is concentrated in a large group and the attitudes of his employer towards the recognition of trade unions. See G. S. Bain, *The Growth of White Collar Unionism*, Oxford, 1969. See also D. Lockwood, *The Black Coated Worker*, London, 1958, pp. 138–55.

6. W. E. J. McCarthy in *The Closed Shop in Britain*, Oxford, 1964, p. 39, estimates that 39 per cent of union members are in jobs covered by closed shop provisions.

7.2 Disposition to Join a Trade Union among Non-Members who were Employed in Workplaces which Include Union Members, 1964

Have not been asked to join, but	
'Would join if asked'	20%
'Don't know'	20
'Would not join if asked'	46
Have refused to join	14
Total of non-members	100%
	(*n* = 399)

(among those at workplaces where there are at least some union members). We shall presently see how revealing are these dispositions of non-members and of voluntary members when we start to analyse the nature of union influence.

In other words, we may think both of voluntary members and of non-members as being arrayed along a dimension describing the strength of their dispositions to join a trade union. Among those who have at some point confronted the question of joining, we may distinguish four degrees of disposition to do so, according to whether the individual did join and the extent of personal motivation that is likely to have been required:

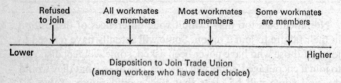

Disposition to Join Trade Union
(among workers who have faced choice)

In a similar way, among those who have not been confronted by the question of joining, we may identify three groups according to the evidence of their disposition to become members:

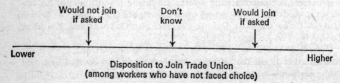

Disposition to Join Trade Union
(among workers who have not faced choice)

We may have some confidence that there is an order within each of these sets of categories, but we do not of course have any way of merging the two or of saying just where on such a hypothetical dimension we should place a given group of those who have or have not faced the question of joining.

Union Membership and Party Allegiance

Plainly there is a vast gulf in party preference between union families and the whole of the rest of the electorate. The support given to the two leading parties in the 1964 election by these two elements in our sample is shown in Table 7.3. The differences shown here would be much the same for the election of 1966.

7.3 Party Preferences of Union and Non-Union Families, 1964

	Trade Union Families	Non-Union Families
Voted: Labour	73%	42%
Conservative	27	58
	100%	100%
	($n = 468$)	($n = 831$)

Considering only Labour and Conservative support, we found seven Labour supporters in trade union families for every four in the rest of the electorate. This trade union support contributed more than half of Labour's strength at the polls.

The problem for anyone who analyses the trade union vote is of course to tell whether and how union members' support for Labour is a result of their union membership. However formidable a difference in partisanship of 31 per cent between union and non-union families, it is still outdistanced by the difference of 50 per cent between the middle and working classes. It is natural, therefore, to begin our analysis by seeing whether trade union members are markedly more Labour than others of the same class. Table 7.4 provides an approximate answer to this from our 1964 data.

7.4 Support for Labour among Union and Non-union Families by Occupational Grade, 1964

	Supervisory Non-manual III	Lower Non-manual IV	Skilled Manual V	Non-skilled Manual VI
Proportion voting Labour				
Among Union families	42%	56%	72%	78%
Among Non-Union families	18%	20%	53%	62%
Difference	24%	36%	19%	16%
	(n = 220)	(n = 121)	(n = 519)	(n = 314)

There is a discernible difference of Labour support between union and non-union families, but it is only in the two non-manual grades that this difference approaches that manifest in the electorate as a whole, a fact to which we shall return. Among skilled manual workers and their families the difference is only 19 per cent. Plainly the political distinctiveness of union families has a good deal to do with class.

In these data the behaviour of union members' wives merits attention. Their party allegiance was within 1 per cent of their husbands'. The widespread notion that the impact of union activity is to some extent cancelled by mutiny in the home finds no support here. Only with the wives of members in the supervisory non-manual grade (III) do we find a divergence of wives towards Conservatism. Moreover, other members of union households appear scarcely less steadfast. Of unmarried sons and daughters or other relatives living in the household of a union member, only 3 per cent fewer voted Labour.

When we interpret the pattern of differences shown in Table 7.4 in the light of the fact that union membership is heavily concentrated in the manual grades, it is clear that the contribution to the disposition to vote Labour which can arise from union membership as such is more modest than at first appeared. Indeed, if we take the original difference of 31 per cent in Labour support between union and non-union members, we find that about a third can be attributed to the class composition of the union and non-union elements of the electorate.[7] None the less, there is still a residual difference of 19 per cent that is not due to simple class composition and that demands explanation. How much of this residual difference in partisanship between union and non-union families can be laid to the influence of the trade unions themselves?

The Question of Union Influence

As is so often the case in social analysis, the key to interpreting the correlation of union membership and party support lies in reaching a reasonable view of their temporal or causal sequence. If union membership were a purely automatic affair, conferred altogether at random on some electors and not on others, we could be sure that a marked divergence of party view between members and non-

---

7. These calculations involve our forming a weighted average of the per cent Labour among non-union families in the several occupational grades, using as weights the proportions of all *union* families found in each of these several grades. In other words we form a percentage of the non-union electors who *would have voted Labour* if the occupational distribution of union and non-union families across grades were identical. The original difference between the per cent q of union families voting Labour and r of non-union families voting Labour can then be partitioned into two components:

$$q - r = (r' - r) + (q - r')$$

The first component represents the portion of the total differences due to the differing occupational composition of the union and non-union groups, the second to influences not to be explained in occupational terms. The values of the quantities in the equation which we have calculated from our sample data for 1964 are these:

$$73 - 42 = (53 - 42) + (73 - 53)$$
$$31 = 11 + 20$$

In other words, something like a third of the total partisan difference between union and non-union families could be attributed to their differing class locations.

members arose from the sequence: union membership →party support. But in fact the processes of becoming a union member are not like this at all. Even those who perceive their membership as compulsory have in fact opted to enter and continue in a trade which necessitates union membership. Moreover, as we have seen, a majority of trade unionists perceive their membership as voluntary, a proportion that is much higher in Britain than in America, despite the fact that the British labour force is much more unionized than the American. At the very least, voluntary membership raises the possibility that partisanship has been among the values and attitudes inclining some men to join unions and others not. The possibility of such an inverted sequence, party support →union membership, puts a very different face on the observed political cleavage between members and non-members.

What does our evidence suggest as to the relative frequency of these alternative sequences? A special case is that of the compulsory member. The strong Labour partisanship of this group (in 1964 Labour won 88 per cent of their votes cast for the two leading parties) cannot have been the cause of their union membership in any immediate sense. But the interpretation of this bond must take account of the traditions of the industries that provide the bulk of compulsory members. Mining, shipbuilding, printing and the dock labour are all trades marked by a largely hereditary recruitment and by a strong *esprit de corps*, greatly reinforced by the special experiences of the interwar period. The same is true, in much less degree, of the railways. Between them these five industries provide over one-third of the compulsory members. The sons who went into their fathers' trade would be most likely to have inherited their fathers' values and partisanship as well. The importance of union organization for the political traditions of these industries can scarcely be doubted. But their mutual ties may well lie deep in the past and have little to do with union influence in the world of the 1960s.

The party allegiance that the compulsory unionists attributed to their fathers suggests the strongly Labour background of this group of workers. Indeed, only the small group of voluntary unionists in workplaces of limited unionization reported so strongly Labour a legacy from parents. Moreover, there is evidence that the compulsory unionists have become somewhat less strongly Labour in their own lifetimes. This evidence is set out in Table 7.5, which compares the present allegiances of these workers with their earliest remembered party preferences. The fact that this group of workers was found, even at the moment of Labour's return to power in 1964, to be less heavily Labour than they were in the first years of political awareness suggests that a unionized work situation in adult life has at most kept them from moving more strongly away from Labour. Many are from solidary working class backgrounds in which unionism is part of the way of life

7.5 Compulsory Unionists' Partisan Self-Images in 1964 by First Remembered Party Preferences

| | | Earliest Party Preference | | | |
		Con	Lab	Lib	
1964 Party Self-Image	Conservative	12	4	3	19
	Labour	2	69	2	73
	Liberal	–	6	2	8
		14	79	7	100%

$(n = 125)$

that includes support of the working class party. But this is a very different image of the relation of union membership to party preference from that which conceives the unions as having a strong persuasive effect on their members' behaviour.

It is the evidence of the voluntary union members, however, that raises the clearest suspicion that party inclination is among the attributes inclining the individual to join a union, rather than the other way round. As we explained earlier, we have assessed the strength of the voluntary member's disposition to join a union by noting whether all, most, or only some of his fellow workers were unionized; the fewer the workmates who are members, the more likely it is that union membership was deliberate choice. It is therefore highly significant that, as Table 7.6 shows, 87 per cent of union members in the least unionized workplaces support Labour

7.6 Labour Preference by 'Voluntarism' of Union Membership

	Proportion Voting Labour, 1964
Voluntary members	
'Some' workmates are members	87% ($n = 38$)
'Most' workmates are members	63% ($n = 96$)
'All' workmates are members	54% ($n = 71$)
Asked to join and have refused	40% ($n = 53$)

compared to 54 per cent in the fully (but not compulsorily) unionized workplaces. Indeed, the latter approach in their partisanship those who have refused to join a union.

These figures together strongly imply that the factors which incline people to be Labour can also incline them to join unions and that this self selection is deeply involved in the greater propensity of union members to vote Labour. Since the voluntarism of union membership is most pronounced in the non-manual occupations, this pattern helps us to understand why the party difference between union members and non-members should be greater in the white collar grades III and IV than in the manual grades V and VI.[8]

8. Had our work been designed mainly to inquire into the party differences between union and non-union workers we should have preferred a more orthogonal design giving similar proportions of union and non-union workers from shops of the same level of unionization. The number of our union respondents precludes us from more than a limited attempt to control for type of industry, size of plant and other factors which affect the degree of unionization. Our hypothesis is, however, that, within shops having the same level of unionization, party preference and disposition to join the union would tend to be part of a common configuration of values, producing party differences between those who belong and those who do not,

Our inferences about the role of the impulse to join a union are strengthened by evidence on the tie between party preference and union inclination among those who have not been asked to join. Table 7.7 shows, once again, how Labour's support falls steadily

7.7 Labour Support among Non-Members in Partially Unionized Workplaces by Disposition to Join if Asked

	Proportion Voting Labour, 1964
Would join if asked	58% ($n = $ 69)
Don't know	34% ($n = $ 69)
Would not join	25% ($n = $ 155)

as the disposition to join lessens. Those who would be willing to join are twice as likely to be Labour as those who would refuse to join. They are indeed more Labour than those voluntary union *members* who work in fully unionized shops, as we saw in Table 7.6.

Means of Union Influence

In the light of these findings some pointed questions can be asked about the effectiveness of the unions' organized efforts to mobilize their members politically. We have attempted a rough evaluation of two means of reaching members: union journals and shop-floor election canvassing. In each case our evidence can hardly be reconciled with any very developed image of the unions directly shaping their members' votes.

Almost all of the substantial trade unions produce monthly journals, some stodgy but some of high quality, which they distribute widely among their members. A remarkably large proportion of trade unionists, 65 per cent, claim to read these journals and two-thirds of these claim to pay 'some' or a 'good deal' of attention to them. However, since these journals give substantial coverage to politics, especially at election time, it is startling to

---

which have nothing to do with the direct influence of unions on the politics of their members.

find that only 30 per cent of their readers, that is to say only 20 per cent of all union members, could recall after the 1964 election having seen any articles on political questions. A still more unsettling finding, set out in Table 7.8 is that readers of union

7.8 Labour Support among Trade Union Members by Readership of Union Journals

	Proportion Voting Labour, 1964
Members who don't see union journals	71% ($n = 125$)
Members who do see union journals	63% ($n = 238$)
Readers who pay 'not much' attention to journals	64% ($n = 82$)
Readers who pay 'some' attention	54% ($n = 80$)
Readers who pay 'a good deal' of attention	73% ($n = 75$)
Readers who noticed political articles	65% ($n = 72$)
Readers who did not notice political articles	62% ($n = 166$)

journals are slightly less likely to vote Labour than other union members. The explanation for this seems to lie in the fact that the white collar unions, where Labour support is weaker, tend to have the most readable journals and, presumably, a membership that is somewhat more inclined to read them. In any event, these figures and the irregular levels of Labour support according to how much attention is paid to the journals and whether the reader noticed political articles would undercut any assertion that union journals are a major source of political indoctrination.

There also is a widespread belief that the shop-floor is a significant forum of electoral activity; but here too the evidence appears scanty – at least to judge by the recollections of our sample when interviewed fairly shortly after the 1964 election. Less than 2 per cent of our union members could remember a union representative approaching them during the campaign and asking them to vote. Moreover, of these few – only seven individuals were involved – one alone voted Labour. This finding may owe something to the tendency of Conservatives to resent pressures that for many others were so informal as to leave no impression. But it clearly implies that organized shop-floor activity is far less important than it is usually supposed to be, by Labour as well as by Conservative officials.

Indeed, it would seem that the unions' communication networks are, from the point of view of achieving their political purposes, at best neutral and possibly even counter-productive in their results. The absence of any evidence that union 'agit-prop' activities affect members' partisan preferences or their propensity to get out and vote may be disturbing to Transport House, but it is quite consistent with the hypothesis that self-selection of union membership by Labour supporters is sufficient to explain the difference in partisanship between members and non-members. What the Labour bias among union recruits implies about the absence of direct union influence is confirmed by the apparent ineffectiveness of two potential means of influence – union publications and electoral persuasion on the shop floor.

Yet it would be remarkable if the politics of a worker were in no way affected by his existence in a unionized industrial setting. Although a man's Labour allegiance may owe more to prior beliefs than it does to his experience as a union member, his union involvement may heighten his political involvement. Our studies in fact supply various indications of the greater political activism of members of trade unions.

The Political Activism of Union Members

The deeper political involvement or activism[9] of the unionized worker is shown first of all by his informal participation in the electoral campaign. The extent to which unionized work settings are exceptionally political is vividly conveyed by the evidence of informal conversations about the campaign among fellow workers. Table 7.9 compares, for example, the frequency with which union and non-union manual workers reported having had such con-

9. Here and in the pages that follow we use political activism specifically to refer to three things done by large numbers – talking about politics, attending political meetings and voting. We do not wish to evoke the quite common connotation – the activism or militancy that characterize the relatively few on whom union operations mainly rest.

7.9 Frequency of Conversations about the Election Campaign among Union and Non-Union Manual Workers (Grades V and VI), 1964

	Union Members	Non-Members
Reported discussing campaign with fellow workers	57%	34%
Did not report discussing campaign with fellow workers	43	66
	100% (*n* = 328)	100% (*n* = 294)

versations at their place of work during the 1964 election. By their own account, union members were very much likelier to have followed the campaign through conversations with other workers. The difference in attendance at campaign meetings between union and non-union workers is also marked, as Table 7.10 shows. To some extent this may be due to the fact that campaign meetings

7.10 Attendance at Campaign Meetings by Union and Non-Union Manual Workers (Grades V and VI), 1964

	Union Members	Non-Members
Reported attending campaign meeting	12%	5%
Did not report attending campaign meeting	88	95
	100%	100%

are often held on the premises or at the gates of large factories, where workers are most highly unionized. In fact, our evidence on attendance would imply that union members supplied something like 54 per cent of all those present at Labour's campaign meetings, although such workers comprised only 36 per cent of the party's mass support.

There is also a suggestion in our evidence that the greater activism of union workers carries over to voting. In 1964 no difference was found in the rates of turnout among union and non-union manual workers. But in 1966 there was at least a small difference in these rates of voting, as shown by Table 7.11, one too small to be statistically significant. A similarly faint

7.11 Turnout of Union and Non-Union Manual Workers, 1966

	Union Members	Non-Members
Voted in general election	87%	83%
Did not vote in general election	13%	17%
	100%	100%
	($n = 269$)	($n = 508$)

difference also appeared among the families of union members. In 1966 turnout among the wives of manual union workers exceeded the turnout of non-union wives by 4 per cent.

In view of the evidence that political orientations can affect workers' disposition towards unions, it would not be surprising if the political activism of union members were also to be explained in these terms. But such predispositions turn out to be less satisfactory as an explanation of political activism than of Labour partisanship. In fact, we would conclude, if anything, that activism tends to be somewhat *less* among those of stronger disposition to join. The evidence for this conclusion is to be found in the levels of activism among the four groups of workers which we distinguished earlier in our discussion of the importance of Labour allegiance in dispositions to join a union. Table 7.12 considers for voluntary union members the level of turnout, of campaign conversations with workmates, and of attendance at campaign meet-

7.12 Political Activism by 'Voluntarism' of Union Membership

	Reported talking about campaign at work, 1964	Reported attending campaign meeting, 1964	Reported voting, 1966
Voluntary members			
'Some' workmates are members	50%	11%	83%
'Most' workmates are members	57%	6%	90%
'All' workmates are members	59%	16%	94%
Asked to join and have refused	56%	4%	95%

ings according to the degree of unionization at their place of work. Once again, we have placed at the bottom of the table, as least inclined to join, workers who have explicitly faced the question of joining and have refused. In terms of turnout and political conversations at work, activism tends to move in a direction *opposite* to the trend in the proportion supporting Labour shown in Table 7.6 on page 200.

When we examine non-members who have not faced the decision whether to join, political conversation is found to be the only form of activism that rises with willingness to join, just as the proportion of Labour supporters was found to rise in Table 7.7. The activism of these non-members is shown in Table 7.13; although some differences appear these do not seem to be consistently related to the worker's willingness to join if asked.

The activism of compulsory union members tends yet again to set them apart. As a comparison of Table 7.14 with Table 7.12 shows, political conversation and attendance at meetings are higher among compulsory than among voluntary members, suggesting how far political involvement is part of some specific industrial cultures, mining providing the outstanding example.

The distinctive ethos of highly unionized industrial settings (and of the residential concentrations that so often go with them)

7.13 Political Activism among Non-Members in Partially Unionized Workplaces by Willingness to Join if Asked

	Reported talking about campaign at work 1964	Reported attending campaign meeting 1964	Reported voting 1964
Workers who have not been asked but:			
Would join if asked	42% ($n = 81$)	6% ($n = 80$)	84% ($n = 62$)
Don't know	35% ($n = 78$)	11% ($n = 79$)	82% ($n = 59$)
Would not join if asked	34% ($n = 182$)	6% ($n = 183$)	89% ($n = 144$)

touches other attitudes as well. Our evidence suggests in particular that members in highly unionized settings are more likely to see politics as a conflict of opposed class interests. When the classification of beliefs about class and party developed at the end of Chapter 4 was applied to the images held by workers in places where membership is compulsory or voluntary but universal, the proportion perceiving politics as a projection of class conflict was found to be measurably higher than it was among members in less unionized industrial settings.[10] The sources of such a difference

7.14 Political Activism among Compulsory Union Members

Reported attending campaign meeting 1964	14% ($n = 177$)
Reported talking about campaign at work 1964	61% ($n = 176$)
Reported voting 1966	85% ($n = 139$)

10. The numbers on which this finding rests are small, since we coded beliefs as to the relationship of class and party for those who held constant (and consistent) class and partisan self-images over three interviews, a group which had to be subdivided still further to make the comparison cited here. But the chance that the difference of the proportions holding a conflict view among members in compulsory or universally unionized

must lie fairly deep in the structure and traditions of different industries, including the role that trade unions play within them.

It seems therefore that a mixed conclusion is to be drawn about the influence of the unions on the worker's political behaviour. There is no doubt of the importance of the unions' presence in the culture of the workplace. In industries with compulsory unionism, especially those with substantial geographic segregation of their work force (with mining as the extreme case), the worker's environment encourages high activism and strong Labour partisanship, although both may have declined with the weakening of the class alignment. In the rest of British industry, a highly unionized workplace encourages activism. But there is remarkably little evidence that the ethos of the workplace, and still less the persuasive efforts of the unions themselves, have much impact on the direction of the worker's party allegiance. On the contrary, the evidence strongly implies that much of the difference of Labour support between union and non-union families in the country as a whole results from the tendency of workers already disposed towards Labour to join unions where membership is optional. Indeed, among workers for whom membership is optional but fairly routine Labour support is no higher than its average among non-union families over the whole of Britain.[11]

But, of course, the influence of the trade unions is not limited to those who for reasons of occupation are, or might become, members. The unions are highly visible in all parts of British society and serve as objects of positive and negative feeling for great numbers of people outside their actual or potential ranks. We should consider several aspects of the influence which the unions may have on the behaviour of the wider electorate.

---

settings (40 per cent did) and in partially unionized settings (27 per cent) was due to sampling accident is less than one in twenty.

11. For a slightly more positive verdict on the importance of trade unionism in fostering Labour support in a particular type of industrial setting, see J. H. Goldthorpe, D. Lockwood, F. Bechhofer and J. Platt, *The Affluent Worker: Political Attitudes and Behaviour*, London, 1968, pp. 62–72.

Trade Unions and the Class Alignment

There can be no doubt about the degree of the country's awareness of trade unions and their actions. Union members are to be found in a very large proportion of British households. Work stoppages are often dramatic confrontations, nationwide in scope, whose consequences can touch the lives of millions of ordinary people. Partly because of this, strikes and threats of strikes receive the widest coverage in the mass media. Indeed, few reference objects are more salient to the mass of the people than are trade unions.

Their salience to the public was plainly evident in our own interviews. Most of our respondents had well-defined attitudes towards the power of the unions and attached strong importance to strikes and work stoppages. In our very long schedule of subjects to be raised with respondents only coloured immigration was more likely to provoke additional, impromptu remarks. Moreover, attitudes towards the trade unions were linked in the minds of many of our respondents to various other political attitudes. For example, middle class electors too showed a tendency to take a different attitude towards the unions according to their beliefs about the relation of class to party.

It would also be impossible to miss the unfavourable opinion of the unions manifest in our interviews. The trade unions do of course find strong support in a large minority of electors, including many in their own ranks, and the attitude of the rest of the electorate is by no means one of unrelieved opposition. A number of our respondents distinguished official from unofficial strikes and showed in other ways as well a mixture of feelings towards the unions and their actions. There are indeed times when the opinion polls have recorded strong sympathy for striking workers, as in the challenge by the postal workers to a Conservative Postmaster-General in 1964.

But the fact that attitudes towards the unions were, on balance, unfavourable in the period of our studies is none the less plain. When we asked our respondents whether their sympathies were generally for or against strikers, 61 per cent of respondents from non-union families, and even 45 per cent from union families, said 'against'.[12] Nearly three quarters of our respondents who were not union members said that the unions have too much power. And very nearly half of respondents from union households expressed the same view. Indeed, the summary of these attitudes set out in Table 7.15 shows that nearly a third of union members who supported Labour in 1964 were prepared to say that the power of the unions was excessive.

7.15 Attitudes Towards Trade Union Power by Union Membership and 1964 Vote

Believes trade unions[a]	Union Member 1964 Vote			Non-Member 1964 Vote		
	Con.	Lab.	Lib.	Con.	Lab.	Lib.
Have too much power	62%	31%	62%	77%	43%	63%
Do not have too much power	32	63	25	15	39	27
Don't know	6	6	13	8	18	10
	100%	100%	100%	100%	100%	100%
	(95)	(238)	(31)	(280)	(179)	(59)

a See Question 24 in the 1964 questionnaire.

The political consequences of the negative feeling towards the trade unions in much of the electorate are likely to depend on the way the public associates the unions and their actions with the political parties. In particular, these attitudes will have a very different significance according to the strength of the link between the unions and the Labour Party in the public's mind. It is therefore noteworthy how weak a connection the public appeared to see between the unions and Labour in the period of our study. Despite

12. The intensity of many of the remarks offered in the generally cordial atmosphere of the survey interview was noteworthy. The Bromley clerk who declared that 'anyone stirring up strikes should be made an example of' and the Folkestone publican who said that 'the unions should be put on crime sheets for unofficial strikes – it's holding up exports' are illustrative of a much wider segment of electors.

their historical and organizational ties it was rare for respondents to project hostility to the unions on to the Labour Party; indeed, only a little more than a score of respondents mentioned the unions as a reason for disliking Labour at any of our interviews.

Moreover, the separation of the trade unions and Labour Party seems to the great bulk of electors a desirable state of affairs. Asked whether the trade unions should maintain close ties to the Labour Party or stay out of politics, the overwhelming majority chose the latter alternative. This was indeed true even of trade union members, as Table 7.16 shows. Only the distinct minority of unionists who seemed to view politics as an arena of conflict

7.16 Views as to Proper Relationship of Trade Unions to Labour Party

	1963	1964		1966
Believes the trade unions[a]	Union Members	Full Sample	Union Members	Full Sample
Should have close ties to the Labour Party	25%	19%	31%	16%
Should stay out of politics	60	69	65	74
Don't know	15	12	4	10
	100%	100%	100%	100%

[a] See Question 76j in the 1963 questionnaire and question 28 in the 1964 and 1966 questionnaires.

between opposed class interests gave appreciably more support to the idea of close ties between the unions and the Labour Party.

The dissociation of Labour from the unions, which so much of the public apparently perceives and endorses, is by no means without a large element of objective truth. Despite the unions' role in launching the party and the ideological belief that each is an arm of a common movement, the unions and the party inevitably pursue different goals. The leaders of the T.U.C. must assert their own and their members' interests to the government of the day, whichever party is in power. For many this involves an unwelcome intimacy with a Conservative government and an unwelcome antagonism to a Labour government. But the need to uphold the unions' interests must none the less guide the behaviour of the unions' leadership in many situations.

On the other hand, the Labour Party, especially when it is the Government, must assert other interests than these, including at times goals which are distinctly general or national. The parliamentary party has progressively established its right to choose the leader of the party and decide questions before Parliament without dictation from the party conference, in which the unions have the dominant voice. This process has no doubt helped to dissociate Labour from the unions in the public's mind. But the belief in their separateness probably comes still more from confrontrations between Labour governments and the unions over industrial disputes and over more general policies affecting the wages and incomes of union members. It is small wonder if the sight of Labour ministers dealing toughly with the leadership of the T.U.C., and with specific unions on major work stoppages, leads the public to believe that Labour and the unions do not see their interests as one, and that the dissociation of the unions from the party is a desirable thing.

The incentives to Labour, especially when it is in power, to establish its independence from the unions in the eyes of the electorate bear strongly on the discussion in Chapter 5 of Labour's loosening identification with the working class. The trade unions are of course not synonymous with the working class, nor are the interests of union members those of all working people. None the less, the unions are still predominantly working class organizations, and the fact that a Labour government sometimes has to take actions that are in sharp conflict with the demands and interests of the unions cannot fail to have blurred Labour's image as a class party. This set of relationships may indeed hold an additional key to the weakening of the class alignment. The negative attitude towards the unions and their strike weapon in much of the electorate gives a Labour government strong inducement to assert a more general or national interest against that of the unions. This sort of motive will be much less important when the party is out of office. But the risks to Labour in power of failing to stand up to a special class-based interest that evokes such wide hostility in the electorate are by no means negligible. Therefore, it may be to a Labour government's own self-interest to protect its standing in the country in the short run by dealing firmly with the unions' demands. But in the longer run the consequence may well be to narrow the perceived differences of the parties in terms of class and to weaken the class alignment which has been the pre-eminent basis of electoral choice in the past generation.

Part Two

	CHANGES OF ALIGNMENT	TRANSIENT VARIATIONS
CONSTRUCTION		
APPLICATION		

8 The Analysis of Issues

The issues of modern politics are extraordinarily varied, but common processes can be seen in the way various issues sway the electorate. We can build a general framework that will allow us to analyse the actual or potential contribution of any issue to electoral change. Elements of such a framework are indeed implicit in our treatment of the 'issues' that underlie the great alignments which have endured for long periods of British politics. Consider the role of social class in electoral change. The simplest conception of the place of class in party choice involves the triangular relationship between elector, class and party that we set out in Chapter 4:

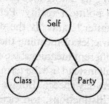

Political change can result from a change in the relationship of self to class. For example, we have seen how the transformation of this bond in the middle class children of wage-earning parents is accompanied by substantial party conversion. Similarly, electoral change can result from a change of the relationship of class to party. Indeed, Labour's emergence as an avowedly working class party early in this century began a conversion process that has not yet run its course.

If we think not just of 'class' but more generally of 'issues' a similar sketch helps us see that several relationships are involved in the influence of issues on the strength of the parties. This influence depends on the links that are formed between issue and party and between self and issue. We shall have to explore in detail

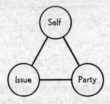

what these links involve and how widely their nature varies. But we cannot deal adequately with the role of issues in electoral change without paying due attention to how both types of bonds bear on the remarkable assortment of issues that confront the electorate over time.

The Limits of Policy-Defined Issues

A 'political issue' is a highly ambiguous concept which has misted up many windows to political reality. Perennial controversies, such as 'Do issues matter?' and 'Is the elector rational?' frequently turn on the varieties of meaning the phrase has acquired. In focusing on these different meanings, we shall not offer a single 'correct' usage but shall instead use the term even more inclusively than is common in everyday speech. But we shall at the same time enforce a number of distinctions, too easily overlooked, which reveal some important differences in the bases of electoral choice.

One of these is the distinction between issues that are defined in terms of alternative courses of government action and issues that are defined more in terms of goals or values that government may achieve. It is natural that the analysis of issues should have a bias towards issues that have meaning in terms of alternative policies. The government's policy decisions constitute much of what politics is about; the interplay between public attitudes or demands, governmental decisions, and the consequences of those decisions provides one of the great challenges of political analysis, a 'feedback' loop at the heart of democratic government.

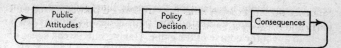

As a result, analyses of political issues often tend to cast the public in the role of an informed spectator at the game of government, one who sees policy issues much as they are seen by the political leaders who play the game. Since the political controversies of Westminster and Whitehall focus upon choices among detailed policy alternatives, why should these alternatives not be taken as defining the issues of the day? In this spirit the newspaper polls take samplings of public opinion on such assorted questions as prices and incomes policy, the issue of D-notices to the press, entry into Europe, increases in family allowances, and even such highly detailed and specific questions as the holding of a referendum in Gibraltar or the decision to set South Arabia up as an independent country with military support to the new régime for the first six months.

But the simplest evidence about the extent of popular attention to the affairs of government must challenge any image of the elector as an informed spectator. Understanding of policy issues falls away very sharply indeed as we move outwards from those at the heart of political decision-making to the public at large. The fall-off is partly a matter of how fully the alternatives are seen. For example, on the issue of Britain's entry into Europe the real insider, the politician or the civil servant involved in preparing the British application, sees a number of alternative courses, distinguished in terms of the conditions of entry, the strategy of approach, the way obligations to other Commonwealth countries are discharged and so on. Many of these are not apparent even to sophisticated observers, such as backbench M.P.s or academic onlookers, who none the less see the choices in complex terms. To great sections of the public, however, the question before the country comes down to the unadorned dichotomy – 'In?' or 'Out?'

The broad public also falls short of the 'informed spectator' role in terms of how well it can link means to ends. Not only is it very incompletely informed of the cards the Government can play; it seldom can understand how putting down a single card is likely to affect the course of the game. Having but a weak sense of how a particular policy line will have an influence on anything it values, the electorate may form only weak and ephemeral preferences even among the policy alternatives it does perceive.

These reservations about the image of the elector as a fully informed spectator are familiar enough. Those who practise or observe politics at an élite level are often reminded how different the political world looks to the broad public. An M.P. returning to a meeting of his constituency party must always be reminded how far, psychologically, he has travelled from Westminster. A lobby correspondent must realize from the conversations he overhears on the train how little of the framework which he has developed for the analysis of policy issues is shared by those who have no daily contact with public affairs.

Yet the true limits of the public's views on policy are likely to be missed. In part this is due to a subtle bias which affects an élite observer's contacts with the general public. The politician, the journalist and the political scientist all tend to encounter people whose interest in politics is grossly unrepresentative of their fellow citizens. Those, for example, whom an M.P. confronts at a local party meeting, innocent though they are by Westminster standards, will still have much more developed ideas about current policy issues than the average elector.

How weak the public's policy preferences really are can be most tellingly demonstrated by studying them over time. Satisfactory evidence on this has seldom been presented.[1] Newspaper opinion polls do frequently put the same policy questions to successive samples and show the wobbles – as well as some meaningful trends – in public sentiment for and against an issue. They also record substantial proportions who admit to being 'Don't knows'. But the ephemeral quality of many of the positive responses

1. But see Philip Converse's seminal analysis of materials from the American panel followed by the Survey Research Center over the four years from 1956 to 1960, 'The Nature of Belief Systems in Mass Publics', in *Ideology and Discontent*, ed. D. E. Apter, New York, 1964, pp. 206–61.

emerges only when the same individual's preferences are followed over a period of time.

This point can be illustrated by changes of attitude towards policy issues which have not been matters of sharp and prolonged conflict between the parties. On the issue of Britain's entry into Europe, for example, fully half of our sample conceded either at the interview in the summer of 1963 or at the interview in the autumn of 1964 that they had no opinion.[2] The views of those who did offer an opinion at both interviews proved quite unstable. Less than four-fifths of this group and therefore less than two-fifths of the whole sample voiced the *same* opinion at both points in time. A highly fluid pattern of individual replies was found beneath the surface of an overall division of opinion that was almost unchanged between the summer of 1963 and the autumn of 1964.

It could, of course, be suggested that the switches represented large blocs of opinion moving in mutually cancelling directions – perhaps of Conservatives reverting to their earlier suspicion of Europe following the Macmillan era and of Labour voters no longer driven to disapprove of Europeanism as a key Conservative policy. The switches might then be seen as genuine changes of attitude, whose volume might be a good deal less at other times. But any such interpretation collides with the evidence: movements in both directions were found in each party, as well as in each class, and in every other category for which an hypothesis as to the direction of change suggested itself. The most reasonable interpretation of the remarkable instability of responses is that Britain's policy towards the Common Market was in 1963–4 a matter on which the mass public had formed attitudes to only a very limited degree.

The limits of popular attitude towards policy issues are even more persuasively attested to by the fluidity of opinion on questions which have been at the heart of the party battle for many

2. The circulation of those giving a 'don't know' response is itself an indication of the fluidity of opinion. At the first interview 38 per cent said they had no opinion; at the second interview 34 per cent did. The turnover of those giving this response was, however, sufficient that fully half said 'don't know' at one interview or the other.

years. An impressive example of this is provided by the nationalization of industry, a matter that for a generation has never been far from the centre of political controversy. At each round of interviews we asked our respondents to choose one from an ordered set of positions on nationalization – or to say that they had no opinion. The overall responses remained quite constant over our three rounds of interviews, as Table 8.1 shows. At each interview something like one elector in six said that he had no opinion

8.1 Profile of Opinion Towards Nationalization of Industry

	1963	1964	1966
A lot more industries should be nationalized	10%	8%	8%
Only a few more industries, such as steel, should be nationalized	14	17	17
No more industries should be nationalized, but industries that are nationalized now should stay nationalized	36	45	42
Some industries that are nationalized should now be denationalized	22	18	19
No opinion	18	12	14
	100%	100%	100%

even on such a long-established policy issue as this. But the distribution of views among those with a declared view seemed quite stable – and appeared to confirm the clear majority against further nationalization recorded in so many public opinion polls over the last twenty years. Indeed the steadiness of the percentages in these interviews over a period of almost three years apparently gives support to the idea that British electors have firmly made up their minds on this perennial issue.

When individual responses are examined, however, the truth is found to be very different. Table 8.2 shows the full turnover of views between our first and second interviews. A glance at the squares in the main diagonal shows that only 39 per cent stuck to an identical and definite position on the broad lines of nationaliza-

8.2 Turnover of Opinion Towards Nationalization of Industry, 1963 to 1964

		Autumn 1964					
		Lot more	Few more	No more	Less	No Opinion	
Summer 1963	Lot more	3	3	3	1	1	11
	Few more	1	6	6	1	1	15
	No more	1	5	21	6	3	36
	Less	1	1	10	9	1	22
	No opinion	1	2	5	2	6	16
		7	17	45	19	12	100%

(*n* = 1473)

tion policy. There was a good deal of wavering between having and not having an opinion and even more between different opinions. By any standard statistical measure, the stability of the entries is decidedly modest.[3] The turnover of opinion carried many respondents across the line between those who believed in more nationalization and those who did not, the critical divide in the struggle over nationalization at the élite level.

This line is blurred still more when we lengthen our time interval and examine the movements of opinion over our three interviews.

3. For example, Kendall's tau-b rank correlation coefficient is only $+0.4$ for this array, even when we exclude those who failed to express a definite opinion on both occasions. The magnitude of this coefficient may have been falsely inflated not only by our exclusion of the explicit 'don't knows' but also by our counting as real and stable opinion the choice of the 'no more' position at both interviews. It is not implausible to suppose that some who gave this opinion both times were expressing a species of 'don't know'.

Even when we collapse our four alternatives into two and consider only whether a respondent was for more nationalization or not, an intricate pattern of change emerges, as Figure 8.3 shows. Fully 26 per cent said in one or more interviews that they had no opinion on nationalization. Only 50 per cent were consistent in either supporting or opposing further nationalization over the three interviews.

8.3 Pathways of Opinion Towards Nationalization, 1963 to 1966

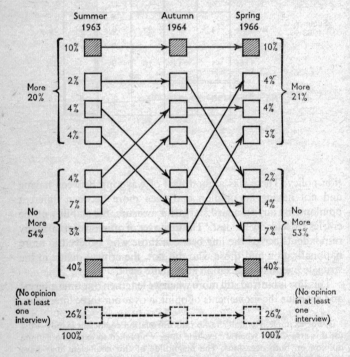

In the case of nationalization, as in the case of the Common Market, there is little empirical support for any hypothesis attributing these cross-currents of change to forces moving blocs of opinion in mutually cancelling directions. It seems more plausible to interpret the fluidity of the public's views as an indication of the limited degree to which attitudes are formed towards even the best-known of policy issues. For it must be stressed that the issue of nationalization is plainly one which has seeped far into the public's consciousness; among those expressing a view, there was virtually no confusion about which party was more likely to go in for further nationalization, as we shall show later. But this stable and almost universal perception contrasts sharply with the changeability of attitude towards the merits of nationalization.

The extent to which the changeability of attitude is a reflection of the sheer uncertainty that surrounds many people's beliefs emerges from another property of opinion revealed by repeated canvassing of individual views. The essence of this property is that substantial short-run reshuffling of views fails to yield the longer-run movement of individual position which we would expect from real and cumulative attitude change. This is a subtle and paradoxical empirical point. There is quite enough circulation of opinion to shatter any idea that the bulk of electors hold to fixed views, as the unchanging total proportions in successive polls might suggest. Yet, if genuine and cumulative attitude change were to occur at the rate of the circulation of opinion between one survey and the next, the correlation of opinions at more remote points of time would decay faster than it in fact does. The slower rate of decay may therefore be seen as further evidence that the circulation of opinion is substantially due to mere uncertainty of response and not to genuine attitude change.[4]

4. The comparison of the actual decay rate and that implied by a Markov chain or other process under which change genuinely cumulative has attracted the attention of several writers. Philip Converse has given an exceedingly interesting treatment, with American examples, of a 'black-white' model under which each of those interviewed over time gives either completely stable or completely random responses. The presence of only these two types of responses in sample data will yield a correlation of opinions over time which does not diminish as the time interval lengthens, a fact which Converse uses to test the fit of actual responses to the model. See P. E. Converse, 'The Nature of Belief Systems in Mass Publics', in *Ideology and Discontent*, ed. D. E. Apter, New York, 1964, pp. 206–61. A

This aspect of popular response to policy issues emerges clearly from the turnover of opinion on nuclear weapons policy. At each round of interviews we asked our respondents which they favoured of the following positions on the issue:

Britain should keep her own nuclear weapons, independent of other countries.

Britain should have nuclear weapons only as a part of a Western defence system.

Britain should have nothing to do with nuclear weapons under any circumstances.

Individual attitudes towards the Bomb were as fluid as those towards nationalization and the Common Market. The correlation between opinions on nuclear weapons expressed in 1963 and 1964 was only $+0.33$ and between 1964 and 1966 only $+0.38$.

But what is significant for our present purpose is a comparison of the rate of change between the two pairs of closer interviews (1963–4 and 1964–6) with the rate between the more distant pair of interviews in 1963 and 1966. Although we shall not develop the point in full detail, the essential idea is plain. If changes of response reflected only genuine attitude change and occurred at a rate fast enough to have produced the very modest correlations between the first and second, and second and third, interviews, then the correlation between the first and third interviews ought to be almost non-existent. Indeed, on these assumptions we would expect the

---

similar empirical property is implied by the 'mover-stayer' model which has been adumbrated by Blumen, Kogan, McCarthy, Goodman and others. See I. Blumen, M. Kogan and P. J. McCarthy, *The Industrial Mobility of Labor as a Probability Process*, Ithaca, New York, 1955, and Leo A. Goodman, 'Statistical Methods for the Mover-Stayer Model', *Journal of the American Statistical Association*, **56** (1961), 841–68. Coleman has proposed a model for the case in which response variation is due partly to response uncertainty and partly to genuine, cumulative change. Under this model the correlation of opinions over time will diminish as the time interval lengthens but not as rapidly as would be true if change were free of response uncertainty. See J. S. Coleman, *Models of Change and Response Uncertainty*, Englewood Cliffs, New Jersey, 1964. This empirical property is fairly typical of policy responses given by our British panel and is additional evidence that considerable uncertainty attaches to these responses.

correlation between 1963 and 1966 to be only $+0.13$.[5] In fact, however, the observed correlation was $+0.31$, not much lower than the correlation between opinions at the two closer pairs of interviews.

Perhaps no one should be surprised that policy questions such as entry into Europe or retention of nuclear weapons, whose consequences for the lives of ordinary people are uncertain and indirect, should be matters on which attitudes are formed only to a limited extent. Even the policy of nationalization, the consequences of which the elector might be expected to know a good deal about as a user of fuel and transport, is really an issue of this kind. There are, however, some issues, such as restricting coloured immigration, which do evoke a strong and well-formed response from the public, as we shall see. But such issues are exceptions and most of the policies which provide the focus of conflict at the élite level excite little reaction in the mass electorate.

From this it follows that in seeking out the issues which are genuinely involved in the public's assessment of the parties it is especially important to inquire into the public's awareness of the policies and the strength of the attitudes it has formed. In this the replies that a pollster receives to a once-only questionnaire may be of very limited help, for it is difficult to distinguish between the questions which the elector cares a good deal about and those which simply collect lightly held and transitory opinions.

The limits of popular orientations to policy also argue for a broader conception of the issue content of electoral politics. Some observers, sensing how little the ordinary man cares about the detailed policy choices facing government, have concluded that issues do not matter. A more useful response is to widen the conception of what issues are about and to ask *in what terms* they are likely to matter, for this may lead to a broader view of the sources of political change.

5. This value has been calculated from the 'expected' turnover table between the first and third interviews which can be obtained by treating change over the three interviews as a (non-stationary) Markov chain.

Issues and the Values Government May Achieve

The pre-eminent means by which the public simplifies the complexity of government action is by shifting its attention from policies to consequences – from government action to the values that government may achieve. We have noted in Chapter 2 that the public tends to focus on certain conditions or values of which it has more direct experience, rather than attempting the more complex assessment of means and ends which in some form must enter the Government's choice among alternative policies. The issue of the handling of the economy provides the outstanding example. How alternative policies affect income, prices and employment is a matter of exceeding complexity. But the conditions that governments seek to influence can be seen and known by ordinary people everywhere.

The connections electors form between these conditions or values and the parties are influenced by the arguments about these links among political leaders and élite observers. But under the British party system these connections are also formed by simple inferences from who is or was in power. A government is credited or blamed for many things while it is in office without the public's having undertaken any serious analysis of the role of government policy in producing the conditions of which it approves or disapproves. The economy once again provides a telling example. A government can profit handsomely from good times without having to prove that prosperity has flowed from its own policies. The Conservatives were able to benefit from the expansion of the 1950s without really having to show that their own role was decisive. In a similar way, a government can be severely damaged by bad times whatever its degree of actual responsibility. We have cited before the analogy of sport: the public may hold a government answerable just as it holds answerable the captain or manager of a losing team – and with even less understanding of what went wrong. This sort of *post hoc ergo propter hoc* reasoning is of course conditioned to some degree by the public's beliefs about what governments can actually affect; the British Cabinet is not answerable for flood damage in Italy, but it can suffer for a fuel shortage in a severe British winter. Yet simple inferences from the control of office are immensely important to the electorate's choice.

It is true that a system of alternating party control introduces an uncertainty into the public's assignment of responsibility. There is plainly some basis for the efforts of party leaders to transfer blame for what the country disapproves of onto their predecessors, or successors; we shall note in Chapter 18 Labour's remarkable success in 1966, eighteen months after taking office, in portraying the country's economic difficulties as a legacy from the Tories.

The conversion of values into electoral issues is of course not limited to values involving material well-being. There are many other values whose attainment, or lack of it, will provide issues between the parties without the public's having penetrated very far into reasons or causes. Threats to peace or to national prestige can easily yield issues of this kind. In America the Republicans' effort to depict the Democrats as the war party for having been in office during two world wars as well as the Korean and Vietnamese conflicts must be one of the purest examples of *post hoc ergo propter hoc* argument in modern politics.

The range of goals or values which can enter the public's assessment of the parties is exceedingly broad. For many people the connection between the parties and such general values as 'freedom' or 'social equality' has a good deal more meaning than the evaluations they are able to form from the calculations of means and ends about the specific policies debated at Westminster. General values of this kind may at times be invoked in particular policy controversies; for example 'freedom' is cited in relation to the issue of nationalization. But even without any clear tie to specific government action, such values can be enough to distinguish the parties in the public's mind.

Indeed some of the values which divide the supporters of the parties are unlikely to become matters of policy conflict. In Chapter 5, for example, we saw how Labour and Conservative voters, in both the middle and the working classes, tend to divide over the role of the sovereign. No one imagines that Labour is a republican party or that the Conservatives wish to restore to the Crown any of the power wrested from it in centuries of constitutional evolution. None the less the higher valuation set by the Conservatives on the symbols of the monarchy is not missed by the broad public.

Thus many of the issues of electoral politics owe more to the voters' orientation towards values or goals than to their assessment of policy alternatives. They tend to start with conditions that they can know from their experience and to connect these to the parties, using whatever cues they are offered. These will at times include some understanding of the relation between means and ends, between goals and policies. But many of the ends which the public cares about will depend on means which are so complex or so conjectural that the link to the parties will be formed in other ways, including inferences from the simple possession of power.

Analysing the Effect of Issues

The distinction between issues defined in terms of policies and issues defined in terms of values does much to clarify the ways of assessing the force of issues on electoral choice. The issues which have altered the party balance in a given period are not to be studied simply in terms of electors' answers to questions about the policies debated at the élite level; we must also discover the goals and values that have shaped the public's response to the parties. The 'image' of the parties – to invoke a much abused phrase – will consist partly of links to these goals or conditions which are valued by part or by all of the electorate but which are not directly reflected in current policy debates. Much of the terminology of party 'images' may be the invention of public relations men. The reality behind it is not. We return in Chapter 16 to the content of the party 'images', examining the way the public associates with the parties' goals or values that are so general or diffuse that they could hardly be given meaning in direct policy terms.

Despite the variety of the issues acting on the electorate it is possible to lay down two conditions that will have to be met if an issue is to exert genuine force on the individual elector. The first involves the individual's orientation to the issue itself – the link, in terms of our initial diagram, between self and issue.

This must entail something more than simple awareness. We have seen how the great bulk of the electorate is aware of nationalization as an issue and knows the relative positions of the parties without having gone on to strongly rooted attitudes towards nationaliza-

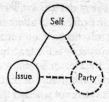

tion. If an issue is to sway the elector it must not only have crossed the threshold of his awareness; he must also have formed some genuine attitude towards it. The more an issue is salient to him and the subject of strong attitudes, the more powerful will be its influence on his party choice. Indeed, given the multiplicity of influences upon the individual elector, only issues that excite strong feeling are likely to have much impact.

The bond we have drawn between self and issue is also designed to suggest important questions about the terms in which the issue is seen. We have already argued the importance of the broad distinction between issues whose content is supplied by alternative policies or government actions and issues whose content is supplied by alternative conditions or values. But important differences also arise from the number and relationship of the alternative actions or conditions. In the simplest case the alternatives are reduced to two. 'Europe, in or out?' must be the form in which Britain's entry into the Common Market had meaning for many electors in the mid-sixties. Similarly, for some people class interests simply pose the issue of whether the government is for 'us' or for 'them'. But the alternatives associated with other issues in the public's mind cover a much wider range. Rhodesia was such a case after the Smith régime had unilaterally declared its independence during the 1964 Parliament. It was widely understood that Britain might take several alternative courses, ranging from settling on Smith's terms to sending troops to put down the rebellion.

Indeed, the range of policies or values entailed by some issues is virtually limitless. How much nationalization? or economic prosperity? The answers could be infinitely varied. In cases of this sort a powerful simplifying device, available to political leaders and the public alike, is to order other alternatives and compare the conditions or policies of the past or future with those of the present. The issue of prosperity is likely to be seen in terms of how much the economy, or the elector's welfare, has moved ahead or slipped back. Similarly, the issue of nationalization may be simplified for the voter in terms of whether there should be more or less of it than now, the elector in effect positioning himself with respect to the present state of affairs along a continuum describing degrees of nationalization:

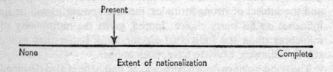

At other times a government proposal, such as the extent of take-over involved when steel is nationalized, will supply the point of reference about which a large set of ordered alternatives is divided. Whether a given issue is seen in these terms is of course an empirical question that is not to be settled by *a priori* argument. But there is no doubt that the interplay between political leaders and the mass of the electorate does frequently entail such a simplification of discourse about issues. We shall draw out some of the implications of this in a moment when we consider the circumstances under which an issue will affect the standing of the parties in the country as a whole.

The influence of an issue on the elector's choice depends on more than the presence of the bond between self and issue. It also depends on the links in his mind between the issue and the parties. However well-formed the individual's attitudes towards an issue, they will not affect his party choice unless the connection he sees between the issue and the parties gives reality to the second of the bonds in our diagram.

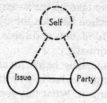

In some cases, this link need involve only one of the parties, especially when it mainly involves judgements upon the government of the day. We shall see in Chapter 18 evidence that the public tends to link economic issues mainly with the Government, judging its performance as satisfactory or not, and giving less attention to the likely performance of the other party. But the link may involve a differing perception of the parties, with the elector judging the relative chance of achieving certain values if one or if the other comes to power. The voter who wishes pensions increased may indeed see one of the parties as far likelier than the other to increase them.

The bonds suggested by our diagram plot the conditions that must be fulfilled if an issue is to sway the individual elector. But we cannot say what impact an issue may have over the whole country without examining these bonds more generally, extending our framework of analysis to the electorate as a whole. Such an extension brings into view some distinctions which can easily be missed so long as our concern focuses on the individual. Let us see what conditions must be met before an issue can be said to have made a net alteration to the strength of the parties.

A first condition is a straightforward extension of the need for the individual to perceive an issue and to form some attitude towards it if it is to influence his behaviour. For an issue to have much impact in the whole electorate the bond of issue to self must be formed in the minds of a substantial body of electors. Many issues have meaning only for tiny fractions of the electorate, but some are salient to much wider portions. The greater the proportion of people to whom an issue is salient and the subject of strong attitudes, the more powerful the impact it can have on the fortunes of the parties. When we take up the issues of the 1960s we shall enforce a rough distinction between those which were of higher salience and attitude formation and those which were of lower salience and attitude formation.

A second condition that must be met for an issue to influence the relative standing of the parties has to do with the balance or skewness of attitudes towards it. What this condition entails is most easily seen in the case of an issue that poses only two clear alternatives. If, for example, the issue of Britain's entry into Europe comes down to a choice between 'In' or 'Out', the issue is likely to affect the relative standing of the parties only if there is a surplus of opinion for one or other of these alternatives. The country might be strongly aroused by such an issue; but unless opinion were strongly on one side or the other, the parties would be unlikely to gain or lose much support by favouring going in or staying out.[6]

What we mean by the balance or skewness of attitudes becomes more complicated when issues that involve more than two alternative policies or conditions. But when these fall into a natural

6. If we exclude the possibility that those on opposite sides will differ in the intensity of their views, an issue that differentiated the parties in the eyes of the electorate would not alter the prior strength of the parties if the division of opinion matched the prior division of party support. The possibility that the intensity with which views are held will differ is a standard point in treatments of the role of public opinion on political issues. See, for example, V. O. Key, Jr, *Public Opinion and American Democracy*, New York, 1961, pp. 206–33, and R. A. Dahl, *A Preface to Democratic Theory*, Chicago, 1956, pp. 90–123. Parties and governments do often pay heed to intense minorities in preference to more passive majorities. In many cases the reasons for this have more to do with money and organizational support and other 'supply' factors of politics than with calculations based on the 'demand' of those who may give or withhold their support at the polling station. But plainly there are some cases where more votes are to be won or lost from the reactions of an intense few than from the reactions of a less intense many.

order, as they do, for example, in the case of degrees of prosperity, the division of opinion may still be determined by comparing the electorate's preferences to present conditions. Once again the issue of nationalization provides a suggestive example. Let us suppose that the electorate is spread along a continuum of support for nationalization:

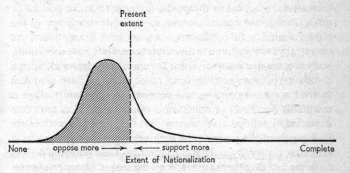

By seeing how opinion is distributed along this continuum, we could see how favourable the country is to additional nationalization; and indeed the debates at Westminster might well give meaning to the issue in this way. In other cases, as we have said, a proposal put forward by a government or party, such as a new level for pensions, will provide a focal point about which the division of opinion in the country can be measured. When we examine the issues of the 1960s we shall distinguish between those which showed a strong trend of opinion and those which divided the country more evenly. It is the first of these, the issues on which the distribution of opinion was a skewed one, that are most likely to shift the balance of support between the parties.

The importance of the skewness of opinion calls attention to issues involving values that are widely shared in the electorate. Many issues present alternative policies or conditions whose value is a matter of disagreement in the country. Nationalization is one of these, but other issues, especially those which are seen in terms of the consequences of government action, involve a virtual consensus in the electorate, and indeed among the parties as well, on the values entailed by different alternatives. The issues connected with the state of the economy offer outstanding examples. There is no body of opinion in the country that favours economic distress, and thereby cancels some of the votes of those who want better times; the whole weight of opinion lies on the side of prosperity and growth.[7] Issues of this sort do not find the parties positioning themselves to appeal to those who favour alternative policies or goals. Rather the parties attempt to associate themselves in the public's mind with conditions, such as good times, which are universally favoured, and to dissociate themselves from conditions, such as economic distress, which are universally deplored. Such a distinction between *position* issues, on which the parties may appeal to rival bodies of opinion, and *valence* issues, on which there is essentially one body of opinion on values or goals, is too often neglected in political commentary. But the parties themselves are well aware of the potential of such valence issues as peace and economic prosperity and national prestige. Their potential derives from the fact that they satisfy so well the second of our conditions for an issue to have impact on the strength of the parties: that the distribution of opinion be strongly skewed.

The third condition for an issue to alter the net strength of the parties is that it be associated differently with the parties in the public's mind. Unless there is a difference of this sort, an issue will not sway the electorate towards one party or the other, however strongly formed and skewed opinion may be. In some cases a difference may arise from the fact that the public links a policy or condition to the governing party and not to its rival; this may be especially true of economic issues, as we shall see. But in other cases the electorate takes account of both parties at once and sees them as having different positions or different capacities to achieve some goal that is universally valued.

Issues do in fact vary widely in the degree to which they differentiate the parties in the public's mind. The extent of these contrasts

7. We shall consider in Chapter 18 the possibility that the 'trade-off' between high employment and price stability is converting the handling of the economy into a 'position' issue.

is illustrated by the issues of nationalization and of Britain's entry into the Common Market. We saw earlier in the chapter that these issues were alike in the low degree of attitude formation towards them in much of the electorate. But these two issues differed profoundly in terms of the separation of parties they achieved in the public mind. This contrast is set out in the entries of Table 8.4.

8.4 Perceived Party Differences on Nationalization and the Common Market, 1964

	Party more likely to extend nationalization	Party more likely to enter Common Market
Labour	90%	22%
	84% difference	22% difference
Conservative	6	44
Not much difference	3	21
Don't know	1	13
	100% (*n* = 1563)	100% (*n* = 1161)

As the gap between the first two percentages in each column shows, the consensus on the party difference was almost four times greater over nationalization than over entry into Europe.

The importance of taking explicit account of the bond the public perceives between issue and parties is illustrated by the problem of industrial conflict. There is no doubt that the British electorate is concerned about strikes and very often denies its sympathy to the strikers. In 1964 some 79 per cent of our respondents said that they thought strikes were a 'very serious' problem (a further 14 per cent thought them a 'fairly serious' problem) and three times as many respondents said that their sympathies were generally against the strikers as said that their sympathies lay generally with the strikers. On this basis, the issue might seem to be excellently suited to the exploitation which it has received, at least implicitly, at the hands of the Conservatives in recent general elections. But the falseness of such a view in the mid-1960s is suggested by the evidence on the public's perceptions of which party has the better approach to strikes. Only one in ten of our respondents said that the Conservatives did, while more than a quarter thought Labour's approach better. The rest saw the parties as much the same or said that they had no clear view. An issue that met all the tests of strength of attitude and surplus of opinion in one direction was effectively de-fused by the electorate's failure to differentiate the parties sharply in relation to it.

The conditions of an issue's influence imply the conditions under which that influence will change. The net 'force' which an issue exerts on the party balance can be altered by a change in the strength of the public's feeling, the distribution of that feeling across alternative policies or goals, or the way the parties are linked to these alternatives in the public's mind. Because each of these conditions is necessary for an issue to have effect, all three must be considered before we can say whether a change in one will alter the issue's influence. In Chapter 15 we shall see that a progressive blurring of party positions in the minds of those most affected by coloured immigration might have undercut this issue between 1964 and 1966 despite the continued public concern and the overwhelming support for control. However, even a progressive sharpening of perceived party positions could not have given this issue great influence on the parties' strength if the public had cared little or been evenly divided.

In Part Four we shall apply this framework to analyse the force of recent issues on the electorate. In Chapter 15 we shall classify a variety of contemporary issues in terms of the three conditions stated here, looking especially for those issues which combine the property of strongly formed attitude, strongly unbalanced division of opinion and strongly differentiated party positions. The goal-defined issues having to do with the economy are so important that we shall devote Chapter 18 to considering them separately.

Moreover, the appeal of the party leaders can in certain respects be brought within this framework. Britain's politics are not so dominated by the parties as collective entities that the leaders fail to enter the voters' calculations; identifying particular leaders with particular actions of government is in fact an important means by which the voter connects his choice to future policies or goals. For example, some who voted Labour in 1966 identified Mr Wilson with defence of the pound, Britain's presence east of Suez, firm handling of strikes, and other actions which were by no means simple extensions of Labour's traditional policies. Even fairly generalized perceptions of a leader as 'able' or 'trustworthy' help the voter to say something about future actions of government on the basis of the leader's past handling of issues. These inferences may be less sure than they would be in a presidential system; the French peasant who trusted de Gaulle may have had a surer guide to the future so long as the President loomed large in it. But these inferences are by no means unknown to the British voter. We shall consider these and other aspects of the appeal of the party leaders in Chapter 17.

For the moment, however, we must note that, in view of the variety of actions governments must take and the variety of values and goals that these will touch, many issues will confront the electorate at a given time. But people have wholly atomistic responses to the issues of politics. Both in Westminster and in the constituencies particular issues are often brought within more embracing frameworks of opinion. Although this tendency is much more evident among political leaders than among ordinary people, a full analysis of the electoral role of issues none the less requires us to pay some attention to the patterns which may be found in the voter's attitudes to several issues at once.

9 Patterns in Political Attitudes

Political change – whether in the individual elector or in the mass electorate – will seldom be provoked by a single issue, standing on its own. Most voters have attitudes towards many issues, and these fall into discernible patterns. Such patterns could obviously have a bearing on the sources of electoral change. Indeed, one of the most familiar frameworks for interpreting change – the schema of left and right – assumes that the public sees a number of political issues in terms of an ideological spectrum and responds to leftward and rightward movements of the parties along this spectrum. But this sort of ideological framework may not be the only source of pattern or structure in attitudes towards issues. We might, for example, suppose that many voters would simply adopt the pattern of issue positions contained in their party's policies.

Parties as Sources of Pattern

Since most electors have partisan dispositions and since the parties themselves offer a lead on most issues, it would be surprising if the parties did not assume a special status in giving structure to attitudes. When they do so, the flow of cause and effect is not from issue to party preference but the other way round, from party preference to belief on the issue. Attitudes towards issues then have only a conserving or reinforcing influence on party choice and not a formative one. How often do the parties in fact shape the beliefs of their followers into a consistent pattern?

Our empirical evidence reveals astonishingly little support for such an interpretation of British electoral attitudes. This is indeed implicit in the last chapter's evidence about the instability of views on policy. If the voter is bound to his party, and if he has fairly stable perceptions of party stands but unstable attitudes of his own, then his 'learning' of party stands cannot have lent much pattern to his views on issues.

It is not that the electorate is ignorant of party stands; on a number of issues there is a clear understanding of the line each party takes. The 'structure' uniting these perceptions is illustrated by the relationship between the positions which their supporters thought their parties were taking on the issues of nationalization and nuclear weapons. There was fairly high consensus that the Conservatives stood for keeping the Bomb and Labour for extending public ownership. Table 9.1 shows how closely the two

9.1 Party Stands on Nationalization and Nuclear Weapons as Perceived by Labour and Conservative Voters, 1964[a]

| | | Party most likely to extend nationalization | |
		Own	Other
Party most likely to keep nuclear Weapons	Other	76%	5%
	Own	24	95
		100%	100%
		(n = 461)	(n = 496)

[a] This table includes all supporters of Labour and the Conservatives who themselves expressed a view on the issues of nationalization and nuclear weapons.

perceptions were related in 1964. Indeed, any standard correlation calculated from the frequencies underlying this table would have a value approaching +0·7.

Nothing like this coherent structure is, however, found when we examine the attitudes that partisan voters expressed towards these same two issues. Table 9.2 shows a very much weaker correlation between these attitudes; by most standard measures it would be little more than +0·1. Plainly the degree to which voters pattern their beliefs on those of their parties, even on key issues, can be very modest.

9.2 Attitudes towards Nationalization and Nuclear Weapons Held by Labour and Conservative Supporters, 1964

| | | Extend Nationalization | |
		Should	Should not
Give up Independent Nuclear Weapons	Should	65%	51%
	Should Not	35	49
		100% ($n = 364$)	100% ($n = 806$)

Even party activists fail to conform. We shall not set out the evidence in detail, but it is striking that the tie between attitudes on nationalization and nuclear weapons was no stronger among those minorities who subscribed to a party or did party work than among the bulk of the electorate. There could be few more forceful comments on the limited extent to which party orientations reach down into the mass public, or on the limited role which tightly clustered policy beliefs play in the motives for party work.

Thus the fluidity of attitudes discussed in the last chapter finds a parallel in the limited interrelationships of such attitudes. Our findings show that, far from comprising a tightly formed cluster of beliefs, attitudes towards such policy issues as nationalization of industry, retention of nuclear weapons, entry into the Common Market and levels of spending on the social services were only weakly related at any of our three rounds of interviews.

The Structure of Stable Opinions

The fact that weakly formed attitudes will tend to change over time suggests an analytic step for us to take in searching for pattern in the attitudes of those who do hold genuine issue beliefs. If we exclude from consideration those whose views wavered between interviews and examine the interrelationships of the attitudes only of those whose views remained fixed,[1] we will be able to clear away most responses that had a random element and allow us to detect any pattern in the beliefs of the minority whose views were more genuine and stable.

Let us begin with a single policy issue, such as the nationalization of industry, dividing our respondents simply by whether they favour more nationalization or not. With the replies to two separate interviews, we can distribute the full sample into four categories.

Should more industries be nationalized?

Earlier interview	Yes	Yes	No	No
Later interview	Yes	No	Yes	No

Since we are concerned only with those who have stable views, we may exclude from the analysis anyone whose variable responses have placed him in one of the shaded cells. Of course, anyone who tossed a coin to decide his response at each interview would have a 50 per cent chance of landing in an unshaded cell, but we have at least eliminated about half the people with high response instability.

The process can be carried further by repeating the question.

1. We do not suppose that all change is response instability; neither do we suppose that constancy is always evidence of genuine attitude. There is some true attitude change in response variation, and some random responses will be consistent from one time to the next for accidental reasons, as explained below. Nevertheless, if we assume that response instability is greater in some people than others, this procedure will take us closer to any true pattern of attitude in the minds of those whose beliefs are relatively well-informed and stable. A good deal of empirical evidence, including many of the later findings of this chapter, supports the assumption that there is normally a gradient in response instability across a sample of the general public. This gradient is not in general such that all respondents have either real and perfectly stable or unreal and random responses, although Converse has shown that this condition may occasionally obtain. But the evidence suggests that the gradient is fairly steep on a good many issues.

With a third interview we can divide our respondents into eight cells. The likelihood of anyone falling in an unshaded cell by giving the same reply by chance at all three interviews would by now be reduced to 25 per cent: three quarters of those with high response instability would now have been eliminated from the analysis.

Should more industries be nationalized?

First interview	Yes	Yes	Yes	Yes	No	No	No	No
Second interview	Yes	Yes	No	No	Yes	Yes	No	No
Third interview	Yes	No	Yes	No	Yes	No	Yes	No

Since we wish to explore the relationship between two or more stable attitudes we may go farther in elimination. If the eight-fold classification of responses on nationalization in three successive interviews is crossed with a similar classification of successive responses to another policy issue, such as whether Britain ought to give up the Bomb, we obtain the sixty-four-fold array shown opposite and reduce the chance of a random answerer falling into an unshaded cell to only one in sixteen.[2]

When this procedure was applied to the pairs of issues for which we have responses at two or three of the interviews, varying proportions of the sample fell into the unshaded cells of such tables. In some cases the fraction giving constant responses on both issues in a pair was as high as half, in others as low as a tenth. The average across all pairs of issues was about three-tenths; our procedure for removing those with unformed or changing opinions has thus on average cut away seven-tenths of the total sample.

2. Assuming a probability of 0·5 for a given response at a given interview, the likelihood of a 'pure' random answerer falling in a given unshaded cell is $(0·5)^6 = 0·0156$. Since there are four such cells, the probability of his landing in one of the four is 0·06. These calculations are of course only suggestive since the probabilities governing the responses of those of high response instability will not in general be as simple as the law governing the toss of a fair coin.

Should more industries be nationalized?

	Yes Yes Yes	Yes Yes No	Yes No Yes	Yes No No	No Yes Yes	No Yes No	No No Yes	No No No
Yes Yes Yes								
Yes Yes No								
Yes No Yes								
Yes No No								
No Yes Yes								
No Yes No								
No No Yes								
No No No								

Should Britain give up the Bomb?

It is important to see that this procedure for removing people of changeable opinion in no way prejudges the relationship of the remaining respondents' attitudes on any two issues. For example, if we draw from the arrays the four unshaded corner cells (describing the joint distribution of the opinions of those who voiced a stable view both on nationalization and nuclear weapons over the three interviews) we do nothing to force a positive or a negative association between these attitudes. Rather, we can now look at the structure of attitudes without its being so heavily overlaid by the effects of random responses.

What in fact emerges from the correlations obtained in this way is that there is no strong pattern linking the attitudes even of those who do have stable attitudes. Compared with the expectation that

Should more industries be nationalized?

	Yes	No
	Yes	No
	Yes	No

Should Britain give up the Bomb?

Yes Yes Yes

No No No

any reader of the *Economist* or *New Statesman*, say, would have about political positions that naturally go together, the actual correlations are strikingly low.

This conclusion emerges clearly from Table 9.3. Each of the figures in the table has been calculated from a four-fold table of constant opinions similar to that shown above. The general consensus of informed opinion, reflecting on the whole the official

9.3 Correlations of Stable Attitudes Towards Issues[a]

	Opposed Nuclear Weapons	Opposed Common Market	Tolerated Immigration	Opposed Death Penalty	Thought Business not too powerful	Thought Monarchy not Important	Thought Trade Unions not too powerful
Favoured nationalization	0·14	0·10	0·06	0·18	0·37	0·26	0·65
Opposed nuclear weapons		−0·26	0·07	0·20	0·09	0·23	0·12
Opposed Common Market			−0·07	0·20	0·00	−0·01	−0·02
Tolerated immigration				0·33	−0·06	0·10	0·18
Opposed death penalty					0·09	0·14	0·18
Thought business too powerful						0·10	0·17
Thought monarchy not important							0·18

[a] The entries in the matrix are Kendall's tau–b rank correlation coefficient calculated from the four-fold table describing stable opinion towards the two items in question, as explained in the text. If both items appeared in all three interviews the figures are in italics and are calculated for opinions that were stable over all three. If both items appeared together in only two of the interviews the correlation is calculated for opinions that were stable between the two waves at which the questions were asked. The detailed wording of items may be found in the Appendix. As also explained in the text, the direction in which the items were scaled conformed to the trend of 'left' and 'right' opinion at an élite level at the outset of the study.

party lines in 1963, explains the direction we have given to the issues. Thus support for nationalization, opposition to nuclear weapons, opposition to the Common Market, tolerance of immigration, opposition to hanging, suspicion of big business, lower esteem for the monarchy and support for trade unions were all treated as if they lay in one direction and the reverse of these positions as if they lay in the opposite direction. There was one case in which such informed judgements as to the direction of items were mildly contradicted by the attitudes held by the mass public. Despite the alignment on the Common Market which the parties assumed under Mr Macmillan and Mr Gaitskell, electors who held the 'left' position on other issues were the more likely to favour *entering* Europe and those who held the 'right' position to oppose it. This reversal is indicated by the negative value of the correlation between attitudes towards the Common Market and attitudes towards nuclear weapons, immigration, the monarchy and trade union power.

The links found in Table 9.3 extend to matters of very dissimilar outward appearance. For example, attitudes towards nuclear weapons were systematically tied to attitudes towards nationalization, as well as to immigration, the death penalty, big business power and the trade unions. People who opposed the recent level of immigration were more likely to be for the death penalty and against the power of the trade unions. Those who discounted the importance of the monarchy were likely to accept nationalization, oppose the Bomb, accept recent immigration, condemn hanging and the power of big business and be tolerant towards the trade unions.

Yet the main impression left by Table 9.3 is of the weakness of the links between attitudes. These figures are based on the drastically reduced groups of electors who held stable opinions on each of two issues over two or three interviews. On average something like 70 per cent of our full sample has been cut away. Yet even when we go to such lengths to confine our attention to the minority of people who have well-formed and enduring views, the association of attitudes is relatively feeble. An occasional correlation, such as that between nationalization and trade union power, rises to an impressive level. But most of these figures are notable mainly for their modest size. There is a mild tendency here for opinion to organize along the left–right lines which would be recognized by political insiders. But by the standards of élite opinion the tendency is very mild indeed.

This aspect of popular thought inevitably raises the question of how important the left–right framework is to the public's appraisal of politics. The looseness of the ties between issues which might be expected to evoke more coherent responses, especially from the minority of electors we have considered here, leads us to examine other evidence as to the importance of conceptions of left and right in the public's response not only to issues but also to the parties and leaders who appeal for electoral support.

The Left–Right Framework of Issues

The notion that policies and leaders can be ranked on an ideological scale running from left to right is perhaps the commonest of all political abstractions. It is not just a piece of academic conceptualization; the words 'left' and 'right' are constantly used in everyday political comment and reporting. The suggestion that matters of political controversy can be interpreted along a continuum from left to right is as old as the French Revolution. A quotation from the 1920s still sums up the widely held approach to the use of the terms.[3]

The broad question which the two-party system asks: 'Do you incline, on the whole, towards the Right, or towards the Left?' is the most sensible question which it is possible to ask of the electorate. It is a question which corresponds far more closely to the realities of human psychology than the more complicated questions which a multiple-party system inevitably raises. The issue is one which presents itself in every department of life. Wherever men take part in collective action, and questions of policy arise, there is a fundamental cleavage between the more adventurous and the more cautious, the more open-minded and the more prejudiced, the more progressive and the more con-

3. H. D. Henderson, *The Nation*, November 5, 1927, quoted in T. Wilson, *The Decline of the Liberal Party*, London, 1966, p. 124. For a brief account of the origins of the terms and their introduction into British political parlance see S. Brittan, *Left or Right: Bogus Dilemma*, London, 1968.

servative. Men fluctuate, of course, pass from the one camp to the other, find themselves ranged on particular issues against those with whom they are normally in sympathy; and some are not quite sure to which camp they normally belong. But the two camps are there. Who does not recognize their existence?

The meaning given to left and right has, of course, varied widely. Indeed much of the usefulness of the terms comes from the openness of possible interpretations. Left and right have been general labels under which a welter of political matters could readily be classified. But the basic picture evoked, both in normal parlance and in academic literature, is of a spectrum or scale along which electors and parties can be placed from Communist on the left to reactionary on the right or, to press the analogy, from infrared to ultra-violet. It is an implied commonplace of contemporary British political discussion that the parties and their leaders, as they contend for mass support, manoeuvre along a line from left to right – and that the electorate too is distributed along that line. Observers have long written about the dilemmas of successive leaders of the Labour Party as they sought to prevent their left-wing activists from becoming too discontented without, at the same time, offending the floating voter in the centre; and about the parallel dilemmas of Conservative leaders in keeping their more right-wing stalwarts happy without having the whole party branded as reactionary. New initiatives by the parties are regularly scrutinized to see whether they represent a move to right or left. Several academic writers, fascinated by the similarities between, on the one hand, the manoeuvring of the parties along a left–right dimension and on the other, the strategic problems faced by firms competing for customers in a linear marketplace – such as a busy High Street or a transcontinental railway – have presented this one-dimensional aspect of the party system in terms of a formal model paralleling a well-known economic model.[4]

4. There is an extensive theoretical literature on spatial models of party competition, much of it inspired by location theory in economics. See in particular H. Hotelling, 'Stability in Competition', *Economic Journal*, **39** (1929), 41–57; Arthur Smithies, 'Optimum Location in Spatial Competition', *Journal of Political Economy*, **49** (1941), 423–9; Anthony

In this left–right model the parties take their place along the spectrum according to the stands which they adopt on issues. Voters too take their place according to their position on issues. The central assumption of the model when it is taken as a theory of electoral behaviour is that a voter's preference for a party depends on how far its position is from his own along the left–right dimension. Thus, he will most prefer the party that is closest to him and least prefer the party that is farthest from him; any other parties will enjoy an intermediate degree of preference. If the parties are too far away the elector may of course not vote at all. But the order of his preferences among the parties will depend exclusively upon their distance from his own ideological position. Because of the central role that this idea of a left–right spectrum plays in most ideological discussion, we should explore in detail how far the left–right spectrum provides a realistic model of the relationship between parties and voters.

A natural approach to the problem is to see how far the assumption that the elector judges the parties by the distance from his own position does in fact fit the preferences felt by voters towards the Conservative, Labour and Liberal Parties. An elector's strength of preference depends of course not on where the parties really are, in some objective sense, along the ideological spectrum, but on where he thinks they are. However, when the number of major parties is small there is likely to be substantial consensus among that portion of the electorate which thinks in these terms on the placement of the parties from left to right. Certainly our own respondents who said that they thought of the parties as being to the left, centre or right politically were virtually unanimous in

Downs, *An Economic Theory of Democracy*, New York, 1957, pp. 114–41; Gerald Garvey, 'The Theory of Party Equilibrium', *American Political Science Review*, **60** (1966), 29–39; and James M. Buchanan, 'Democracy and Duopoly: A Comparison of Analytical Models', *American Economic Review*, **58** (1968), 322–40. For interesting efforts to extend such models to more dimensions than one, see Otto A. Davis and Melvin Hinich, 'A Mathematical Model of Policy Formation in a Democratic Society', in Joseph L. Bernd, ed., *Mathematical Applications in Political Science, II*, Dallas, Texas, 1966, pp. 175–208, and Gordon Tullock, *Toward a Mathematics of Politics*, Ann Arbor, 1967.

placing Labour to the left, the Conservatives to the right and the Liberals somewhere in between. Fewer than one in twenty ranked the parties in an order that differed from the conventional one.

It is, of course, quite possible to have a sophisticated view of politics and yet to say that Labour is now right-wing and that the Conservatives are the progressive party. Articles about the conservatism of Labour and assertions of the Liberals' claim to be left-wing are frequently to be found. Such paradoxes are, however, the preserve of a negligible minority. None among the few respondents who claimed to think in left–right terms, but who placed the parties in other than their conventional order, gave any evidence in the rest of their replies that they were taking an ultra-sophisticated position. They were not drawn from those who were particularly interested in politics and there is little doubt that their eccentric placing of the parties reflected political innocence rather than independence of judgement.

General agreement on the ordering of the parties helps in testing the assumption that party preference is based on ideological proximity, since it limits the number of ways in which a voter can arrange his preference among the parties. Consider a simple representation of the placing of the British parties on a dimension divided into three regions – left, centre and right – a dimension along which the electorate too could be distributed.

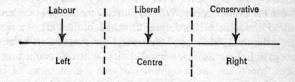

If ideological closeness were in fact the basis of preference, all voters in the left region would like Labour best, the Liberals next best and the Conservatives least. Similarly all voters in the right region would like the Conservatives best, the Liberals next best and Labour least. Voters in the centre region would like the Liberals best but their second and third choices would depend on whether they were to the left or right of a point half-way between

Labour and the Conservatives. Nevertheless, voters in the centre must have one of only two orders of preference and every voter one of only four orders of preference:

1 Labour	1 Liberal	1 Liberal	1 Conservative
2 Liberal	2 Labour	2 Conservative	2 Liberal
3 Conservative	3 Conservative	3 Labour	3 Labour

There are, however, two other sequences in which a voter might order his preferences:

1 Labour	1 Conservative
2 Conservative	2 Labour
3 Liberal	3 Liberal

But to have either of these orders of preference would be to contradict the assumption that ideological closeness is the basis of party choice. If the model is true, no one who most prefers the party which is farthest to the left should have as his next choice the party which is farthest to the right – or vice versa.

Yet in fact many voters do order the parties in this way. Among Labour supporters in the summer of 1963 fully a third preferred the Conservatives to the Liberals as a second choice and among Conservatives more than a quarter preferred Labour to the Liberals despite all the talk on television and in newspapers (much of it inspired by the left–right model) about the Liberals as an alternative to the Conservatives. What is more, there was little tendency for these 'inadmissible' orderings to vanish in the heat of a campaign. After the 1964 General Election 21 per cent of Conservative voters gave Labour as their second choice. When we probed these choices, moreover, we sought to remove the problem of the 'wasted vote', the sense that voting Liberal was futile, by asking the voter which of the three parties, named in turn, he would prefer to see 'form a government' if the party he preferred most did not do so.

Removing considerations of tactical voting does not of course mean that the Liberals' perceived weakness as a governing party had no influence on the preference order given by our respondents; on the contrary, we have evidence that such a perception was held by many of the people who placed the Liberals last. The point to be made in the present context is that there is at least a second dimension, perceived competence in governing or something like it, cutting across the left–right dimension in shaping the orderings of preference offered by our sample of electors.[5] No one-dimensional model of party distance can account for the fact that some Conservative and Labour partisans reach right over to the other side of the spectrum and name the opposite major party as their second choice rather than the party that is ideologically closer to their own.

How are these inadmissible orderings to be explained? The failure of the preferences of so many electors to conform to the dimensional model has implications reaching far beyond the discussion of left and right. It is a finding that casts doubt on any one-dimensional model of this kind, whether content is supplied to the dimension by social class or by a psychological orientation such as tough- and tender-mindedness, or by perception of issues and parties in terms of left and right.[6] We focus attention here on the concepts of left and right because they seem to offer the only possibility within the contemporary British political culture of organizing a wide range of political issues in terms of a single dimension. But the more general implications that must be drawn from the presence of inadmissible preference orderings should be kept in mind.

One possibility is to imagine that preference is related to ideological distance in some much more complicated way. It could be suggested that ideological closeness, in some circumstances,

5. But perceptions of Liberal strength held nothing like a full explanation of the discrepant preference orderings. Even among those who rated the Liberals as a 'strong' party the frequency of preference orderings inconsistent with the traditional left–right ordering of the parties was high.

6. Moreover, our demonstration that a single-dimensional model does not account for preferences for the three parties at once in no way depends on our having *a priori* knowledge of what the likely order of the parties is. For convenience of exposition we have availed ourselves of the consensus among the few who think in left–right terms that Labour is to the left, the Liberals in the middle and the Conservatives to the right. But the method of unfolding analysis would have disclosed the presence of inadmissible preference orders without our having such advance knowledge.

breeds hostility or contempt, as it occasionally does between some rival parties of the left within European multi-party systems. The Communist who hates Social Democrats more than he hates adherents of bourgeois parties might have his analogue in the Conservative who is furious with the Liberals for letting the Socialists in. There is no evidence, however, that this sort of response was involved in the preferences of those who gave the inadmissible orderings. The feelings that these electors expressed in answer to questions about the Liberal Party were in fact remarkably neutral.

A much simpler explanation is that many electors do not in fact see politics in terms of a single ideological dimension. There is no point in devising complex reasons why the left–right model fails to account for popular preferences if in fact a substantial proportion of the public is quite innocent of the left–right distinctions that are so constantly employed by insiders. Let us therefore try to measure more directly the extent to which the notions of left and right are comprehended by British electors.

Recognition of the Concept of Left and Right

Because our findings are at variance with widely held preconceptions we should begin by recording that in 1964 and 1965 we put to a number of leading politicians and political journalists the question 'To what proportion of the electorate would you say the terms "left" and "right" are meaningful, even in the shadowiest of ways?' The replies ranged widely, but the great majority put the figure as high as 60 per cent and some went up to 90 per cent. Among political insiders, it would appear, the words are so universally employed that they find it difficult to conceive that anyone for whom contemporary politics had the slightest meaning could fail to recognize them. The sophisticated are of course aware of the ambiguities of the concepts and of the confused and confusing way in which they are employed, but almost none escapes from using them – and from assuming that they are generally intelligible.

A first indication of the limited extent of ideological thinking at the mass level comes from the electors' answers to the question 'Do you ever think of the parties as being to the left, the centre or the right in politics or don't you think of them in that way?' Not many of them do – only 21 per cent of our respondents answered 'yes'. Given the opportunity to confess the remoteness of such terms most people took it.

In a widely separated place in our interview we asked our respondents if they ever thought of themselves personally as being to the left, centre or the right in politics. Only 25 per cent said that they did so; three-quarters of our sample indicated that these concepts were not among their working stock of ideas when they thought about politics. These figures contrast sharply with the fact that 96 per cent of our respondents conceded readily enough to some degree of party commitment. Allegiance to party is one of the central facts of the British elector's political awareness. Identification with the ideological symbols of left and right is clearly one of the more peripheral facts of such awareness. We shall return later to the intriguing differences between the 25 per cent who thought of themselves as being to the left or right and the 21 per cent who thought of the parties in this way.

These sobering proportions do not of course show the full extent to which these ideological symbols are recognized. There is a clear difference between associating the symbols of left and right with a party or with one's own attitudes and merely having some minimal recognition of the words. In order to see how many among that vast majority of electors who do not think in these terms none the less have some awareness of them, we included in our interviews an alternative approach to the question. Our respondents were asked to rate the parties along a series of scales involving such polar extremes as United/Split, Expert/Clumsy, Middle Class/Working Class, and among a number of other qualities, Left-wing/Right-wing.[7] Our respondents found these questions quite comprehensible. On eleven scales almost everyone

7. We followed a modified version of the semantic differential technique, which proved in this instance an admirable means of drawing replies from reluctant subjects. The standard work on the semantic differential technique is C. E. Osgood, G. J. Suci and P. H. Tannenbaum, *The Measurement of Meaning*, Urbana, Illinois, 1957.

was able to give a rating to the parties: only about one in twenty said 'don't know'. But on the Left-wing/Right-wing scale more than one elector in five was too baffled to give any reply at all, a proportion which suggests the difficulty the public has in using these terms.

Let us look more closely at the places given to the Labour Party along this Left-wing Right-wing scale for evidence of the limits of ideological awareness. To begin with, among the 78 per cent of our respondents who would place Labour at all, a further 17 per cent of the total sample placed Labour in the middle position on the scale, as Figure 9.4 shows.

9.4 Ideological Perceptions of the Labour Party

	Very	Fairly	Slightly	Neither	Slightly	Fairly	Very	
Left wing	30%	13%	7%	17%	2%	4%	5%	Right wing

In view of the almost complete consensus among the ideologically aware section of the electorate that Labour is to the left, it is reasonable to think that the 'neither' position was chosen as a way of evading a genuine answer by respondents seeking to conceal their bafflement. Hence we are left with 61 per cent who gave Labour a position other than 'neither'. But a further 11 per cent chose a point on the right side of the scale. Once again on the basis of the consensus that Labour is to the left, we may label these replies as no more than guesses. And if we assume that a guesser was as likely to say left as right we may add to the 11 per cent who guessed 'wrong' by putting Labour on the right a further 11 per cent who presumably guessed 'correctly' by putting it on the left. Deducting, therefore, a further 22 per cent from 61 per cent we end up with 39 per cent who could be presumed to connect the left and right symbols correctly with Labour. The arithmetic by which we would identify the proportion correctly placing the Conservatives gives very similar results.

That only about two electors in five had any real recognition of the terms left and right is confirmed by examining the consistency of answers between the summer of 1963 and the autumn of 1964. Of respondents who were asked at both interviews to place Labour along the left–right scale, we find 29 per cent who confessed at one interview or the other that they were unable to do so. We find another 28 per cent who at one interview or the other placed Labour at the middle or to the right. Moreover, since 3 per cent put Labour on the right both times, we can assume that a further 3 per cent were guessing when they put Labour on the left both times.[8] Thus we end up with approximately two-fifths of the electorate who can be presumed to connect the left and right symbols with the Labour Party in a meaningful way.

Total sample asked to place Labour at both interviews		100%
Said 'don't know' at one interview or other	29	
Placed Labour in middle or on the right in at least one interview	28	
Placed Labour on the left both times by guessing	3	60
Genuinely perceived Labour as on the left		40%

In other words, in addition to the 20–25 per cent who said that they thought in terms of left and right, there was an additional stratum of 15–20 per cent who showed some ability to link these ideological symbols with the parties. But we are still left with a substantial majority of the British people unfamiliar with these concepts.

In some respects, however, the most impressive evidence of the lack of ideological thinking in the British comes from the fifth of the public who claimed that they did think of the parties in terms of left and right. It would be very wrong to imagine that all of them interpret the words anything like as fully as most political activists do. Some may, but most have a much less elaborated understanding of the terms. In some cases the understanding is very nominal indeed.

8. The advantage of longitudinal data is of course that it makes unnecessary our assuming that all those who placed Labour in the middle or right (and an equal number who placed Labour to the left) at a given interview were offering insubstantial responses. Their insubstantial nature is plain enough in the way those who gave them wobbled between interviews, by contrast with those who genuinely saw Labour as being to the left.

Levels of Ideological Interpretation

To probe what meaning the words left and right imparted we asked those of our respondents who said they thought of the parties in such terms what they had in mind when they said a party was to the left, centre or right politically. Their replies could be sorted into three levels of ideological sophistication. The highest involved a well-elaborated interpretation, one in which the concepts of left and right seemed to organize the respondent's attitudes to several issues at once. Such interpretations seemed also relatively 'dynamic', in the sense of providing the grounds on which the elector might decide that the parties, or he himself, had moved to the left or the right. An interpretation of this sort is reflected in the remarks of a London Transport supervisor:

> To the left means increased social and welfare benefits, the elimination of private wealth, and nationalization. To the right means the preservation of private wealth and the reduction of expenditure on social benefits.

By a fairly generous classification not more than one in ten of those who associated the words with the parties (which means only two in a hundred of the entire electorate) gave answers at this level.

A second level involved a less developed interpretation in which the concepts were given meaning in terms of only one kind of content, usually identifications with a social class. Interpretations at this level seemed not only less capable of organizing attitudes towards various issues at once but also more static in the sense that the parties' behaviour in relation to contemporary issues, or changes of the voter's own issue beliefs, would be unlikely to change his placement of the parties or himself on the left–right spectrum. Such an interpretation in terms of a single attribute is illustrated by the remarks of an Edinburgh man:

> The Conservatives are to the right, the Liberals are in the middle, and Labour is left. The Conservatives favour the middle and upper classes and Labour only the working class.

Just under three out of four of those who associated the terms with the parties gave answers at this level (or about 14 out of 100 of the entire electorate). Remarks such as the ones just quoted illustrate a tendency among those who gave less developed interpretations to understand the terms nominally, to maintain that the Conservatives *are* the right and Labour *is* the left.

A third level of interpretation was provided by respondents who seemed unable to give any meaning to the concepts other than such a purely nominal one. They had learned to know which term was linked with which party – but nothing more. Consider, for example, the remarks of this Sheffield lubricating engineer:

Well, when I was in the Army you had to put your right foot forward, but in fighting you lead with your left. So I always think that the Tories are the right party for me and that the Labour Party are fighters. I know that this isn't right really, but I can't explain it properly, and it does for me.

Plainly the meaning given the words here is nothing more than a memory device for attaching ideological names to the parties. This 'meaning' is unrelated to any left–right spectrum along which individual or party positions could move. Similarly a number of our respondents clung to the fact that the Conservatives were the 'right' party because their policies were 'correct' or 'upright'. In all, nearly one in four of our respondents who said they thought of the parties as being to the left or to the right could offer only an empty, nominal interpretation of this sort.[9]

This evidence of how often the interpretation is purely nominal suggests a key to the puzzle about why some respondents said they thought of themselves as being left or right but denied thinking of the parties in these terms. An explanation now emerges. Some of

9. As suggested on p. 258, one of the criteria used in classifying people into these several levels was the ease with which their interpretations of left and right could provide a basis for perceptions of changes of position along the left–right spectrum. It is therefore interesting to note the frequency with which those at the three levels reported perceiving changes of party positions when we probed for such perceptions in a separate question. Of those we coded at the highest level of interpretation, 72 per cent said they thought one of the parties had moved; at the second level the figure was only 36 per cent; and at the third level only 12 per cent.

those who have learned a set of ideological labels for the parties have also come to think of themselves, in a wholly nominal way, as being left or right according to their party persuasion. To such people, being asked whether they think of *themselves* as left or right means nothing more than being asked whether they have a preference for one of the leading parties. But the question whether they think of the *parties* as being to the left or to the right is more likely to be seen as asking whether they have any concept of the meaning of the terms as applied to the parties. Some whose use of the terms is purely nominal will say 'no' even though they have reported thinking of themselves as left or right. The elector who 'knows' his own ideological location simply because he knows which party he supports stands in flat contradiction to our ideological model; he has stood on its head the basis of political choice which it assumes – his 'ideology' follows his partisanship, not his partisanship his ideology. But our evidence leaves little doubt that this is a very common phenomenon: voters come to think of themselves as right or left very much as a Conservative in Birmingham or Scotland used to think of himself as 'Unionist' because that is what his party was called locally.

By adding to these three levels of ideological sophistication the two remaining categories into which the electorate can be placed – those who can at least connect the terms left and right correctly with the parties when obliged to do so and those who cannot – we summarize in Table 9.5 the ideological awareness of the mass public. Even with full allowance for the approximate nature of the methods leading to this distribution, we must regard it as a remarkable profile of popular acceptance – or rather non-acceptance – of left–right framework.[10]

10. The extent of this sort of cognitive organization in different political cultures is an interesting problem for comparative study. Repeated surveys in France have found that 85 to 90 per cent of French electors are prepared to place themselves along a five-point scale extreme left/moderate left/centre/moderate right/extreme right, and other evidence from these surveys suggests that the terms were in fact meaningful to a much larger fraction of French than of our British respondents. See E. Deutsch, D. Lindon and P. Weill, *Les Familles Politiques*, Paris, 1966.

9.5 Levels of Interpretation of Left–Right Concepts

Fully elaborated dynamic interpretation	2%
Partially elaborated static interpretation	14
Nominal interpretation	4
Minimal recognition	20
No recognition	60
	100%

Ideological Awareness and the Organization of Issues

We may now return to our findings on the small degree to which individual political attitudes are organized. The low awareness of the left–right concept helps to explain why 'left' and 'right' positions on issues are so little reflected in popular thought. But our classification of ideological awareness now offers a way of identifying parts of the electorate in which there should be a relatively greater consistency in the organization of attitudes. Let us see how the degree of a voter's ideological awareness is related to the structure of his political attitudes and to the link between his beliefs on issues and his self-identification in left–right terms.

Nationalization, so long at the heart of the struggle over socialism in Britain, provides an excellent example of the relevance of ideological symbols to an elector's position on an issue. Figure 9.6 on the next page shows the relationship of the respondent's position on this issue to his placement of himself in left–right terms, at each level of ideological awareness (except the lowest). The decline of this association as we move down the hierarchy of awareness suggests the declining importance of the ideas of left and right in shaping responses to issues once we leave the tiny fraction of the electorate which thinks in ideological terms in a fully developed way.

But ideological interpretation can scarcely be tested in terms of a single issue; what really distinguishes those who think ideologically is the extent to which their attitudes to several issues are organized

9.6 Relationship between Attitude towards Nationalization and Own Left–Right Placement, by Ideological Level[a]

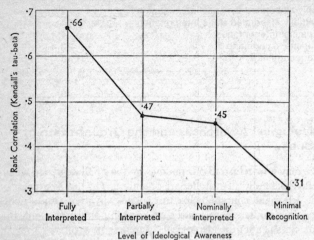

[a] The minimum recognition group are the few people, discussed above, who said that they thought of themselves as being to the left, centre or right politically but went on to say later in the interview that they did not think of the parties in those terms. We may therefore expect that this sub-group of the full set of respondents with 'minimal recognition' will, if anything, be relatively more familiar with the terms.

into a clear structure. Left and right positions can be identified by the ideologue on issues as dissimilar in subject matter as colonialism and the handling of sex offenders. Indeed the reduction of a multiplicity of issues to a single ideological dimension is, as we have seen, necessary for the ideological model to work.

The greater coherence of attitudes towards issues among those at the highest ideological level is illustrated by Figure 9.7, which shows the declining correlation of attitudes towards nationalization and expenditure on the social services as we move down the hierarchy. Among the most sophisticated the correlation is fairly high, but it falls away sharply even at the next highest ideological level and decreases almost to vanishing point among those who

9.7 The Correlation of Issue Attitudes by Level of Ideological Interpretation

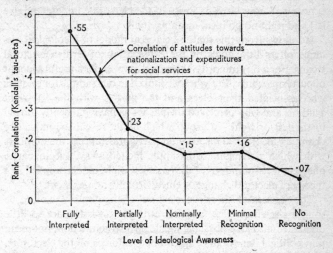

Correlation of attitudes towards nationalization and expenditures for social services

are not able even to recognize the symbols of left and right. A similar pattern of relationships obtains between attitudes towards a number of other political issues.

From all that has been said, it is clear that the theory that a voter chooses among parties on the basis of their distance from his own position along a left–right spectrum is very far from describing how the great bulk of British electors make their choice. The assumption that people order their preferences for the parties according to the parties' distance from their own position on the spectrum is contradicted by the preferences expressed by many of our respondents. The assumption that voters see themselves or the parties on a left–right dimension at all is contradicted by our evidence on the slightness of the role that the words left and right play in the political thought of the British mass public. A thin layer of the most ideologically aware does seem to use left and right to organize their views about where they and the parties stand on current issues. But such people are vastly outnumbered by those who have more impoverished and static interpretations of the concepts. And a large majority of the electorate apparently give left and right no political meaning at all.

It follows from this that the classical model of ideological distance offers little towards the explanation of British electoral trends. For a tiny minority, the model may render a useful account of partisan change. But when we looked in our sample for electors who associated themselves and the parties with the left–right symbols and who perceived the parties as having recently moved to the left or right – a group which might reveal the impact of changing ideological distance on party preference – the numbers with which we might work simply melted away. Electors who obeyed the assumptions of the basic left–right model, applied as a theory of electoral change, seemed virtually non-existent.

The sources of short-run electoral change must therefore be sought elsewhere. The fact that attitudes on issues are so little organized into an embracing ideological structure does not mean that political issues can be discounted as forces on the electorate. Individual political issues, especially those defined in terms of the goals which matter to wide sections of the public, can have substantial impact as they reach the ordinary voter through the channels of political communication.

10 The Flow of Political Information

Political change must depend in large part upon the flow of political information. New information sets in motion the processes by which individual attitudes are formed and modified. Exchanges of information alter the political outlook of the family and other small social groups. The information about politics reaching the public through the mass media changes the support accorded to the parties and their leaders. In the long term there may be certain processes of change at work – differences in mortality rates, for example – which alter the balance of party strength without any new inputs of political information. But in the short term, marked changes are scarcely imaginable except in response to some information flow.

Academic students have given increasing recognition to the central role that the flow of information must play in any political system.[1] The value of this approach is peculiarly evident in Britain, where political élites conduct so much of their affairs through the subtle and extraordinarily intricate communications networks of Westminster and Whitehall. When we turn to the mass level, where the channels of communication are very different, an understanding of how information is transmitted proves to be no less important to the understanding of attitudes and behaviour.

Developments in mass communications – the coming, first of the popular press, then of radio and now of television – have transformed mass politics. Our understanding of the precise impact of

1. This view is perhaps most systematically and forcefully expressed by Karl Deutsch in *The Nerves of Government*, New York, 1963. For two interesting British approaches, see Lord Windlesham, *Communication and Political Power*, London, 1966, and R. Rose, *Influencing Voters*, London, 1967.

these media is still fragmentary, partly because the impact is so imperceptible and long-term. This point is often made by critics of short term, empirical studies.[2] We recognize that, despite the attention we shall give to the long-run impact of the oldest and most partisan of the media – the press – our evidence is insufficient for us to do more than speculate about many of the cumulative effects of exposure to the mass media.

Our concern here will be first with extent of the electorate's *exposure* to political communication and, second, with the *channels* through which political information flows to the public, especially the influence that may be attributed to the partisan press. Questions having to do with the content of political communication will also concern us. But they are of course raised throughout this book; indeed, they are central to the discussion of change in the previous two chapters and the companion chapters (15–18) of Part Four. Since the flow of information is conditioned by the structure of the networks of communication we begin with a brief account of the changing sources of political communication.

The Sources of Information

The modern voter has a variety of sources of information. He may choose to rely on personal conversation or on one of the mass media – the press, magazines, radio, television, even films. But the situation is not one of alternatives. Those who are in the habit of talking about politics with family and friends do not constitute a separate, isolated part of the British culture. On the contrary, the information which the voter receives in communications of this sort will normally have had its origin in the mass media, even though it may have undergone various transformations along the way. Lazarsfeld and Katz have described this evident link between the mass media and personal conversation as a 'two-step' flow of communication, although of course more than two steps may be involved.[3] The extent to which personal conversation is penetrated

2. See for example J. D. Halloran, *The Effects of Mass Communication, with Special Reference to Television*, Leicester, 1964.
3. The 'two-step' hypothesis was first discussed in P. F. Lazarsfeld, B.

by content from the mass media puts obvious difficulties in the way of describing the effect of different forms of communication.

A further difficulty inherent in any *simpliste*, single cause view of communication lies in the interpenetration of the mass media themselves. Their lack of independence is partly a result of the heavy overlap of the media audiences. There are, of course, some people who rely mainly or exclusively on one of the media, and we shall capitalize on this fact as we explore the effects of the different media. But millions of people read the press – often more than one newspaper – as well as watching television or listening to radio. There are even a few who read books as well as doing all these other things. As a consequence it is difficult to isolate a set of electors whose exposure to one of the media has been 'pure'.[4]

The interpenetration of the mass media is partly an élite phenomenon. Those who determine the political content of the media rely on a variety of common sources, including the press agencies and the parties; their very awareness of the overlap of their audiences makes them sensitive to excessive disparities of content. An instance of this has been the effect on the partisan press of the trend in television and radio towards fuller and franker political reporting; it is widely held that since politics began to receive extensive television coverage there has been a diminution of newspaper bias. Such convergence lessens the distinctness in the content of the rival media and, with it, the possibility of separating their effects.

None the less, substantial differences of content remain, some of which are intrinsic to the nature of the media. It is hardly possible, for example, for the press and television to give identical treatment to the party leaders. Nor are the media audiences completely

Berelson and H. Gaudet, *The People's Choice*, New York, 1944, although it was treated more fully in E. Katz and P. F. Lazarsfeld, *Personal Influence*, Glencoe, Illinois, 1955. See also E. Katz, 'The Two-Step Flow of Communications: an Up-to-Date Report on a Hypothesis', *Public Opinion Quarterly* **21** (1957) 61–78.

4. A vigorous statement of this difficulty is given by H. Blumer, 'Suggestions for the Study of Mass Media Effects', in *American Voting Behavior*, eds. E. Burdick and A. J. Brodbeck, Glencoe, Illinois, 1958, pp. 197–208.

overlapping. Let us, therefore, consider briefly the several sources of communication and the public's reliance on each.

Private conversation is, from the point of view of politicians, one of the most tantalizing sources of political information, since what is said and what sinks home is so largely outside their observation and control. They suspect that it is the most important cause of changes of mood and voting intention and at every election widespread reports of 'deliberate whispering campaigns' (baseless though such reports almost always appear to be) give evidence of the neuroses that can build up about what may be happening in millions of casual, unrecorded political conversations.

Both in 1964 and 1966 about three-fifths of our sample claimed to have had such conversations, but their incidence varied greatly with personal circumstances. Obviously, an elderly spinster, living alone with no one to talk to, is situated very differently from the publican who has to listen to his customers' ideas about politics – and everything else – as a necessity of business.

Table 10.1 shows, for the 1964 campaign, the marked differences

10.1 Personal Conversation About Election Campaign by Sex and Work Status, 1964[a]

	Per cent of Men With Jobs	Per cent of Women With Jobs	Per cent of Women Without Jobs
Talked about campaign with:			
Husband/wife	12	12	14
Other family	11	15	19
People at work	55	29	—
Friends	22	23	27
'Everyone'	4	2	6
Others	1	—	1
Didn't talk about campaign	26	43	53

[a] Each entry of this table is the per cent of those in a given sex and work status who reported a given conversational pattern. The entries sum to more than 100 per cent by column because some respondents reported more than one pattern of conversation.

in the extent both of men's conversation as compared with women's and of the conversation of those who went out to work as compared with those who did not. Perhaps the most interesting finding in the table is the reciprocal nature of talking politics at work and not at all: the falling-off of political conversations at work across the three columns of the table is paralleled by the rise in the proportion not discussing politics at all. But more than the housewife's absence from a work-place is involved, as the difference between employed women demonstrates; it recalls our findings in Chapter 7 about the greater activism of trade union members.

The electorate itself sees the mass media as a more important means of following politics. Whereas two-fifths of our samples said that they did not talk about politics to anyone, only 12 per cent in 1964 and 14 per cent in 1966 reported that they did not follow the campaign from newspapers, television or radio. The medium with the largest political audience – about three-quarters of the electorate by their own report – is television. This ascendancy is of very recent origin. Although, as Table 10.2 shows, television has over twenty years moved steadily to something like nationwide saturation, it was slow to develop full and forceful coverage of politics.

10.2 Percentage of British Households with Television

1950	10
1955	40
1959	75
1964	88
1966	90

In its early days it had been influenced by the B.B.C. tradition of caution which, until 1959, led to the suppression of all references to election speeches from the news bulletins lest the Corporation be suspected of partiality. But with changing attitudes and with the stimulus of competition between a public service network and a commercial one, more and more prominence was given to politicians and their doings. In the 1964 and 1966 elections at least a quarter of the population over the age of five watched each of the nightly party broadcasts and even more saw the specially extended daily news bulletins.[5]

Very nearly as large a fraction of the public reported following politics in the press as on television. In a nation whose proportion of newspaper readers is the highest in the world, 66 per cent said in 1964 and 59 per cent in 1966 that they had followed the campaign in the press, proportions which attest to the continued importance of newspapers in the process of political communication. Yet when electors were asked to evaluate their relative use of television and the press in following the campaign, television was much preferred. In 1964 fully 65 per cent of those who followed the campaign at all said that they had relied more on television,[6] and only 28 per cent that they had relied more on the press.

By contrast with the press and television, radio has a very secondary audience. Radio in its heyday never came into its own politically – despite the impact of party election broadcasts from 1931 onwards and of Churchill's wartime addresses. The liberalization of political broadcasting in the late 1950s arrived too late; television had pre-empted radio's place. In 1964 only 23 per cent and in 1966 only 20 per cent of our respondents said they had followed the campaign by radio. Of those who had followed the campaign by any medium, a mere 7 per cent (in 1964) reported that they relied most on radio.

These facts as to the sources of political information are brought together in Table 10.3. The first three columns show the propor-

5. See *The British General Election of 1964*, pp. 168, 182, and *The British General Election of 1966*, pp. 143–5, for detailed viewing figures.

6. This figure is the sum of those who followed the campaign only by television and of those who gave television first place among several media by which they had followed the campaign. The relative weight given these media in terms of a single, inclusive measure of importance is supported by the more differentiated measure used in the Leeds studies of television's influence. The respondents in these studies rated television ahead of the press in terms of helpfulness for weighing up political leaders, helpfulness for understanding political issues, up-to-dateness, impartiality and trustworthiness. Only in terms of fullness of account of political events was the press rated ahead of television. See J. Blumler and D. McQuail, *Television and Politics*, London, 1968, p. 42–4.

10.3 Sources of Political Information

| | Per cent following politics/ campaign by given medium or channel[a] | | | Per cent saying given medium of channel most important 1964 | |
	Summer 1963	Autumn 1964	Spring 1966	Of all media	Of all channels
Television	55	75	72	65	48
Newspapers	48	66	59	28	20
Radio	19	23	20	7	5
Conversation	27	60	63	—	19
Didn't follow campaign/ politics	30	8	8	—	8
				100%	100%

[a] The entries in these three columns add to more than 100 per cent, because many respondents followed politics or the campaign by more than one medium.

tions of our sample who followed politics in the summer of 1963 or the election campaigns of 1964 and 1966 through each of the several forms of communication – or through none at all. The two right-hand columns convey the electorate's own judgement about the sources they relied on most in the election campaign of 1964.

Exposure to Communication and Partisan Change

The evidence of interview studies from several countries has suggested that voters who pay less attention to politics and absorb less political information are more likely than the better informed to change their party support.[7] The disturbing implication has seemed

7. These findings have variously explored the links between exposure to communication, the possession of political information, and the degree of the voter's interest or emotional involvement in politics on the one hand and changes of preference between elections, changes within a single campaign, and reported strength of party attachments on the other, although the relationships defined by different pairs of these 'independent' and 'dependent' variables are of course by no means fully interchangeable.

to be that the making and unmaking of governments depends most on those who are least qualified to reach an informed judgement. But the studies which have put forward this ironic view have come under sharp attack, and the relationship between the amount of an elector's knowledge and his propensity to change party has become one of the standard controversies in the field of voting behaviour.[8]

In fact the correlations adduced to show that the poorly informed are most likely to alter their votes have been fairly weak ones. Moreover, Daudt is right in saying that the original evidence had more to do with wobbles within a single election campaign than with those changes between elections on which the lives of governments actually depend.[9] It might also be said that there was something over-simple in the original contention that the propensity to change must always rise, or always fall, with the amount of political information. Converse's sensitive analysis of American re-interview data has suggested a less monotonic relationship; voters with no new input of information are exceedingly stable in their partisanship, even though stability does rise with increased information over most of the range of information found in the American electorate.[10]

The relationship between exposure to political communication and constancy of party preference revealed by our own surveys was in accord with the findings of earlier studies: the less exposed tended to be more changeable. This relationship can be seen in

The earliest American findings go back to the Erie County study in 1940, the earliest British findings to the studies of Greenwich in 1950 and of Bristol North-East in 1951 and 1955. See especially R. S. Milne and H. C. Mackenzie, *Straight Fight*, London, 1954, and *Marginal Seat*, London, 1958.

8. For a sceptical view of the early evidence, see H. Daudt, *Floating Voters and the Floating Vote*, Leyden, 1961, pp. 141–50.

9. ibid., pp. 141–50.

10. See P. E. Converse, 'Information Flow and the Stability of Partisan Attitudes', *Public Opinion Quarterly* 26 (1962); reprinted in A. Campbell, P. E. Converse, W. E. Miller and D. E. Stokes, *Elections and The Political Order*, New York, 1966.

Table 10.4; those who were more attentive to political communication proved more likely to support the same party in both 1964 and

10.4 Stability of Party Preference, 1964–66 by Exposure to Political Communication

	Exposure to political communication[a]				
	Lowest ⟷	⟷	⟷		Highest
Proportion supporting same party in general elections of 1964 and 1966	57%	71%	75%	80%	83%

[a] The index of exposure was formed from the respondent's report of the number of 'channels' – conversation, press, television and radio – by which he followed politics in 1964 and 1966 by classifying respondents according to the larger number of channels reported at the two interviews. Thus someone was placed at the lowest level of exposure if he said at both interviews that he did not follow politics by any channel, at the highest level if he said in at least one interview that he followed politics by all four channels and so on.

1966. Comparable arrays show that the tendency of our respondents to keep to established party ties increased also with the amount of their political information and with the degree of their interest in politics.

Why should greater exposure to political communication be associated with less political change? The classical hypothesis was enunciated by Lazarsfeld and his associates in their 1940 Erie County study. Their hypothesis was that party constancy rises with exposure because the more committed voter is more likely to expose himself to political communication. In this sense the relationship is spurious: both exposure and constancy depend on the strength of the voter's pre-existing party ties. Lazarsfeld and his co-authors also stressed the importance of selective exposure, arguing that the committed voter screens out information that might contradict his preference by concentrating his attention on news sources that he expects to find sympathetic. More recent studies of the process by which the individual reduces 'cognitive dissonance' have suggested a variety of additional means by which the partisan voter copes with discordant political messages.[11] The ways in which new political information can be made to fit old partisan biases are many.

Our interviews offer ample evidence that in Britain the more strongly partisan voter is indeed more likely to expose himself to political information.[12] Table 10.5 illustrates this tendency in terms of attention to politics through the newspapers. Although a number of voters without very strong party attachment report

10.5 Proportion Following Politics in the Newspapers by Strength of Partisan Disposition, 1963

	Strength of Partisan Disposition		
	Not Very Strong	Fairly Strong	Very Strong
Proportion reporting following politics in newspapers	35%	50%	58%

following politics in the press, the link between exposure and party commitment is plain. A similar relationship is found for each of the other sources from which the individual may receive political information.

Despite this evidence the Erie County hypothesis offers a very inadequate explanation of the stable partisanship of the more attentive voter in Britain. If the hypothesis were well-founded we would expect the relationship between higher exposure and higher constancy to disappear as soon as voters were separated according

11. A concise but lucid summary is to be found in R. E. Lane and D. O. Sears, *Public Opinion*, Englewood Cliffs, N.J., 1964.

12. The question of why exposure and strength of partisanship should run together is complex. Many observers have thought that the partisan seeks out news of politics, much as the sports fan seeks out news of his team on the sports page. Blumler and McQuail have made an interesting empirical contribution to this problem by identifying in their samples a group of partisans who seem to find gratification in exposing themselves to political information and reinforcing their existing preferences. See *Television and Politics*, London, 1968, pp. 64 ff.

to the strength of their pre-existing party ties. Indeed, we would expect that, once strength of partisanship had been taken into account, the relationship between exposure and stability would be *reversed* – that among voters with an equivalent tie to party (whether a strong or weak one) those exposed to more political communication would be *more* likely to change their minds.

Such an expectation is not fulfilled. Even among voters whose existing party attachments are especially strong, those exposed to a larger amount of political information are still the less likely to change. The nature of this more complex three-cornered relationship between strength of partisanship, exposure and stability of choice is set out in Table 10.6, where the proportion of voters

10.6 Stability of Party Preference by Strength of Partisanship and Level of Exposure to Mass Media, 1964–66[a]

		Strength of Partisan Self-Image, 1964		
		Very Strong	Fairly Strong	Not Very Strong
Exposure to Political Communication	Highest	83%	71%	78%
		84%	77%	68%
		79%	70%	55%
		78%	62%	59%
	Lowest	53%	58%	49%

[a] Each entry is the proportion of respondents of a given strength of partisanship in 1964 and level of exposure to the mass media in 1964 and 1966 who remained constant in their party preference between the two years. The number of the question used to assess the strength of the individual's partisan self-image is 49b of the 1964 questionnaire. The details of the exposure index are explained in the note to Table 10.4 above. Those who failed to vote in either year are excluded from this array.

whose party preferences remained constant between five levels of exposure to political communication.

This table shows, as might be expected, that those who start with a stronger sense of party attachment are less likely to change their vote; a mild decline, at least, is seen across the entries of each row. But a much more notable aspect of Table 10.6 is the decline of party constancy with a decline of exposure, at each level of party commitment. Within each column it is the least exposed voter who emerges as least stable in his party preference.

What is to be made of this pattern? The fact that changeableness does not increase with exposure, even when strength of partisanship is taken into account, quite evidently requires an explanation involving something more than the Erie County hypothesis. It must be partly due to the increasing redundancy of political messages to those who are exposed to more of them. An elector may be somewhat more disposed to accept a party's current arguments if he hears them six times rather than once. But the impact will be nothing like six times as great. Studies that have relied heavily on measures of sheer exposure have tended to neglect this diminishing marginal utility of communication to the voter. But the fact that its utility will diminish is implied by the very definition of 'information' proposed by modern communications theorists.[13] Presumably in politics as in other fields the capacity of additional messages to dispel the individual's uncertainty decreases as the volume of messages increases.

The diminishing marginal utility of communication helps to explain why the rate of change does not *rise* with exposure; it does nothing to explain why changeableness should actually *fall* with exposure, even when the strength of the voter's partisanship is allowed for. It seems to us that the probable key to this relationship is to be found in the greater elaboration of frameworks for interpreting political information which goes with higher exposure. The elector who pays more attention to politics and government is more likely to have developed frameworks for interpreting new political messages, and this must give a more settled character to

13. See, for example. G. A. Miller, 'What is Information Measurement?' in G. A. Miller, ed., *Mathematics and Psychology*, New York, 1964, and W. R. Garner, *Uncertainty and Structure as Psychological Concepts*, New York, 1962.

his responses to the parties. For example, someone who was knowledgeable about the background to Central African events, including the actions of past British governments, might be less swayed by a dramatic prime ministerial statement on Rhodesia's break-away than someone who had scarcely any prior awareness of the Rhodesian position. More is involved here than the strength of the elector's *affective* ties to party; greater stability may also result from the fuller cognitive development of those who customarily expose themselves to political information.[14]

The image of an information processing machine may catch part of the reality that lies behind these data. The elector who is consistently exposed to information about party politics will form over time a complex circuitry to receive and interpret additional messages of this kind. What is new will be interpreted in terms of connections that have been built up before, and fresh exposure is unlikely to dislodge the elector's choice of party from the framework of beliefs of which it forms part. By contrast, the elector whose exposure is normally less is more easily swayed by the few simple messages that he does receive about the way the Government or the parties affect the things he values. The factory hand who is on short time under a Labour Government may react directly and simply, whereas a banker in the City who fears the Conservatives have mishandled the economy may have a far greater aptitude for interpreting away the implications this might have for his party choice.

There may, however, be circumstances in which the elector with greater exposure is the likelier to change. If political communication were limited to complex messages of the kind that required sophisticated frameworks of interpretation, a strong new input of information might well leave a greater impress among those of

14. If this difference is seen in terms of the amount of past information retained by the elector, we may say that the highly exposed voter, though he receives more new political messages than the less exposed voter, will be less swayed by them because the ratio of new to retained information is lower. Converse argues this point in terms of the physical analogy of the 'force' of new information on a given 'mass' of stored information. See 'Information Flow and the Stability of Partisan Attitudes', in *Elections and the Political Order*, p. 141.

greater exposure. Support is lent to such a view by the very different ways in which the stability of certain attitudes towards issues is related to the extent of the voter's exposure to political information.

Reactions to the issue of Britain's entry into Europe provide a remarkable example of this difference. Throughout the period of our studies the Common Market was an issue that evaded the comprehension of many electors. We have seen in Chapter 8 how many of the replies to a question about entry were 'don't know' and how very many of our respondents fluctuated in their opinion between successive interviews. From the autumn of 1964 to the spring of 1966, however, there was a profound shift of opinion towards going in. Whereas in 1963 and 1964 opinion was fairly evenly divided on the issue, by 1966 three-quarters of those who voiced an opinion wanted Britain in Europe.

This change was very closely related to the extent of the voter's exposure to political information. Figure 10.7 shows that in both years those of higher exposure were more likely to have an opinion and that there was at all levels of exposure an increase in the

10.7 Whether Held Opinion on Common Market, 1964 and 1966, by Level of Exposure to Political Communication

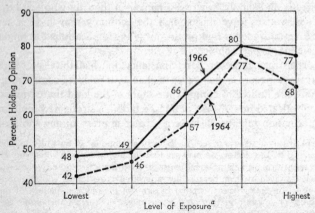

[a] Details of the index of exposure are given in the footnote to Table 10.4.

salience of the issue between the two years, although the overall level of attitude formation was still low in 1966. But the more important aspect of the change lies in the shifts towards Britain's entry at different levels of exposure. Although the Common Market gained ground at all levels between 1964 and 1966 it was among those who were most exposed to political communication that the most spectacular increase occurred. Indeed, the most attentive group swung from an even division in 1964 to a four to one majority for entry in 1966, whereas opinion in the least informed group remained nearly evenly divided, as Figure 10.8 shows.

10.8 Support for Britain's Entry into Common Market, 1964 and 1966, by Level of Exposure to Political Communication

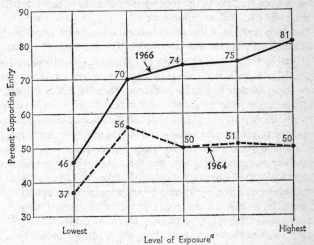

[a] Details of the index of exposure are given in the footnote to Table 10.4.

Nothing could put the case more strongly for the differing effects of exposure on different political attitudes than a comparison of the pattern of change in Figure 10.8 and that in Table 10.4. While the most exposed were swinging most strongly towards Europe, it was the least informed who were swinging most strongly to

Labour. The key to this difference lies in the demands which the two kinds of problem made on the voter. The appraisal of alternative European policies remained throughout the period a task that was beyond much of the electorate. But appraising the parties in terms of the values entailed by various goal-defined issues or other simple grounds of choice was a task that nearly everyone could undertake in some way.

The relationship between exposure and stability of party preference seems to depend very little on what the sources of the individual's information are, and we have thus far treated the various channels of communication as interchangeable. But much of the interest in political communication centres on the impact of particular media. A wide variety of academic and popular hypotheses have been offered about the contrasting influence of press, broadcasting and personal communication.

Our own findings in this field are for the most part surprisingly negative. Indeed, in several ways the media seems to us more interchangeable than is often supposed. Much has been made, for example, of television's greater capacity to convey an impression of political leaders to a mass audience. There is indeed evidence that the public itself thinks that this is part of television's *raison d'être*.[15] From this we might suppose that someone who relies mainly or solely on television would have a different and perhaps fuller image of the party leaders than would someone who relies mainly or solely on the press. But this is not what our evidence suggests. We shall not present detailed findings on this point; but the image of the leaders formed by the average press reader was found to be no less full than that formed by the average television viewer, even when due account is taken of other background factors, such as the voter's education, which might obscure such a difference. Much the same could be said about the absence of differences between newspaper readers and television viewers in relation to their consciousness of issues. The media, of course, do give attention to the same issues, events and men; they borrow extensively from each other; and their audiences have many dispositions and beliefs in common. As a result, the experience of

15. See J. Blumler and D. McQuail, *Television in Politics*, pp. 51 ff.

following politics by print and broadcast is in many ways more alike than different.[16]

The difference may however become a good deal larger as parties and producers develop new arts in the presentation of political television. It seems that television has at times had a sharp impact on the public's evaluation of politics and politicians, as it probably did while 'That Was The Week that Was' gathered its audience in 1962–3 or while the 'Army–McCarthy' hearings held the American public transfixed nine years earlier. If dramatic confrontations of party leaders, as in the Kennedy–Nixon debates, were to become a feature of British elections, television's potential might become more apparent.

The effects of specific mass media which we have explored farthest are those of the popular press. This decision flows mainly from the enduring partisanship of the mass circulation dailies. The persistent angling of their coverage of politics raises a number of interesting questions about the matching of partisanship between paper and reader. The subtle combination of persuasion and self-selection involved in this matching gives the press a distinctive place among the communications media.

Partisan Dispositions and the National Press

Eight national morning newspapers are available at breakfast time to the overwhelming bulk of British households.[17] In 1964 they

16. In this connection it is interesting that one of the most notable instances in which political television has been thought to be influential – the gain of Liberal strength during the 1964 campaign – was more a matter of exposure than of the nature of the medium *per se*. Blumler and McQuail argue that because the Liberals (largely on the basis of their strength at the time broadcasts were allocated two years earlier) were allotted three-fifths as many broadcasts as the larger parties, the exposure of television viewers to the party was suddenly much increased during the 1964 campaign, with a consequent rise in Liberal support. See *Television and Politics*, pp. 197 ff.

17. There are in fact ten serious national dailies produced in London. But because of their specialist nature and the size of their circulation we do not deal here with the *Financial Times* (150,000) or the *Daily Worker/Morning Star* (65,000).

provided 92 per cent of the 18 million morning newspapers sold each day and they reached over 80 per cent of households – a higher proportion than in any other country.[18] Because of this centralization, fully established for a couple of generations, Britain has a smaller total of independent morning newspapers than any comparable nation.[19] On the other hand, the individual citizen, with at least eight different papers reaching his locality, has an unusual range of choice. One consequence of the centralization of the press is that the market tends to be divided up, each paper angling its presentation to a limited segment of the population. And since each paper has its own independent newsgathering and editorial resources, each manages to be fairly strongly differentiated from its rivals in style and in politics.

The mass circulation papers are all explicit in their partisanship, and all to some degree carry their partisanship from their editorial to their news columns. Though seldom slavish in their party orthodoxy, the *Daily Express*, *Daily Mail*, *Daily Telegraph* and *Daily Sketch* are Conservative while the *Daily Mirror* and *Daily Herald/Sun*[20] are Labour. The 'élite' papers, *The Times* and the *Guardian*, are harder to place. In 1964 and 1966 *The Times*, in the end, gave very qualified advice to vote Conservative while the *Guardian* abandoned its traditional Liberalism to ask support for the Labour Party.

A newspaper's readers tend to be remarkably faithful to it. Most people read only one morning newspaper and go on buying it for

18. In 1964 there were seventeen provincial morning newspapers (in no case with a circulation of more than 130,000). There were seventy evening newspapers, with a total circulation of over eight million, which tended to be primarily local in their coverage. There were also eight Sunday morning newspapers, with a total circulation of 24 million. The circulation of newspapers per head of population is 66 per cent greater in Britain than in the United States. For morning newspapers it is three times as great.

19. One reason for our special focus on the morning press in this chapter is that electors give it precedence over the other newspapers. While 60 per cent of our respondents claimed to have followed the campaign in their morning newspaper only 11 per cent mentioned a Sunday paper as a political source and only 6 per cent an evening newspaper.

20. The *Daily Herald* was transmuted into the *Sun* on September 15, 1964.

very long periods. Morning newspaper circulations, despite vast promotion efforts, only edge up or down by, at most, a few per cent a year. In 1964 the circulation of every national daily was within 10 per cent of where it had been four years earlier, apart from the *Daily Sketch* (down 20 per cent) and the *Guardian* (up 20 per cent). Although it is a simple thing to change one's delivery order at the newsagent or pick up a different paper at the station bookstall, few people do so. Less than 4 per cent of our sample admitted to ever having switched morning newspapers. Indeed, over successive interviews only the distribution of characteristics such as age and sex showed greater stability than readership of the morning dailies.

What bearing does the partisanship of a newspaper have on the partisan preferences of its readers? It is clear, to begin with, that the partisan bias of the newspapers is reflected fairly faithfully in the biases of their readers. In every case, as Table 10.9 shows, a preponderant group of readers of the mass circulation dailies

10.9 Partisanship of Newspaper Readers, 1963

Readers' Partisanship	Conservative				Labour		Less Committed	
	Tele-graph	Sketch	Mail	Express	Mirror[a]	Herald/Sun	Times	Guardian
Conservative	78	54	48	48	18	9	60	23
Labour	9	29	28	38	66	83	20	33
Liberal	6	13	18	10	11	3	10	37
Other or none	7	4	6	4	5	5	10	7
	100% (n = 111)	100% (n = 48)	100% (n = 190)	100% (n = 434)	100% (n = 445)	100% (n = 128)	100% (n = 10)	100% (n = 30)

[a] This figure includes *Daily Record,* the Glasgow version of the *Daily Mirror.*

shared the paper's traditional partisanship – overwhelmingly in the case of the *Telegraph* and the *Sun* and by a substantial margin in every other case except that of the *Guardian* (which has a long Liberal tradition). If only those who had read their paper for ten years or more were considered, the proportion of readers favouring the paper's choice of party was higher in almost every case. The proportion of Conservative-minded *Express* readers rose from 48 per cent to 52 per cent; and for the *Telegraph* from 78 per cent to 82 per cent. The proportion of Labour-inclined *Sun* readers rose from 83 per cent to 86 per cent. The two exceptions are not surprising: the veteran readers of the *Guardian* appeared unpersuaded by the paper's switch to Labour support – even more of them were Liberal. The veteran readers of the *Mirror* were not more Labour-inclined than the new young readers the paper had won in the last ten years.

The combined circulation of the Conservative papers exceeded by half that of the Labour papers. Whether this gave the Conservatives an advantage, and if so whether it was a short-term or a long-term one, are questions which we can answer only by considering the effects of reading a partisan newspaper. It is none the less true that more than a fifth of Labour's supporters in 1963 were exposed to a Conservative newspaper, whereas only a tenth of the Conservatives' supporters were exposed to a Labour paper. Because the *Mirror*'s angling towards youth is balanced by the elderly readership bequeathed to the *Sun* by the *Herald*, there is little difference of age between the readership of the two groups of partisan newspapers.

The cross-reading of newspapers favouring the other party is complemented by the phenomenon of people who do not recognize that their newspaper is partisan. We asked readers of each paper which party it supported. Very few gave the 'wrong' party, but, apart from readers of the *Telegraph* and the *Herald*, only a bare majority, if that, named the 'correct' party, as Table 10.10 shows. Well over a third of all readers thought that their paper was neutral.

The profiles of reader partisanship in Table 10.9 and of attributed party bias in Table 10.10 bear obvious resemblances. The papers with the most purely partisan followings, the *Telegraph* and the *Herald*/*Sun*, are also those whose partisan angle is seen most clearly. The relationship between the reader's own agreement with his paper and his detection of party bias is summarized in Table 10.11 opposite which shows that it is the readers who agree with their newspaper's bias who are most likely to perceive it. But the table also shows that many readers who see clearly what their

10.10 Reader's Recognition of His Newspaper's Partisanship, 1963

Attributed Partisanship	Tele-graph	Sketch	Mail	Express	Mirror	Herald/ Sun	Times	Guardian
Conservative	72%	25%	52%	44%	1%	—	30%	—
Labour	—	11	2	4	52	76%	—	17%
Liberal	1	2	2	1	—	—	—	37
None	24	54	36	42	34	18	70	43
Don't know	3	8	8	9	13	6	—	3
	100% (n = 111)	100% (n = 48)	100% (n = 191)	100% (n = 434)	100% (n = 448)	100% (n = 127)	100% (n = 10)	100% (n = 30)

paper's bias is do not themselves agree with it. Conscious cross-reading is the daily habit of a good many British electors.

All of this scarcely begins to unravel the problem of the press's partisan influence, a problem that is made more difficult by the fact that readership and partisanship may both reach far back into the past. The distinctive partisan colouring of those who read the morning dailies could be taken as evidence of the press's influence only if it is clear that the choice of a newspaper preceded the choice of a party. But it is, of course, quite possible either for a paper to be chosen for its partisanship or for the choice of both paper and

10.11 Detection of Newspaper Bias by Agreement of Reader's Partisanship with His Newspaper's Partisanship, 1963

	Reader has partisanship consistent with newspaper's	Reader does not have partisanship consistent with newspaper's
Reader perceives newspaper's partisanship	57%	44%
Reader does not perceive newspaper's partisanship	43	56
	100% (n = 812)	100% (n = 333)

party to reflect the influence of a family or class milieu. In such a case, the press might play a role in conserving a party tie; it would not have created it.

These alternative possibilities supply the only plausible explanations for the way in which parents' partisanship is echoed in their children's adult choice of newspaper, as shown by Table 10.12. The reflection of early family partisanship in newspapers taken by voters from politicized homes casts a new light on the political

10.12 Partisanship of Present Newspaper by Party of Childhood Family, 1963

		Family was[a]		
		Conservative	Other	Labour
Respondent	Conservative newspaper	66%	55%	35%
Now	Labour newspaper	22	36	55
Reads[b]	Other	12	9	10
		100%	100%	100%
		($n = 393$)	($n = 589$)	($n = 405$)

[a] 'Conservative' or 'Labour' homes are those in which both parents had this partisanship or one did and the other had none. 'Other' homes are those of mixed, Liberal or no partisanship.

[b] 'Conservative' or 'Labour' readers are those seeing only newspapers from one partisan group. 'Other' readers are those who see newspapers from both or neither party group.

distinctness of those who read the morning dailies, since the correlation seen here is the work of factors that will also increase this distinctness without any need for newspapers to have influenced their readers. The correlation shown in Table 10.12 cannot result from the voter's family having influenced the paper's editors. And today's editors cannot have influenced the family in the voter's childhood. The correlation is most likely to have been produced by the family's passing on a partisanship which the child has matched by his choice of paper, or by its passing on a more general social location to which both paper and party are appropriate. If the voter's report on his family is accepted, it is clear that newspapers often profit from, rather than shape, their readers' party ties.

We should not, however, discount the press's role in conserving partisanship. When the agreement of child with parent is examined separately for those who read a paper consistent with their parent's party and those who do not, as is done in Table 10.13, we see an impressive difference in the survival of parental partisanship

10.13 Party Support by Partisanship of Respondent's Family and Respondent's Present Newspaper, 1963

		Family was[a]			
		Conservative Respondent's newspaper is[b]		Labour Respondent's newspaper is[b]	
		Conservative	Labour	Conservative	Labour
Respondent's	Conservative	79%	44%	25%	5%
Own	Labour	13	42	62	86
Party	Other[c]	8	14	13	9
		100%	100%	100%	100%
		(n = 259)	(n = 85)	(n = 141)	(n = 221)

[a] See fn. a, Table 10.12.
[b] See fn. b, Table 10.12.
[c] Includes Liberals, other parties and voters without a party.

according to the child's current reading habits. Too simple a view ought not to be taken of these findings; once again the adult may have kept or changed his partisan reading habits to accord with his evolving partisan beliefs or his changed social conditions. None the less, it is difficult to think that the conserving and reinforcing effect of the partisan press has nothing to do with these differences.

What is more, the formative role of the press may be somewhat larger in the case of voters whose political legacy from their family was mixed or relatively weak. Table 10.14 divides such people by whether they now read a Conservative or Labour newspaper. The cleavage in the current partisanship of these two groups is at

10.14 Party Support by Partisanship of Newspaper Among Persons from Other than Conservative and Labour Families, 1963

		Partisanship of Newspaper[a]	
		Conservative	Labour
Respondent's	Conservative	48%	14%
Own	Labour	28	66
Partisanship	Other[b]	24	20
		100%	100%
		(n = 321)	(n = 231)

[a] 'Conservative' or 'Labour' readers are those who see no morning paper except one or more from their own partisan group.
[b] Includes Liberals, other parties and voters without a party.

least suggestive of the influence of the press in forming or sustaining a party tie.

The ambiguities which surround the analysis of the press's role in forming and changing party ties are less severe when we turn to short-term movements of partisanship. The chance to dispel some of these uncertainties in treating shorter-term changes was greatly enhanced by the fact that our study bridged a period when newspaper partisanship fluctuated greatly in intensity if not in direction. In the winter of 1962–3 the national press became unprecedentedly critical of the Conservative Government. Its attacks on the handling of general public issues may have owed something to a particular grievance that had grown up between Fleet Street and Downing Street. Mr Macmillan seems to have felt that he had been hounded by quite unjustified press innuendos into accepting the resignation of Mr Galbraith, a junior minister indirectly involved in the Vassall spy scandal. The Radcliffe tribunal which the Prime Minister set up to inquire into the affair was given terms of reference which were interpreted by much of Fleet Street as a mandate to pillory the press, and in the course of the hearings two reporters were sent to prison for refusing to reveal their sources. Journalistic *amour propre* was involved and it was widely argued that the splash treatment given to the Profumo scandal in June

1963 had some elements of revenge in it. Whether or not that was the case, it is plain that the Conservatives, who could normally rely on reasonably sympathetic coverage in most of the national press, were at an exceptional disadvantage throughout the year 1963.

By 1964 the tide had turned. The Conservative press had, with the disappearance of Mr Macmillan, abandoned any vendetta it may have had against the Government. There is no doubt that those exposed to the mass media in 1964 were receiving substantially less anti-Conservative material than in 1963. The difference can be demonstrated by a tabulation of the tone and number of political lead stories and editorial comments. The results of such a content analysis are presented in Table 10.15. As the table shows, in Conservative papers the balance of party advantage was not too unequal in 1963, but by 1964, and above all in the month before the election, it was almost as rare to find an article giving comfort to the other side in a Conservative as in a Labour paper. The picture of the Conservative papers rallying to their traditional party attachment is shown graphically in Figure 10.16, which combines the measurements for the four Conservative papers and two Labour papers. The graph makes clear that we have chanced upon a kind of 'natural experiment' under which the readers of Conservative newspapers were exposed to very different political coverage in mid-1963 and in late 1964, whereas readers of Labour papers were treated to an almost perfectly unrelieved pro-Labour view in both periods. Since the Conservatives did in fact gain in support during these fifteen months, it is natural to wonder whether this variation in stimulus was not in part responsible.

The Press and Partisan Change

We may assess the short-run influence of the press by examining changes of preference among readers of Tory and Labour papers. These changes give unmistakable evidence of the stronger attraction which a party that is favoured by a given paper has for the paper's readers. Those who already support the party are more likely to remain steadfast; those not already supporters are more likely to become so. The nature of these findings can be suggested

10.15 Partisanship in Front-Page Articles and Editorial Comments[a]

| | Conservative Newspapers | | | | | | | | Labour Newspapers | | | |
| | Telegraph | | Sketch | | Mail | | Express | | Herald/Sun | | Mirror | |
	Pro Govt	Anti Govt	Pro Govt	Anti Govt	Pro Govt	Anti Govt	Pro Govt	Anti Govt	Pro Govt	Anti Govt	Pro Govt	Anti Govt
Lead story												
March–May 1963	10	3	2	2	4	4	3	8	0	10	1	4
July 15—October 15, 1964	13	4	10	0	6	2	8	1	0	12	1	14
September 15—October 15, 1964	8	0	8	0	4	2	3	1	0	9	1	9
Other front page story												
March–May 1963	7	5	1	3	5	2	0	6	0	6	0	1
July 15—October 15, 1964	19	2	4	0	9	1	8	1	0	7	0	6
September 15—October 15, 1964	11	1	3	0	5	1	6	1	0	4	0	3
Editorial												
March–May 1963	18	3	5	2	8	4	15	16	2	15	3	9
July 15—October 15, 1964	35	0	17	0	18	2	23	3	0	30	0	11
September 15—October 15, 1964	17	0	9	0	14	0	11	2	0	13	0	3

[a] The figures in this table are for the number of stories of each type which appeared in each paper in each time period. For the purposes of this table only articles with fairly specific party connotations have been counted. Even some which bore on contentious questions but were strictly neutral in tone have been excluded. Articles suggesting that the Government had done something praiseworthy or that contained bad news about the opposition's fortunes are classed as pro-government. Articles that suggested the reverse are classed as anti-government.

10.16 Direction of Partisanship of Editorials and News Stories of Labour and Conservative Newspapers, 1963 and 1964[a]

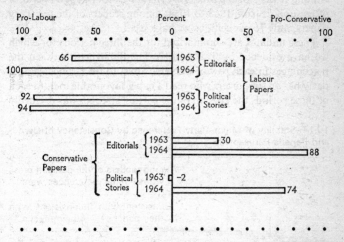

[a] Each bar of the figure is formed by subtracting the percentage of editorials or political stories in a given period that was inconsistent with the papers' normal partisanship from the percentage consistent with this partisanship. '1963' refers to the three-month period from March 1 to May 31, '1964' to the three-month period from July 15 to October 15. For this figure we have combined 'lead' stories and other front-page political stories.

by the physical analogy of magnetic force. Readers who are already close to their paper's party will tend to be held close; those at some distance will tend to be pulled towards it.

The tendency of a reader to keep to his newspaper's partisanship is confirmed repeatedly in our studies. For example, among readers of the Tory press who favoured one of the two main parties in the summer of 1963, the Conservatives kept 86 per cent of their support through to the General Election of 1964, whereas Labour kept only 76 per cent of theirs. This difference does not simply reflect a general trend to the Conservatives during this period, since the Conservatives retained at the 1964 election the support of only 63 per cent of readers of the Labour press who were Tory in the summer of 1963. Moreover, an exact parallel of this finding can be seen in Labour's stronger hold in this period on its supporters who were also readers of a Labour paper. Among readers of the *Mirror* or *Herald* Labour kept 84 per cent of its support from 1963 to 1964; among readers of the five Tory papers, only 76 per cent, as we have seen.

These findings are summarized for the three periods for which we have evidence by Table 10.17. The differences between the percentages in each row of the table attest to the stronger hold a party has on supporters who read a paper favourable to it. In each of these periods the erosion of the parties' strength was decidedly

10.17 Stability of Major-Party Preference by Consistency of Own and Paper's Partisanship

| | | Among readers of the partisan press whose initial preferences were | |
		Consistent with their paper's	Inconsistent with their paper's
Proportion Retaining Preference From	1959 to 1963	83%	63%
	1963 to 1964	85%	73%
	1964 to 1966	86%	81%

more marked among supporters who were exposed to papers whose partisanship contradicted their own.

There is equally general evidence of the dynamic attraction a party has for uncommitted electors who read a paper favourable to it. For example, among electors who did not have a major-party preference in the summer of 1963 but who ended up voting for one of the major parties in 1964, the Conservatives won a substantial majority of votes among readers of the Tory press and Labour a substantial majority among readers of the Labour press. And the voter who made a straight switch between the major parties in this period was more likely to have gone from Labour to the Conservatives if he read a Tory paper and from the Conservatives to Labour if he read a Labour paper.

These findings are summarized for the three intervals of change

within our studies by Table 10.18 and 10.19. The entries of the
rows of Table 10.18 show that newly-crystallized party preferences

10.18 Crystallization of Preference Among Readers of Partisan Press Who Were Previously Uncommitted

Period of crystallization	Moved towards their paper's party	Moved towards opposite party	Totals
1959–63	66%	34	100%
1963–64	63%	37	100%
1964–66	73%	27	100%

in each of these periods tended to follow the party bias of the
reader's paper; those who ended one of these periods in a major-
party camp, but who began it outside either camp, were more
likely to have joined the Conservatives if they read a Tory paper,
Labour if they read a Labour paper. The entries of Table 10.19

10.19 Movements of Support between Major Parties Among Readers of the Partisan Press

		Among major-party supporters whose initial preferences were	
		Inconsistent with their paper's	Consistent with their paper's
Proportion Switching	1959 to 1963	19%	4%
Between Major	1963 to 1964	11%	5%
Parties	1964 to 1966	10%	3%

make the complementary point that the likelihood of an elector's
leaving one camp for the other was in each of these periods
measurably greater if he were moving towards the party supported
by his paper rather than away from it. These findings convey a

clear sense of the greater pull of a party for the elector whose normal reading practices expose him to a paper favouring it.

On the other hand, these findings do not imply that the readers of each group of partisan papers are moving towards a single, homogeneous preference. In fact, the process of change implied by Tables 10.17, 10.18 and 10.19 will be in rough equilibrium when the division of party preference within each group of readers falls a good deal short of homogeneity. To clarify the reasons for this let us divide the readers of papers with a common editorial slant into two groups: those whose preferences agreed with their paper's and those whose preferences did not – either because they supported the other party or the Liberals or because they did not have a preference. Let us denote by m_1 the relative proportion or mass of readers falling in the first of these groups, by m_2 the mass falling into the second. And let us denote by p_1 the probability that a reader who supports his paper's party will move away from it over a given period and by p_2 the probability that a reader who is not aligned with his paper's partisanship will become so over this same period. In other words, we have reduced a fairly complex set of changes to the simplest kind of process, one involving only two 'states' and two 'transition probabilities' describing the rates of change between these states.

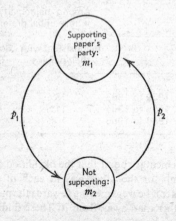

What the evidence of Tables 10.17, 10.18 and 10.19 tells us is that p_2 tends to exceed p_1, that is, that non-supporters tend to move towards their paper's party at a higher rate than supporters move away from it. This relationship is of course very much prey to the influence of short-run electoral tides, which typically flow in both readership groups at once. Unless there were large-scale and appropriately timed transfers of readers between the newspaper groups themselves, or unless change were to come entirely from non-readers of the party press (ideas that are implausible on their face), swings of party fortune could be achieved only by a raising and lowering of p_1 and p_2, and we shall see that these changes tend to occur in both readership groups together. But these swings do not obscure the underlying tendency of the reader of a partisan newspaper to move towards, rather than away from, his paper's party.

And yet this tendency may not increase the partisan one-sidedness of a readership group at all. The key to this apparent puzzle is that among such a group those who are already aligned with their paper's editorial view are more numerous than those who are not. Hence, a lower *rate* of defection can produce an actual *number* of defectors that is as large as the number of the party's new recruits from readers who were previously not aligned with it. The way such offsetting movements can yield a rough dynamic equilibrium is illustrated by changes of partisanship among readers of the Labour press between the general elections of 1964 and 1966. The chance that a reader who failed to vote Labour in 1964 would support the party in 1966 was almost twice as large as the chance that a reader who voted Labour in 1964 would fail to do so in 1966. And yet, since the readers of the Labour press who were already aligned with the party were twice as numerous as those who were not, the resulting transfers of strength to and from Labour were almost perfectly offsetting. These exchanges are summarized in terms of the statistical quantities we have previously defined by Figure 10.20, where the virtual equality of the products p_1m_1 and p_2m_2 indicates that Labour's strength among this group of press readers remained in rough equilibrium over this period. A little less than a tenth of the entire group of readers moved away

10.20 Transfers of Strength to and from Labour Party Among Readers of Labour Newspapers Between General Elections of 1964 and 1966

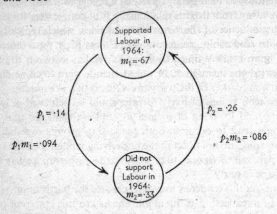

from Labour; about the same fraction of all readers moved towards Labour.

The equality of numbers flowing in the two directions by no means implies that these newspapers are without influence on party strength. The dynamic equilibrium which these flows sustain is one under which the proportion (m_1) of readers aligned with their paper's party exceeds the proportion (m_2) of readers not so aligned and greatly exceeds the proportion (not more than a part of m_2) who are aligned with the opposite major party. If the papers were to somehow *de*magnetize the parties, the probability (p_1) of defection would rise; there would be a massive flow from m_1 to m_2 and equilibrium would be restored at very different levels of part strength. Such at least is the hypothesis.

It is here that we can usefully return to the behaviour of the Conservative press in the dark days of 1963 and examine the flows of party strength in the specific periods for which we have evidence. Is it possible that by 1963 the Tory papers had to some degree 'demagnetized' the parties for their readers, with a consequent

loss of Conservative strength? When we reconstruct the partisan
shifts of their readers between 1959 and 1963, the deterioration of
Tory strength is indeed impressive. To begin with, and quite
against the general pattern of the findings we have presented,
the rate of defection from the Conservatives was actually higher
than the rate of the attraction among readers of the Tory press.
As Figure 10.21 shows, the probability that a reader who had
supported the party in 1959 would leave it by 1963 was almost

**10.21 Transfers of Strength to and from Conservative Party
Among Readers of Conservative Newspapers, 1959 to 1963**

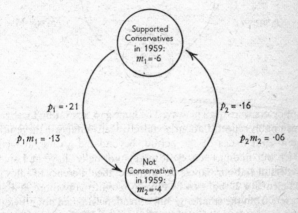

Supported
Conservatives
in 1959:
$m_1 = \cdot 6$

$p_1 = \cdot 21$

$p_2 = \cdot 16$

$p_1 m_1 = \cdot 13$

$p_2 m_2 = \cdot 06$

Not
Conservative
in 1959:
$m_2 = \cdot 4$

half again higher than the probability that a reader who had
not supported the Conservatives in 1959 would be ready to do so
in 1963. Applied to the preponderant share which the Tories had
of such readers in 1959, this desertion rate produced a substantial
haemorrhaging of party strength.

Any idea that this was the only portal through which the
Conservatives' strength ebbed away during this period is, however,
dispelled by comparable figures for readers of the Labour press.
As Figure 10.22 shows, the rate at which readers of Labour newspapers who were not Labour voters in 1959 were drawn to the
party by 1963 vastly exceeded the rate at which the party's 1959

10.22 Transfers of Strength to and from Labour Party Among Readers of Labour Newspapers, 1959 to 1963

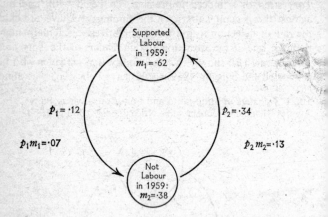

supporters were drawn away. The huge gap separating these rates presumably reflects Labour's 'objective' advantages in the political events and issues of the period, beyond the greater attraction which our findings suggest it might 'normally' have had among readers of Labour papers. In any case, the difference of rates was sufficient for Labour to be able to recruit many more new supporters from the smaller group of readers who had not previously supported it than it lost through defections from the much larger group of readers who had previously supported it. The Conservative press may have demagnetized the parties for their readers and increased the loss of Tory strength. But there was also a parallel gain of Labour strength among readers of the Labour papers.

We may gain added insight into the effects of the unusually mixed treatment of politics in the Conservative press by early 1963 if we compare the rates of change of the 1959–63 period with those of the 1963–4 period. This comparison, as set out in Table 10.23, does show a remarkable shift of the rates of Conservative gain and loss among readers of the Tory press. In the earlier period, as we

10.23 Rates of Change of Party Preference Among Readers of the Partisan Press

	1959–63	1963–64
Among readers of Conservative papers:		
Probability of Conservatives losing supporter (p_1)	0·21	0·14
Probability of Conservatives gaining supporter (p_2)	0·16	0·21
Among readers of Labour papers:		
Probability of Labour losing supporter (p_1)	0·12	0·15
Probability of Labour gaining supporter (p_2)	0·34	0·30

have seen, the rate of defection sufficiently exceeded the rate of renewal to produce a sharp Tory loss. But as the line taken by the Conservative press hardened over the 1963–4 period there was a dramatic reversal of these proportions. The rate of gain did not exceed the rate of new loss by enough in this period to account for the greater number of readers already aligned with the Conservatives and produce a net gain for the Tories. Here again, the advantage which a favoured party enjoyed in terms of rates of change did no more than sustain its strength, and we shall not find in this group the source of the mild Tory revival before the 1964 election. And yet the shifting rates of change among readers of the Conservative papers – contrasting with the more stable rates among readers of Labour papers – do suggest that the disaffection of the Tory press somewhat demagnetized the parties for their readers and permitted a short-term run-off of Conservative support in the middle years of the 1959 Parliament. The evidence of this particular loss strengthens the view of the importance which the partisan papers customarily have in sustaining their party's preponderant support among their readers.

We may therefore attribute to the press some role in changing the relative strength of the parties in the short run as well as in forming and conserving more enduring allegiances. Yet it would be wrong to see most short-term political changes as the product of short-term angling by the press. The parallel movements of party strength among readers of both groups of partisan newspapers suggest that readers are absorbing more than their editor's bias. A great deal of common information flows out to the mass British electorate through media which are heavily overlapping and which are describing political issues and events that they have seldom done anything to shape.

Part Three

	CHANGES OF ALIGNMENT	TRANSIENT VARIATIONS
CONSTRUCTION		
APPLICATION	▨	

11 The Evolution of Party Strength

Few party systems in the world have as long a past or as settled a character as Britain's. Yet the last two generations have brought profound changes both in the basis of political alignment and in the identity of the leading parties. This span of time has seen the Liberals displaced as a major party after having held power intermittently over the whole of the preceding century. The place of the Liberals was taken by Labour, which became the second major party after one world war and an equal contestant for power after another. Yet we ought not to assume too easily that Labour inherited the Liberals' mass support. The transition was accompanied by a fundamental change in the basis of party allegiance, especially the rise of the class alignment which has dominated electoral politics since the interwar period. As we trace the evolution of party strength the pattern of change may at times prove unexpected.

The broadest facts of the evolution of party strength are set out in Figure 11.1, which shows the share of the major-party vote won by the three parties at each general election in this century. The figure makes clear that two leading parties have always possessed the overwhelming bulk of votes, except in the 1920s. The century indeed divides in these terms into three distinct phases: the pre-1914 struggle of Conservatives and Liberals, the period of party realignment in the 1920s and the phase of clear-cut Conservative–Labour contest which has now lasted for forty years.

There are elements here both of continuity and of change. The collapse of the Liberals from a dominant to a minor role emerges clearly enough, together with the notable fact that their vote as a minor party has fluctuated proportionately more than when they were serious contenders for power. But support for the

Conservative Party appears almost deceptively constant. The Conservatives, strikingly undamaged by their debacles in 1906 and 1945, and indeed 1966, have scarcely strayed outside a range of 40 to 50 per cent, apart from a peak in the early 1930s. After its upward leap at the end of the First World War the Labour Party kept on a 30 to 40 per cent plateau until its further leap upwards in the Second World War. Since then it has never exceeded 50 per cent nor fallen below 44 per cent of the three-party vote.

In this stability of voting there have of course been some fairly sharp changes. Five elections of this century, though none more recent than 1945, have seen one party's share of votes go up or down by 10 per cent or more. In each of these cases, 1906, 1918, 1924, 1931 and 1945, a gain or loss occurred which tended to persist through subsequent elections, reflecting the processes of realignment which have remade the party system over successive decades.

As we describe change over so long a period we must inevitably emphasize the procession of cohorts through the electorate. Almost the entire electorate of 1906 had gone by 1966, and of those who were qualified to vote in the latter year, more than half were too young to have voted before the Second World War. Partisan parents may of course transcend their own mortality through the allegiances they form in their children, as we saw in Chapter 3. But the years of adolescence and early adulthood are also ones in which the young are unusually open to the forces that are shaping a partisan realignment, and these forces leave some impress in the later phases of the political life cycle as well. Moreover, some parents achieve more political immortality than others by having more children; when birth rates differ by party, as they have in modern Britain, fertility is itself a factor in partisan change. As we trace the evolution of party strength we shall want ultimately to consider each of the four kinds of demographic and political processes to which we called attention at the close of Chapter 3 – fertility, the socialization of the young, the conversion of the aging, and mortality. We may begin this reconstruction of the past by seeing what a comparison of the cohorts in the present electorate can reveal about the trends of party support over recent decades, especially the displacement of the Liberals by

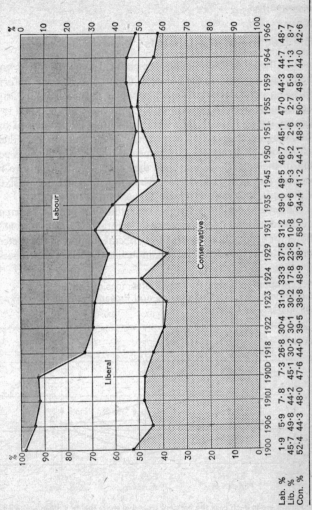

11.1 Labour, Liberal and Conservative Proportions of Total Votes Cast in General Elections 1900 to 1966

	1900	1906	1910J	1910D	1918	1922	1923	1924	1929	1931	1935	1945	1950	1951	1955	1959	1964	1966
Lab. %	1·9	5·9	7·8	7·3	26·8	30·4	31·0	33·3	37·5	31·2	39·0	49·5	46·7	45·1	47·0	44·3	44·7	48·7
Lib. %	45·7	49·8	44·2	45·1	30·2	30·1	30·2	17·8	23·8	10·8	6·6	9·3	9·2	2·6	2·7	5·9	11·3	8·7
Con. %	52·4	44·3	48·0	47·6	44·0	39·5	38·8	48·9	38·7	58·0	34·4	41·2	44·1	48·3	50·3	49·8	44·0	42·6
	100·0	100·0	100·0	100·0	100·0	100·0	100·0	100·0	100·0	100·0	100·0	100·0	100·0	100·0	100·0	100·0	100·0	100·0

Labour and the new balance of strength between Labour and the Conservatives.

The Decline of the Liberals

In 1906 the Liberals dominated the political scene. They had won the largest majority in the House of Commons since the Reform Bill; even without their parliamentary allies, the new Labour Party, they secured over 50 per cent of the popular vote. Less than two decades later, although they were still getting 30 per cent of the vote, they were struggling desperately for survival. In 1929 their last serious challenge for governmental power won them 23 per cent of the vote. Since that time they have never risen above 12 per cent and in 1951 and 1955, when they fought barely a sixth of the seats, they sank to a mere 2·5 per cent of the vote.

The Liberal decline is vividly sketched by the past and current preferences found in our successive electoral cohorts. Figure 11.2 shows for each cohort the trend of Liberal support in the preferences of our respondents' fathers, in their own earliest preferences,

11.2 Proportion Liberal of Party Preferences of Fathers, Respondents' Earliest Preferences, and Present Partisan Self-images, by Cohort[a]

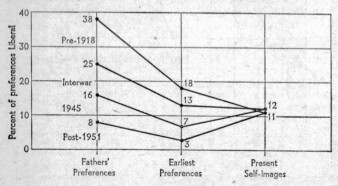

[a] Figures are in each case the per cent Liberal of those within a given group who held a preference, excluding those who had none or for whom none could be recalled.

and in the partisan self-images they held at the time of our studies. The convergence of Liberalism in these four cohorts towards a common level in the 1960s is remarkable. From wide differences of Liberal support in the fathers' generation,[1] which are still reflected in the respondents' own earliest preferences, Liberal strength in each cohort moved towards a proportion just above a tenth in the present partisan self-images. In the case of the two youngest cohorts (voters who entered the electorate in the aftermath of the Second World War and those who entered in the 1950s and 1960s), this result required a net increase in Liberal strength between the respondents' earliest and present preferences; in the youngest cohort it required a net increase over the Liberalism remembered among fathers as well. But in the electorate as a whole the pattern is one of Liberal decline between father and child and across the cohorts.

Where the support released by this decline went is of course a central problem of British electoral history. Those who left the Liberalism of their fathers or of their own earliest years must have gone elsewhere, even if only to non-voting or non-alignment; a law of the conservation of political matter must apply to movements of this sort.[2] Our evidence on this question is set out in Table 11.3, which shows the partisan self-images of those who recalled their fathers as Liberal or who gave their own earliest preferences as Liberal. The table makes clear how strong is the continuity be-

1. There is evidence that the recall of partisanship by children somewhat understates the proportion of Liberalism in the fathers' generation. We would expect some of those whose fathers were in fact Liberal to have failed to recall a party preference for their fathers, who were therefore excluded from the percentage for fathers in Figure 11.2. This tendency probably has little effect on the pattern of Liberal decline shown here, but we shall be concerned at a number of points in the subsequent analysis with the effects that this frailty of recall can have on our findings.

2. Such a law must of course apply to changes over the life cycle of a given cohort, but is inexact as applied to changes between generations, since some Liberal fathers will have died without leaving progeny whose partisanship must be taken into account and others will have reproduced themselves more than once. For the moment we defer a consideration of the problems introduced by differential fertility.

11.3 Partisan Self-Images Held by Those Whose Fathers Were
Liberal or Whose Own Earliest Preferences Were Liberal

| | Among those whose | |
	Fathers Were Liberal	Earliest Preferences Were Liberal
Partisan Self-Image Is		
Conservative	40%	25%
Labour	34	19
Liberal	23	53
None	3	3
	100% (*n* = 300)	100% (*n* = 165)

tween historic Liberalism and Liberal support in the 1960s. More
than half of those whose own earliest preferences were Liberal still
thought of themselves as Liberal, and nearly a quarter of those
who recalled their fathers as Liberal still held such a self-image.

The outstanding feature of this table, however, is its evidence on
the flows of Liberal strength into the other parties. Despite the
fact that the Labour Party succeeded to the Liberals' place as the
Conservatives' main opponent in the British party system, only a
minority of historic Liberal support went to Labour. Indeed, the
proportion that went to the Conservatives is found to be greater
both among those whose fathers were remembered as Liberal and
among those who gave their own earliest preferences as Liberal.
This is true despite the fact that our information was gathered in an
era of peak Labour strength in the early 1960s, when many of those
whose partisan self-images were weakly formed might have been
expected to call themselves Labour. The fact that a greater share
of Liberal strength went over to the party's historic opponents, the
Conservatives, rather than to Labour as the successor party of the
left, provides an outstanding instance of the uncertainties of
the conclusions that are often drawn from historical series of the
sort set out in Figure 11.1.

The analysis carried through in Chapters 5 and 6 suggests, however, that the rise of the class alignment must have divided the
Liberals' support along class lines. If we disaggregate the data of
Table 11.3 we find quite different flows within the middle and
working classes. This separation is shown in Figure 11.4. The two
lines at the top of the figure show the dominant flows of Liberal
support to the Conservatives in the middle class and to Labour in

11.4 Proportions Conservative and Labour Among Earliest
Preferences and Current Partisan Self-Images of Those Whose
Fathers Were Liberal, by Occupational Grade[a]

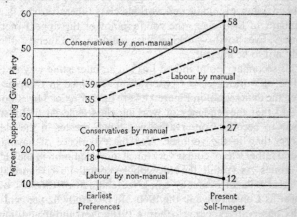

[a] Figures are the proportions supporting a given party among earliest or current
preferences for all parties, including Liberals. Non-manual is defined as occupational
grades I–IV, manual as occupational grades V–VI. The separation of occupational
grades bteween grades III and IV would make almost no difference to these results.

the working class. These flows are already evident in the earliest
preferences reported by these children of Liberal fathers and are
more pronounced in their current party self-images. Indeed, by the
time of our study at least half of those in each class group of historic
Liberals had aligned themselves with the party that was dominant
within their own class.

By contrast the support in each group evoked by the party of the opposite class is relatively weak. But it is not entirely missing. Indeed, the greater appeal of the Conservatives for the children of working class Liberals is part of the reason why the Conservatives have inherited more of the Liberals' former support than Labour. Among middle class children of Liberal parents support for Labour is negligible: not much more than a tenth of such respondents called themselves Labour even in the strongly Labour years of the early 1960s. But among the working class children of Liberal parents Conservative support was far from negligible: more than a quarter of such respondents called themselves Conservatives in this strongly Labour period. Although the main point of Figure 11.4 is the flow of middle and working class Liberals to the party dominant in their class, the counterpoint of the appeal of the Conservatives to the working class children of Liberal fathers ought not to be missed.

This secondary point indeed links in an interesting way to the decline of working class Conservatism examined in Chapter 5. When the data set out in Figure 11.4 are further refined by cohort, we find that the tendency of working class children of Liberal fathers to become Conservative was much greater in the older cohorts than in the younger. And the experience of having a Liberal father was of course very much more common in the older age groups. As a result, the older cohorts contribute to Figure 11.4 the great bulk of manually employed children of Liberals who appear as Conservative in the 1960s. In fact, fully 62 per cent of such Conservatives belong to the pre-1918 cohort and an additional 28 per cent to the inter-war cohort. By contrast not more than 9 per cent belong to the 1945 cohort and a mere 1 per cent to the post-1951 cohort. We are, in other words, speaking of a process of conversion which in most cases lay years in the past.

Such a perspective reinforces our interpretation of the greater Conservatism of older working class electors set out in Chapter 5. Most working class Conservatives who had had Liberal parents were confronted when young by a party system in which Labour was not yet a full contestant. Indeed, many would have seen Labour's challenge largely in terms of the damage it did to the Liberal Party, the party to which their families had formed an allegiance. In view of the 'intrinsic' values which Liberal success would have had for many of these children, it is possible to suppose that the Liberals' eventual displacement by Labour could have left a residue of ill-will in some, which countered Labour's appeal as a working class party and drew them to the Liberals' ancient foe. Support recruited to the Conservatives in this way would have contributed to the unequal appeal which Labour and the Conservatives had for the 'opposite' class in later years without necessarily involving factors, such as social deference, that may be cited when motives for working class Conservatism are sought in the political and social attitudes of the present.

The flows of support away from the Liberals therefore played an important role in fashioning the partisan alignment of recent decades. As we have seen, the Liberals left a larger legacy of strength to the Conservatives than to Labour, despite the fact that Labour succeeded the Liberals as the Conservatives' main opponent in the British party system. The movements into the main parties over several decades deserve closer study, and we should see what a comparison of cohorts can reveal about the background of Labour and Conservative support in the 1960s.

The Making of the New Alignment

Labour's electoral strength matured over an extended period. As recently as the onset of the First World War the party was a minor element in the party system. Labour had only a small bridgehead in parliament and although it was a very solid one, with most members firmly entrenched in their seats, it gave no evidence of expanding. Between 1906 and 1914 the party made no headway in adding to its representation; indeed, by 1914 it had only thirty-eight M.P.s compared with an effective peak of fifty-three at the end of the 1906 parliament, and from the by-elections of 1911 to 1914 it seemed that the party might even be declining.

Against such a background the importance to Labour of the First World War is difficult to overstate. The war disturbed the social order in profound ways and brought a vast growth of trade unionism. In political terms it interrupted the stable competition of Conservatives and Liberals. Indeed, the split in the Liberal leadership after 1916 gave Labour the priceless opportunity of becoming the largest opposition party, even with the mere sixty-three seats won in 1918. Throughout the interwar period Labour polled at least 30 per cent of the vote at each General Election, and the results in 1924 and 1929 brought Labour cabinets to power.

The Second World War added a fresh increment of Labour strength. Something in the experience of the war years broke the established attitudes of many people; moreover, a very large segment of new voters entered the electorate in 1945. We have seen in Chapter 3 how strongly Labour this new segment was. Fragmentary evidence suggests that some time after the Battle of Britain there was a sharp change in national political mood. Despite the wartime party truce which prevented direct confrontations between Conservative and Labour candidates, Conservatives began to fare very badly in by-elections, and when the Gallup Poll resumed questioning about voting intentions in 1943 Labour was well ahead of the Conservatives. In 1945 Labour was swept into office on a landslide with a 12 per cent swing in votes compared to 1935. In the twenty years following the war the balance of strength between Labour and the Conservatives was remarkably stable. Labour had become an equal contestant for power, and its electoral support levelled off after several decades of growth.

The rise of Labour and the new class alignment is most plainly reflected in our cohort data for the manual working class. Figure 11.5 on the next page shows the Labour proportion among the preferences which our manual respondents attributed to their fathers and gave for themselves. The trend upwards as one moves rightwards along the curves both for fathers and sons shows the strong growth of Labour support in the manual working class as the century wore on. Not more than a quarter of working class respondents in our pre-1918 cohort said their fathers were Labour, and if we were to allow for those unable to give a partisanship for their fathers the proportion would fall to less than a fifth. By contrast, Labour's share of fathers' allegiances remembered by working class respondents in the post-1951 cohort was 69 per cent. The fact that the curve for respondents is located above that for their

11.5 Proportion Labour of Preferences for the Three Parties Attributed to Fathers and Held by Manual Respondents, by Cohort[a]

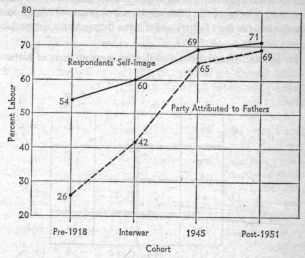

[a] Figures are per cent Labour of Labour, Conservative and Liberal preferences attributed to their fathers and of current party self-images held by respondents in grades V and VI of the several cohorts.

fathers shows the continued growth of Labour's strength over the life cycle of these manual workers. The growth was most spectacular in the older age-cohorts, where Labour's prior strength was least. But it reached its highest levels in the younger cohorts, because there the working class elector was more likely to have grown up in a Labour household.

This profound alteration of party allegiance among manual workers did not result simply from the conversion of Liberals, as we have seen. Several streams contributed to the rising strength of the Labour Party. There were some conversions to Labour among the children of Conservative parents. But our evidence suggests that Labour's new strength was achieved most of all by mobilizing the support of manual workers who grew up in relatively non-political homes.[3]

Evidence on this point is set out in Table 11.6, which shows the full turnover between the party allegiance our manual respondents remembered for their fathers and the one they gave for themselves.

11.6 Party Self-Image of Manual Respondents by Party of Father

Partisan Self-Image

		Lab	Con	Lib	Other None	
	Lab	30·5	4·1	1·7	1·4	37·7
	Con	6·5	9·4	2·2	1·2	19·3
Party of Father	Lib	6·1	3·3	2·3	0·5	12·2
	Other None	18·4	7·7	2·3	2·4	30·8
		61·5	24·5	8·5	5·5	100·0%

$(n = 1229)$

The first percentage at the right-hand margin of the table shows that 37·7 per cent of fathers were remembered as having been Labour, whereas the first percentage at the bottom margin shows that 61·5 per cent of these manual workers were themselves Labour in the early 1960s, an increase of 23·8 percentage points. This increase is the result of the movements towards and away from Labour reflected by three pairs of interior entries of the table. The first of these reflects the direct exchanges between the Conservatives and Labour: 6·5 per cent of these manual workers reported their fathers as Conservative and themselves as Labour, whereas only 4·1 per cent travelled an exactly opposite route. The result of

3. By 'manual worker' we mean all those in our sample living in a household where the head of household was of occupational grade V or VI as defined in Chapter 4, whether or not the respondent was employed in a manual occupation.

this exchange was a small net increase of Labour strength. A rather larger gain to Labour came from movements involving the Liberal Party: 6·1 per cent of these manual workers reported their fathers as Liberal and themselves as Labour, whereas only 1·7 per cent had moved away from Labour to the Liberals by the early 1960s. But much the largest source of the increase in Labour strength reported between generations is due to the recruitment of support among manual workers who could not associate a party allegiance with their fathers. Of this working class sample 18·4 per cent did not link their fathers to a party but described themselves as Labour, whereas only 1·4 per cent remembered their fathers as Labour and gave no party allegiance for themselves. The arithmetic of these various components of change is summarized in Table 11.7.[4]

11.7 Source of Increase of Labour Strength Between Generations Reported by Manual Working Class Sample[a]

	Movements towards Labour	Movements away from Labour	Net Increase
Alternative position:			
Conservative	6·5	4·1	+ 2·4
Liberal	6·1	1·7	+ 4·4
No allegiance	18·4	1·4	+17·0
	31·0	7·2	+23·8

[a] The entries of this table are taken from the turnover between the party allegiances manual working class respondents remembered for their fathers and gave for themselves, as shown by Table 11.6.

In every cohort manual workers whose fathers were not remembered as having a partisan alignment were an important source of

4. We do not consider here the party preference which our respondents remembered their mothers as having, although we have seen in Chapter 3 that this could have an independent influence on the partisanship of children, when mother and father disagreed. In the great majority of cases, however, the party of the mother agreed with that of the father or was not recalled by the respondent. We have therefore simplified our analysis of change between generations by considering only the party of the father.

new strength for the Labour Party. The relative importance of the several sources of additional Labour support across cohorts is shown by Figure 11.8, which gives for each cohort the net change

11.8 Source of Increase of Labour Strength Between Generations in Manual Working Class by Cohort[a]

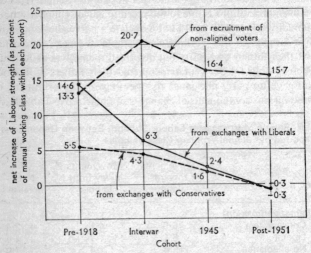

[a] Figures are percentages describing net increase of Labour strength within the manual working class sample of each cohort analogous to those given for the manual working class sample as a whole by Table 11.7. The figures given here are not strictly comparable to those in Figure 11.5, where we have excluded fathers not remembered as having a party allegiance from the base on which the proportion of fathers Labour is calculated.

between generations due to exchanges with the Conservatives and the Liberals and to the recruitment of manual workers whose fathers were not remembered as having a partisan alignment. This figure shows an interesting pattern of differences across cohorts. The most important source of new Labour strength among the oldest cohort was the conversion of Liberals; the conversion of Conservatives also made an important contribution among manual workers in this age group. In the interwar cohort the conversion of Liberals and Conservatives still contributed a substantial increase in Labour strength. But in the two youngest cohorts exchanges with the other parties yielded little net change in Labour's strength among manual workers. In all cohorts, however, the recruitment of those who did not attribute a partisanship to their fathers made the balance of allegiances which workers gave for themselves far more Labour than the balance they remembered for their fathers.

These data on successive cohorts help to explain the pattern of strong Labour growth earlier in the century and of more moderate growth in later years. Despite the diminishing net gains to Labour from exchanges with the Conservatives and Liberals, Labour still attracted a *proportion* of workers with Conservative or Liberal fathers that was much larger than the proportion of workers with Labour fathers that it lost to the other parties; in all four cohorts it was much more likely that workers with Conservative or Liberal fathers would become Labour than it was that those with Labour fathers would become Conservative or Liberal. But, as the century wore on, these unequal rates of conversion were applied to workers of progressively more Labour background. As a result, the loss of even a small proportion of working class sons of Labour fathers could offset the recruitment of a much larger proportion of working class sons of Conservative or Liberal fathers. In the post-1951 cohort, for example, less than an eighth of workers with Labour fathers had become Conservative, whereas more than a third of workers with Conservative fathers had become Labour. But because so many more workers had Labour fathers, these very unequal conversion rates produced roughly equal flows of support towards and away from Labour in this cohort, as Figure 11.8 shows.

The role of recruitment to Labour of workers who did not attribute a partisanship to their fathers is more complex. In all cohorts this movement helped to make the allegiances which manual workers gave for themselves more Labour than those they remembered for their fathers, as we have seen. But we should be cautious about regarding this as indicating a net increase in Labour's strength, since a father could in fact have been Labour, even though his offspring was unable to recall his partisanship. The chance that this was the case was of course less earlier in the century, when fewer fathers were Labour, than in later years. Indeed, some non-alignment before 1918 was linked with actual disfranchisement of the working class.[5] Hence, the recruitment to Labour of workers who did not associate a partisanship with their fathers probably produced a diminishing net gain for Labour as the century wore on, just as exchanges with the Conservatives and the Liberals between generations also produced a diminishing net gain.

These trends describe the historical process by which Labour took possession of preponderant support in the working class. The way was prepared for this process by certain early formative circumstances, including the enfranchisement of workers, the identification of the new party with working class interests, and the Liberal split that gave Labour the priceless opportunity of achieving the major-party status that is so strongly rewarded by the British electoral system. Given these initial conditions, Labour came to exert a strong attraction for working class electors not aligned with it. The pull was not so strong as to break all at once the bonds to the other parties. Many working class voters remained firmly Conservative, as we have seen. Moreover, it is at least a plausible conjecture that many others were hostile towards Labour for having undercut the Liberal Party. None the less, the pull of the working class party converted to Labour many younger voters whose fathers had been Conservative or Liberal or were not seen as having a clear allegiance. We have noted in Chapter 5 how much of the 'drift' towards Labour between parents and

5. The extension of the franchise to the working class, begun by the great Reform Acts of the nineteenth century, was completed only within the lifetime of much of today's electorate. Until 1918 British franchise legislation was very complicated: only those who had a year's residence in one place could vote, and even then some categories of lodger and of sons living with their parents were not entitled to be put on the register. The registered electorate in the early years of the century constituted less than 60 per cent of the total British adult male population. But after 1918 the law and practice of registration denied very few men over 21 (and after 1928 very few women over 21) the right to vote in parliamentary elections. It is impossible to characterize very exactly the 40 per cent of adult males who were left off the register before 1918, but it is safe to assume that they were drawn very disproportionately from the working class.

children in the working class was already reflected in the earliest partisan inclinations recalled by our working class respondents.

We may indeed conceive this historical process in terms of a simple model, a model which assumes there is a substantial probability that a working class child whose parents were not Labour will himself be Labour as an adult and a much lower probability that a working class child whose parents were Labour will himself not be Labour as an adult.[6] When it is applied to the entry of successive cohorts into the electorate such a model readily generates the pattern of growth we have observed, with a rapid early increase of Labour strength tapering off as Labour takes possession of the support of a larger and larger proportion of working class parents. This pattern of growth would not be essentially different if we took account of the differences of the rates of flow between Labour and the two other parties and the circulation of electors having no party allegiance, including the differing chances that fathers of various party hues will be seen by their children as having no allegiance.

We may be sure that such a model captures an important aspect of the process by which Labour acquired dominant working class support. Yet we may also be sure that the actual process was subtle and intricate. The complexity was primarily due to the factors that conditioned the several conversion rates that we have discussed. But there are additional intricacies linked with the composition of the class groupings. We have indeed tended to treat the working class as if it remained a distinct element of the electorate throughout this period. But there was in fact substantial circulation

6. A very simple model of this kind would be a Markov chain in which the movement between two alternative states, Labour and non-Labour, is governed by a matrix of transition probabilities that is completely specified by the two conversion rates mentioned above. If it were to govern the transmission of party allegiance between parents and children in successive cohorts such a model would lead the proportion of working class support for Labour to converge in a very few generations on an equilibrium value, which would be the same for all cohorts. For an interesting discussion of the growth of support for working class parties under alternative models of conversion see Gösta Carlsson, 'Time and Continuity in Mass Attitude Change: The Case of Voting', *Public Opinion Quarterly*, **29** (1965), 1–15.

between classes from father to son, as we saw in Chapter 5, and these movements must have affected the growth of Labour's support in the electorate.

Three differences relating to social mobility would have modified the historical process suggested by our model. The first is the greater extent of upward mobility. The evidence on the incidence of upward and downward mobility is far from conclusive, but it seems probable that there has been a long-term fall in the proportion of the electorate performing manual occupations and that this trend has been more marked since the Second World War.[7] Since those who change their social position show some tendency to conform to the partisan hue of their new class, this difference would have made Labour's growth in the whole electorate less rapid than would have been true with equal upward and downward mobility.

A second difference tending to the same result is the greater political impact of upward mobility. We have seen evidence in Chapter 5 that the Conservatives' share of middle class electors from Labour working class backgrounds was greater in the early 1960s than Labour's share of working class electors from Conservative middle class backgrounds, despite the strongly Labour climate of the period. This finding is consistent with evidence from a number of other studies in Britain and elsewhere.[8] Such a difference would also have made Labour's growth in the whole electorate less rapid than would have been true had upward and downward mobility been equal solvents of prior party loyalties.

7. G. S. Bain has estimated that the proportion of the work force engaged in manual occupations fell 5 per cent between 1950 and 1965. See 'The Growth of White Collar Unionism in Great Britain', *British Journal of Industrial Relations*, **4** (1966), 304–35. A somewhat different assessment of the evidence of an earlier period may be found in D. V. Glass, ed., *Social Mobility in Britain*, London, 1954. Further evidence of a long-term increase in the proportion of the population performing non-manual occupations is set out in Rose Knight, 'Changes in the Structure of the Working Population', *Journal of the Royal Statistical Society*, **130**, Part II (1967), 408–22.

8. See especially S. M. Lipset and R. Bendix, *Social Mobility in Industrial Society*, Berkeley, 1959.

The effect of these two differences was, however, partly offset by a third contrast, the greater tendency of the children of Conservative working class parents to be the ones who achieve middle class status as adults. We have commented in Chapter 5 on the evidence that aspirations of upward mobility for one's children may, together with Conservative allegiance, belong to a wider set of values held by a part of the working class, values that seem also to include the norm of smaller family size. If we see this aspect of upward mobility as limiting the proportion of the working class who lose their parents' allegiance to Labour by becoming middle class, it is a factor that must have lessened one of the constraints on Labour's growth in the modern period.

The contrasts between cohorts visible in the modern electorate make it worthwhile to set out a somewhat more general image of the link between political change and the movement of successive cohorts through the electorate. Such an image helps to focus attention on several processes, especially the impact of birth and death, which are too often neglected in political analysis. The idea of a stratum of new voters entering the electorate is sufficiently familiar for consideration of what their preferences may do to the party balance to have seeped fairly far into political commentary. However, the idea that differences in fertility may have weighted the political composition of this group by contrast with their fathers' generation is much less familiar, and the idea that differences in mortality rates by party may alter the balance of political strength has scarcely attracted any attention at all.

Yet each of these factors has effects which deserve sustained study. It is indeed impossible to move from an analysis of change *within* the life cycle of given cohorts, treating information about parents as a kind of starting-point for later change in the individual's life cycle, to a serious comparison of change *between* generations without taking differences of fertility into account. Let us see what insights may be derived from a model of political change which follows the movement of successive cohorts through the electorate.

Generations and Political Change

The period from the beginning of the century to the early 1960s is roughly spanned by two thirty-year generations or four half-generations of fifteen years each. Our four cohorts entered the electorate approximately during these four successive half-generations of time, and we show here an idealized sketch of their movement upwards through the age structure. This idealization

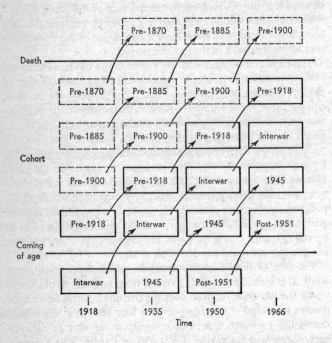

stops at four points in time – 1918, 1935, 1950 and 1966 – the continuously-moving process by which individual electors come of age, advance through the life cycle, and pass out of the electorate through death. The electorate of the middle 1960s was comprised of the four cohorts for which we have direct evidence. In 1950, a half-generation before, the post-1951 cohort had yet to enter the electorate, all other cohorts were less old, and a 'pre-1900' cohort had yet to pass out of the electorate. In 1935, a half-generation still farther back, the 1945 cohort had yet to enter the electorate, and a cohort which came of age before 1885 had still to leave the electorate through death. The cohorts for which we do not have direct evidence are drawn more faintly in the sketch.

The two thresholds suggested by the sketch offer a simplification of reality. In the case of the threshold of entering the electorate there is the additional complication of restrictions on the franchise of women under 30 before 1928 and of all women and various categories of men before 1918. But the greater simplification is the threshold of departing the electorate, since death does not remove a cohort during a single span of half a generation. From the moment a cohort comes of age (indeed even before), death begins to take its toll, although in Britain these losses only become at all heavy after a cohort passes middle age. We may therefore see the pre-1918 cohort in the middle 1960s, for example, as the surviving element of a larger cohort which entered the electorate between 1900 and 1918 and was steadily diminished by death over the next four decades.

These reductions do not fall equally on the supporters of all parties. We have noted in Chapter 3 the difference of life expectancy between men and women, whose political inclinations have been measurably divergent in recent decades, and between the middle and working classes, whose party preferences have been even more sharply divergent. Moreover, there is no evidence that the difference of life expectancy by class has lessened with the introduction of the National Health Service and other welfare measures which might be expected to have ameliorated the conditions of life for the working class. On the contrary, the age-specific death rates for the lowest of the Registrar General's categories of social class (Class V) actually *rose* between the 1951 and 1961 Censuses of Population in the older age groups, whereas the death rates for the higher social classes were falling.[9]

9. For example, the age-specific annual rates of death per 100,000 of population in England and Wales given by the 1951 and 1961 censuses for

What these differences may imply for party support can be seen by charting the contrasting death-rates among the several political elements comprising a cohort. Let us suppose a cohort to be composed in partisan terms of only two elements, electors who would give undeviating support to the Conservatives and to Labour throughout life. In the context of British society and politics the second of these elements would be more heavily working class and male and therefore of shorter average life. This discrepancy may be represented by a hypothetical graph showing the cumulative proportions of these two elements that will have died as the cohort moves through the electorate:

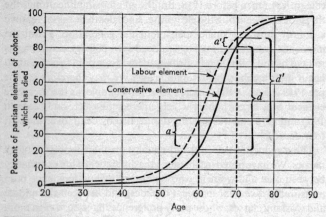

men within the Registrar General's social classes I and V, as defined in the 1951 census, were these:

	Class I		Class V	
Age group	1951	1961	1951	1961
25–34	162	76	214	179
35–44	230	165	386	381
45–54	756	528	1,027	1,010
55–64	2,347	1,765	2,567	2,716
65–69	4,839	4,004	4,868	5,142
70–74	7,614	6,278	7,631	8,390

See *The Registrar General's Decennial Supplement for England and Wales, Occupational Mortality, 1951, Part II, Vol. 2,* pp. 23–7; 1961, unpublished figures from the Registrar General.

The Labour element within the cohort has the higher death rates early in the life cycle and therefore the greater cumulative proportion dead throughout. In an election when the cohort was aged 60 or 70, this difference would cost Labour a real group of votes (a and a').[10] But the graph makes also the important companion point that the party that loses a greater fraction of its initial support through death early in the cohort's life cycle will lose a smaller fraction of its initial support later in the cycle. In the long run everyone in both partisan elements will be dead. Therefore, if more of the Labour element die early, more of the Conservative element must die later and move the party balance within the cohort back towards Labour. In our hypothetical example, the support lost to the Conservatives through death between ages 60 and 70 (d) is substantially greater than the support lost to Labour in the same interval (d'), despite the fact that the Conservatives are in an absolute sense benefited by average life expectancy throughout this interval. If the two parties were even when the cohort entered the electorate the pattern of mortality shown by the figure would increase the Conservatives' strength until the cohort was of late middle age and reduce the Conservatives' strength thereafter.

The shifts of relative party strength that differential mortality has produced within each of the cohorts that have moved through the electorate in modern times may be quite substantial in a system where the main parties are evenly matched. We shall not offer precise estimates on this point, but we are impressed by the magnitude of the differentials in mortality by class. Figure 11.9 sets out the cumulative deaths among men which we would expect in the highest and lowest of the Registrar General's social classes if mortality between the ages of 20 and 75 were governed by the age-specific death rates reported by the 1961 census for social classes I and V, as defined by the 1951 census (see note to page 323). The curves shown by Figure 11.9 diverge as widely as those drawn in our hypothetical sketch on the preceding page. We would need to know the partisanship of the two classes to translate this illustrative

10. To translate the divergence of the two curves at a given point in time into an actual difference of votes we would of course need to know the relative initial size of the two partisan elements.

11.9 Specimen Cumulative Distributions of Deaths Among Men in Registrar General's Highest and Lowest Social Classes[a]

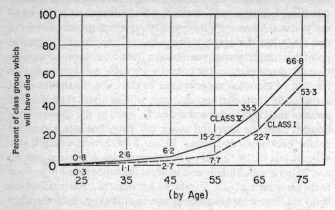

[a] These distributions are based on the age-specific mean annual rates of death reported by the 1961 census for England and Wales among males within social classes I and V, as these classes were defined by the 1951 census. Apart from the death rates for men in these classes between the ages of 20 and 24, the rates are those given by the footnote to pages 323–4 above. Probabilities that males within each of these classes would die in each of the successive five- or ten-year intervals were derived from these age-specific rates and the expected proportions dying cumulated across intervals to obtain the curves shown by the figure.

divergence into party advantage. But if we assume that social class I will be generally Conservative and social class V generally Labour, this difference in life expectancy would plainly work substantially to the Conservatives' advantage. It seems probable that the greater life expectancy of the middle class (and to a lesser extent of women) has made each cohort that has moved through the modern electorate increasingly Conservative over time. Indeed, if we took account of class differentials in infant mortality as well, the relative benefit that selective death gave to the Conservatives would be found to have been even more marked.

An additional aspect of the effect of differential mortality on political change emerges only when we extend our view beyond a single cohort and take account of deaths in several cohorts at once.

Death rates differ by age more than they do by any other factor, including class and sex. Hence the cohorts at the top of the age structure in a given period will move out of the electorate much more rapidly than those below. The political significance of this becomes evident when we note that the older and younger cohorts can have very different partisan composition, owing to the influence of earlier experiences, especially the issues and events that dominated the political scene when each entered the electorate. As a consequence, a party whose strength is more heavily concentrated in the older cohorts may lose far more support than its rival from selective death even in a fairly brief span of years. We shall see in Chapter 12 that this happened during the 1959 parliament, when deaths in the older age-cohorts, which were more strongly Conservative, produced a net shift towards Labour.

It is a fairly straightforward extension of this logic to use our knowledge of death rates to project future changes of party strength as the cohorts comprising the present population move out of the electorate. Such projections must be understood to be *ceteris paribus*: we may say what effect differential mortality would have under certain assumptions as to other conditions that will hold in the future, although these assumptions are certain to be wrong in detail. Indeed, the death rates that will actually govern the future mortality of the cohorts in the present electorate will themselves change in ways that cannot now be entirely foreseen. None the less, such projections are interesting in themselves and help to demonstrate that the movement of cohorts out of the electorate can have measurable consequences for the strength of the parties. In this spirit we have drawn in Figure 11.10 a curve showing the net benefit that would accrue to Labour from the death of the cohorts comprising the electorate in the middle 1960s if individual party preferences remained as they were in the period from 1963 to 1966.[11] On such an assumption we would expect a swing to Labour

11. Of course we do not suppose that there will be no net change of party support among those who survive from the middle 1960s to later decades. Indeed, the experience of the later 1960s makes clear that substantial net flows of party support are to be expected in the surviving electorate.

11.10 Projected Swings to Labour from the Death of the Cohorts Comprising the Electorate, 1963–6[a]

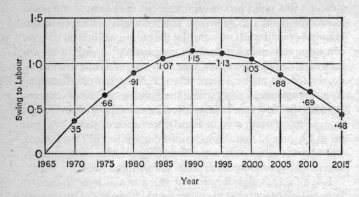

[a] The entries of this figure were obtained by tabulating party strength by sex and age for Scotland and for England and Wales within a combined sample of more than 120,000 electors interviewed by National Opinion Polls between 1963 and 1966; reducing this sample of the electorate at successive half-decade intervals by applying the age-specific probabilities of survival by sex in Scotland and in England and Wales set out for the period of our work in N. Keyfitz and W. Flieger, *World Population: An Analysis of Vital Data*, Chicago and London, 1968, pp. 538–9 and 544–5; comparing the relative strength of the parties in the element of the 1963–6 electorate which could be expected to survive a given number of years with the relative strength of the parties in the electorate of the 1963–6 period; and multiplying these swings due to selective death in 1963–6 electorate by a fraction expressing the ratio of the size of the surviving element of this electorate to the expected total size of the electorate at a given future point of time as estimated from figures set out by *Economic Trends, 139*, Her Majesty's Stationery Office, May 1965, p. 10. Quite apart from the assumption of unchanging individual allegiance, these projections are given a provisional quality by the fact that the estimated probabilities of survival we have used here take account of differences by age and sex (and between Scotland and England and Wales) but not by social class.

as the century progressed and death claimed a heavier toll from the older cohorts, in which the Conservatives were disproportionately strong. Indeed, if we were to confine our attention to the electorate surviving from the middle 1960s and ignore electors who would have come of age after that, the swing to Labour due to selective death would reach 4 per cent by the end of the century. The swings shown by Figure 11.10 are smaller than this, since they take account at each future point in time of the probable size of the full electorate, in which electors surviving from the mid-1960s would be a progressively smaller element. The curve of Figure 11.10 is a suggestive one, even though we may feel no certainty that the two parties or the two-party system will in fact survive the century.

Movements across the threshold leading out of the electorate are likely to change the party balance less rapidly than movements across the threshold leading into the electorate. Since death claims electors in several cohorts at once, the party views of those who die are in some degree an average of several cohorts, whereas those coming of age belong to only a single cohort which may be quite distinctive in party outlook as, for example, the 1945 cohort plainly was. The distinctiveness of the young can be the result of their greater responsiveness to the forces that dominate politics when they come of age. But the party composition of those in a new cohort may diverge from that of their parents' simply because of the differing extent to which different parts of the electorate reproduce themselves. If all children were to inherit their fathers' party allegiance, the party balance in the new generation would still swing towards the party of those who had most children.

Fertility would be a factor in political change even if it did not differ by party in the parents' generation. Unless this generation were precisely representative of the whole electorate, its average fertility would affect the party balance in the electorate. If the downward trend of births in the inter-war period had continued through the Second World War and beyond the age distribution and politics of Britain in the middle 1960s – and 1970s and 1980s – would have been measurably different.

But the importance of fertility is added to by the fact that supporters of one of the parties may reproduce themselves more than supporters of the other. Several types of evidence suggest that this sort of differential has been present during much of the period in which the modern electorate was born. Glass and Grebenik's analysis of live births to wives of manual and non-manual husbands who were married during four successive intervals earlier in the century shows that the ratio of seven births in the manual group to five in the non-manual group was remarkably stable, despite the fall of the birth rate in both groups.[12] Such a ratio implies a gain in Labour's relative strength between generations. This implication is consistent with the evidence of several interview surveys that attest the difference of fertility between the supporters of different parties. Of Conservative respondents in the 1965 Gallup sample analysed by Kelvin only 47 per cent said they grew up with three or more brothers and sisters, whereas 60 per cent of Labour respondents grew up in a family of this size.[13] Our own studies found the average number of minor children in the homes of Conservative parents aged 20 to 39 to be 1·57, whereas the average number in the homes of Labour parents within this age group was 1·77. Moreover, survey evidence suggests that a gradient in fertility by party may be found *within* the class groupings. Kelvin reported that the proportion of respondents who grew up with three or more siblings was 36 per cent among Conservative non-manual respondents, 49 per cent among Labour non-manual respondents, 56 per cent among Conservative manual respondents, and 69 per cent among Labour manual respondents.[14] Our own studies found

12. See D. V. Glass and E. Grebenik, *The Trend and Pattern of Fertility in Great Britain: a Report on the Family Census of 1946*, Part I, p. 106. Their figures on the average number of live births to manual and non-manual women married below the age of 45 according to the period of marriage are these (when weighted to compensate for the bias caused 'by the selection of earlier ages at marriage to which all fertility censuses are subject'):

Date of marriage	Status group I (non-manual)	Status group II (manual)	ratio of I to II
1900–9	2·75	3·88	1·41
1910–14	2·32	3·27	1·41
1915–19	2·05	2·86	1·40
1920–4	1·89	2·67	1·41

In view of the technical difficulty and conceptual ambiguity of identifying the occupation of the father in the case of illegitimate births, it is natural that most fertility data by class refer to legitimate births. But we may suppose that the rates of illegitimate births differ even more sharply by class.

13. See R. P. Kelvin, 'The Non-Conforming Voter', *New Society*, November 25, 1965, pp. 8–12.

14. ibid., p. 9. These differences do not strictly speaking measure fertility differentials by class in the parents' generation, since some respondents

a marked difference in fertility by party within the working class. Working class parents aged 20 to 39 who identified with the Conservatives had an average of 1·35 minor children in the home, whereas Labour working class parents in this age group had an average of 1·76 children in the home.

A series of analytical steps are required if we are to allow for the roles played by fertility and mortality, as well as by partisan changes from parent to child and conversions later in the life cycle, when we attempt to reconstruct the evolution of the strength of the parties according to the generational model set out above. Our estimates of the effects of various of these factors are too imprecise for our reconstruction to be sharply accurate. But we can still suggest how such a reconstruction would proceed, and we can set out some very tentative estimates from the evidence that we do have.

We begin with the distribution of party support in the cohorts for which we have direct evidence and from our knowledge of the relative size of each cohort within the electorate as a whole. The party division of the total electorate in the 1963–6 period can be regarded as a weighted average of the division within each of our four cohorts, where the weights are given by the relative magnitude of each cohort in the whole adult population. As we carry the reconstruction back one half-generation in time, we must unravel the effects of several types of changes. First of all, the cohorts that comprised the electorate in 1950 will have been diminished by death by 1966. These losses will be relatively light in the 1945 cohort, heavier in the interwar cohort and still heavier in the pre-1918 cohort. They will have been heaviest of all in the pre-1900 cohort, which our sketch represents figuratively as having crossed the threshold leading out of the electorate during this period. Estimates of the partisan division of the 1945, interwar and pre-1918 cohorts before death took its toll can be built up from what we know of class and sex differences in party preference and mortality and of

---

will have moved above or below their parents' social location. Yet it is most improbable that these differentials within class in the children's generation are purely a consequence of social mobility.

shifts of party preference among those in these cohorts who did not die between 1950 and 1966.

Reconstructing the party division of the pre-1900 cohort as it might have been in 1950 requires other means, since virtually no one from this cohort survived to the 1960s to give us direct evidence of their party preferences. We have done this by relying on the reports of parents' partisanship given by those who may be regarded as the children of the pre-1900 cohort. Such reports offer indeed a more general opportunity of pushing our inquiry back in time to encompass cohorts which have passed out of the electorate. Each of our cohorts, as we have defined them, is comprised of those entering the electorate during the same half-generation of time; hence, each is comprised of those born during the child-bearing years of the second cohort preceding them in the age structure, since the average difference in age between father and child is about 30 years. We may therefore establish a parent–child relationship between alternate cohorts in our sample and beyond it and identify the interwar cohort as the children of the pre-1900 cohort, collectively speaking.[15]

To resurrect such a missing cohort we must allow, first, for the fact that those who comprised the pre-1900 cohort were not equally present in the memories of the interwar cohort. There was no one to tell us the votes of those now dead who never married or who remained childless.[16] The true cohort was transformed into the remembered one by differentials both of fertility in the parents' generation and of mortality in the children's generation, which had already been diminished by death. We must therefore use our

15. Since a parent-child relationship can be identified between two of the pairs of cohorts for which we have direct data (the 1945 cohort are the children, collectively, of the pre-1918 cohort and the post-1921 cohort are the children of the inter-war cohort), we may use this fact to gain some insight into errors involved in the recall of parents' party allegiance, when due allowances are made for the effect of differential fertility and mortality and changes of party support in the parents' generation between its child-rearing period and the middle 1960s.

16. We have noted the importance of differential fertility in distorting the memory of a historical cohort when we reconstructed the religious cleavage in the pre-1900 and pre-1885 cohorts in Chapter 6. See p. 167.

evidence on how fertility and mortality have differed across the social and political elements of these cohorts to remove the partisan distortion inherent in this transformation. And we must of course also allow for the net shifts of party support among those in the pre-1900 cohort who survived to 1950 from their child-rearing years earlier in the century.

With these estimates of the partisan division and the relative size of the cohorts comprising the electorate in 1950 we could form a weighted mean giving the partisan division in the whole electorate at that time. And by successive application of these procedures to earlier periods we might reconstruct the party composition of the cohorts comprising the electorate at intervals of half a generation back to the earliest decades of the century. Other factors might be taken into account in a full reconstruction of the past. The class differentials in fertility and mortality suggest the importance of taking rates of upwards and downwards mobility into account. And we might well relax the assumption that the British electorate has been closed to migration and study the effects of emigration and immigration on the social and political composition of the population.

Our own reconstruction is still quite preliminary, and we offer here much less than the estimates which might issue from an exhaustive modelling of these processes of change. We set out in Table 11.11 a tentative sketch of the party composition of the cohorts which have comprised the electorate in this century. These estimates of the proportions Conservative, Labour, Liberal, and unattached in successive cohorts are especially frail where they depend on the memories within a living cohort of the political allegiances of parents who have died, corrected for the distortions we are able to observe in the memories of fathers' allegiances held by cohorts whose parents, collectively speaking, were still represented in our samples from the 1963–6 period. As our studies extend into periods of very different party advantage we may expect to learn more about these frailties of memory and the allowances that should be made for them.

None the less, the estimates given by Table 11.11 offer additional insight into the electoral past, especially into the decline of the

11.11 Party Composition of Successive Cohorts Comprising the Electorate[a]

	Pre-1885	Pre-1900	Pre-1918	Interwar	1945	Post-1951
Conservative	43%	46%	45%	43%	34%	33%
Labour	12	20	39	40	49	50
Liberal	38	27	11	11	11	10
None	7	7	5	6	6	7
	100%	100%	100%	100%	100%	100%

[a] Estimates of the party composition of the four cohorts comprising the electorate in the 1963–6 period are based on the preferences given by our samples during this period. Estimates of the party composition of cohorts which have passed out of the electorate are based on the recollection of parents' preferences held by members of the cohorts which are comprised, collectively speaking, of their children. These estimates were adjusted for the greater fertility of the class and for the mean bias of recall observed in estimating the party composition of the pre-1918 cohort from the recollection of parents' perferences held by the 1945 cohort and the party composition of the interwar cohort from the recollection of parents' preferences held by the post-1951 cohort. In the case of the pre-1885 cohort an adjustment was also made for selective death in the pre-1918 cohort (the cohort of children of the pre-1885 cohort) over the years since it formed its impressions of parents' party allegiance.

Liberals and the rise and diffusion of Labour support as the century wore on. The full array can indeed be seen as underlining the importance that the physical turnover of the electorate has for the broadest and most lasting electoral changes. Some of the change recorded in these estimates reflects transient shifts of support among those who remained in the electorate between successive periods, and these shifts would be of greater importance if we sought to account for fluctuations of party support within such periods, as we do in Chapter 12. But our estimates here show most of all the role which the replenishment of the electorate has played in the great changes of alignment that have characterized British politics in this century.

12 Partisan Change 1959–66

Many electoral changes of the twentieth century cannot now be reconstructed. In the last chapter we drew a broad description of the long-term changes of party strength which have accompanied the movement of successive political generations through the British electorate. But we were able to say little as to short-run changes within various eras, changes that depended primarily on the shifting preferences of people who continued as members of the electorate. However, when we come to the early 1960s we can say a good deal about these more intricate patterns of change.

Our surveys recorded the party preferences of the British public at four points in recent years – the election of 1959 (as recalled in 1963), the summer of 1963, the election of 1964 and the election of 1966. By following the same people between these successive points we are able to trace the remarkable variety of paths along which individual preferences may shift. This chapter examines the simple movements from one time to another. The next chapter will look at the more complex patterns of change which emerge when we consider several periods of time at once.

Pathways of Change

In the past twenty years it has become common in Britain to combine all individual changes of vote into the single concept of 'swing'. Such a concept reflects the need for a summary measure of the change of the two main parties' strength in the electorate between two points of time.[1] It is plain that a summary measure of

1. The measure established in the Nuffield studies since 1950 (the average of the Conservative gain and the Labour loss as percentages of the total vote cast) is the one more commonly used, but it is by no means the only

this kind is useful even when we have full information about all the individual changes of behaviour whose net effect is 'swing'. Just as we find it useful to compare the relative strength of parties in classes and other groupings within the electorate at one point in time so also we need to compare the relative strength of parties across time – in the electorate as a whole and in various of its parts. Such comparisons are indispensable in much of the analysis of later chapters.

Yet for some analytical purposes it is essential to distinguish the several patterns of individual change which together yield the net shifts of strength that we see in election results. It is indeed probable that prolonged exposure to descriptions of net change has induced in many a false sense that swing typically reflects direct, one-way transfers of the vote between the main parties. In fact many streams and counter-eddies of change flow together to make up a given movement of party strength; the interpretation of the change must differ according to their relative magnitudes.

The possible variety of individual changes is suggested by Table 12.1, which cross-classifies people according to their positions at two points of time. The twenty-five cells of this table are of three kinds. First, there are the five shaded cells representing those whose behaviour is unvarying; the number of people who fall in these cells, especially the first three, has great significance for the outcome of each election but none for electoral *change*. Second, there are the twelve lightly shaded cells representing those whose change leaves the relative strength of the main parties unaltered; the death of a previously inactive voter, for example, has no effect on the existing party balance.

It is in the third region of the table, the eighteen unshaded cells, that the keys to change in major party strength are to be found.

---

one possible. See M. Steed in *The British General Election of 1964*, pp. 337–8, and *The British General Election of 1966*, pp. 271–2. H. Berrington's report on the 1964 election in the *Journal of the Royal Statistical Society*, Series A, **128** (1965), pp. 17–66, discusses the advantages of measuring swing as a percentage of the total Conservative and Labour vote. Henry Durant and James Douglas have offered enlightening calculations of swing on the basis of the total electorate rather than total votes.

12.1 Pathways of Change (1)[a]

First Point of Time / Second Point of Time

	Conservative	Labour	Liberal	Other Party	Non-Voter	Dead
Conservative	Constant Conservative					
Labour		Constant Labour				
Liberal			Constant Liberal			
Other Party				Constant Other Party		
Non-Voter					Constant Non-Voter	
Too Young						

[a] The diagram is not quite exhaustive. The cell in the bottom right-hand corner is omitted since we are concerned only with those who qualified to vote at the first or second point of time. In any case the number of people who die after coming of age but before voting is negligible.

These cells describe the behaviour of changers who supported Conservative or Labour at least once.[2] We may identify in these cells five distinct processes by which the party balance may be altered.

1. *Replacement of the electorate.* The turnover due to deaths and comings of age is between 1 and 2 per cent each year.[3] This turnover is represented by the last row of Table 12.1, 'incoming electors',

2. Perhaps it is worth pointing out that we stretch this idea of 'changing' here to include dying, even though the dead ought not to be charged with political infidelity, and coming of age, even though the new elector may express a party preference which he has held for some time.

3. It is not quite an exact change. The electorate in the 1950s and 1960s grew by about 100,000 annually (0·3 per cent).

and the last column, 'dying electors'. For our present purposes we consider the 'incoming electors' as young people coming of voting age: but immigrants who qualify for the vote also fall into this category (however, even in the 1959–64 period, their total contribution to the electorate was under 1 per cent). Similarly emigrants, an equally small category, should here be subsumed under dying electors. There is also a still more minute group which gains or loses statutory disqualifications from voting either through acquiring or through shaking off the status of convict, certified lunatic or peer of the realm.

The relative strength of the two major parties is, however, affected only by those electors who fall into the top two squares in the 'dying electors' column and left hand two cells in the 'incoming electors' row; major party strength is left unchanged by the entry into and exit from the electorate of non-voters or minor party supporters. In fact young voters have been more Labour and older voters more Conservative; at least in the early 1960s Labour's lead in votes was increased by its larger share of incoming electors, according to the arithmetic difference:

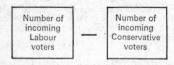

And Labour's lead in votes was increased by the Conservatives' greater share of electors who had died according to the difference:

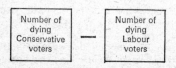

Therefore the change of Labour's lead owing to the physical replacement of the electorate was the sum of these two differences:

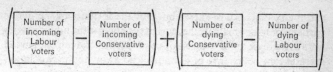

We shall offer a similar presentation for each of the processes which contribute to a net shift of party strength.

2. *Differential turnout.* Since a majority of people who go to the polls support the same party as last time, decisions on whether to vote at all may do more to decide an election outcome than decisions on how to vote. The parties strive hard to convert potential support into actual votes and their varied success in doing so is a familiar theme in electoral post-mortems. Equally familiar is the idea that electoral tides can sometimes be explained in terms of differential turnout – a fall in participation among supporters of the losing party and, perhaps, a rise in participation among their rivals. If we confine our attention to non-voters who previously supported the Conservatives or Labour and to Conservatives or Labour supporters who previously did not vote, we may represent the change of Labour's lead in votes owing to differential turnout by the sum of these differences:

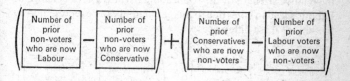

3. *The circulation of minor-party supporters.* In recent contests barely one-sixth of the electorate have been confronted by candidates from other than the three leading parties. Only 1 per cent of all votes have been cast for such candidates and most of these have gone to Irish, Welsh or Scottish Nationalists, or to Communists in seats where these groups have fought regularly and in which they have retained some continuing support. But there do remain some voters who shift towards, and away from, such minor candidates

and the significance of these shifts for the fortunes of the major parties would be greater if the level of support for the minor parties were to increase at the expense of major parties. We can once again represent the net change of Labour's lead owing to the circulation of minor party supporters as the sum of two differences:

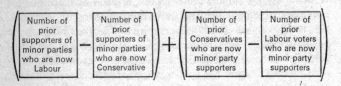

4. *The circulation of Liberals.* Over the elections from 1955 to 1966 the Liberal party's strength varied from 2·5 per cent of the total vote to 11·2 per cent and the number of Liberal candidates from 109 to 365. Even in seats fought regularly the party's support was remarkably variable. We shall see evidence enough of what a large number of voters circulate to and from the Liberals relative to the size of the Liberal vote at any given time. The flow of former Liberals to Conservative or Labour and the flow of Conservative or Labour voters to the Liberals can have substantial influence on the relative strength of the two leading parties. The net change of Labour's lead in votes due to this circulation can be represented by the sum of these differences:

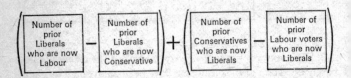

5. *Straight conversion.* Lastly, there is direct movement between the two parties of those who were Labour and have become Conservative or *vice versa.* This is the sort of change most commonly evoked by the term 'swing' but, as we have seen, it is only one of several types of movement which can alter the relative strength of

the major parties. It differs from all the others, however, in that it counts twice in calculations of the lead of one party over the other: making a Conservative of a non-voter, for example, is a gain for the Conservatives, but making a Conservative of a Labour voter is both a gain for the Conservatives and a loss for Labour. Therefore, while only one pair of terms enters the formula expressing the net change of Labour's lead in votes because of straight conversion, we must count these terms twice as we calculate the net change of party strength.

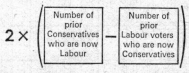

$$2 \times \left(\begin{array}{c} \text{Number of} \\ \text{prior} \\ \text{Conservatives} \\ \text{who are now} \\ \text{Labour} \end{array} - \begin{array}{c} \text{Number of} \\ \text{prior} \\ \text{Labour voters} \\ \text{who are now} \\ \text{Conservatives} \end{array} \right)$$

We may now complete the analytic framework by treating these several types of change together. Having written a separate statement of what each source of change contributes, we may now combine these into a single statement – one that separates the change of lead into its five components. It is convenient for this purpose to return to the earlier table and to denote each of its unshaded cells, as well as each total of Conservative or Labour strength at the margin of the table, by an explicit symbol (see Figure 12.2). We shall express each of these figures as a percentage of the total number entering all cells of the table. The total of these entries $p_{..}$ is thus equal to $100 \cdot 0$.

From these definitions it follows that the change of Labour's percentage lead over the Conservatives from time 1 to time 2 can be written as follows:

$(p_{.2} - p_{.1}) - (p_{2.} - p_{1.})$	*Source*
$= 2(p_{12} - p_{21})$	Straight conversion
$+ [(p_{13} - p_{23}) + (p_{32} - p_{31})]$	Circulation of Liberals
$+ [(p_{14} - p_{24}) + (p_{42} - p_{41})]$	Circulation of minor party supporters
$+ [(p_{15} - p_{25}) + (p_{52} - p_{51})]$	Differential turnout
$+ [(p_{16} - p_{26}) + (p_{62} - p_{61})]$	Replacement of electorate

The sums on the two sides of this 'accounting' equation will be

12.2 Pathways of Change (2)

Second Point of Time

	Conservative	Labour	Liberal	Other Party	Non-Voter	Dead	
Conservative		P_{12}	P_{13}	P_{14}	P_{15}	P_{16}	$P_{1.}$ lead at time 1
Labour	P_{21}		P_{23}	P_{24}	P_{25}	P_{26}	$P_{2.}$
Liberal	P_{31}	P_{32}					
Other Party	P_{41}	P_{42}					
Non-Voter	P_{51}	P_{52}					
Too Young	P_{61}	P_{62}					$P_{..} = 100\%$

First Point of Time

$P_{.1}$ $P_{.2}$ lead at time 2

positive when Labour increases its strength from one time to another, as it did from 1959 to 1963 and from 1964 to 1966. But the sums will be negative when the tide moves the opposite way, as it did to some degree from 1963 to 1964.

The period to which we have applied this framework was one of strong electoral tides. The swings of party fortune, as recorded by the Gallup Poll, are charted in Figure 12.3. This time series and the results of parliamentary by-elections and of local government elections suggest three main turning points. The first of these came in the winter of 1960–61 when a long period of Conservative decay and Labour gain began. The second came in the winter of 1963–4 when the Conservatives began the recovery which almost carried them to another victory in 1964. The third came during the 1964 parliament when the Labour Party began the consolidation of power that was capped by the triumph of 1966. Therefore our own measurements of the public's preference in 1959, 1963, 1964 and

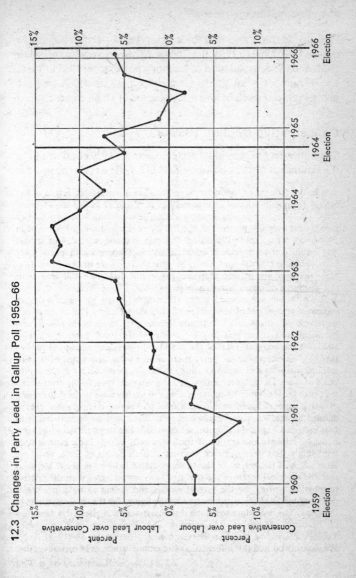

12.3 Changes in Party Lead in Gallup Poll 1959–66

1966 divide the period into three natural eras – the Conservative decline from 1960 to 1963, the Conservative recovery from 1963 to 1964, and the consolidation of Labour's power from 1964 to 1966. Let us now see what the framework of analysis which we have just set out can disclose about the sources of change in each era.[4]

Conservative Decline 1959–63

The full variety of individual preference at the 1959 election and in the summer of 1963 is shown by Table 12.4.[5] The table shows a net

4. In the tables that follow we have introduced one simplification of the exhaustive possibilities of change set out in Table 12.2. We have treated the votes for minor parties as abstention. The total vote for minor parties represented only 0·4 per cent of the full electorate in 1959, 0·7 per cent in 1964 and 0·9 per cent in 1966 and it was very unevenly spread. Our sample was insufficient to provide reliable estimates of where minor party votes (cast chiefly for Welsh and Scottish Nationalists) were drawn from. It is plain that, for our present purposes, no serious distortion will arise from this disregard of minor party support.

5. We should say a word about the detailed steps by which we have estimated the entries of this table and of Tables 12.5 to 12.8. First of all, we have used census data to estimate the marginal totals of the row for the previously too young and of the column for the dead. Second, we have allocated the marginal total of the previously too young across the cells of that row by examining the party preferences at the later point of time of respondents who had been too young to be qualified electors at the earlier point of time. Third, we have allocated the marginal total of the dead across the cells of that column by applying census mortality rates to the distribution of party support found within each of a number of demographic groups defined by age, sex, social grade and marital status in a manner similar to that used in Chapter 11. Fourth, we have used the turnover data from our panel to estimate the entries of the main body of the table representing individuals who were qualified electors at both points of time. Fifth, we have adjusted the entries of the table, as estimated by the above steps, so that the marginal totals of the first five rows would agree with the relative proportions voting for the several parties and failing to vote in 1959 as disclosed by the election returns and by the figures for the total electorate in that year. The procedure by which this adjustment was effected is described in Frederick Mosteller, 'Association and Estimation in Contingency Tables', *Journal of the American Statistical Association*, **63** (1968), 1–28. We have introduced this information so that our estimates of certain entries,

[Continued on p. 346]

12.4 Pathways of Change 1959–1963

		Con.	Lab.	Lib.	None Don't know	Dead			Percent of 1959 Electorate
				1963					
1959	Con.	22·8	1·8	3·3	5·7	2·7	36·3	} −2·9	38·5
	Lab.	0·6	26·2	1·5	3·3	1·8	33·4		35·3
	Lib.	0·2	0·4	3·5	0·2	0·2	4·5		4·7
	Didn't vote	2·9	4·7	1·9	10·3	0·4	20·2		21·5
	Too young	1·1	2·8	0·3	1·4		5·6		
		27·6	35·9	10·5	20·9	5·1	100·0		
			+8·3						
	Percent of 1963 electorate	28·9	37·6	11·0	22·5				100·0

change of percentage lead between the 1959 election, which the Conservatives won, and the summer of 1963, when Labour was far ahead, of more than 11 per cent.[6] The contributions to this net shift made by each of the sources of change were these:

Straight conversion $2 \times (1\cdot8 - 0\cdot6)$	+ 2·4
Circulation of Liberals $(3\cdot3 - 1\cdot5) + (0\cdot4 - 0\cdot2)$	+ 2·0
Differential turnout $(5\cdot7 - 3\cdot3) + (4\cdot7 - 2\cdot9)$	+ 4·2
Replacement of electorate $(2\cdot7 - 1\cdot8) + (2\cdot8 - 1\cdot1)$	+ 2·6
	——
Net change in Labour's lead	+ 11·2

These detailed figures throw fresh light on the politics of the period. The most striking fact is that barely a fifth of the change in party lead was due to straight conversion between Conservative and

[Footnote 6 is on p. 346]

Labour while the much publicized Liberal upsurge contributed even less to the change in major party fortunes (in part because former Liberals were still drawn more to the Conservatives than to Labour even in a period when considerably more Conservative than Labour voters were deserting to the Liberals). The physical replacement of the electorate was more important; three fifths of major party supporters who died were Conservatives as compared with barely a quarter of those who came onto the electoral register. In fact, of the total swing against the Conservatives, a tenth could be attributed to the net effect of deaths and a seventh to the net effect of coming of age. In a period of strong pro-Labour movement, it was the young, with their less-established voting habits,

---

especially those involving abstainers, will be less affected by non-response. It will be clear from the subsequent tables that we have also introduced the known marginal totals for 1964 and 1966 where appropriate.

The figures for the gap between the two main parties in 1959, 1964 and 1966 may surprise readers familiar with those normally presented. They are to be reconciled with the usual figures in three ways: (1) We are concerned with the figures for Great Britain not the United Kingdom; this reduces any Conservative lead by up to 2 per cent. (2) We use the total electorate and not just those voting as the basis of calculation; with up to 25 per cent abstention, this may in fact cut down the percentage gap between the parties by about a quarter. (3) We bring into our calculations all those who were in the electorate at either of two points of time; this further reduces the proportion of active voters contributing to the major party percentages.

As in many places in the book we rely here on our respondents' recall of their 1959 vote several years after the fact, a procedure which is known to introduce some errors of report. The marginal totals for 1963 in this and the later tables are calculated from our own sample in that year, with two exceptions; we have fixed the marginal totals of the dead and the previously too young on the basis of demographic evidence, as explained above; and we have raised the total of potential abstentions to a level consistent with actual abstentions in 1959 and 1964, the two 'adjacent' elections for which we have such figures.

Although, to avoid excessive rounding errors, we present our figures to one decimal point, we should warn our readers that considerations of sample size, as well as of inaccurate recall, mean that too much reliance should not be placed on the exact figures quoted here.

6. This is, of course, based on the full number of people in the table, not all of whom voted or were intending to vote. If the percentages are based only on the active electorate the shift of lead is even more.

who were most influenced. The aged were less susceptible to such short-term factors. But the aged were more likely to die, and those who died were mostly Conservative: in this period the higher rate of death among the aged, who tended to be Conservative, was only partially offset by the higher rate of death among men and the working class, groups which tended to be Labour. But the largest apparent source of change lay in differential turnout: 1959 Conservatives were much more likely than 1959 Labour supporters to say they wouldn't vote and 1959 non-voters were much more likely to support Labour than Conservative. What people said on this score must be taken with some caution, for the 1963 interview was not conducted in an election situation. None the less the potential contribution of turnout to electoral tides is manifest.

Conservative Recovery 1963–4

The Conservative slump after 1960 had come unexpectedly; the Conservative recovery in 1963–4 was even more unexpected. The large reduction in the Labour lead in the fifteen months before the 1964 election coincided with a period of economic expansion, but it also coincided with the Conservative leadership struggle and the row over resale price maintenance. None the less, opinion polls, local elections and by-elections agreed in charting a recovery that went on until September 1964, when the party entered the election on almost level terms with Labour.

Table 12.5 sets out the changes between the voting intentions expressed by our panel in the summer of 1963 and their actual behaviour on 15 October 1964. Once again we can focus on those which affected the party lead:

Straight conversion $2 \times (1 \cdot 3 - 2 \cdot 5)$	$- 2 \cdot 4$
Circulation of Liberals $(1 \cdot 1 - 1 \cdot 5) + (1 \cdot 7 - 3 \cdot 2)$	$- 1 \cdot 9$
Differential turnout $(3 \cdot 9 - 6 \cdot 4) + (4 \cdot 4 - 4 \cdot 1)$	$- 2 \cdot 2$
Replacement of electorate $(0 \cdot 6 - 0 \cdot 7) + (1 \cdot 0 - 1 \cdot 5)$	$- 0 \cdot 6$
	$\overline{}$
Net change in Labour's lead	$- 7 \cdot 1$

The Conservatives' rally was insufficient to offset their earlier

12.5 Pathways of Change 1963–1964

		1964						Percent of 1963 Electorate
		Con.	Lab.	Lib.	Didn't Vote	Dead		
1963	Con.	21·2	1·3	1·1	3·9	0·6	28·1	28·9
	Lab.	2·5	25·5	1·5	6·4	0·7	36·6	37·6
	Lib.	3·2	1·7	3·5	2·1	0·2	10·7	11·0
	None, Don't know	4·1	4·4	2·2	10·2	0·4	21·3	22·5
	Too young	1·5	1·0	0·3	0·5		3·3	
		32·5	33·9	8·6	23·1	1·9	100·0	

+8·5 (between Con. and Lab. 1963 totals)

+1·4 (below 32·5)

					Percent of 1963 Electorate
Percent of 1964 electorate	33·1	34·6	8·8	23·5	100·0

decline. Even fewer voters remained in an identical position from 1963 to 1964 than from 1959 to 1963, but their changes were more mutually cancelling. Among those who were in the electorate on both occasions as many wavered between the latter two moments as between the former two; one elector in three had a different electoral stance in 1964 from his position in 1963. The replacement of the electorate contributed much less to change in this period because the time that elapsed was shorter. Even so it contributed doubly to the Conservative trend. Labour's earlier advantage in terms of differential mortality (chiefly because Conservative electors, being more elderly, died at a higher rate) was now offset by the fact that the death rates were being applied to a greater pool of Labour than of Conservative supporters – in 1963 there were a third more of the former than of the latter. New electors, too, showed their plasticity by tending to the Conservatives now that the tide was flowing in that direction. In 1963–4 straight conversion comes to the fore as, marginally, the largest contributor to the Conservatives' net gain; in some measure, as we shall show in Chapter 13, this represents the recovery of earlier losses. The Conservatives also gained substantially from the Liberals as well as from the fact that the Liberals were on balance gaining from Labour. But the change in turnout was more important; once again we must allow for the difference between hypothetical behaviour in 1963 and actual behaviour in 1964 yet it is significant that the Conservatives benefited much more than Labour from those who declared a preference in 1963 but did not vote when it came to the point in 1964. The traditional pre-election recovery of the party in power came, according to our data, almost equally from direct transfers between the main parties and changes in the turnout pattern.

Change 1959–64

Although the summer of 1963 was a high-water mark for Labour, it had no significance in terms of the actual transfer of power. It is therefore of interest to examine the turnover of preference between the elections of 1959 and 1964 in order to identify the types of change which ultimately brought Labour to office. This turnover during the full life of the 1959 Parliament is set out in Table 12.6. The composition of the net change in Labour's lead over the five years separating these elections is made up from the following contributions by our several types of change:

Straight conversion $2 \times (2{\cdot}1 - 1{\cdot}8)$	$+ 0{\cdot}6$
Circulation of Liberals $(2{\cdot}9 - 1{\cdot}4) + (0{\cdot}7 - 1{\cdot}0)$	$+ 1{\cdot}2$
Differential turnout $(4{\cdot}4 - 5{\cdot}2) + (4{\cdot}9 - 3{\cdot}3)$	$+ 0{\cdot}8$
Replacement of electorate $(3{\cdot}5 - 2{\cdot}4) + (3{\cdot}1 - 2{\cdot}5)$	$+ 1{\cdot}7$
Net change in Labour's lead	$+ 4{\cdot}3$

There is a notable contrast between the findings for 1959–64 and 1963–4. Over the full parliament the two factors that were strongest in the final phase – straight conversion and differential turnout –

12.6 Pathways of Change 1959–1964

1959 \ 1964	Con.	Lab.	Lib.	Didn't vote	Dead			Percent of 1959 Electorate
Con.	22·3	2·1	2·9	4·4	3·5	35·2	−3·0	38·5
Lab.	1·8	21·4	1·4	5·2	2·4	32·2		35·3
Lib.	1·0	0·7	1·8	0·6	0·2	4·3		4·7
Didn't vote	3·3	4·9	1·6	9·3	0·6	19·7		21·5
Too young	2·5	3·1	0·5	2·5		8·6		
	30·9	32·2	8·2	22·0	6·7	100·0		
	+1·3							
Percent of 1964 electorate	33·1	34·6	8·8	23·5				100·0

were the least important. Easily the largest contribution to Labour's return to power came from the physical renewal of the electorate. Indeed, the higher death rate of the Conservatives by itself supplied the last vital margin of Labour's victory: if the 1964 vote had been cast by the 1959 electorate, the Conservatives would have been returned a fourth successive time with a quite adequate majority. The Liberals, taking votes from the Conservatives, also emerge as an important factor. Yet here we must be cautious in attributing a decisive effect to their appeal for, as we shall suggest in Chapter 14, many of those who switched from Conservative to Liberal might have gone all the way to Labour in the absence of a Liberal candidate. It is significant that differential turnout made much less contribution to the net result as between the two elections than it did in swings measured hypothetically to a point (Summer, 1963) well clear of any contest. The small net contribution of straight conversion to Labour serves as a salutory warning to anyone who automatically interprets 'swing' simply as a direct and one-directional switch from one side to the other and not as the complex product of a large number of often contrary movements.

Labour Consolidation 1964–6

In the 1966 election Labour gained the biggest increase in majority any British party has ever won after a term in office. Table 12.7 shows the pathways by which the electorate changed in the first seventeen months of Mr Wilson's government. The accompanying breakdown of Labour's marked increase of lead shows some interesting contrasts with the earlier surge in Labour strength from

12.7 Pathways of Change 1964–1966

	1966							
1964	Con.	Lab.	Lib.	Didn't vote	Dead			Percent of 1964 Electorate
Con.	24·6	2·3	0·8	3·9	0·8	32·4	+1·0	33·1
Lab.	0·7	27·6	1·1	3·2	0·8	33·4		34·6
Lib.	1·8	1·3	3·8	1·6	0·1	8·6		8·8
Didn't vote	3·4	4·3	0·6	14·2	0·4	22·9		23·5
Too young	0·4	0·8	0·1	1·4		2·7		
	30·9	36·3	6·4	24·3	2·1	100·0		
	+5·4							
Percent of 1966 electorate	31·5	37·0	6·6	24·9				100·0

1960 to 1963. The components of Labour's increase in lead were these:

Straight conversion $2 \times (2 \cdot 3 - 0 \cdot 7)$	$+ 3 \cdot 2$
Circulation of Liberals $(0 \cdot 8 - 1 \cdot 1) + (1 \cdot 3 - 1 \cdot 8)$	$- 0 \cdot 8$
Differential turnout $(3 \cdot 9 - 3 \cdot 2) + (4 \cdot 3 - 3 \cdot 4)$	$+ 1 \cdot 6$
Replacement of electorate $(0 \cdot 8 - 0 \cdot 8) + (0 \cdot 8 - 0 \cdot 4)$	$+ 0 \cdot 4$
Net change in Labour's lead	$+ 4 \cdot 4$

We saw that direct conversions accounted for little more than a quarter of the Conservative decay in the period up to 1963. But from 1964 to 1966 such conversions were of paramount importance, accounting for three-quarters of the net increase in Labour's lead. This contrast suggests that the fact of a Labour Government, established in power, made the act of voting Labour much less difficult for many former Conservatives. The size of the step involved in such changes may have appeared a good deal smaller in 1966 than it did three or four years earlier; if that were so, such half steps as voting Liberal or staying at home would have appeared less attractive. It is significant that 1964–6 provides the only example where one of our sources of change worked in the opposite direction to all the others: our data suggests that the net effect of the circulation of Liberals may have hurt Labour marginally, and we return to this in Chapter 14. As in 1963–4, time was too short for the replacement of the electorate to have much net effect on party fortunes although Labour's two to one advantage among new voters is noteworthy. Once again a national tendency may have been exaggerated among those less set in their ways; but the national tendency also had the unusual effect of encouraging Conservatives to abstain in greater numbers than their opponents.

Change 1959–66

We may now sum together our three periods of change and inquire into what happened over the full seven years between the elections of 1959 and 1966. This total pattern is set forth in Table 12.8 on the next page. When the entries in this table are analysed in terms of our four components of change, the importance of the physical

12.8 Pathways of Change 1959–1966

		1966					Percent of 1959 Electorate
	Con.	Lab.	Lib.	Didn't vote	Dead		
Con.	20·5	2·8	1·9	4·9	4·3	34·4	38·5
Lab.	1·1	21·4	1·2	4·5	3·1	31·3	35·3
1959 Lib.	0·9	1·0	1·2	0·8	0·3	4·2	4·7
Didn't vote	3·8	5·2	1·2	8·1	0·8	19·1	21·5
Too young	2·5	3·5	0·5	4·4		10·9	
	28·8	33·9	6·0	22·7	8·5	100·0	
	+5·1						
Percent of 1966 electorate	31·5	37·0	6·6	24·9			100·0

(Con. to Lab. bracket: −3·1)

replacement of the electorate remains apparent but straight conversion emerges as the largest factor.

Straight conversion $2 \times (2·8 - 1·1)$	$+ 3·4$
Circulation of Liberals $(1·9 - 1·2) + (1·0 - 0·9)$	$+ 0·8$
Differential turnout $(4·9 - 4·5) + (5·2 - 3·8)$	$+ 1·8$
Replacement of electorate $(4·3 - 3·1) + (3·5 - 2·5)$	$+ 2·2$
Net change in Labour's lead	$+ 8·2$

The pattern over seven years conceals some of the trends that were important in shorter periods. By 1966 the Liberals had fallen back nearer to their 1959 position and there was little trace of the impact they were having in 1962–4. The contribution to change made by the replacement of the electorate is linked to the passage of time: Labour's great electoral victory in 1966 depended a good deal on the death of Conservatives and the advent of new voters during the long years of opposition. The primary role of straight conversion is to be ascribed mainly to the final period when the party was at last endowed with power.

We have examined the pathways linking behaviour at two points of time, inspecting the turnover of preference over the shorter intervals of 1959–63, 1963–4 and 1964–6, as well as over the longer intervals of 1959–64 and 1959–66. By breaking down the net change in each of these intervals into its several components, we have added to our knowledge of electoral behaviour in these years. Yet the successive measurements of preference yielded by our panel have much more to offer. It is worth looking now at the intricate patterns of change that emerge when preferences at more than two points of time are considered. We have shown how large is the gross proportion of the electorate that acts differently between two elections. In the next chapter we shall see whether it is the same people who waver in successive intervals of time, examining new evidence on the continuities of party disposition.

13 Patterns in Change

The most notable feature of the shifts in individual preference is their sheer volume. Our evidence indicates that the movements of party strength between successive elections may involve a turnover of something like a third of the electorate.[1] Indeed, in the three intervals of change that we have examined in the 1960s, there were never more than seven-tenths of the public positively supporting the same party at two successive points of time; the fraction remaining steadfast through several successive intervals of change was even smaller. Such figures indicate how widely the sources of change are dispersed through the electorate. Electoral change is due not to a limited group of 'floating' voters but to a very broad segment of British electors.

The increase in political volatility so manifest in the 1960s raises important questions about Britain's electoral system. It is natural that most observers should have stressed the virtues of electoral fluidity, arguing, for example, that the expectation of a future swing of the pendulum and a change of government is essential if the opposition is to attract and retain the parliamentary talent it needs. But all such arguments have assumed that swings will be moderate; for this reason the way in which swings in votes are exaggerated in terms of parliamentary seats has been regarded as a cardinal virtue of the single-member constituency system. But if the parties' consistent support were to be drastically reduced and turnovers of party strength were to involve a vast majority of electors, a very different verdict on the electoral system might be called for.

1. We include among changers here those who voluntarily abstained at one election. The extent of turnover would be larger still if we were to include deaths and comings of age.

Table 13.1 summarizes the rates of change in the three political intervals for which we have evidence – 1959–63, 1963–4 and 1964–6. These entries are obtained by combining the much more elaborate data given for these periods in Tables 12.4, 12.5 and 12.7, excluding only those who have come of age and those who have

13.1 Rates of Individual Change in Three Political Intervals

Interval	Position changed	Position remained constant[b]	Totals
1959–63[a]	30%	70	100%
1963–64	36%	64	100%
1964–66	26%	74	100%

[a] We have relied on our respondents' recall of their 1959 preference; as noted above, this procedure understates somewhat the true rate of change.

[b] We include among those whose position remained constant; any electors who abstained or were without a preference at the beginning and end of a given interval.

left the electorate through death. It is clear from the table that the rates of change in these intervals were very substantial indeed; they challenge us to ask how many of each party's supporters have remained constant over more extended periods of time.

The Cumulation of Change

In certain respects the rates of change in relatively brief intervals can give a misleading picture of the amount of change during more extended periods. If we were to impute a cumulative quality to change, assuming that at each successive interval of change every voter was equally likely to switch, the rates shown by Table 13.1 would have involved the vast majority of electors in some sort of motion across these four points of time. Indeed, if the changes shown by the table had cumulated across all three intervals, less than 40 per cent of the electorate would have held to a constant position, including abstention, at the four points which define these intervals.[2]

2. The meaning we give to 'cumulative' here is simply that changes in

But, as might be expected, a cumulative assumption conflicts with the evidence. Its failure is linked to two distinct and important aspects of change over longer periods of time. The first of these is that the propensity to change, not surprisingly, is far from being uniform throughout the electorate. If the image of a nation sharply divided into 'stalwarts' and 'floaters' is false to reality, so is the opposite image of an electorate in which everyone is equally likely to change. Our evidence suggests that those who change in one interval are much more likely than those who do not to shift again in a successive interval.

This aspect of our panel's behaviour is illustrated by Table 13.2, which crosses the occurrence of changes in the months prior to the election of 1964 and the months between the elections of 1964 and 1966. Plainly changes in these successive intervals were substantially interlinked. People who had moved between 1963 and 1964 were almost three times more likely to move again between 1964 and 1966. And six-sevenths of those who remained fixed over

13.2 Rates of Change 1964–66 by Change 1963–64

| | | Between 1963 and 1964 | |
		Constant	Changed
Between 1964 and 1966	Constant	85%	56%
	Changed	15	44
	Totals	100%	100%

the first period remained fixed over the second compared to four-sevenths of those who switched. The consequence of this difference is that the fraction of the electorate which keeps to a constant position over a fairly extended period of time is very much larger than it would be if all change were cumulative, with all voters always equally at risk.

---

any two intervals are statistically independent; that is, that these changes conform to a first-order Markov process – although not in general to a stationary one!

The cumulation of change is limited by a second and perhaps less evident aspect of the electorate's behaviour, the tendency of change to be in the direction of a position which the elector has taken before. Any conception that change in one interval is independent of change in prior intervals is false not only because some electors are more prone than others to change at all; it is also false because the direction of change shows the marks of the voter's prior partisan history. Our evidence on this point is illustrated by Table 13.3, which compares the rates at which movers shifted towards the Conservative Party between the elections of 1964 and 1966 according to whether they had been Conservative

13.3 Proportions Moving to the Conservatives between 1964 and 1966 by 1959 Preference

| | Among movers whose 1959 preference had been | |
	Conservative	Other than Conservative
Proportions moving to the Conservatives between the elections of 1964 and 1966	67%	17%

in 1959. The table seeks to answer this question: among those voters who did not vote Conservative in 1964 but who were going to shift their position by 1966, how did the likelihood of the shift being towards the Conservatives compare among those who had been Conservative in 1959 and those who had not? The contrast of the two groups is very marked. The likelihood of a mover's becoming a Conservative between 1964 and 1966 was vastly greater among those who had been Conservative at the General Election of 1959.

The influence of prior partisanship in movements to Labour over the same period is shown by Table 13.4. The likelihood of a mover's shifting towards the Labour Party between the elections of 1964 and 1966 is seen to have been far greater among those who

13.4 Proportions Moving to Labour from 1964 to 1966
by 1959 Preference

| | Among movers whose 1959 preference had been | |
	Labour	Other than Labour
Proportion moving to Labour between the elections of 1964 and 1966	74%	28%

supported Labour in 1959 than among those who did not. This pattern is indeed quite general in our evidence. It holds for both of the major parties – and for the Liberals as well, although we reserve evidence on this point to the next chapter. Moreover, it holds for whichever three of the four points of time for which we have evidence – 1959, 1963, 1964 and 1966 – that we choose to look at. The pattern is, for example, just as apparent in changes during the seventeen months prior to the election of 1964 as it is in changes between the elections of 1964 and 1966.

The combined effect of the 'gradient' in propensity to change and the 'homing' tendency of those who do change is to prevent change from being as widely dispersed across the electorate over an extended interval as we would expect by observing rates of change within briefer intervals. This combined effect can be summarized in two turnover tables which show the changes of party preference between the relatively remote points represented by the 1959 and 1966 General Elections calculated in two contrasting ways. The first of these tables is hypothetical and is based on the assumption that the changes observed from 1959 to 1963, 1963 to 1964 and 1964 to 1966 were in fact cumulative over the whole period from 1959 to 1966.[3] The other table gives the actual turn-

3. As indicated on p. 356, we have interpreted the idea of perfectly cumulative change in terms of a (non-stationary) Markov chain. Thus, for each of our three intervals of change we may calculate from the observed turnover of party preference a transition matrix whose generalized elements we may denote as:

[Continued on p. 361]

over of party preference observed between the elections of 1959 and 1966.

As set out in Table 13.5, the contrast between these two arrays is very marked indeed. The entries of Table 13.5a, formed under the

13.5 Turnover of Party Preference Between Elections of 1959 and 1966

a. *Assuming Cumulative Change*

		Preference in 1966			
		Con.	Lab.	Lib.	Abstained
	Con.	51%	20	6	23	100%
	Lab.	14%	58	6	22	100%
Preference in 1959	Lib.	33%	28	15	24	100%
	Abstained	28%	36	7	29	100%

b. *Turnover Actually Observed*

		Preference in 1966			
		Con.	Lab.	Lib.	Abstained
	Con.	68%	9	6	17	100%
	Lab.	4%	76	4	16	100%
Preference in 1959	Lib.	23%	25	31	21	100%
	Abstained	21%	28	7	44	100%

assumption of perfectly cumulative change, show a marked diffusion over the table, with less concentration along the ridge of the main diagonal from upper left to lower right, the cells that represent electors with unchanged positions. In the true turnover table, 13.5b, this ridge is much higher. Considerable erosion has moved electors into the 'low' regions on either side of the main diagonal, but this movement is less marked than the assumption of independent or cumulative change would lead us to expect. The contrast of expected and actual erosion is summarized by the curves drawn in Figure 13.6.

13.6 Proportions of Electors Holding the Same Position, 1959 and 1966

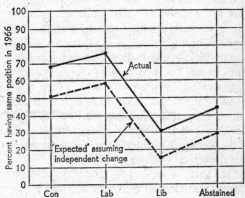

Sources of Traditional Behaviour

How are we to account for the 'homing' tendency seen among changers? In some cases this type of behaviour could be described

$$p_{ij1}, p_{ij2} \text{ and } p_{ij3}$$

respectively for our three intervals. If change were in fact perfectly cumulative the probability

$$p_{ij}^{(3)}$$

that an elector who preferred the ith party in 1959 prefers the jth party in 1966 would be the sum of the probabilities of the occurrence of all possible paths which lead between these two positions, or

$$p_{ij}^{(3)} = \sum_{\eta\nu}\sum p_{i\eta 1} p_{\eta\nu 2} p_{\nu j 3},$$

where the probability of the occurrence of any given path is the product of the probabilities of each of its steps, in accord with the idea of independent or 'cumulative' changes.

as the return to a traditional party allegiance by those who consistently expressed such a partisan self-image and who voted for another party while still professing loyalty to their old party. A number of people in our panel did return between two points of time to vote for the party they had supported at an earlier time and with which they expressed a generalized identification at all three points of time. In such cases what mainly needs explaining is the deviating, rather than the homing, behaviour.

But a generalized party tie of this kind can supply an explanation of the behaviour only of a minority of those in our sample who shifted back to a position they had had before. In fact, less than a third of those who exhibited this pattern of choice could be said to have been returning to vote in conformity with the partisan self-image they had held throughout. A commoner pattern, as the evidence of Chapter 2 suggested, was for current electoral choice and more generalized partisan self-image to vary in tandem. We could in fact exhibit tables similar in form to 13.3 and 13.4, but showing instead the tendency of voters to return to a partisan self-image that they had temporarily abandoned. In such cases we must find the source of traditional partisan self-images as well as of traditional electoral choices.

Generalized partisan self-images restore the deviating voter to an accustomed position less often in Britain than in America, but in Britain, too, the elector's long established habits of looking at politics can be a powerful influence restoring him to a traditional voting pattern. Voters develop over time a set of impressions about the actors who play roles on the political stage, and some of these ideas will readily enough survive a change of the voter's preference or partisan self-image. A man who came to think of the Tories as the party of good times by comparing the postwar austerity under Labour with life in the 1950s could be drawn by this belief back to the Conservatives in the latter 1960s, even though he voted Labour in 1966 and described himself then as Labour in a more generalized sense.

Probably no attribute of the parties is more pervasive in this sense than the way in which they are associated with the two main classes. The links of party to class survived in the minds of many electors whose party preferences shifted during the period of our research and these perceptions must often have contributed to a return to traditional preferences. Evidence for this is provided by Table 13.7, which compares the strength of the 'homing' tendency

13.7 Proportion of Movers Returning to 1963 Preference between 1964 and 1966 by Consistency of Change with Voter's Class Self-Image

| | Among movers for whom a return to earlier preference would be | |
	Consistent with their class self-image	Inconsistent with their class self-image
Proportion returning to 1963 party preference between 1964 and 1966	80%	55%

among those whose shifts were consistent or inconsistent with their class self-images. The entries of the table make it clear that movers were much more likely to return between 1964 and 1966 to a preference they had held in 1963 if this change would align them with the party having dominant support in the social class with which they identified themselves.

It would, however, be misleading to think of the difference shown by Table 13.7 entirely in terms of influences that are within the voter's mind. Membership of a social class carries with it a number of 'external' influences, including the likelihood of involvement in informal conversations favourable to the party enjoying dominant support in the individual's class. For this reason the elector who has strayed from his party has, by the mere fact of his class, a higher probability of being restored to it; the homing tendency seen among those whose return to a former preference makes them consistent with the majority of their class is a phenomenon that must rest both on internalized class loyalties and on these more external influences provided by social milieu.

A similar mixture of influences must be present in the behaviour of those who are exposed to the partisan press. Table 13.8 compares the strength of this tendency among those whose return to an

13.8 Proportion of Movers Returning to 1963 Preference between Elections of 1964 and 1966 by Consistency of Change with Partisanship of Newspaper[a]

	Among movers for whom a return to earlier preference would be	
	Consistent with their newspaper's partisanship	Inconsistent with their newspapers' partisanship
Proportion returning to 1963 party preference between 1964 and 1966	72%	35%

[a] Analysis limited to those who consistently read newspapers having a Conservative or Labour editorial line.

earlier preference would have been consistent or inconsistent with the editorial line of their morning newspaper. The findings of Chapter 10 would lead us to expect such shifts to come more readily when they are consistent with the newspaper's partisanship, and this expectation is generously confirmed by the entries of the table. Some of the difference of these entries must be attributed to the influence of images of the parties persisting in the voter's mind, built up in part by past exposure to his paper's angling of the news. But some of the difference must also be laid to the immediate 'external' influence of the press between 1964 and 1966. A voter's return to a prior preference is more likely when it coincides with his paper's editorial line because the paper's interpretation of political reality continues to exercise its influence.[4]

The importance of the individual's social ambience to his pattern

4. Because newspaper readership is related to class, we have given attention here as in Chapter 10 to the possibility that differences in the behaviour of the readership groups over time are artifacts of their different class composition. The number of cases available for such an analysis is small yet large enough to show clearly that readership and class membership have independent effects on changes of party preference.

of choices over the long run is by no means to be identified solely with the influence of class. Indeed, we ought perhaps to put the matter the other way round and say that changes of preference over time tend to run with social class because the voter is likely to exchange ideas mainly with people from his own class. We saw in Chapter 6 that the social environment can have effects which modify those of class; in particular, a party that is already dominant in a local area, such as mining areas or resorts, enjoys a degree of strength that goes beyond what would be expected on the basis of the area's class composition alone.

The role which the social environment can play in the formation of political opinion would lead us to expect a stronger tendency for the voter to return to a prior preference if such a change were to bring him into line with the party that is dominant in the local area. Evidence of such a difference may be seen in the tendency of those who had been Conservative in 1963 to move towards the Conservatives again between 1964 and 1966 according to whether they lived in safe Conservative or safe Labour seats. This evidence is set out in Table 13.9. The table does show a clear difference in

13.9 Proportion of Movers Returning to 1963 Conservative Preference between Elections of 1964 and 1966 by Consistency of Change with Partisanship of Constituency

| | Among 1964–1966 movers who were Conservatives in 1963 and lived in constituencies which were | |
	Safe Conservative[a]	Safe Labour[a]
Proportion returning to Conservative preference between 1964 and 1966	62%	43%

[a] Seats are defined as 'safe' if a given party polled at least 60 per cent of the vote cast for the two main parties in 1964.

the propensity of those who moved between 1964 and 1966 and who had deserted the Conservatives between 1963 and 1964 to shift back to the Conservatives in 1966 according to the partisan climate of the local constituency. The complementary findings for the renewal of Labour preferences are set out in Table 13.10. The propensity of movers who were Labour deserters in 1964 to shift

13.10 Proportion of Movers Returning to 1963 Labour Preference between Elections of 1964 and 1966 by Consistency of Change with Partisanship of Constituency

| | Among 1964–1966 movers who were Labour in 1963 and lived in constituencies which were | |
	Safe Labour[a]	Safe Conservative[a]
Proportion returning to Labour preference between 1964 and 1966	69%	58%

[a] Seats are defined as 'safe' if a given party polled at least 60 per cent of the vote cast for the two main parties in 1964.

back to Labour in 1966 was measurably stronger in safe Labour than in safe Conservative seats.

We have therefore a portrait of the elector being led back to accustomed partisan behaviour by a variety of influences. Some are internal to his own mind; the straying elector is helped to return to his former position by a matrix of established motives, attitudes and beliefs which he links to the parties. Indeed, in some cases, the return to a former preference merely reasserts an allegiance which the voter is well aware he has never vacated. But the individual is also led back to accustomed behaviour by a wider matrix of external influences. Reading a partisan newspaper will expose him to political information. Belonging to a social class and the informal groupings which run with class will tend to expose him to political conversation that has some persuasive effect. These social influences, added together in relatively homogeneous local areas, increase the tendency for the elector to be restored to a preference that is consistent with the party that is dominant in his constituency.

This pattern of individual change within local areas has interesting consequences for changes observed in the aggregated election returns. In fact it holds a key to the puzzle of why net shifts of party strength should be so uniform across the country, an aspect of electoral change which presents a profound, if only partially recognized, paradox. This implication is worth considering here both for its own interest and for what it can add to our understanding of the nature of influences on the voter within a local political and social milieu.

The Sources of Uniform Swing

No electoral phenomenon in Britain has been more widely remarked on than that of 'uniform national swing'. In election after election since the Second World War, the net shift of strength between the parties had amounted to a remarkably similar fraction of the electorate in the great bulk of constituencies across the country.[5] The degree of this uniformity has encouraged the view that national political issues and events are of paramount importance for the voter and that his chances of moving from one party to another are virtually identical everywhere.[6]

Yet such a view leads to a contradiction. If the electors in each constituency were to respond to national political influences in an identical way we would *not* see the same fraction of the electorate, or total vote, change hands between the parties in each constituency. The simplest calculations will show why this is so. Let us suppose that it were everywhere true that someone who had voted Conservative at the last election had one chance in five of voting Labour at the next and that everyone else kept the same preference. A fifth of the support which the Conservatives had enjoyed in each constituency would then be transferred to Labour. But this would represent very different fractions of the total electorate in different

5. See p. 172 above.
6. We may state this proposition more formally by saying that the transition probabilities governing the shifts between successive elections would be virtually identical in all constituencies; that is, that turnover tables of the kind shown in Chapter 12, if they were percentaged to add one hundred in each row, would look virtually the same everywhere.

constituencies. In a seat where the Conservatives had had 80 per cent of the vote the drop would be to 64 per cent; but in a seat where the Conservatives had had 30 per cent of the vote the drop would be only to 24 per cent. The fraction of the total vote changing hands in the safe seat would be 16 per cent; in the hopeless one, a mere 6 per cent.

In fact, if national influences were completely paramount, we should expect swings to involve not identical fractions of the total vote or electorate in each constituency but a fraction proportional to the prior strength of the party that was losing ground. This fact has indeed led Berrington to propose that swing should be calculated in proportional terms, advancing an argument that has not been adequately answered.[7] At a simple empirical level the answer is of course that observed swings do not fit this alternative formula. Instead of being proportional in each constituency to the prior strength held by the party losing ground nationally, the fraction of the total vote changing hands has been remarkably similar in Conservative and Labour seats, whether safe or marginal. This uniformity in four successive pairs of General Elections is shown by Table 13.11, which gives the mean percentage of the total vote

13.11 Deviation from Overall Mean Swing[a] by Prior Strength of Parties in Seats Involving Straight Fights[b]

	Conservative vote in prior election		
	Less than 40%	40–60%	More than 60%
1951–55	−0·5	+0·1	−0·1
1955–59	−0·2	+0·1	−0·3
1959–64	−0·4	+0·1	+1·4[c]
1964–66	+0·1	0·0	+0·9[c]

[a] In the case of straight fights swing may be defined as simply the increase of the gaining party's percentage of the total vote between successive elections; a negative entry means a less than average swing, a positive entry a more than average one.

[b] Entries are the mean percentage deviation in the category from the overall mean percentage swing.

[c] These entries are averaged from the swings for only ten and three seats respectively.

7. See H. Berrington, 'The General Election of 1964', *Journal of the Royal Statistical Society*, Series A, **128** (1965), 17 ff.

changing hands in safe Labour, marginal and safe Conservative seats which had only straight fights between the two main parties. The uniformity is not complete, but there is no sign of any marked tendency for swings to be proportional to the prior strength of the party that is losing ground.

But such an answer does not adequately deal with the questions that are raised by the failure of swing to be proportional. The real significance of this failure is that it implies the presence of influences which modify the effect of uniform national forces. When the tide is running against his party, why should an elector in a hopeless seat be three or four times as likely to change his voice as a fellow-partisan in a safe seat? We cannot escape from this mystery by denying that national forces are of immense importance and seeking to explain swing entirely in other terms. The evidence for the existence of national forces, including the homogeneity of change, is far too persuasive. What is needed is additional insight into the processes which modify the influence of national forces so that the fraction of the total vote changing hands is roughly the same in all constituencies instead of being proportional to the parties' prior strength.

Let us restate this puzzle in terms of a simple diagram in which we place constituencies along a 0–100 scale showing the Conservatives' percentage of the two-party vote at a given election. And let us put three specimen constituencies along the scale; in Constituency A the Conservatives received 25 per cent of the major party vote, in Constituency B 50 per cent and in Constituency C 75 per cent. It follows from the argument we have given that, if the electorates in these three constituencies were to respond in an

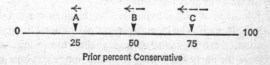

Prior percent Conservative

identical fashion to common national forces, the net transfers of strength would be very unequal. If, as in our earlier example, one Conservative in five transferred his support to Labour and no one else shifted, there would be a change of 5 per cent of the total vote in Constituency A, of 10 per cent in Constituency B and of 15 per cent in Constituency C. The relative size of these swings is suggested by the arrows we have drawn above the constituencies. Yet the empirical reality is very different, as Table 13.11 showed. Broadly speaking, the experience of recent years would lead one to expect the arrows to be of equal length.

What is the explanation for this conflict between what is actually observed and what might reasonably be expected? It is here that we return to the clue offered by our earlier findings regarding the tendency of a party to draw additional strength to itself in areas where it is already dominant. The evidence of Chapter 6 as to the relationship of class to party in one-party seats and the evidence given above as to the stronger homing tendency among those who are returning to a party that is dominant in their local area imply the presence of processes that modify the impact of more national forces. We may illustrate our hypothesis concerning the effect of these local processes by drawing a new set of arrows over our scale of prior party strength. Any such local processes would tend to move the strongly Labour seat, Constituency A, farther in Labour's direction. They would have no net effect in the marginal seat, Constituency B, where neither party is ascendant. And they would

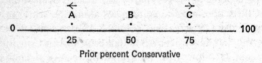

Prior percent Conservative

tend to move the strongly Conservative seat, Constituency C, farther in the Conservatives' direction.

The relevance of such a hypothesis to the phenomenon of uniform swing is plain. The local processes of opinion change which are postulated would retard swings against the losing party in seats where the party had been strong and amplify swings against the party in seats where it had been weak.[8] If we return to our

---

8. This possibility seems first to have been hinted at by H. Berrington during the discussion of his paper on the 1964 election. See *Journal of the Royal Statistical Society*, Series A, **128** (1965), 62.

hypothetical case in which the tide is running against the Conservatives we may suggest how the overlay of local on national forces may change proportional swings into swings that are more nearly blind to prior party strength:

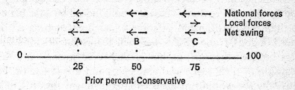

The intricacy of any such interplay of forces is not to be disposed of by a simple diagram, and before turning to the question of empirical support for such a hypothesis we should consider the nature of the influences involved. Other research would suggest that these consist mainly of the persuasive nature of personal conversation, a conjecture that is supported by findings that we shall set out in a moment.[9] If this is the case the tendency towards homogeneity of political opinion in seats where one of the parties is already dominant would reflect the fact that the persuasive contacts in such an area are mainly in one direction. The persuasive influence of personal contact may be felt in every area, including those as evenly balanced as our hypothetical Constituency B. But when such influences are summed across a constituency they are likely to have worked in mutually cancelling directions in a mixed area, and to have benefited the dominant party in a more homogeneous area.[10]

The voter's social ambience need not of course lie within his

9. See especially R. D. Putnam, 'Political Attitudes and the Local Community', *American Political Science Review*, **60** (1966), 640–54.

10. The relationship between the persuasive events which we posit at an individual level and the tendency towards homogeneity of opinion at an aggregate level would of course involve a number of additional complexities, as, for example, the limit to further change when complete homogeneity is approached. Nevertheless, a variety of models of opinion change at the individual level will produce, in aggregate, something like the tendency towards homogeneity that we have postulated.

constituency. Often the constituency does provide his social environment; and even in some cases where it does not, such as the stockbroker who commutes from a comfortable suburb but talks politics mainly with his associates in the City, the partisanship of his constituency may be a serviceable guide to the political hue of his contacts elsewhere (in this case it would indeed be a far better guide than the partisanship of some wider area such as all of Greater London). None the less there will be mismatches for some electors between the partisanship of their constituency and the partisanship of their real social ambience, and this is one of the reasons why we would not expect the adjustment towards uniformity of swing to be everywhere equal.

There is a further complexity about the relationship between swing and the relative strength of the parties that must be taken into account. Our contrived example of the influence of national forces assumes that change will be in one direction only and that voters will move only from the party that is losing ground to the party that is gaining. But this simplification, as we saw in Chapter 12, is quite false to reality. National politics at any moment will present a mixture of forces, and individual voters move in many contrary directions, even when the national party tide is fairly strong.

If the proportional swings attributable to national forces involved partially offsetting flows in each direction, these swings would be more variable across the scale of prior party strength than our contrived example has made them. We may illustrate this by supposing that the net transfer of 10 per cent of the electorate in our evenly matched constituency B is really the result of two opposite flows, one carrying two-fifths of previously Conservative voters (or 20 per cent of the total vote) over to Labour and the other carrying one-fifth of previously Labour voters (or 10 per cent of the total vote) over to the Conservatives. The net result of these opposite flows in constituency B would be a 10 per cent swing from the Conservatives to Labour as before.

But the effect of these opposite flows in our hypothetical safe seats would be very different. In constituency C, where the Conservatives have a very large prior vote 'at risk', the movement from

Conservatives to Labour would be 30 per cent of the total vote (two-fifths of the 75 per cent previously won by the party) and the movement in the opposite direction would be only 5 per cent (one-fifth of the 25 per cent previously held by Labour). The net result would be a net movement of 25 per cent – appreciably larger than the 15 per cent which we obtained when the flow was only in one direction.

The more interesting result, however, would be obtained in constituency A, where Labour rather than the Conservatives have a large prior vote at risk. In this case the identical application of our mixed national forces would move 10 per cent of the total vote (two-fifths of the 25 per cent previously held by the Conservatives) from the Conservatives to Labour. But it would also move 15 per cent of the electorate (one-fifth of the 75 per cent previously held by Labour) from Labour to the Conservatives. Since the second of these flows is the larger the application of the hypothesized national forces has in this case produced the remarkable result of a swing *against* the national tide:

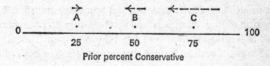

This example involves flows of individual electors which are very large by modern British standards. But the possibility of swings against the national tide, especially in seats still more one-sidedly Labour or Conservative than these, underlines the challenge of explaining the processes which modify the effect of uniform national forces so that such negative swings – or even swings much below the national average – in seats where the winning party is already strong occur very seldom. For as Table 13.10 showed, the pattern of swings has not looked remotely like the one that we have sketched here.

We must now present our evidence for our hypothesis that observed swings are the sum, first, of the more proportional swings due to national forces, and, second, of the tendency towards homogeneity in the local constituency which retards such swings where they are strong and amplifies them where they are weak. If this sort of interplay of forces in fact took place we would expect national influences to be more apparent when they are relatively stronger. It is therefore of interest that the strongest tide of British politics in the past generation – that from 1935 to 1945 – also produced swings which were most nearly proportional to prior party strength. Indeed in seats with straight fights or with triangular contests involving the Liberals both in 1935 and 1945 the correlation of the Conservatives' strength in 1935 with their loss between 1935 and 1945 was not less than 0·55. But the analogous correlation has been very much lower in subsequent pairs of elections when the tide of change has run less strongly. When these forces have been weakest the relationship has essentially vanished.

There is, however, a more direct way of examining the adequacy of such a model. Electors differ in their sources of information about politics. We saw in Chapter 10 that some feel they get their information mainly from television and the national press and are therefore primarily exposed to political stimuli that are broadly similar in all parts of the country. But some apparently get their information mainly from personal conversation and are therefore exposed to political stimuli that depend more on their local social milieu. Some, of course, receive their information in both of these ways.

This rough classification of electors by sources of information can be connected to our model by dividing each group again into those living in safe Labour, marginal and safe Conservative seats and inspecting the pattern of swing found within each. Let us consider first those who seemed to follow politics through the national media. If we divide these respondents into three groups, according to the past Conservative strength in their constituencies, we find in each group the swings between 1964 and 1966 shown in Figure 13.12.[11]

11. Following our procedure in Chapter 12, we have based swing on the full electorate, subtracting Labour's positive or negative lead over the Conservatives in 1964 (expressed as a per cent of the full electorate) from its lead in 1966. A negative swing therefore indicates a net movement of support to the Conservatives rather than to Labour between the two years.

13.12 Swings among Nationally-Oriented Respondents
1964–66 by Partisanship of Constituency

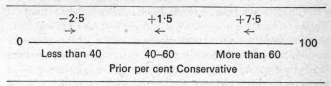

In view of the almost uniform swing to Labour across the constituencies of the country between 1964 and 1966 the pattern found here is a remarkable one. The swing to Labour among nationally-oriented respondents was very much stronger in the constituencies where the Conservatives had the larger vote at risk than it was in the relatively marginal constituencies. But what catches the eye most of all in these figures is the swing *away* from Labour among nationally-oriented respondents in seats where Labour had been traditionally strong. Without our having some theoretical grounds for expecting such a result, it would seem very odd indeed.

Let us now turn to the swings in these same groups of constituencies among respondents whose sources of information about politics seemed more locally based. The pattern is equally remarkable, as Figure 13.13 shows.

13.13 Swings among Locally-Oriented Respondents 1964–1966
by Partisanship of Constituency

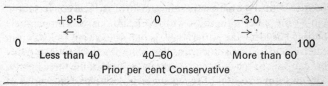

In each of the traditional party areas, the swings among locally-oriented respondents were the reverse of those found among respondents whose information came from the national media. In both the strong Labour and strong Conservative areas we find a tendency towards even greater solidarity with the local majority. And on the Conservative side this required a swing *against* the prevailing national tide, a result which might also seem strange if we had no basis for interpreting it. Indeed, Figures 13.12 and 13.13 show a complete reversal of the direction of the arrows drawn for respondents in safe Labour and safe Conservative seats, a pattern that would seem very odd except in the light of our theory. The phenomenon observed here is of trivial importance in comparison with the bending of the sun's light as it passes the planet Mercury, but it is just as much an example of a puzzling empirical observation becoming comprehensible only with the aid of an adequate framework of interpretation.

We may compare these sharply contrasting patterns of swing with the swings found among respondents whose sources of political information appeared more mixed. Figure 13.14 shows

13.14 Swings among Respondents of Mixed Orientation 1964–1966 by Partisanship of Constituency

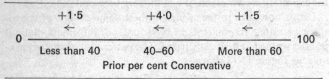

the changes of preference among those who said they followed politics both in the national media and through local conversation. Unlike the patterns for those whose orientations seem more purely national or local, the pattern here is of a mild swing to Labour in each group of constituencies. Sampling fluctuations can easily have produced the difference in the magnitude of the three figures. The uniform direction of swing suggests, however, the overlay of local and national forces which can produce swings that are more nearly uniform. Of course this summation of forces need not occur within the psyches of individual electors; the adding together of the votes of electors whose orientations are primarily national and of electors whose orientations are primarily local can produce a uniform aggregate swing out of fundamentally contrasting individual patterns of change.

In reporting these data we feel obliged to a quite exceptional degree to make clear the slenderness of the empirical foundations of our findings. The difficulties of measuring the elector's sources of information cut away part of our sample. When we further divide those who seem to have national, local and mixed orientations into sub-groups on the basis of the relative party strengths in their constituencies we are left with very few cases on which to base a measure of swing. We have no doubt whatsoever that the detailed patterns in Figures 13.12, 13.13 and 13.14 are partly the work of sampling accident. We are also aware of the additional blur that would be introduced into these findings by using somewhat different definitions of swing or other periods of time. Our findings are set out simply in the spirit of arguing the empirical plausibility of a hypothesis which seems to us capable of resolving what has remained a substantial, if only partially recognized, paradox of electoral change in Britain.

The volatility of choice which has concerned us here – and the tendency of voters to return to a prior choice – is nowhere more apparent than among those who have sympathy for the Liberal cause. In much of our analysis we have put Liberals on one side, giving attention mainly to the patterns of change between the Conservative and Labour parties. But the Liberals have played an important role in the patterns of change of the recent past. This role is of interest in its own right and it also holds some implications for the balance of strength between the larger parties.

14 The Liberal Presence

In the early 1960s three national parties were appealing for votes. The Liberals, who forty years earlier had ceased to be a serious contender for power and by 1951 appeared on the verge of extinction, revived sufficiently a decade later to secure the votes of a tenth of the electorate and the sympathy of many more.[1] The Liberal presence in our period is of interest for its own sake; but it is of equal interest for what it shows about the support of the two larger parties and the transfers of strength between them.

The Liberal revival during the 1959 Parliament was very striking. A party which in 1951 and 1955 had been reduced to a fortieth of the total national vote and a hundredth of the members of Parliament managed in the early 1960s to put itself forward as a real challenger to the Conservative and Labour parties. Its triumph at Orpington in March 1962 was only the most outstanding among a number of spectacular by election performances. For one brief heady moment after Orpington, National Opinion Polls showed the Liberals with more support nationwide than either Conservative or Labour. But for almost the whole period from 1961 to 1966 Liberal support only varied between 10 and 12 per cent, as the Gallup findings in Figure 14.1 show.

1. Total U.K. figures:

	Liberal candidates	Liberal seats	Liberal percent of total vote	Average Liberal percent per candidate
1950	475	6	9·1	11·8
1951	109	6	2·5	14·7
1955	110	6	2·7	15·1
1959	216	6	5·9	16·9
1964	365	9	11·2	18·5
1966	311	12	8·5	16·1

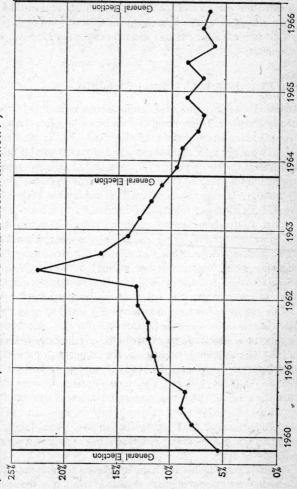

14.1 Gallup Poll Findings on Liberal Support, 1960–6 (quarterly averages of monthly reports on the question 'How would you vote if there was a General Election tomorrow?')

Our own surveys found 10 per cent of electors saying that they regarded themselves as Liberals in 1963, 11 per cent in 1964 and 10 per cent in 1966. The Liberals polled 11·2 per cent of the votes in 1964 (with 365 candidates) and 8·5 per cent in 1966 (with 311 candidates).

The Circulation of Liberal Strength

Repeated sampling can yield results whose apparent stability is largely deceptive. This is peculiarly the case with Liberal strength. From the constancy of the Liberal percentage over most of this period we might infer that the party had attracted a stable band of followers, some inherited from the past and some 'new' Liberals, to whom it sought to add as it climbed towards major party status. By analogy, we might think of a well defined satellite body attracting additional bits of matter as it orbited about a main mass of electors. But such an image would be wholly misleading. In fact the Liberals' support during this period was derived not from a stable and well-defined body of electors but from a constantly changing group. A more realistic analogy would be with a peripheral cloud of particles emitted almost at random from a larger mass, to which most would return after a brief separation.

This quality of Liberal support emerges very forcibly from the materials set out in Chapter 12. Consider, for example, the seventeen months between the summer of 1963 and the General Election of 1964. Our interviews suggest that the proportion of the electorate supporting the Liberals declined only marginally between June 1963 and October 1964. But this was only because of a coincidental balance in the very large movements in and out of the fold. When it came to the 1964 election, two-thirds of those who in 1963 intended to support the Liberals failed to do so. And of those who voted Liberal in 1964 nearly 60 per cent had expressed some other intention in 1963.

These flows, which were huge in relation to the total Liberal strength, were of course much smaller in relation to the strength of the major parties. Once again we have the phenomenon of a rough equilibrium in the net change brought about by very different rates of change among very different sized groups. Figure 14.2[2] shows this dynamic equilibrium in 1963–4 in the terms we used when discussing a comparable two-state process in

14.2 Circulation of Liberal Support, 1963 to 1964

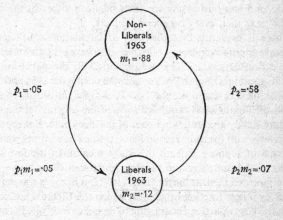

Chapter 10. Among the 88 per cent of electors who were not Liberals in 1963 (m_1) the chance of being Liberal in 1964 was not greater than one in twenty (p_1), whereas among the 12 per cent of the electorate who were Liberal in 1963 (m_2) the chance of leaving the party in 1964 was over one in two (p_2). But worse odds than these would have been needed for a sharp drop in net Labour support. Applied to drastically unequal masses of electors, these very unequal rates of exchange resulted in a net movement of about 6 per cent of the total electorate in each direction (p_1m_1 and p_2m_2).

The very unequal groups of electors supporting the Liberals and the two larger parties suggest both strengths and weaknesses in the Liberal situation. On the one hand, since the party could address its appeals to the great mass of electors, its potential rate of growth

2. In Figure 14.2 and again in Figure 14.3 more elaborated data has been rounded off to two decimal points. The evidence presented in these Figures should be taken as merely indicative.

was high; only a small proportion of non-Liberals needed to succumb to these appeals for the party to gain an important new increment of strength. On the other hand, such strength was likely to be evanescent. The party's minority status meant that it had more difficulty in sustaining its claims for support; its adherents would find less buttressing for their position either in the mass media or in their everyday social contacts.

There is evidence that this sort of circulation characterizes Liberal support even over so brief an interval as the few weeks of an election campaign. This was manifest in the panel surveys which National Opinion Polls conducted during the 1964 and 1966 campaigns. For example, the N.O.P. samples in four successive weeks during the 1964 campaign showed the Liberals' strength as holding steady at about 9 per cent of the electorate. But repeated interviews with the same respondents revealed how strong were the currents of support beneath this surface calm. In the few short weeks of the campaign the Liberals lost two-fifths of those who had supported them at the first interview; but this loss was entirely offset by a new fraction of support which the Liberals had taken from the larger parties. By drawing to their side only one in twenty of those who had not supported them, the Liberals could afford to give up nearly eight in twenty of their own supporters and still improve their position slightly, as Figure 14.3 shows. These very unequal rates of exchange applied to even more unequal masses of electors resulted in a small net gain for the Liberals. We shall look at these campaign shifts in more detail in Chapter 19.

The rapid circulation of individual support could thus leave the Liberals' strength remarkably undisturbed. But, equally, even modest changes in the rates at which the Liberals attracted and lost supporters could yield net changes of support that must be regarded, proportionately, as very large indeed.

There can also be marked short-term shifts in the *pattern* of the Liberal gains and losses from the main body of electors. Although to treat the rest of the electorate as an undifferentiated mass helps to show the rapid circulation of Liberal support, the kind of exchange pictured in Figures 14.2 and 14.3 could have involved exchanges with Conservatives, with Labour supporters, or with

14.3 Circulation of Liberal Support during 1964 Campaign

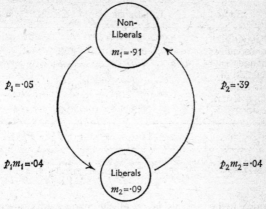

Source: National Opinion Polls

voters previously unaligned. The Liberals, moreover, may also
have gained and lost support by the appearance of young electors
and the death of old. Therefore we should extend the framework of
analysis devised in Chapter 12, identifying components of the
change in Liberal strength which are analogous to the components
of the shifts of lead in the one major party over the other.[3]

Such an analysis reveals some notable differences between the
several intervals of change encompassed by our studies. Let us
first examine the sources of the impressive Liberal gain between
1959 and the summer of 1963. Table 14.4 records the extent to
which this increment – fully 6 per cent of the total electorate – had

3. Extending the notation of Table 12.2 we may define four components
of change of Liberal strength as follows:

Exchanges with Conservatives $= p_{13} - p_{31}$
Exchanges with Labour $= p_{23} - p_{32}$
Circulation of non-voters $= p_{53} - p_{35}$
Replacement of the electorate $= p_{63} - p_{36}$

These components supply the values entered in the 'net change' columns
of Tables 14.4, 14.5 and 14.6 below.

14.4 Changes of Liberal Strength, 1959–1963[a]

Source	To Liberals	From Liberals		Net Change
Exchanges with Conservatives	3·3	−0·2	=	+3·1
Exchanges with Labour	1·5	−0·4	=	+1·1
Circulation of non-voters	1·9	−0·2	=	+1·7
Replacement of electorate	0·3	−0·2	=	+0·1
Totals	7·0	−1·0	=	+6·0

[a] Entries are percentages of total of electors who were qualified either at the election of 1959 or the summer of 1963. See Table 12.4 and accompanying text.

its source in the Liberals' favourable exchange with Conservatives. Although this accounted for more than half the Liberals' net gain, a sizeable contribution was attributable to the net impact of exchanges with Labour; exchanges with non-voters also accounted for a further quarter, reflecting in part the absence of Liberal candidates in 1959 in two constituencies out of three. Compared with these new increments of strength, the element in Liberal support that was a carry-over from 1959 was almost trifling. Only one in three of those preferring the Liberals in 1963 had voted Liberal in 1959.

By contrast with the growth from 1959 to 1963, the 1963–4 and 1964–6 periods saw a marginal decline of Liberal strength. But the individual circulation which lay behind this trend followed a somewhat different pattern before and after the 1964 election, as Tables 14.5 and 14.6 show. Conservative gains from the Liberals, which accounted for virtually all of the party's decline in 1963–4, accounted for only half of its slump in 1964–6. In the latter period the party's share of the vote was equally hurt by movements to abstention, based partly on the withdrawal of Liberal candidates between 1964 and 1966. In each period the Liberals' exchanges with Labour, although visible, produced almost equal flows in both directions and played only a trifling net role in the party's moderate decline.

14.5 Changes of Liberal Strength, 1963–1964[a]

Source	To Liberals	From Liberals		Net Change
Exchanges with Conservatives	1·1	−3·2	=	−2·1
Exchanges with Labour	1·5	−1·7	=	−0·2
Circulation of non-voters	2·2	−2·1	=	+0·1
Replacement of electorate	0·3	−0·2	=	+0·1
Totals	5·1	−7·2	=	−2·1

[a] Entries are percentages of total of electors who were qualified either in the summer of 1963 or at the General Election of 1964. See Table 12.5 and accompanying text.

14.6 Changes of Liberal Strength, 1964–1966[a]

Source	To Liberals	From Liberals		Net Change
Exchanges with Conservatives	0·8	−1·8	=	−1·0
Exchanges with Labour	1·1	−1·3	=	−0·2
Circulation of non-voters	0·6	−1·6	=	−1·0
Replacement of electorate	0·1	−0·1	=	0·0
Totals	2·6	−4·8	=	−2·2

[a] Entries are percentages of total of electors who were qualified either at the General Election of 1964 or at the General Election of 1966. See Table 12.7 and accompanying text.

Dispositions towards Liberalism

The very fact of the circulation of the party's supporters means that the number of people with latent Liberal predispositions has far exceeded the fraction of the electorate with crystallized Liberal intentions at particular moments.[4] The same conclusion could be drawn from a number of poll findings, most notably from the repeated readiness of something like a third of the electorate to tell Gallup interviewers that they would vote Liberal if they thought the party would get a majority.[5]

What was the source of these Liberal predispositions? The answer lies partly in the past. The Liberals' position as a former major party meant that a substantial fraction of electors in the early 1960s had an early history of Liberal voting or, at least, were of Liberal parentage, as we saw in Chapter 11. Occasionally the distant origins of Liberal sympathies were vividly conveyed by the image of the party in the minds of our respondents. Asked in the summer of 1963 what they liked about the Liberals, a number spoke admiringly of Lloyd George and the policies of Liberal Governments early in the century. A carpenter in Bridgwater recalled that 'they done good in their time – they got the National Insurance'; a grocer in Lytham St. Anne's said, 'they couldn't be bettered in Lloyd George's time'; a Henley lathe turner remembered that 'Lloyd George did bring in the unemployment benefit and did try to put the screws on the rich'; while a retired garage hand in Guildford actually used the slogan of half a century ago: 'there was the ninepence for fourpence scheme in 1909 or 1910 . . . I've a sneaking regard for them.' His attitude was widely shared.

The religious preferences and the geographic location of modern Liberals also echoed the past. We noted in Chapter 6 the Liberals'

4. Those who supported the Liberals at one or more of our three interviews comprised fully 20 per cent of our total sample. And this proportion will have missed those who moved towards the Liberals after one interview and away again before the next. The N.O.P. evidence of the short-term circulation of Liberals, cited on pp. 382–3, suggests that this additional fraction was far from negligible.

5. The question, 'Would you be likely to vote for the Liberals if you thought they would get a majority?', elicited affirmative replies from 30 per cent of the electorate in May 1955, 33 per cent in March 1958, 41 per cent in August 1962, 33 per cent in February 1964 and 35 per cent in March 1966. In the autumn of 1968 the Opinion Research Centre found that 52 per cent of a sample replied 'yes' to the question, 'If you thought that Liberals stood a chance of forming a Government would you ever consider voting for them?'

remarkable, though declining, strength among non-conformists, especially those of the middle class. Such attachments plainly go back to the ancient wars of church and chapel which reached a climax over the 1902 Education Act. Partly as a consequence, the Liberals have more easily re-established themselves in parts of the Celtic fringe and in quite specific constituencies or even wards where they were once especially strong. A surviving or reviving local Liberal organization may sometimes have played a part but clearly the endurance of old Liberal sympathies among individual electors has often been an essential element.[6]

Yet the location of Liberal support in the 1960s should warn us against excessive reliance on the historical explanation for Liberal strength. The Liberal revival spread right across rural and suburban Britain, and, indeed, Liberal councillors were elected in almost every large urban area. In many of these places, not least in Orpington, the party's upsurge involved voters with no past history of Liberalism.

What factors disposed these new supporters towards the Liberals? The minority position of the party and the turnover among its declared sympathizers suggest that in many cases we are dealing with idiosyncratic and short-lived causes, such as an individual's favourable response to a Liberal broadcast or to a doorstep appeal by a canvasser. There were, of course, supporters of all parties who held their preferences for light or transient causes. But the temptation to project too coherent a set of reasons into the minds of voters should particularly be resisted in the case of the new Liberals.

One evident appeal of the Liberals in this period was that of novelty. As an established element of the British party system the Liberals did not have to arouse the passions that would have been needed to launch a new party. Yet as a party that had been relatively dormant the Liberals could exploit a genuine novelty value as they renewed their drive nationally and locally.[7] By a remarkable

6. There may even be fairly widespread recollections of local Liberal traditions, as in the case of a respondent from the North East who declared, 'Darlington used to be a Liberal town'. (Darlington last had a Liberal M.P. in 1910.)

7. This was evident in the comments of many of our respondents. For

argument, the party's long sleep was sometimes thought to enhance its claims. Having roused themselves from obscurity the Liberals seemed to some electors to deserve a new turn or innings. The Liberals had once ruled Britain; in view of the tradition of party alternation, fairness required that they should have their day again. Thus a Cheadle housewife offered as her main reason for voting Liberal in 1964, 'They should be given a chance'; and an old-age pensioner in Blackpool who had no trace of Liberalism in her past felt that the Liberals 'deserve to have a try in Parliament – they did very well in the old days'.

Both the appeal of novelty and the desire for alternation were easily linked to disenchantment with the main parties, and the views of many of the new Liberals reflected rejection of the Conservatives and Labour as much as acceptance of the Liberals. A number of our respondents echoed the view of a technical college lecturer who said of the Liberals, 'The only thing I like about them is that they are neither Labour nor Conservative.' Some who rejected all party politics embraced the Liberals as a kind of 'anti-party', as the party least like a party. But many others who had come to dislike aspects of both the Conservative and Labour parties' performance or policies found in the Liberals a form of rejection which allowed them still to fulfil their civic duty of voting.[8] One in six of Liberal electors in 1964 and one in four in 1966 gave hostility to the major parties as the main reason for their vote, proportions far exceeding those of Conservative or Labour

---

example, a 34-year-old Harborough woman said she became a Liberal supporter 'to see what they would do if elected'. A record-press operator in Middlesex said he liked the party 'because it's new, something different – we might get a few ideas from them'. A musician's wife in Kingston-on-Thames favoured the Liberals 'because they are trying to bring in the winds of change (although) I find it rather difficult to find out a lot about them – their policies seem to be a bit obscure to the uninitiated'.

8. Asked why she supported the Liberals, a Sevenoaks housewife said, 'I really don't know. I don't agree with the Conservatives and I don't agree with Labour.' A Hampshire tenant farmer described his Liberal vote as mainly 'protest against other parties'. A policeman's wife in Paisley voted Liberal in 1966 'because I don't like the other parties' policies'.

electors who attributed their preference to opposition to the other main party.

The place of hostility towards the major parties in the Liberal revival is attested to by Table 14.7, which divides our 1963 respondents into nine groups, according to their attitudes towards

14.7 Frequency of Liberal Vote Intentions by Attitudes towards Major Parties, 1963[a]

		Attitude towards Labour[b]		
		Positive	Neutral	Negative
Attitude towards Conservatives[b]	Positive	8%	14%	13%
	Neutral	7%	13%	18%
	Negative	5%	17%	32%

[a] Each entry is the proportion intending to vote Liberal among respondents having a given pattern of attitude towards each of the major parties.
[b] Attitude towards parties is measured according to whether a respondent offered more positive or negative comments about a party in replying to questions 6a and b and 7a and b of the 1963 questionnaire. See Appendix.

the two main parties at once. The table shows that Liberal preferences were running at more than 30 per cent among those who were disaffected with both parties. But when hostility to either of the parties was coupled even with neutrality towards the other the rate of Liberal support was very much lower.

This dual rejection of the Conservatives and Labour helps explain the marked rise of Liberal strength in the early 1960s. We have seen in Table 14.4 how much of the Liberals' new support came from the Conservatives, far more indeed than from any other source. These new legions were in the main comprised of those who had become disillusioned with the Conservatives but who also felt some reserve about Labour. We shall see below how many of these new supporters, when they left the Liberals at a later time, returned to the Conservatives and how very few, indeed almost none, went on to the Labour Party. Therefore, the Liberals grew stronger in the period from 1961 to 1963 by gathering in the support of those who had become disenchanted with a governing party without becoming enchanted with its leading opponent either for class or other grounds.

Many Liberals expressed this blend of rejection and acceptance in terms of the imagery of the 'happy medium', 'taking the middle course' and other language suggesting the absence of the extremes associated with the Conservatives and Labour.[9] No other theme was offered as often as this one. When some definite meaning was given to the extremes which the Liberals were thought to avoid, it was most often expressed in class terms. A number of the Liberals plainly looked with equal disfavour on the Tories as the party of aristocracy and business and on Labour as the party of the trade unions and the working class. Some described the Liberal Party as actually promoting the interests of an intermediate class element, but it was more commonly seen as standing clear from any dominant class interest. Liberals were much more likely than major-party supporters to say that business and the trade unions alike had too much power.[10] These attitudes by no means implied a denial of the reality of class itself. Liberals were as prone as anyone else to identify themselves with a particular social class. Indeed more of the new Liberals than of any other partisan group in our sample expected conflict between classes. The implication seemed rather to be that they opposed links between party and class which would carry over these conflicts into the political arena.

The leadership of the party made a very favourable impression as it exploited the legacy of the past and the new dissatisfaction with the major parties. Mr Grimond in particular evoked an exceptionally sympathetic response. He was not as well known as

9. For example, a machine shop foreman in Don Valley approved the Liberals for 'staying in between – they don't go too far either way'; a widow in Blackpool felt that 'they are sort of halfway between, which is always a good thing to be'; and a Cornish fisherman observed, 'they are the halfway party'.

10. In the summer of 1963, for example, 45 per cent of those calling themselves Liberal held that *both* big business and the trade unions were too powerful whereas only 30 per cent of those calling themselves Conservative or Labour did so.

his Conservative or Labour counterparts, but the public's reactions to him were quite one-sidedly positive, and he must almost certainly be seen as one of the reasons for the Liberals' gains in this period.[11] The Liberals also registered a very favourable impression in many local areas. The proportion of Liberal voters saying that the local candidate or party campaign was the main reason for their vote, although not large, was twice as high as it was among supporters of either of the major parties.

Yet the Liberals had formidable difficulties in converting good-will from these sources into actual support. Throughout this period only a fraction of those who were well-disposed towards the Liberals actually voted Liberal or even intended to. Moreover, among those who did, many soon drifted away, as we have seen. Our evidence makes clear that two kinds of constraints acted to reduce the Liberals' strength in the polling station below what might have been expected on the basis of historic loyalties, or of dissatisfaction with the other parties, or of the positive appeal of the contemporary Liberal Party.

Constraints on Liberal Voting

The first and most obvious barrier between dispositions and votes was the absence of a Liberal candidate in so many constituencies; the Liberals' potential could not be realized where no candidate stood. In 1964 less than 60 per cent of the electorate had a chance to vote Liberal because the party only put up 361 candidates in the 618 seats in Britain. In 1966 the proportion sank to 50 per cent as the Liberals fought 308 seats. The importance of this constraint is fully confirmed by our interview data. In 1964 a quarter of those who described themselves as Liberals were denied a Liberal candidate; in 1966 the proportion was two-fifths. If we return to the circulation of Liberal support over the seventeen months before the General Election of 1964, pictured in Figure 14.2 on

11. In the summer of 1963 our sample offered only half as many comments about Mr Grimond as about Mr Macmillan and only two-thirds as
many as about the newly-chosen Mr Wilson, but in Mr Grimond's case
the ratio of favourable to unfavourable remarks was roughly three to one.

page 381, 42 per cent of the flow away from the party occurred in constituencies where no Liberal stood in 1964 although these contained only 25 per cent of our 1963 Liberals. We have no means of determining how much of the decline of Liberal strength during the weeks of the campaign shown in Figure 14.3 represented Liberals who came to realize that they were without a candidate, but the proportion must be quite significant.

Both in 1964 and in 1966 a number of our informants who were confronted by a straight fight between Conservative and Labour said they would have voted Liberal if a Liberal had stood.[12] Indeed, as Table 14.8 shows, the proportions saying they would

14.8 Major-Party Voters Disposed to Support a Liberal Candidate If One Had Stood

Would you have voted Liberal if a Liberal candidate had stood in this constituency?	1964	1966
Would have	18%	16%
Might have	10	8
Would not have	72	76
	100%	100%
	(n = 551)	(n = 750)

definitely have done so closely matched the Liberal share of the vote actually cast in seats the party contested – 18·5 per cent in

12. The frustration of lacking a candidate was expressed by a number of our Liberal respondents. A bride in the Handsworth division of Birmingham told us in 1963 that she was Liberal 'because of my husband' but cared little about politics herself. In reply to a question asking what she liked about the Liberals she said, 'I don't know. I don't care about these things at all but just live in a world of my own.' By the autumn of 1964, however, some learning had taken place. Her husband's role was still prominent, but she had a sharp conception of the virtues of the local Liberal candidate: 'My husband has taken great interest in the Liberals and also theirs is a very good man – he has done a lot of welfare work locally.' But by 1966 the Liberal candidate had withdrawn and her gathering enthusiasm found no means of expression; reluctantly, she voted Conservative.

1964 and 16·1 per cent in 1966. Since Liberals on the whole stood where their strength was greatest, we may discount some of these hypothetical and retrospective claims, especially of those who said only that they might have voted Liberal, although the presence of this additional group is in itself an interesting indication of the extent of sympathy for the Liberals.[13]

An incomplete slate of Liberal candidates does more than prevent the party from harvesting its full potential of votes. Party *dispositions*, when they cannot be expressed in the act of support, are themselves weakened. If political attitudes are learned and are, in the absence of reinforcement, subject to decay – as we have suggested in Chapter 3 – we would expect some reduction of Liberal sympathy among those who had no chance of expressing it at the polling station.

Support for this idea can be found in the contrasting rates of decay of Liberal self-images where the party did and did not stand. For example, among respondents who described themselves as Liberals in 1963 and lived in constituencies fought by the Liberals in 1964, two-thirds still called themselves Liberal where they had a chance to vote for a Liberal again in 1966, whereas only a quarter still called themselves Liberal in seats where they had no chance of voting Liberal in 1966. The survival of Liberal self-images where the party stood may be due partly to canvassing and other party activities. But the importance of allowing Liberal dispositions to be expressed at the polling station can scarcely be doubted.

But the electoral system reduces the Liberal vote not only by discouraging Liberal candidatures. It also discourages many of those who do have a chance to vote Liberal from actually recording a Liberal preference. The spectre of the wasted vote is the second great constraint inhibiting the conversion of Liberal sympathies into Liberal votes. Local tactical considerations may be far from

13. To these fractions we may add the proportion of the electorate that abstained altogether from voting when deprived of a Liberal candidate, a proportion that has been placed between 1 and 3 per cent on the basis of changes in turnout with Liberal intervention or withdrawal. For estimates of Liberal abstention based on the election returns, see *The British General Election of 1964*, p. 344, and *The British General Election of 1966*, p. 275.

the minds of most Liberal voters. Many support the party without any thought that the Liberal will win, in the belief that a good Liberal showing nationally or locally will enhance the party's influence, or reward an admired leader or candidate, or fulfil a promise to a canvasser. But where the outcome of the local contest and, indirectly, the choice of a government have entered the voter's calculations, tactical considerations have weighed heavily against the Liberals ever since they dropped behind the Labour Party between the wars.

The importance of this constraint can be illustrated by the occasional examples in recent years of tactical voting in the Liberals' favour. The 'wasted-vote' argument has plainly worked in reverse in North Cornwall, North Devon and Orpington, where the Labour percentage has been squeezed down to a level far below that in neighbouring seats because the Liberals have demonstrated that they offered the likeliest means of keeping the Tories out; in Colne Valley, on the other hand, Conservatives have plainly flocked to the Liberal candidate as the likeliest means of defeating Labour. But for every such case there are dozens of others in which the Liberals, as the weakest party, have been hurt by calculations of this kind.[14]

Our interview data show how heavily these considerations hindered the Liberals' realization of their potential support. For example, Table 14.9 shows that the fall-off of Liberal votes among self-described Liberals living in contested seats varied according to their perception of how well the Liberals might do. The decline in

14. These contrasting results were sometimes illustrated by the behaviour of particular respondents in successive elections. For example a carpet fitter and his wife in the rather special constituency of Huddersfield West (a Liberal seat in all the elections of the 1950s owing to the Conservatives leaving the field clear) preferred the Liberals in the summer of 1963 but voted Conservative in 1964 because they thought the Liberal had no chance and they knew 'what Labour would do if they got in' (in fact the Liberals came second to Labour in a close three-cornered race). In 1966, however, the Liberals benefited from this couple's revised estimate of who could win. In the wife's words: 'I thought the Liberal would get in so I voted for him to keep the Labour man out and because I thought the Conservatives had no chance of getting the seat' (this time, in fact, the Liberals came a poor third).

the rate at which sympathy is converted into support across the three columns of the table is such that the Liberal share of the vote in these constituencies would have been something like 20 per cent larger if support for the local Liberal candidate had been as high among those who thought he had little or no chance as it was among those who thought he would come fairly close.

Perhaps equally noteworthy in Table 14.9 is the fact that, among self-described Liberals who thought their candidate had no chance at all, three-fifths persisted in voting Liberal. Why should the fear

14.9 Proportion of Self-Described Liberals Who Voted Liberal in Seats Fought by the Party at the 1966 Election by Perception of How Close the Liberals Would Come to Winning the Seat

| | Thought Liberals Would Come | | |
	Fairly close	Not very close	Not at all close
Voted Liberal	79%	68%	62%
Did not vote Liberal	21	32	38
Totals	100%	100%	100%
	(n = 37)	(n = 29)	(n = 44)

of a wasted vote not have squeezed Liberal support even more? Part of the answer, as we have said, is that many Liberals stood by the party for reasons which had nothing to do with the outcome of the local contest. But part of the answer is that many Liberals were sufficiently indifferent to the local outcome between the Conservatives and Labour for them to have little motive to abandon the Liberal candidate even if they thought his cause a hopeless one. Only the Liberal sympathizer who also cared whether Labour or the Conservatives won could think of a Liberal vote as 'wasted' and see a greater utility in voting for his second choice.

The relative indifference of many Liberal sympathizers towards the two major parties emerges from several kinds of evidence from voters in seats fought by the Liberals. For example, Figure 14.10

contrasts the evaluations of the major parties and their leaders that were offered, on the one hand, by self-described Liberals and, on the other, by electors in these constituencies who described themselves as usually Conservative or Labour. The curves for both groups show a mild bias towards Labour, reflecting the country's general Labour mood in 1966. But what distinguishes the two

14.10 Distribution of Attitude towards Labour and Conservative Parties and Their Leaders Expressed by Self-Described Liberals and Major-Party Supporters in Seats Fought by the Liberals in 1966[a]

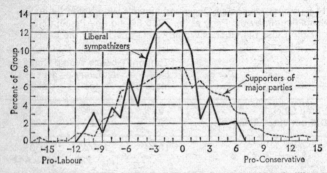

[a] Respondents are placed on this dimension according to the arithmetic difference of the number of their pro-Conservative or anti-Labour replies and the number of their pro-Labour or anti-Conservative replies to a series of free-answer questions asked about the parties and their leaders in 1966 (see questions 7 to 15 in the Appendix). A respondent who gave many more replies favourable to the Conservatives would have a positive score and be placed to the right on this scale. One who gave many more replies favourable to Labour would have a negative score and be placed to the left. One who gave more neutral or mixed replies would be placed near the neutral point of the scale.

curves is the fact that self-described Liberals are grouped fairly closely about this average in a zone of relative indifference or neutral feeling. By contrast, the curve for electors who call themselves Conservative or Labour spreads out much farther about the neutral point, indicating that many more of these voters had strongly differing valuations of the two main parties.

None the less, Figure 14.10 shows that some Liberals did on balance have a preference between the two major parties. It is therefore interesting to discover that these voters were especially prone to abandon the Liberal candidate at the polling station. Table 14.11 divides Liberal sympathizers in these constituencies according to whether they thought the Liberal had a good chance

14.11 Per cent Voting Liberal Among Self-Described Liberals in Seats Party Contested in 1966 by Perception of Liberal Chances and Attitude Towards the Main Parties

| | | Thought Liberal Candidate Had | |
		Good chance	Fair chance or no chance
Attitude towards Labour and Conservatives[a]	Neutral or mixed	86%	74%
	Favoured one party more than other	69%	52%

[a] Respondents were classified as neutral or mixed or as more favourable to one of the parties according to whether they occupied a position between −2 to +2 on the dimension shown by Figure 14.10 or lay outside this interval of relative indifference.

of winning or only a fair or poor chance. And it divides each of these groups of Liberal sympathizers again according to whether they had strongly differing attitudes towards the two main parties. The table makes clear that those whose differing estimates of Labour and the Conservatives gave them a motive for abandoning the Liberal standard were more likely to do so. Indeed, among those who also gave the Liberal little chance the rate of abandonment rose almost to half. We see here a kind of behaviour that is often attributed to voters in multi-party systems.[15] Voters who feel they have little chance of contributing to their most-desired outcome may feel that the most rational course is to seek a next-most-preferred outcome if they have clear preferences among the alternatives. Had we some means of selecting out of Table 14.11's lower right-hand cell those who saw the contest between the major parties as close we might well find that the rate at which they con-

15. See in particular Maurice Duverger, *Political Parties*, London and New York, 1954, p. 226.

verted their Liberal sympathies into votes actually was well under 50 per cent.

The reluctance to waste one's vote, like the absence of a Liberal candidate, has consequences which reach beyond the vote itself to the formation of the dispositions that lie behind it. A belief that the Liberals have no chance does not simply hinder the conversion of Liberal sympathies into votes; it hinders the formation of Liberal sympathies. We might perhaps speak more appropriately of a reluctance to waste one's sympathy. Indeed, if the Liberals enjoyed much wider sympathy in the electorate yet still remained plainly the third party (and an enormous gain in votes would be needed to give it second party status), we would imagine a situation in which the fall-off of Liberal voting among those who gave the party no chance would be far greater than in Tables 14.9 and 14.11. This indeed may have been the situation in the 1920s and 1930s when the Liberals first dropped into third position and were deserted at the polls by large numbers of people who had long-standing attachments to the party. If we could reconstruct for the interwar years figures comparable to those shown in Tables 14.9 and 14.11 we might well find that the Liberals then realized far less of their potential – that the rate of Liberal voting among sympathizers who thought the party's cause to be hopeless was very much lower than it was in the early 1960s.

Evidence that the party's weakness has inhibited the recruitment of new Liberals can be seen in the voting behaviour of those who do not ordinarily think of themselves as being Liberals. Table 14.12 shows the extent of voting for the Liberals in 1966 among those who did not call themselves Liberal, divided according to their perceptions of the Liberals' chances. The table shows that the recruitment of new Liberal votes, like the harvesting of votes from existing Liberals, depended a good deal on the voter believing that the party's cause was not hopeless. At a very much lower level of overall strength, Table 14.12 shows the same fall-off of support among people who gave the Liberals little or no chance.

The interplay of attractions and constraints which determines the Liberals' strength is of interest for its own sake. But the Liberal presence is of interest too for its effect on the strength of the main

14.12 Proportion Voting Liberal of People Not Calling Themselves Liberal by Perception of How Close the Liberals Would Come to Winning Seat, 1966

| | Thought Liberals Would Come | | |
	Fairly close	Not very close	Not at all close
Voted Liberal	16%	5%	3%
Did not vote Liberal	84	95	97
Totals	100%	100%	100%
	($n = 120$)	($n = 156$)	($n = 435$)

parties. We have seen in Chapter 12 that the circulation of Liberals altered the balance between the Conservatives and Labour. Let us now examine some additional aspects of the Liberals' impact on the strength of the leading parties.

The Liberal Presence and the Strength of the Larger Parties

The possible role of a third party in modifying the strength of two dominant parties is obvious enough, but to measure its actual effect during a given period of change is far from simple. Any such assessment requires us to compare the actual allocation of party strength with what it might have been had the third party not intervened. Moreover, the impact of the third party may differ according to whether it is present or absent throughout the period or intervenes or withdraws only before an election.

Some insight into these effects in the case of the Liberals can be derived by questioning voters about what they would have done if a Liberal had, or had not, stood. In each campaign since the 1930s we can think of Liberal intervention as dividing the country into two great electoral segments, one with a Liberal presence and the other not. We may ask electors in the first segment what they would have done if there had not been a Liberal candidate; we may ask electors in the second what they would have done if there had been a Liberal candidate.

The use – and the limitations – of such evidence can be clarified by a simple classification of the alternatives open to the elector with a Liberal standing and without a Liberal standing. For the moment let us put on one side the complications of minor parties and abstention and distribute the electorate according to the proportions which would choose each of the two alternatives available in a straight fight or each of the three alternatives available with the Liberals in. We may represent such a matrix of choices thus:

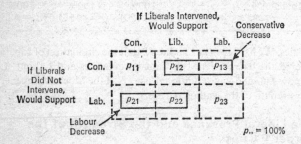

If we knew for certain how the electorate was distributed over these six cells, could we say whether Liberal interventions did the Conservatives or Labour more harm?

We may begin by dismissing the upper left- and lower right-hand entries, p_{21} and p_{23}, since these represent electors whose behaviour will be unchanged whatever the Liberals do. These entries help to determine the prevailing levels of party strength but have nothing whatever to do with changes of party strength according to whether the Liberals intervene. The remaining four entries divide into two natural pairs. The first pair (p_{12} and p_{13}) represent the votes the Conservatives will lose if the Liberals intervene; the second pair (p_{21} and p_{22}) represent the votes Labour will lose.

Closer inspection of the choices facing the elector suggests that the upper right-hand and lower left-hand entries in this matrix are likely to be of little consequence empirically. Consider the upper right-hand entry, p_{13}; by our definition, this represents electors who choose one major party, the Conservatives, if the Liberals stay out and choose the opposite major party, Labour, if the Liberals intervene. Such a pattern of choice seems distinctly odd but it is not impossible to imagine. For example, a disaffected Tory might first be induced to consider leaving his party by the appearance on the scene of a Liberal candidate and only later on (perhaps under the weight of the wasted vote argument) move all the way to Labour, a step he would never have taken had the emotionally easier first step to the Liberals not been available. We shall return in a moment to the question of whether many electors in fact belong in this cell or in the opposite cell, p_{21}, which represents an equally odd, yet possible, pattern of choice.

It is clear, however, that the key entries of this matrix are those in the middle column, p_{12} and p_{22}, representing electors who would vote Liberal if a Liberal stood and Conservative or Labour if not. How are we to estimate these entries on the basis of our evidence from the two segments of the country formed by Liberal intervention and non-intervention? We can first, examine the second preferences expressed by Liberal voters where the Liberals did in fact intervene, in effect asking the electors who placed themselves in the middle column of our matrix by actually voting Liberal whether they belonged to the first or second row; that is, whether they would have voted Conservative or Labour if no Liberal had stood. Our evidence about the second preferences of Liberal voters differed substantially between 1964 and 1966, as Table 14.13 shows. A three to two ratio of Conservative to Labour second choices in 1964 turned into a two to three ratio in 1966. These

14.13 Second Preferences of Liberal Voters[a]

	1964	1966
Conservative	59%	40%
Labour	41	60
	100%	100%
	($n = 115$)	($n = 95$)

[a] We exclude the 19 per cent of Liberal voters in 1964 and 9 per cent in 1966 who did not have a second preference.

figures seem to imply that Liberal intervention hurt the Conservatives in the first of these elections and Labour in the second. But such a judgement is premature, as we shall see in a moment.

Second, we have from electors who were deprived of a chance to vote Liberal their report of whether they would have supported a Liberal candidate if one had stood. We, in effect, asked electors who placed themselves in the first or second row of our matrix by actually voting Conservative or Labour in straight fights whether they belonged to the middle column; that is, whether they would have voted Liberal if a Liberal had intervened. The proportions of Conservative and Labour voters in straight fights who showed a strong Liberal inclination are set out by Table 14.14.

14.14 Disposition of Voters in Straight Fights to Have Voted Liberal, by Party

Would you have voted Liberal if a Liberal candidate had stood in this constituency?	1964 Conservative Voters	1964 Labour Voters	1966 Conservative Voters	1966 Labour Voters
Would have[a]	19%	14%	18%	14%
Would not have or only 'might have'	81	86	82	86
	100%	100%	100%	100%
	(n = 236)	(n = 315)	(n = 281)	(n = 469)

[a] As explained in the text above, we regard only those who were fairly definite in their Liberal inclination as being probable Liberal voters.

We may now use both types of evidence to assemble the matrix of preferences that describes the effects of the Liberals' presence on the major parties. If the Liberals chose on a purely random basis the constituencies they would contest we would expect the matrix describing the electorate's conditional preferences to be roughly the same where Liberals stood and where they did not. If this were the case we would indeed be able to judge the effects of Liberal intervention simply by comparing the relative strength of the main parties in the two segments of the country into which the Liberals had divided it – consulting, in effect, the relative magnitude of the Conservative and Labour vote in straight fights ($p_1.$ and $p_2.$) and triangular contests ($p._1$ and $p._3$) as these were presented by the actual returns.

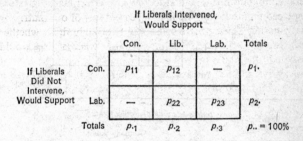

| | | If Liberals Intervened, Would Support | | | |
		Con.	Lib.	Lab.	Totals
If Liberals Did Not Intervene, Would Support	Con.	p_{11}	p_{12}	—	$p_1.$
	Lab.	—	p_{22}	p_{23}	$p_2.$
	Totals	$p._1$	$p._2$	$p._3$	$p.. = 100\%$

In fact, however, Liberal intervention has been highly selective. Liberals have in particular tended to stand more in Conservative than in Labour seats in recent years, and this factor would by itself be enough to confound hopelessly any effort to gauge the effect of Liberal intervention by inspecting the relative strength of the Conservatives and Labour where there were Liberal candidates and where there were not. We have therefore used our evidence on the second preferences of our respondents to reconstruct a matrix of conditional choice for each of these segments of the country with a view to seeing whether consistent judgements can be given from each as to the effects of the Liberal presence in a given year.

The results of such an analysis for the election of 1964 are set out in Table 14.15. The entries at the margin of the matrices shown here demonstrate that the Liberals did indeed tend to stand in Conservative areas; the Conservatives polled no more than 40 per cent of the actual votes cast by our respondents in straight fights, whereas they would have received a clear majority of votes in seats with triangular contests if these too had been straight fights. But what is mainly of interest here is the very limited effect of Liberal intervention or withdrawal on the relative strength of the

14.15 Conditional Preferences of 1964 Voters

a. In seats with straight fights

| | | If Liberals Had Intervened, Would Have Voted | | | |
		Con.	Lib.	Lab.	Totals
Actually Voted	Con.	33·1	7·3	—	40·4
	Lab.	—	8·4	51·2	59·6
	Totals	33·1 (39·3)	15·7	51·2 (60·7)	100·0% (100·0%)

b. In seats with triangular fights

| | | Actually Voted | | | |
		Con.	Lib.	Lab.	Totals
If Liberals Had Not Intervened, Would Have Voted	Con.	45·9	7·8	—	53·7
	Lab.	—	5·5	40·8	46·3
	Totals	45·9 (52·9)	13·3	40·8 (47·1)	100·0% (100·0%)

major parties. If we ask of the matrix of conditional preferences in straight fights (14.15a), what would have happened if the Liberals had intervened, the answer is a very slight swing to Labour, one which could easily be the consequence of sampling error. Labour's share of the actual vote in these constituencies stood at just less than 60 per cent; our best guess as to Labour's share of the major-party vote if the Liberals had intervened is just more than 60 per cent, representing a swing of about 1 per cent.

A very similar judgement as to the effect of the Liberal presence can be made from the lower matrix (14.15b), which describes the conditional preferences of respondents who were confronted by triangular contests. Its entries suggest that Liberal withdrawal from these contests would have produced a very slight swing to the Conservatives. Labour's share of the major-party vote actually cast by our respondents in these constituencies stood at just over 47 per cent; our best guess as to Labour's share if the Liberals had withdrawn is just over 46 per cent, a difference representing a swing of less than 1 per cent. Therefore, in each case there is evidence of a trace of benefit to Labour and of harm to the Conservatives from the Liberals' presence. But what mainly emerges from these figures for 1964 is how remarkably little difference the Liberal presence made.

The results of the companion analysis for the election of 1966 are set out in Table 14.16. The entries at the margin of the matrices show once again how diffident the Liberals were about contesting Labour seats. Indeed, in 1966 the Conservatives polled little more than a third of the votes cast by our respondents in straight fights.

14.16 Conditional Preferences of 1966 Voters

a. In seats with straight fights

| | | If Liberals Had Intervened Would Have Voted | | | |
		Con.	Lib.	Lab.	Totals
Actually Voted	Con.	29·8	6·2	—	36·0
	Lab.	—	8·6	55·4	64·0
	Totals	29·8 (35·0)	14·8	55·4 (65·0)	100·0% (100·0%)

b. In seats with triangular fights

| | | Actually Voted | | | |
		Con.	Lib.	Lab.	Totals
If Liberals Had Not Intervened, Would Have Voted	Con.	44·3	5·2	—	49·5
	Lab.	—	7·8	42·7	50·5
	Totals	44·3 (50·9)	13·0	42·7 (49·1)	100·0% (100·0%)

The conclusions to be drawn from these matrices as to the effects of the Liberal presence are somewhat more mixed. The upper matrix suggests that Liberal intervention into straight fights would have yielded something like a 1 per cent swing to Labour, whereas the lower matrix suggests that the Liberals' actual intervention into triangular contests yielded a comparably slight swing away from Labour. What is mainly impressive about the 1966 findings, however, is how little net impact the Liberals probably had.[16]

Where the Liberals would go – or come from – if the pattern of candidature at a given election were different needs to be sharply distinguished from the question of where the Liberals actually came from, or went to, between one election and the next. Failure to separate these questions confused many of the commentaries on the Liberal growth in the early 1960s. There is little doubt that this growth was due mainly to shifts away from the Conservatives. From this it was widely assumed that if the Liberal recruits fell away from the party, either because they were denied a candidate or because they were reluctant to waste their vote on a hopeless Liberal candidacy, the Conservatives would reclaim what they had lost.

The actual flows to and from the Liberals in the period of our work were set out earlier in this chapter and in Chapter 12. We must look to the more complex pattern of these flows over several intervals of time, however, to see whether voters tend to move from

16. This conclusion as to the Liberals' slight effect is generally consistent with the findings of those who have used the election returns to measure the swings of major-party strength where the Liberals have intervened and withdrawn between successive elections. This type of analysis has indeed become a standard part of the repertory of those who inspect election returns. See, e.g. *The British General Election of 1964*, p. 275, *The British General Election of 1966*, p. 350, or H. Berrington, 'The General Election of 1964', *Journal of the Royal Statistical Society*, Series A, **128** (1965), pp. 39–48 and 'The 1966 Election', *Swinton Journal*, Autumn 1966, 3–10. Some analyses, notably by region and by classes of constituencies, can be made of election returns which are beyond the reach of a national survey. Probably the most important of the findings from such work is Berrington's demonstration that the Liberals have tended to draw their strength from Labour in Conservative-held seats and from the Conservatives in Labour-held seats.

the Conservatives to Labour, or vice versa, *via* the Liberals. The incidence of such two-stage defection is of interest in its own right and also for its bearing on the effect of Liberal intervention on the vote for the other parties. If the Liberals offer a half-way house for many voters it could be argued that their presence makes the full journey from one of the two larger parties to the other an easier one to travel.

A most unequivocal answer can be given to this question in terms of the longer-run movements of voters during the years of our work. Liberal support was sufficiently evanescent for our samples to include many electors who moved to the Liberals from one of the major parties only to move away again. But in almost every case this second move was back to the same party. For example, of those in our sample who moved from Labour to the Liberals between 1963 and 1964, not a single one moved on to the Conservatives in 1966. That may not seem very surprising in view of the Labour tide that was then flowing, but a very similar picture is offered by those who moved from the Conservatives to the Liberals between 1963 and 1964 and then changed again: fully 94 per cent of them moved back to the Conservatives despite the Labour tide. There were many voters in our sample who moved from the Conservatives to Labour between 1963 and 1966. Almost none used the Liberals as a half-way house. The pattern of changes between 1959, 1963 and 1964 or between 1959, 1964 and 1966 was very similar. In the light of this, it is difficult to support the idea that the Liberals' presence encouraged a traffic of electors between the two larger parties. Indeed it may well have retarded it by giving the voter who had lost enthusiasm for his own party a means of not taking the greater plunge.

This need not mean that the Liberal presence damped the overall swings of party strength. Although they may have provided an escape for some who might otherwise have gone all the way to the other side, they also may have given some who would never have gone right over an opportunity for more limited protest. In fact, if the Liberals cut more into the strength of the Conservatives in 1964, we would say, other things being equal, that they increased the party swing from 1959 to 1964.

Therefore, although the Liberals' support in the early 1960s could give them no significant representation in the House of Commons under the existing electoral system,[17] the party did have a measurable impact on the strength of the two larger parties.

But these movements of Liberal strength in the 1960s are only one among the factors in the electoral changes which this section of the book has been concerned to measure. If we are to understand the background of the movements of party strength in this period, especially the shifts of the relative strength of the two main parties, we must examine a much wider configuration of political issues as well as the standing in the country of the parties and leaders who give these issues meaning for the mass electorate.

17. For our evidence on what a different electoral system might have done for the Liberals, see D. Butler, A. Stevens and D. Stokes, 'The Strength of the Liberals under Alternative Electoral Systems', *Parliamentary Affairs*, **20** (1969), 10–15.

Part Four

	CHANGES OF ALIGNMENT	TRANSIENT VARIATIONS
CONSTRUCTION		
APPLICATION		▨

15 Issues and Change

Elections seldom turn narrowly on issues of government policy. We have seen in Chapter 8 how little the mass of voters could be said to respond to the policy alternatives at Westminster in judging the claims of the rival parties. If we are to deal very fully with the issues swaying the electorate we must use a framework of analysis that admits of a wider class of issues. We have indeed argued that a framework of this sort can be applied to influences which are often thought not to be properly issues at all, including the images of the parties, or the pull of the leaders, or the country's feelings of economic well-being. This chapter applies a general framework of analysis to the issues which may have shifted the party balance in the 1960s. We defer till later chapters the related forces which were involved in changes of party strength in this period.

A Framework for Issues

In Chapter 8 we explored the conditions which must be met if an issue is to alter the relative standing of the parties. First of all, the issue must be one that involves attitudes which exist or can be evoked in a substantial part of the electorate. The vast majority of issues fail such a test. Most never achieve any public salience at all. Of the fairly restricted number that are brought before the public by political debate and the mass media we may conclude that only a few become matters that excite genuine and strong attitudes in significant parts of the electorate. Yet unless an issue touches values that make it a matter of widespread popular feeling, it cannot have a major impact on the relative standing of the parties.

Even if it does, two other conditions must also be satisfied. One is that opinion on the issue must be skewed rather than equally balanced. An issue which divides the country fairly evenly can sway the behaviour of many individual voters but it cannot greatly alter the net strength of the parties. The other condition is that the public must see the parties differently in relation to the issue. Unless one party or the other is more closely linked to the values or policies which give the issue content for most electors, the issue cannot shift the balance of party strength, however strongly formed and skewed the opinion it excites.

The sharpest impact on party strength will be made by issues which simultaneously meet all these three conditions, that is to say by issues on which attitudes are widely formed, on which opinion is far from evenly divided and on which the parties are strongly differentiated in the public's mind. We may represent the confluence of these properties as one region in an eight-fold geometric figure suggested by the joint classification of how well these three conditions are satisfied.

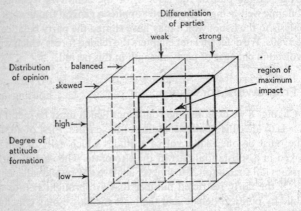

There is, of course, no reason to think of properties such as the differentiation of parties in the simple dichotomous terms suggested by the diagram; each of the ideas represented here can be regarded as a continuum, capable of many gradations. But to simplify the argument that follows we do treat them as roughly dichotomous. On this basis, only one of the cells in this eight-fold classification will include the issues that have maximum impact on the party balance. In each of the other seven the issues will lack one or more of the necessary properties.

Where, within such a framework, did the issues of British politics during the early 1960s fall? Our evidence suggests that they varied widely in the extent to which they fulfilled our three prerequisites. Moreover, there were several notable cases in which an issue's properties changed quite abruptly, altering its capacity to influence the party balance. Our analytic framework suggests some new insights into the impact of some of the issues of the 1960s. The issues to which the parties gave most prominence were not always those which had the greatest potential.

Issues of Strongest Impact

In the non-economic field the most persuasive case can be made for the impact of a set of domestic issues involving social welfare. To begin with, there can be no doubt of the salience of the values associated with welfare issues, especially housing and pensions, during this era. In our 1963 survey, we asked our respondents to tell us what they thought were the most important problems facing the Government, without confining their answers in any way. The replies to this question, as summarized by Table 15.1 on the next page, show vividly how prominent pensions and housing and related issues were in the electorate's thinking. A sample of two thousand mentioned just under five thousand 'problems' in all. Almost half of these involved social welfare. By contrast the whole realm of foreign affairs and defence provided less than one in ten of the problems mentioned. The newspaper polls throughout this period offer a similar picture. When they asked people to choose the most important problems, housing, pensions and education invariably came in the top five. Only the cost of living and taxation attracted a comparable number of mentions.[1]

1. In the 1963–4 period the Gallup Poll, for example, found that respondents who chose a domestic problem as the most important facing the country outnumbered those who chose a problem of external affairs by three to one. The problems most frequently chosen were housing, pensions, education and economic affairs.

The salience of issues of this kind was not, of course, peculiar to the early 1960s. The values underlying them are easily understood by the mass of people; the rise and endurance of the Welfare State is directly related to this fact. Variations in the impact of these issues over time must have depended principally on the two other conditions – the skewness of opinion and public differentiation of the parties.

Certainly our evidence indicates how one-sided the public's support for increased outlays for the social services was in the early 1960s. The spontaneous reference summarized in Table 15.1

15.1 Most Important Problems Perceived as Facing Government, 1963[a]

Type of Problem		Frequency of Mention	
Social welfare, including		1160	25%
Pensions and old people's welfare	787		
Health service	167		
Give family allowances only to needy	101		
Housing, including		1122	24%
Build more houses	566		
Improve standards, clear slums	192		
Keep house and mortgage prices down	189		
Reduce rents	115		
Economic problems, including		788	17%
Keep down cost of living	193		
Reduce unemployment	193		
Bring jobs to particular areas	153		
Education		420	9%
Defence and international affairs		344	7%
Transport		286	6%
Taxation		277	5%
Immigration		100	2%
Industrial relations		73	2%
All other problems		176	3%
		4746	100%

[a] This table shows the total number of items volunteered by our 2,009 respondents in the summer of 1963 when asked the question 'What do you yourself feel are the most important problems the Government should do something about?' (See Question 16 in the 1963 questionnaire.)

were overwhelmingly angled towards increased government expenditure on pensions and housing. Of those who mentioned social welfare issues, fewer than one in ten touched restrictionist themes, such as confining family allowances to the needy. Of those who mentioned housing, even fewer raised themes, such as the charging of economic rents for local authority housing, designed to reduce the burdens on government. Even if all references to the need to cut taxes were interpreted as implicit calls for the limitation of spending on social services, an interpretation that could hardly be sustained, the negative view would still be very much a minority one. The public mood in this period was, in this field at least, strongly interventionist.

The evidence is equally clear that this mood benefited Labour more than the Conservatives. Those who in 1963 mentioned as a problem the need for some expansion of the social services were asked which party could handle the matter best. As Table 15.2

15.2 Perceived Ability of Parties to Expand or Curtail Social Services, 1963

	Party Perceived as Better Able to Achieve Goal				
	Conservative	Labour	No difference	Don't Know	
Respondent favours[a]					
Expanding social services	18%	51	20	11	100% (1537)
Curtailing social services	28%	23	28	21	100% (113)

[a] The perceptions included in this analysis are those associated with the respondent's identification in the 1963 interview of the major problems facing the Government. Responses advocating that the pension be put up, more houses be built, etc. were counted as wanting to expand the social services, while those advocating that family allowances be cut, a higher rent be charged for municipal council housing, etc. were counted as wanting to curtail the social services. After each problem mentioned the respondent was asked, 'What would you like to see the Government do about that?' and 'Which party would be most likely to do what you want on this, the Conservatives, Labour, the Liberals, or wouldn't it make much difference?'

shows, Labour was seen as very much more likely to expand the services. The point is reinforced by the tendency of those few who sought some curtailment of the social services to see the Conservatives as somewhat more likely to achieve such a result: thus, had curtailment been a dominant public desire, Labour would have benefited much less from the differentiation of parties so clearly shown by the entries of Table 15.2.[2]

These perceptions remained almost equally sharp throughout our study. As Table 15.3 shows, the view that Labour was more likely to increase social service spending was even stronger in 1964

15.3 Perceived Position of the Parties on Increased Spending for the Social Services, 1964 and 1966

Which party would be more likely to spend more on the social services?	Conservatives	Labour	Not much Difference	Don't know	Totals
Autumn 1964	8%	69	16	7	100%
Spring	7%	64	23	6	100%

and 1966 than in 1963. Undoubtedly the Labour Government's action in giving first priority on taking office to a substantial increase in pensions helped to reinforce the distinctness with which its position in this area was perceived.[3]

During this period the social services thus provided an issue that satisfied the three conditions. The evidence suggests that the issue's effect was substantial. Table 15.4 compares the swing to Labour from 1959 to 1963 among three groups: those who wanted the

2. It would, however, be difficult not to see the slight extent of the Conservatives' advantage in the eyes of those who would *curtail* the social services as evidence of a far more general decline of support for the party. This is a question to which we return.

3. In November 1964 despite the economic situation, the new Government announced that the election promise to raise pensions would be met as soon as possible. In March 1965 the basic rate was increased by 20 per cent.

15.4 Swing to Labour 1959–63 by Attitudes on Social Services

	Wanted social services expanded and preferred Labour handling of issue	Did not mention social services	Wanted social services curtailed and preferred Conservative handling of issue
Swing	+9·6%	+2·0%	−1·9%

social services to be expanded and saw Labour as better able to do so, those who did not mention the social services in 1963 and those who wanted the social services curtailed and saw the Conservatives as better able to do so. Since, as we have seen, the first of these groups was very much larger than the third this issue worked strongly to Labour's advantage.

Although throughout our period, the issue of the social services helped Labour, there is interesting evidence that the public desire for their expansion was partially satisfied between 1964 and 1966 and that the skewness of opinion lessened on this issue. Both in 1964 and 1966 we inquired whether our respondents thought that expenditures for the social services should be increased or should be kept at their existing level. The change during the course of the 1964 Parliament is set out in Table 15.5. Apparently the action

15.5 Perceived Need for Increased Spending on Social Services, 1964 and 1966

Do you feel that the Government should spend more on pensions and social services or do you feel that spending for social services should stay about as it is now?	Autumn 1964	Spring 1966
Should spend more	77%	54%
Should stay about as it is now	20	42
Don't know	3	4
	100%	100%

of the new Labour Government in putting up pensions and removing prescription charges for medicines had lessened the gap between what the average elector felt desirable and what he thought government was doing. Following a line of reasoning employed in Chapter 8 we can suggest the nature of this change between 1964 and 1966 in terms of a dimension showing degree of support for the social services on which we can place a distribution of voter preferences for government spending on social services together with their perception of the extent of present government spending. The situation in 1964 might be represented as follows:

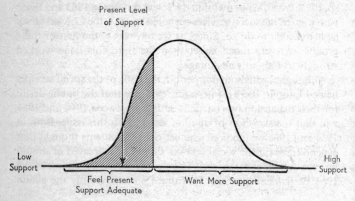

The perceived level of existing support for the social services was low enough to satisfy only a minority of electors, those who are shown in the interval marked 'feel present support adequate'. The majority had preferences far enough above what they perceived the existing level to be to record themselves as favouring an increase in spending. These are the people who fell in the interval marked off for those who 'want more support'.[4] By 1966, however,

4. We have prepared these sketches to convey a few main ideas for which empirical warrant seems clear. We do not at all regard them as literal representations of reality. We do not know the shape of the electorate's distribution along such a dimension or even the extent to which it sees such a continuum of support for the social services. A fully realistic representation would have to take account of a number of further complications, especially the differing perceptions individuals would have of the existing level of support.

the actions of the Labour Government presumably had shifted the perceived level of existing support, so that opinion was much less skewed in favour of additional spending:

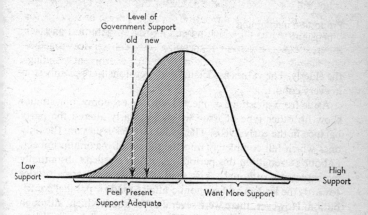

Whether this shift altered the effect of the issue is a question that is not easily answered. It is possible that Labour's advantage was not diminished because the Conservatives were seen as likely actually to reduce the level of support for the social services if they were returned to power. The parties remained sharply differentiated in the public's mind, as we have seen. If substantial numbers of electors thought the Conservatives would restore the *status quo ante*, Labour's advantage might have remained intact. It seems more probable, however, that the force of this issue was somewhat lessened by 1966.

Issues surrounding the social services are presumed to have this great potential because they touch the lives of so many within the electorate. Yet their impact will vary with the importance accorded to these outputs of government by different parts of the electorate. A very clear example of this is the greater interest of older people in the question of the size of pensions. Table 15.6 shows how in 1963 the salience of the pension issue increased with age. But it would be wrong to think of this issue as being of concern only to

15.6 Spontaneous Mention of the Issue of Pensions
by Cohort, 1963

	Pre-1918	Interwar	1945	Post-1951
Proportion mentioning pensions	39%	35%	34%	28%

the elderly. The values associated with pensions were plainly seen
in every cohort.

Aside from questions connected with the economy, our studies
show no other type of issue which so clearly altered the party
balance in the early 1960s. The social services issues are the only
ones which fall completely into the region of maximum impact.
Labour's strength in this period was plainly swelled substantially
by these issues, although, as we shall see in later chapters, attitudes
towards the leaders and economic affairs made a parallel contribution. However, there were several other issues which, although
high in potential influence, failed to meet fully our three conditions
for maximum impact upon the party balance.

Issues of High Potential

The explosive possibilities of the issues raised by coloured immigration were only partially recognized during the early 1960s.
Yet the question was very salient to the mass of the people. As
Table 15.1 showed, immigration was spontaneously mentioned
in 1963 by a substantial number of our respondents, even though
it was then playing a relatively small role in public debate.
Moreover, a specific question about immigration elicited fewer
'don't knows' than any other issues question in our survey,
except for one about the importance of the Queen and Royal
Family. Indeed a remarkable proportion of our respondents –
fully a quarter – felt strongly enough to go beyond the 'closed'
question and to offer spontaneous elaborations of their hostility
to coloured immigration.[5] In 1964 and 1966 we found that more

5. Spontaneous objections centred on competition for housing and jobs

than half our sample felt 'very strongly' on immigration and a further third felt 'fairly strongly'.

The evidence for the one-sidedness of the public attitude is equally overwhelming. Table 15.7 shows the undeviating opposition to coloured immigration reflected in each of our interviews.

15.7 Attitudes Towards Immigration

Do you think that too many immigrants have been let into this country or not?	Summer 1963	Autumn 1964	Spring 1966
Too many	84%	81%	81%
Not too many	12	13	14
Don't know	4	6	5
	100%	100%	100%

Its entries match closely the findings of the opinion polls.

The degree of concern with this problem varied between classes and generations. Those in the higher occupational grades were less opposed to immigration and were markedly less likely to feel strongly about the issue. Indeed, the proportions feeling strongly that too many immigrants had been let in rose almost without a break across our six occupational grades from 28 per cent among higher managerial (I) to 48 per cent among unskilled manual (VI). This difference of attitude according to the closeness of the individual to the consequences of immigration parallels a difference by geographic proximity that we shall observe in a moment.

There was also a fairly steep gradient in opposition to immigration by age. The proportions recording themselves as strongly opposed to the entry of so many immigrants were quite different across our four cohorts. Among the pre-1918 cohort 52 per cent did so, and among the inter-war cohort the proportion, 47 per

('there's not enough work for our own as it is') and the deterioration of health and living standards the immigrants were thought to bring ('up in Birmingham they crowd twenty into a house'; 'it's the way they're let in without any medical checks, bringing tuberculosis and things like that').

cent, was only slightly less. Yet among the 1945 and post-1951 cohorts the proportions strongly in opposition were only 35 and 37 per cent.

But the immigration issue, although in 1964 it lost the Labour Party three seats against the tide and probably prevented them from winning several others, never exercised anything like its potential impact on the party balance, because the public failed to differentiate the party positions. This was partly because the parties themselves were each visibly divided. Moreover, while the Labour Party had opposed the Conservatives' Commonwealth Immigrants Act of 1962, the first restriction on immigration, it was a Conservative Government that had been in power during the period in which mass immigration had taken place. When Labour came to power in 1964, after a campaign which in Smethwick and a few other constituencies had revealed the dynamite that lay in the issue, the new Government quickly moved to a position on immigration control that was quite as tough as that of its predecessor.

Our respondents gave clear evidence of failure to differentiate the parties' positions. When asked which party would be more likely to keep the immigrants out, the great majority, both in 1964 and 1966, saw no difference between the parties or confessed that they did not know, as Table 15.8 shows. These figures suggest how limited the influence of the issue can have been on the strength of the parties across the country as a whole.

15.8 Perceived Position of Parties on Control of Immigration

Which party is more likely to keep immigrants out?	Autumn 1964	Spring 1966
Conservative	26%	26%
Labour	19	13
No difference	41	53
Don't know	14	8
	100%	100%

There is, however, evidence that the issue may have had a stronger influence in particular areas. The concentration of coloured immigrants in a few cities makes it natural that the salience of the issue should have varied widely. We divided our sample into those who lived in areas with substantial, moderate or neglible numbers of immigrants. In the areas of high concentration, as Table 15.9 shows, the proportion volunteering the issue was appreciably greater than elsewhere. In areas which had

15.9 Frequency of Spontaneous Comments on Coloured Immigration by Concentration of Immigrants[a]

	In areas of		
	High Concentration	Low Concentration	No Significant Concentration
Proportion offering spontaneous comments on coloured immigration	44%	26%	21%

[a] Entries are proportions offering spontaneous additional comments about coloured immigration in replying to question 25 of the 1963 questionnaire.

virtually no immigrants, one respondent in five made such comments, and in intermediate areas the proportion was scarcely higher; but in areas of high concentration nearly one in two did so.

Even more striking is the extent to which the electorate's perception of party difference on this issue varied with the degree of immigrant concentration. The country as a whole saw only a moderate difference between the parties, but in the areas most affected the perception of difference was much sharper. Table 15.10 shows this contrast for 1964. Where there had been negligible immigration, virtually equal numbers of respondents saw each party as the more likely to shut off the flow. But where immigration had been substantial, three times as many people thought the Conservatives would be more restrictive.

15.10 Differentiation of Parties Perceived Position on Immigration by Degree of Immigrant Concentration, 1964

Which party is more likely to keep immigrants out?	Degree of Immigrant Concentration in Local Area		
	None	Low	High
Conservative	22%	31%	43%
Labour	21	14	14
No difference	42	45	31
Don't know	15	10	12
	100%	100%	100%

This pattern survived to 1966. Table 15.11 records a rise in all areas in the proportions who saw no difference in the party positions on immigration control. But a sharp gradient is still evident in the extent to which the parties were seen as having different positions.

15.11 Differentiation of Parties' Perceived Position on Immigration by Degree of Immigrant Concentration, 1966

Which party is more likely to keep immigrants out?	Degree of Immigrant Concentration in Local Area		
	None	Low	High
Conservative	22%	30%	37%
Labour	15	10	11
No difference	54	52	45
Don't know	9	8	7
	100%	100%	100%

Too much ought not to be made of these differences. Even in areas of high immigrant concentration, voters were much less likely to have a clear perception of party difference on this issue than on, for example, nationalization. Moreover, only a small fraction of the electorate lived in such areas. Yet these differences offer additional testimony to the potential influence of the issue. The campaign and the outcome in Smethwick show how candidates who appreciated the possibilities could exploit them.[6]

We may therefore place the issue of immigration in the region of our schematic diagram which is adjacent to the region where issues have their maximum impact on party strength:

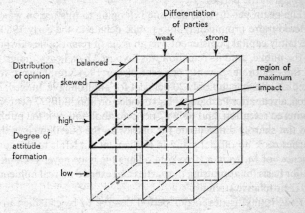

It was an issue that involved the necessary salience and the necessary skewed opinion – but it failed to involve sufficiently widespread differentiation in the perceptions of the parties' positions. There can be little doubt that, if this third condition had also been met, the issue could have altered the party balance sharply.

What distinguished immigration from the other issues of this period that might be allocated to this region was the very real possibility that its full potential might have been realized through a further differentiation of the parties' stands in the public's mind.

6. In April 1968 the extraordinary response to an inflammatory speech on immigration by Enoch Powell, then on the Conservative front bench, underlined the great potential of the issue. It also stressed the forbearance of those in both parties who, perhaps against their short-term electoral advantage, had over the previous few years sought to take the heat out of the issue.

By contrast a number of other issues that might be placed in such a region concerned questions that scarcely differentiated the parties at all. An example is the 'issue' of the monarchy. The institutions of monarchy are salient to the people and their retention is overwhelmingly favoured. If one of the parties were thought, rightly or wrongly, to be threatening their destruction the issue could well become one of great significance for the relative strength of the parties.

The death penalty was an issue belonging to this region which entered more prominently into public debate in the early 1960s. Certainly capital punishment was an issue of remarkable salience to the public. And its retention was favoured by a heavy majority of the electorate. Seventy per cent of our 1964 sample were for keeping hanging and only 20 per cent for abolishing it. Indeed, in 1966, a year after Parliament had decided on abolition, 77 per cent favoured retention, and only 17 per cent abolition. But the public did not sharply differentiate the parties on the question since the parties took no official stand in Parliament but left it to the consciences of M.P.s in a 'free vote'. Thus the issue never became a major basis for appraising the parties and exerted no real influence on their relative strength.[7]

Few, if any, issues in our period deserve to be classified in a second region which also lies adjacent to the region of maximum impact. Our schematic classification allows for issues which are highly salient and which strongly differentiate the parties but on which opinion is fairly evenly divided between competing policies or goals. When they occur these are the issues which divide a society most profoundly. In the 1880s Irish Home Rule may have been one such case. But in the early 1960s, although there were issues on which opinion was fairly evenly divided, none of these was a matter both of strong feeling in the country and of sharply differentiated party positions. As for the other issues which had

7. In fact Labour Members were much more strongly abolitionist than Conservatives. But some Labour M.P.s did support retention of the death penalty and a large number of Conservatives, including some very prominent ones, consistently voted for abolition. This appears to have been sufficient to blur in the public mind the differentiation between the parties on this issue more than was in fact justified.

currency in this period, they all seem to have been of much lower salience for the mass electorate.

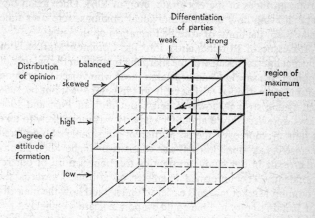

Issues of Less Potential

The vast majority of issues which gave content to political debate within the parties and at Westminster during our period plainly belong in the lower tier of our schematic diagram in one of the regions of low attitude formation. In Chapter 8 we discussed the interesting case of nationalization. Our data showed that the public differentiated the party positions on this very clearly and, furthermore, that a clear majority of the electorate expressed opposition to further nationalization. Yet our data made plain, especially in the instability of individual opinion over time, the slight extent to which the issue of nationalization was a matter of genuine attitude formation among the mass electorate.

A very similar judgement can be made about the issue of nuclear weapons. Before Labour came to power in 1964 the parties were perceived as having strongly divergent positions on the nuclear deterrent (although this perception had become much more blurred by 1966). Opinion on the issue, although less one-sided than on nationalization, leaned heavily towards the retention of

British nuclear weapons. But what made the Bomb ineffective as an issue was the limited hold it had on either the attention or the strong attitudes of the electorate, even in 1964. Once again our data showing how unstable individual opinions were over time make plain the limits of attitude formation on the issue.

The issue of Britain's entry into the Common Market is of unusual interest because of the sharp fluctuations in the balance of opinion. We saw in Chapter 10 that those who voiced an opinion on this issue divided fairly evenly in 1963 and 1964, but by 1966 had swung strongly towards entry. But both in 1964 and 1966 views were very mixed about which party was more likely to take Britain in; moreover, the proportion of our sample who declared themselves as 'don't knows' was consistently higher than on any other issue in our study, amounting to about a third of our respondents. The unformed character of attitudes towards the Common Market makes it easier to understand how the majority for Britain's entry in 1966 could evaporate again so quickly.[8]

Somewhat less clear is the impact of Rhodesia, which became a prominent issue with the unilateral declaration of independence by the Smith government in November 1965. The issue made headlines throughout the autumn and early winter. The Prime Minister projected himself as a national leader defending the Crown and the Commonwealth. The Conservatives were deeply divided: a compromise arrangement to avoid a vote at their party conference in mid-October was presented as a capitulation to Lord Salisbury and the right wing, and in November and December when the issue was debated in Parliament the party split three ways between opposition, abstention and support on a motion approving the Government's policy.

The issue was undoubtedly given prominence by the mass media and there is no doubt that the parties were differentiated in the electorate's mind. Figure 15.12 shows the clear tendency of the public to see the Conservatives as favouring a compromise with or

8. Over several surveys between August 1966 and January 1967 the Gallup Poll found majorities of at least four to one in favour of a British application for membership. A year later surveys were showing the public as evenly divided, even before General de Gaulle's second veto.

15.12 Perceived Positions of Parties on Rhodesia, 1966[a]

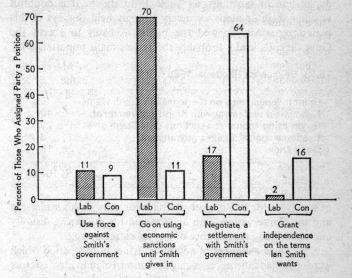

[a] The values given are the proportions of those assigning a given party to each of several alternative positions in response to questions 30b and 30c of the 1966 questionnaire. Those who replied 'don't know' (9 per cent in the case of Labour, 15 per cent in the case of the Conservatives) are excluded from the analysis.

an outright grant of independence to the Smith government and to see Labour as committed to going on with sanctions. A few in our sample could not associate a position with Labour, and somewhat more were unable to place the Conservatives. But of those who could, the great majority were clear that Labour stood for tougher handling of the Smith government.

The extent to which the electorate had well formed opinions of its own on the issue is more doubtful. Few of our respondents volunteered Rhodesia as one of the main issues of the 1966 campaign or as a ground for liking or disliking either of the main parties or their leaders. One in five of our respondents said they did not have any opinion on Rhodesia. Of those who did endorse one of the several alternative positions, a narrow majority came down on the side of a negotiated settlement rather than the continued application of sanctions, as Table 15.13 shows. It is doubtful whether these opinions were very strongly held. Surveys of this period repeatedly showed the public as likely to accept the Government's lead.[9] Probably the issue's main importance lay

15.13 Opinion on Rhodesia, 1966

Grant independence on the terms Ian Smith wants	5%
Negotiate a settlement with Smith's government	40
Go on using economic sanctions until Smith gives in	29
Use force against Smith's government	8
Don't know	18
	100%

in supplying Mr Wilson with a vehicle for showing his leadership and the Conservatives with an occasion for displaying disunity and underlining the presence of a vocal extreme wing.

There were a number of additional issues in this period which were of limited salience, engaging the concern of individual electors or groups of electors but having little hold on the electorate as a whole. The impact of each such issue on the relative strength of the parties must have been small, although taken together they had, of course, an influence on the choices of a large number of people. For example, however faint the issue of the nuclear deterrent for the great bulk of the electorate there is no doubt that it mattered enormously to many thousands of individuals.

If perceptions of the parties' ability to deal with a number of distinct issues are inspected closely, it becomes plain that the electorate tends to gain or lose confidence in a party in several

9. In October 1965, for example, National Opinion Polls recorded 82 per cent of the electorate as accepting the Government's position with the encouragement offered by this question: 'The British Government insist that independence can only be granted to Rhodesia if the conditions are acceptable to the people of Rhodesia as a whole, and not just to whites. Do you think this is right or wrong?' The same survey showed that the ratio of whites to blacks in Rhodesia was known only to a very small fraction of the public.

areas at once. During the period of our work Labour was the more successful in instilling a fairly general confidence or trust, which extended to its putative performance on many (though not all) of the particular issues which engaged our sample's concern. A similar study from the later 1960s, when Labour was in a deep trough of public disfavour, would undoubtedly show a reversal of this picture, with confidence in Labour having drained away across almost the whole range of issues.

This phenomenon draws attention to more general aspects of popular attitudes towards the parties, in particular to elements of the parties' images that are susceptible to marked change over time. Therefore we shall now go beyond the electorate's perception of the parties' positions or abilities in relation to particular issues and explore the more generalized impressions of the parties in the public's mind.

16 Images of the Parties

In the 1960s, as for a century past, the behaviour of the electorate was shaped by generalized attitudes and beliefs about the parties far more than by any specific policy issues. People respond to the parties to a large extent in terms of images they form from the characteristics and style of party leaders and from the party's association, intended or not, with the things governments may achieve. The importance of such images has been recognized since Graham Wallas' day, and the terminology of party images moved from academic to popular discussion in Britain in the later 1950s.[1]

Some of the most general and salient beliefs about the parties are very slow to change. The outstanding examples in Britain are of course the links of the Conservatives with the middle and upper classes and of Labour with the working class. We have argued that there has been a profound change in the beliefs about the relation of class and politics over the past generation. But the pace of this change, depending as it has on the entry of new cohorts into the electorate, must be fairly glacial.

Other elements of the parties' images, however, are much more plastic. The electorate may in a fairly short span come to associate qualities with the parties which have a substantial influence on its choices at the polling station. Indeed, the presumption that this is so underlies the very considerable efforts by the parties themselves to help form the images that the public holds. Towards the end of the 1950s the Conservative Party sought with considerable skill to

1. See G. Wallas, *Human Nature in Politics*, London, 1908; R. S. Milne and H. C. Mackenzie, *Marginal Seat*, London, 1958; J. Blondel, *Voters, Parties and Leaders*, London, 1965, pp. 81–4; P. Pulzer, *Political Representation and Elections*, London, 1958, pp. 113–14; and D. E. Butler and R. Rose, *The British General Election of 1959*, London, 1960, pp. 17–34.

heighten the public's sense that it was the party of good times; the 'life's better with the Conservatives – don't let Labour ruin it' campaign is still a model of its kind. At the start of our studies, in the years 1963–4, the public was subjected to an unprecedented amount of advertising by both parties, each trying to associate itself with the symbols of modernization, optimism and strong leadership.[2] We examine here the nature of the images of the parties formed by the public, giving particular attention to evidence of how these may have helped to account for fluctuations of party strength in the 1960s.

The Nature of Party Images

Much in the discussion of issues in the preceding chapter anticipates our treatment of party images here, and we shall not draw any sharp distinction between the two. Indeed, once issues are conceived more broadly than in terms solely of competing policies we move into realms of attitude and belief that are frequently associated with the concept of image, as our reference to the class images of the parties suggests. If a distinction is to be enforced it seems to us most natural that it should be drawn in terms of whether at least a vaguely defined class of potential outputs of government is involved. The 'issue' of class benefit evokes some set of possible effects of government action, however diffuse and general the set may be. But some qualities of party image, such as strength or modernness or reliability, are so broad that they could be linked to almost any set out of government outputs. A party may be seen as trustworthy or as bound to make a mess of things without any necessary reference to the area in which it can be trusted or in which it is bound to make a mess. Indeed, some image qualities have much more to do with 'intrinsic' values of party, which are not related to the outputs of government at all. The value of a party to the voter who finds it 'exciting' rather than 'dull' may be the psychic gratification of breaking the dullness of most political news.

2. See R. Rose, *Influencing Voters*, London, 1967, and Lord Windlesham, *Communication and Political Power*, London, 1966.

The intimate link between issues, broadly conceived, and party images argues the utility of applying a common framework to the effects of each on party strength. The framework for the analysis of issues set out in Chapters 8 and 15 can also give insight into the impact which image properties may have on the electorate's choice. To begin with, we may inquire which properties are genuinely salient to the electorate. What are the qualities which the public tends to see in the parties? The salience of different properties may of course be influenced by political leaders, either through explicit propaganda or through the subtler processes by which the conceptions developed by those near the centre of politics radiate outwards, via the mass media, to those who are more peripheral. There is a parallel here with the importance that political leadership has in shaping the bond between issue and self in the voter's mind.

But we may in some cases be sceptical about the insider's idea of the terms in which the parties are viewed by the mass electorate. Those on the stage of politics often see in the reaction of their audience perceptions that are in fact held only by the actors themselves. To what extent, for example, does the public weigh up the parties in terms of how united they are? Those immersed in the affairs of Westminster frequently express the view that the public cares a good deal about party unity, and this argument enters discussions of the need for cohesion in the division lobbies or in statements to press and television. But the salience of this and other image qualities to the electorate is really an empirical question on which little evidence is available.

In a similar way, we may ask how 'skewed' are the electorate's preferences among alternative properties the parties may exhibit. The example of cohesiveness is again instructive. Not only is it unclear how much the public sees the parties in terms of whether they are united or split. It is also unclear which of these the public likes its parties to be. This is again an empirical question that is not to be settled by *a priori* argument. The standard assumption at Westminster, as we have noted, is that the public approves of unity and abhors disunity: a party must after all, in the conventional phrase, 'show that it knows how to govern'. But there is really very little evidence that the public may not at times love a party better if it exhibits a little disorder, which may help to lessen the ennui of the evening paper and to show that its leaders are independent and care.

The question of the skewness of opinion about image qualities is one that can be brought within the distinction between 'valence' and 'position' dimensions that we set out on page 236. Probably it is true that most image qualities belong to dimensions on which there is high consensus about where a party should be. A party should be 'wise' rather than 'foolish', 'strong' rather than 'weak', 'expert' rather than 'clumsy', perhaps even 'united' rather than 'split'. The presumption that this is true explains why the party managers invest so much effort in projecting image properties to the mass electorate: the votes gained by persuading the country that a party is 'forward-looking' are not partially offset by the lost votes of those who want a party to be 'backward-looking'. But we shall apply at least a limited test to the possibility that some of the dimensions of party image are ones on which there are differences of opinion about where a party should be. Plainly there are some qualities that are central to the parties' images about which tastes differ. The electorate lacks a united view about whether a party should be 'middle class' or 'working class'. It is not altogether unreasonable to think that tastes may also differ about whether a party should be 'traditional' or 'modern'.

Finally, we have to take account of the extent to which the parties are differentiated in terms of the various properties which define their images in the public's mind. This question is closely linked with our first point in that the qualities which are likely to be most salient are precisely those on which the parties are most sharply set apart. But it is also of interest to see how well the public differentiates the parties in terms of various generalized qualities; clearly the relative standing of the parties in the country can be affected only by qualities which set them apart in the electorate's eyes.

Our assessment of the images of the parties in the early 1960s relied chiefly on two types of data. On the one hand we asked our sample to say freely in their own words what they liked and disliked about each of the parties. From these unprompted responses there emerged a remarkable portrait of the parties as the British electorate saw them at successive moments over a three-year period. The advantage of such an approach was that it allowed a representative group of electors to choose the concepts they spontaneously associated with the parties, favourably or unfavourably; the answers that were volunteered give above all an indication of the relative salience of various properties of the party images. But they also reveal a good deal about how the electorate values these properties and about the extent to which it distinguished the parties in terms of them.

Our second main approach was to ask our sample to place the parties on each of a dozen scales designed to assess how they were seen in terms of simple image properties such as good/bad, or honest/dishonest. The properties we measured were chosen in the light of some extensive exploratory interviews.[3] The majority of these scales were 'valence' dimensions of the sort that we have cited, on which the electorate's valuation could be presumed to be heavily skewed towards one end of the scale.

Themes Associated with the Parties

We have already explored several of the ideas that are most central to the electorate's images of the parties. In Chapters 4 and 5 we showed how enormously class and other group associations entered into the image of the Labour Party and, to a lesser extent, of the Conservative Party. In each of our rounds of interviews references to group and class associations accounted for between 10 per cent and 20 per cent of all the spontaneous comments offered about the parties. Those who made these remarks used

3. In its main outlines the empirical technique we have followed here is that of the 'semantic differential' due to Charles Osgood and his colleagues. See C. E. Osgood, G. J. Suci and P. H. Tannenbaum, *The Measurement of Meaning*, Urbana, 1957. For the preliminary work on the selection of scales appropriate to the British parties we are grateful to John Clemens of Marplan Ltd who conducted research in this field for the *Sunday Times* early in 1963.

class imagery in a way that was, on balance, overwhelmingly pro-Labour and anti-Conservative as Figure 16.1 shows.

16.1 Attitude Expressed in Class- and Group-Related References to the Parties[a]

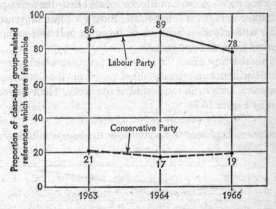

[a] Each entry is the proportion favourable of all spontaneous class- and group-related references to a given party in reply to question 6a to 7b in the 1963 questionnaire, 9 to 12 of the 1964 questionnaire, and 7 to 10 of the 1966 questionnaire.

In Chapter 15 we also discussed how the parties were seen in relation to various themes of domestic and foreign affairs. Very few of our respondents' comments were focused in any precise way on the policy debates of Westminster, but quite a number touched more generally on policy-defined or goal-defined issues; indeed between 20 and 30 per cent of all these spontaneous references to the parties dealt with issues in this very loose sense. At each round, references to domestic issues far outnumbered those to foreign and defence affairs, with the Labour Party, as we have seen, always enjoying a strong advantage.

In our present context, however, two additional types of references are of particular interest. The first were references to the leadership of the parties. Some of these, which we shall reserve to the next chapter, dealt with the Prime Minister and the Leader of the Opposition. But some concerned the leadership of the parties in a more general or collective sense. A Bridgwater nurseryman, for example, liked the Conservatives because of 'their type of men – higher education gives them a better grasp of things', while a Birmingham fitter liked Labour because of 'the level-headedness of their top men'. A clerk in Blackpool said that 'the atmosphere with the Conservatives is sober and there's a common sense approach, with a decent amount of breeding and well-mannered behaviour towards opponents'.

It is notable how much the balance of favourable and unfavourable feeling in such references shifted away from the Conservatives and towards Labour in the period of our work. These trends are shown by Figure 16.2.

16.2 Attitude Expressed in Spontaneous References to Leadership of the Parties[a]

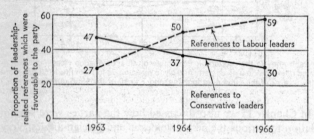

[a] Each figure is the proportion favourable of all spontaneous references to the leaders of a given party, other than the party leader himself, in reply to questions 6a to 7b of the 1963 questionnaire, 9 to 12 of the 1964 questionnaire, and 7 to 10 of the 1966 questionnaire.

Whereas positive and negative references to the Conservative leaders were fairly evenly balanced in 1963, the proportion which were favourable fell to 37 per cent in 1964 and to 30 per cent in 1966. The shift of the balance of feeling in spontaneous references to Labour's leaders was even more striking. In 1963 little more than a quarter of such references were positive, suggesting the deep reservations held by many electors about a party that had then spent twelve years in Opposition. But by 1964 the proportion of references which were favourable rose to half and by 1966 it stood at almost three-fifths.

These shifts paralleled the changing image of the parties' general ability to govern the country. The trend of favourable and unfavourable feeling in this closely related category of spontaneous references to the parties is set out in Figure 16.3. At our first round

16.3 Attitude Expressed in Spontaneous References to the Parties' Ability to Govern[a]

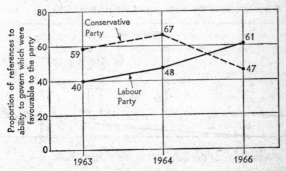

[a] Each entry is the proportion favourable for all spontaneous references to a given party's ability to govern in reply to questions 6a to 7b in the 1963 questionnaire, 9 to 12 of the 1964 questionnaire, and 7 to 10 of the 1966 questionnaire.

of interviews in 1963 the balance of such references was in the Conservatives' favour; and this balance had become even more favourable over the period of Conservative recovery from 1963 to 1964. But with the Conservatives out of power from 1964 to 1966 the reduction of positive feeling towards the party in these terms was fairly marked while the trend of such references to Labour became increasingly favourable. In 1963 there were still on balance more negative than positive references to Labour in these terms. But feeling was evenly balanced by the time of Labour's accession to power, and over the period of the 1964 Parliament there was a further increase in the proportion of favourable references to Labour's ability to govern.

The growing acceptance of Labour's capacity to govern as our period advanced is consistent with the changing appraisals mirrored through our 'semantic differential' scales. At each interview we asked half our respondents to say where they would put each of the parties on a seven-point scale ranging from weak to powerful. In 1963 the electorate perceived little difference in the average placement of the two main parties although the Liberals were seen as relatively weak, as Figure 16.4 shows. In 1964 the position of the parties was much the same, as Figure 16.5 shows. But when we

16.4 Perceptions of the Strength of the Parties, 1963

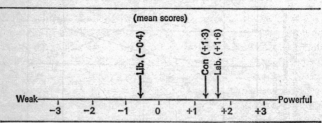

16.5 Perceptions of the Strength of the Parties, 1964

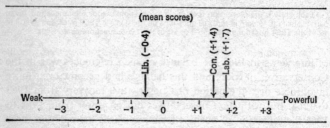

turn to the 1964–6 period this scale reveals a growing belief in Labour's strength. Labour was indeed seen at the time of the 1966 election as much stronger and the Conservatives as much weaker, as Figure 16.6 shows. This array provides fresh evidence of the erosion of one of the generalized perceptions of the Conservatives that for so long had helped to sustain them in power.[4]

4. The average positions shown in these figures do not reveal the reserva-

16.6 Perceptions of the Strength of the Parties, 1966

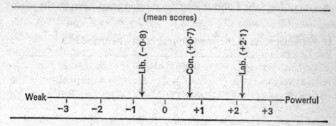

Other aspects of the parties' images include qualities less obviously related to the business of government. The explorations that preceded the construction of our image scales suggested that the parties were also differentiated in the public's mind in terms of qualities that had to do with their freshness and interest and responsiveness to change. The belief that governments grow tired in power is much more than a cliché of the élite observer. We therefore sought evidence about perceptions of this sort and about the bearing they might have on party strength during the period of our studies.

The Image of Newness

We included in our questionnaire three related scales that sought to tap this aspect of the electorate's image of the parties. In the first of these the respondent was asked to place the parties in terms of a

---

tions about Labour that were evident in the spontaneous comments on the parties' capacity to govern. No doubt this was due partly to the fact that our two devices were tapping slightly different aspects of the parties' imagery and partly to the fact that the scale approach involves the average of the answers of *all* respondents. When we examine how the sub-group of respondents who spontaneously referred to the parties' qualities of strength of leadership placed the parties on the strong/weak scale, a rather different picture emerges. This part of our sample, to whom the question of party competence seemed salient, did have a view of the relative forcefulness of the parties which was on balance appreciably less favourable to Labour than the image held by the electorate as a whole.

scale ranging from 'out of date' to 'modern'. As Figure 16.7 shows, in 1963 the Labour Party was on average seen by the mass

16.7 Perceptions of the Modernness of the Parties, 1963

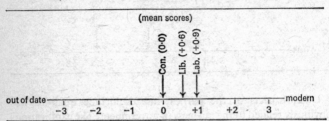

electorate as the most modern of the three parties. The ordering of the parties remained unchanged throughout the years from 1963 to 1966 but Labour was in fact able slightly to increase its relative advantage in these terms, as Figure 16.8 shows.[5]

16.8 Perceptions of the Modernness of the Parties, 1963–66

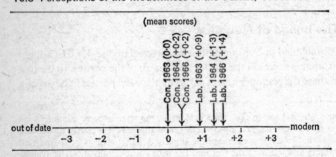

A similar ranking of the main parties could be seen on a second scale, ranging from 'old' to 'young'. Figure 16.9 shows the average

5. Although the Liberal scores are not presented here, at each wave of interviews the Liberals were given an average position between the larger parties.

positions for 1963. In this case the Conservatives were seen as old in an absolute as well as a relative sense, whereas both Labour and

16.9 Perceptions of the Youthfulness of the Parties, 1963

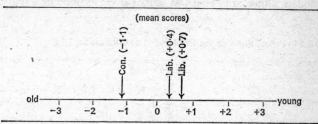

the Liberals were placed towards the younger end of the scale, the Liberals having the most youthful image. Between 1963 and 1966 there was little change in Labour's distance from the Conservatives, though as Figure 16.10 shows, both moved towards a younger image. Indeed by 1966 Labour was placed closer to the 'young' end of this scale than the Liberals. The fact that the Conservatives appeared so much younger in 1966 may have owed a good deal to the replacement of Sir Alec Douglas-Home by Edward Heath.

16.10 Perceptions of the Youthfulness of the Parties, 1963–66

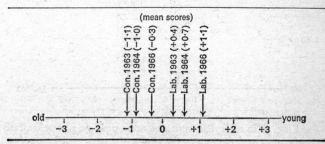

A final related aspect of the greater attractiveness of Labour's image in the 1963–6 period is revealed in our respondents placing of the parties on a scale ranging from 'dull' to 'exciting'. Figure 16.11 shows that in 1963 the differentiation of the parties was only modest, although Labour was ranked as the most exciting party.

16.11 Perceptions of the Excitement of the Parties, 1963

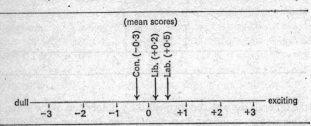

Between 1963 and 1964, however, the difference became much more marked and this increase of difference was fully maintained in 1966. As Figure 16.12 shows, the Labour Party was clearly seen, on balance, as 'exciting' and the Conservative Party as 'dull'.

16.12 Perceptions of the Excitement of the Parties, 1964–66

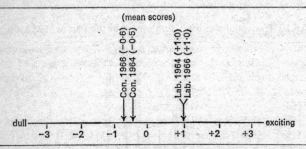

The Liberals in each year were assigned a position just perceptibly on the more exciting half of the scale.

As we gauge the impact which these differences of image may have had on the party balance, we can assume that we are largely dealing with 'valence' properties and that the electorate's 'ideal' would lie overwhelmingly on the side of a party's being modern, youthful and exciting. Such an assumption finds clear justification in the party preferences of our respondents; for example, among Conservative and Labour supporters who in 1963 saw one of the parties as 'modern' and the other as 'out of date' 89 per cent supported the party which they saw as the more modern. We do not from this suppose that these aspects of the party images are pre-eminent in determining party choice; the extent of agreement between the two is largely due to electors' making their images of the parties fit their pre-existing preferences. But in either case, the close relationship between party choice and perceptions of the modernness of the parties shows the high valuation placed on the 'modern' position by the vast majority of electors.

We did, however, probe further to see whether a fraction of the electorate might actually have preferred a party whose image was the less modern. In 1963 we asked our respondents directly whether they preferred things that were 'traditional and well-tried' or 'modern and up-to-date' and a heavy majority came down on the modern side. We could test whether traditionally inclined respondents preferred the less modern party by investigating whether those who perceived one of the parties as modern and the other as not were more likely to support the less modern party. In fact there proved to be no difference of this kind; traditionally inclined respondents were just as prone as the rest of our sample to prefer the party they saw as the more modern. We have therefore felt more confidence in the inference that the difference of party image disclosed in Figures 16.9 to 16.12 is one which carried a genuine, if small, advantage for Labour, especially in 1964 and 1966.

Our confidence that we are here touching upon an aspect of the parties' image which influenced their standing in the country in the middle 1960s is strengthened by the very null results obtained from our measures of other image qualities. At each round of interviews we also probed the public's view of the parties as honest or dishonest, united or split, foolish or wise, and other dimensions along which perceptions might differ. For the period of this work, the results were outstandingly negative. Many voters did tend to associate their own party with the more approved of two concepts defining such a scale. However, across the electorate as a whole these tendencies were mutually cancelling. But this was not true, as we have seen, of perceptions of the interestingness and modernness and youthfulness of the parties. In each case Labour apparently enjoyed a modest advantage in the eyes of the typical elector.

Since our evidence belongs entirely to the 1963–6 period, we cannot say how transient the advantage was. There are reasons why the Conservative Party might be seen as 'older' throughout the period since the Second World War; indeed the distribution of party support between successive age-cohorts might help to create such an image. But there are other reasons why such a difference could be especially strong in the early 1960s; the Conservatives had been long in power, longer than any government in this century, and they were led by an aging Prime Minister whose Edwardian style was underlined by its contrast with the new Kennedy era; the cadre of Conservative leaders which had seemed fresh in the 1950s could not appear so novel or interesting in the 1960s. On the other hand the Labour Party had in 1963 acquired a leader who was of the Kennedy generation and who showed unrivalled skill in associating himself with the ideas of youth and modernization. When Labour took office in 1964 it was bound for a while to have a novelty and appeal that its predecessors could scarcely match. A choice between these alternative interpretations requires additional evidence on changes in these image qualities over the full cycle of Labour's tenure of power.

Several of the qualities of the party images emphasize the importance of the party leader. The parties do plainly owe some of their personification in the public's mind to their identification with those who lead them, and a great leader, a Disraeli or a Roosevelt, may impart something of themselves to images of their parties that are held long after they have gone. But the leaders may make a more direct contribution to their parties' strength. The visibility of the men at the head of the parties is sufficient for them to affect more immediately their parties' standing in the country. We should therefore inquire further into the role of the leaders in electoral change.

17 The Pull of the Leaders

Politics in Britain, to a remarkable degree, are based on the competition between cohesive parties which act together in the national legislature and offer unified appeals for the support of the mass electorate. A member almost never goes against the party whips in the division lobbies, and very few candidates diverge from the party line in their election appeals.[1] The familiar American phenomenon of the candidate who plays down his party affiliation and emphasizes local rather than national issues is much less common in Britain.

In our search for the influence of personalities on voting we can largely ignore candidates at the constituency level, although in Chapter 19 we shall return to their role. The results of every election since the war have been sifted for traces of 'personal' votes and the findings are impressively negative. The national swing in votes shows a notably uniform pattern and such variations as there are seem linked to regional variations or third party intervention far more than to individual candidates.[2]

In the light of the evidence about the limited influence of personalities at the constituency level, it is sometimes assumed that those standing for the premiership, the party leaders, have negligible impact too. Elections can be portrayed as plebiscites between alternative governments, each with their own policies, the choice being made in terms of the parties as a whole, not their leading

1. See, e.g. *The British General Election of 1964*, pp. 142–4.
2. See, e.g. *The British General Election of 1966*, pp. 287–8. However, P. M. Williams, after analysing the returns from a series of elections, concludes that certain candidates have had a very mild cumulative influence on the swing in their constituencies. See *Parliamentary Affairs*, 20, 1966–7, 13–30.

spokesmen. But the opposite view has at least equal currency. A large part of modern British electioneering displays the personalities of the two main leaders. The Prime Minister and, to a lesser extent, the alternative Prime Minister are now seen as very much more than the 'first among equals' of the traditional textbooks. The increasing complexity of government and the extension of the system of Cabinet committees have made the premier appear more and more presidential. His share in the moulding of his party's image has been much enchanted by the coming of new styles in journalism and even more by the advent of television. It is understandable that pre-eminent electoral importance should often be attributed to the two rival leaders.

Yet it would be wrong to present the dominance of the leaders as a wholly new development. It is true that the mass media focus a sharper spotlight on the leaders than before. Perhaps Mr Attlee could not have survived as the head of his party for twenty years in a television age. But the hero-leader, made the vehicle for all sorts of issues and emotions, is hardly a new phenomenon. The qualities of Gladstone and Disraeli – and even Baldwin – were projected as central issues in election campaigns.

In fact, little has been known about how a leader's image intertwines with his party's image or with the other issues of politics in the voter's mind. We may, however, apply to the effect of the leaders the same analytical tests that we have applied to issues and the parties' images. The impact of the leaders too may be assessed in terms of their salience to the public, the skewness of opinion towards them and their differentiation by party in the public's eyes, although the last of these tests can in this case hardly fail to be met. Let us see what such a framework would suggest about the pull of the leaders on the electoral tides.

The Salience of the Leaders

There can be no doubt that the Prime Minister and the Leader of the Opposition are highly visible figures who excite a great deal of feeling, both positive and negative. But their salience may vary widely. For example, we found that in the summer of 1963 a series of free-answer questions about the party leaders elicited nearly 40 per cent more comment about Harold Macmillan, then near the end of his long premiership, than about Harold Wilson, who had led the Labour Party for only four months; but Harold Wilson in turn elicited 40 per cent more comment than the Liberal leader, Jo Grimond.

The relative salience of Mr Wilson and the Conservative leader altered dramatically over the next three years. By the autumn of 1964 Mr Wilson attracted as much comment from our respondents as the retiring Conservative Prime Minister, Sir Alec Douglas-Home, and by the spring of 1966 he had achieved a greater level of visibility than any other leader in the period of our studies. As Figure 17.1 shows, the number of remarks volunteered about him were a third greater than about Mr Heath, the new Conservative leader.

17.1 Salience of the Party Leaders, 1963–66

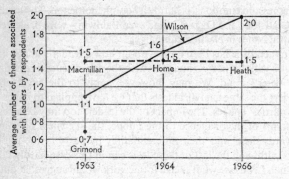

Further insight is offered by comparing the volume of comments made about the leaders with the volume of replies given to a very similar series of questions on likes and dislikes about the parties. The replies to these questions show that in each case about the same number of comments were volunteered about a leader as about his party. In particular, as Figure 17.2 shows, the increasing salience of Mr Wilson over the period was associated with a rise in the salience of the Labour Party itself, as it took possession of government after long years in opposition.

17.2 Salience of the Parties and Leaders, 1963–66

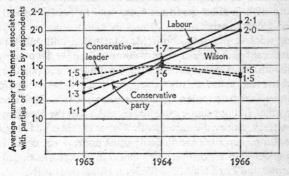

Indeed an interesting comment on the limits of 'presidentialization' in British politics lies in the contrast between these data and comparable figures from the United States. In each presidential election since 1952 the Survey Research Center has used a parallel series of questions to elicit from the American electorate likes and dislikes about the Republican and Democratic parties and their candidates for president. The candidates have regularly excited roughly one and a half times as many remarks as their parties, whereas in Britain leader and party are commented upon equally.[3]

It does seem clear, however, that the party leader in Britain is vastly more salient than his colleagues; the only possible exceptions in recent times, apart from ex-Prime Ministers, have been Mr Bevan and Mr Powell. Survey evidence suggests an absence of public awareness of the secondary leaders of the parties that many insiders find hard to credit. We cited earlier the example of a

3. The only exception to this American generalization in the period from 1952 to 1964 was Adlai Stevenson, who in 1952 attracted fewer comments than the Democratic Party and in 1956 only about the same number. The volume of comments about Eisenhower (twice), Kennedy, Nixon, Johnson and Goldwater exceeded the volume of comment about their respective parties by from 25 to 75 per cent.

Sunday Times survey in 1962 which showed that, in spite of all the coverage given to front benchers by the mass media, a majority of the electorate was unable to give the name of any front bencher in either party aside from the party leaders themselves.

Our own findings are in the same vein. In 1963 we asked our respondents to express their feelings about any other party leaders after we had inquired about Mr Macmillan and Mr Wilson. Remarkably few names were volunteered either favourably or unfavourably. George Brown attracted the strongest positive and negative responses (slightly more positive than negative) but fewer than 3 per cent of people spontaneously referred to him and scarcely any other Labour figure attracted mention. On the Conservative side, R. A. Butler, Edward Heath, Ernest Marples and Reginald Maudling were each mentioned by just under 1 per cent of our respondents in a positive way; similar numbers mentioned Mr Marples and Lord Hailsham (Quintin Hogg) negatively.

In 1964 the situation was similar. On the Conservative side Mr Butler, presumably because of sympathy over his leadership defeat, and Mr Maudling, who had served as spokesman at the Conservatives' campaign press conferences, were mentioned favourably by 4 per cent of our respondents, while 5 per cent commented unfavourably on Quintin Hogg in the wake of his campaign explosions. On the Labour side George Brown leapt to new prominence, with no less than 12 per cent mentioning him unfavourably and 2 per cent favourably.

Table 17.3 shows our sample's feeling towards the secondary leaders in 1963 and 1964. It is striking how similar are the figures for the summer of 1963, when there had been no campaign, and the autumn of 1964, just after the politicians had had such full exposure during the election. The very large proportion of the sample with neutral feelings or no feelings and the stable and fairly symmetrical distribution of the remainder suggest that we were not tapping very deep or widespread attitudes. The parties may project more or less sharply-defined images of their ability to lead or govern, as we have seen in the preceding chapter, but these depend little on the public's capacity to distinguish particular figures in the parties' secondary leadership.

17.3 Attitudes Towards the Secondary Leaders, 1963–64

	Towards Conservative leaders		Towards Labour leaders	
Nature of feeling[a]	1963	1964	1963	1964
Strongly likes	2%	3%	3%	3%
Likes	19	25	20	24
No feelings, mixed, don't know	68	61	64	57
Dislikes	8	8	11	13
Strongly dislikes	3	2	2	3

[a] Each respondent was asked, 'Apart from Macmillan (or Home or Wilson), how do you feel about the other Conservative (or Labour) leaders? Do you generally like them, dislike them or don't you have strong feelings about them?'

The Content of Leader Images

In what terms is a leader seen? There is an obvious distinction to be drawn between perceptions that have to do with his personal characteristics and perceptions that have to do with policies or outputs of government. It is quite imaginable that a leader might be seen largely in instrumental terms, with his image formed out of his perceived association with government actions or goals or class interests; in short, the leader's image might repeat many of the themes that are found in the images of the parties.

Our evidence suggests, however, that the image of the leader is a much more personal one. Table 17.4 shows that at each round of interviews the vast majority of the positive and negative themes spontaneously associated with the Conservative and Labour leaders were personal rather than ones whose content was supplied by the goals which the leaders were seen as the instrument for achieving. This does not necessarily represent a triumph of the cult of personality in British politics or the pre-eminence in these reactions of non-rational factors deep in the psyche of the individual elector. Plainly images of a leader do give scope to such psychological factors. But many of the references to the leader's personal characteristics can also be seen as 'intrumental' in a broader sense. The leader's experience, his intelligence, his sin-

17.4 Content of Likes and Dislikes About Leaders 1963–66

	1963	1964	1966
References to Wilson[a]			
Personal characteristics	79%	84%	84%
Philosophy and goals, issues, class or group interests	14	14	13
Other	7	2	3
	100%	100%	100%
References to Conservative Leader[a]			
Personal characteristics	86%	85%	87%
Philosophy and goals, issues, class or group interests	10	10	11
Other	4	5	2
	100%	100%	100%

[a] References tabulated here are the distinct themes volunteered by our samples in response to the questions: 'Is there anything in particular that you like (or dislike) about Harold Wilson (or Harold Macmillan, Sir Alec Douglas-Home, or Edward Heath)?' Up to five likes and dislikes about each leader were coded for each respondent at each round of interviews.

cerity, his calmness, his eloquence, his likeability – or his short-comings by these standards – can be regarded as qualities which will affect the likelihood of his achieving goals which electors value.

Tables 17.5 to 17.8, which set out the positive and negative themes mentioned in each round of interviews, give a fascinating collective portrait of the Conservative and Labour leaders from 1963 to 1966. The most notable element in the picture of Mr Wilson was the sense, growing throughout this period, of his straightforwardness. The view of him as tricky or devious, so widely held among insiders, was not at that time nearly so prevalent in the mass public (even though in their responses it was one of his two weakest points, the other being a more generalized distaste for his manner). But the general verdict was very favourable; his intelligence and industry, his speaking ability ('he's another Churchill for talking'), his likeableness and his qualities of leadership all drew increasingly positive mention.

The three Conservative leaders in our period evoked a more mixed reaction. All were commended for sincerity, all appealed to people who just 'liked' them, and all attracted some general commendation as good leaders. Although Mr Macmillan was much more appreciated than his successors for leadership, industry and steady nerve ('he's a strong man let down by his party'), it was the negative comments on the three men that varied most. Mr Macmillan was especially condemned for his age, Sir Alec for his looks, his weakness, and his poor speaking, and Mr Heath for his manner and for his unmarried state ('he wouldn't understand family problems').[4] More personal types of disaffection seemed to be inspired by Sir Alec and Mr Heath than by Mr Macmillan and the net balance of comments on them was more unfavourable, as we shall see.

Therefore, since the party leader undoubtedly constitutes an element of salience in British politics, he meets the first test for a force that can genuinely deflect the party balance. A second test is plainly met as well; the party leaders are, in the nature of things, differentiated on a party basis. A third test, then, is the crucial one; the electoral effect of the leader will depend primarily on how unevenly balanced are the favourable and unfavourable elements in his image.

The Net Direction of Attitudes towards Leaders

Over the period of our studies the balance of positive and negative comments on the leaders varied even more than their relative

4. But the idea that Mr Heath, as a bachelor, was especially disowned by women finds scant support in our data. Of the hundred respondents who volunteered Heath's marital status as a reason for not liking him, 57 were women and 43 men, a ratio that differed little from the 53 to 47 ratio of women to men in the sample. Moreover, the ratio of favourable to unfavourable comment about Heath in the whole sample was by a small margin *higher* among women.

17.5 Favourable References to Personal Characteristics of Wilson, 1963–66[a]

Nature of reference	1963	1964	1966
Good man, well qualified, good leader	261	256	415
Experienced, informed, knows job	17	47	87
Intelligent, able, shrewd, wise, astute	92	137	137
Honest, sincere, fair, straightforward, keeps promises	270	462	590
Strong, decisive, courageous	58	138	133
Hard-working, dedicated, efficient, gets things done	99	126	175
Steady nerve, calm under fire (esp. from hecklers)	13	54	91
Age: not too old, young	35	51	7
Physical appearance – handsome, homely	34	67	55
Manner – dignified, gracious, humble	34	67	55
Personally likeable, 'I just like him'	64	138	199
Education, well educated, university background	23	43	16
Good speaker. Like his TV appearances	115	319	385
Other personal references	72	204	145
Total references to personal characteristics	1187	2105	2542

[a] In this and Tables 17.6 to 17.8 we report the actual frequency with which each theme was mentioned at each round of interviews, after adjusting the frequencies for the second and third rounds so that their sample size is in effect set equal to the sample of 2000 electors interviewed at the first round.

17.6 Unfavourable References to Personal Characteristics of Wilson

Nature of reference	1963	1964	1966
Not a good man, not qualified, poor leader, poor P.M.	65	28	29
Inexperienced	11	13	2
Unintelligent, stupid, foolish	5	3	7
Dishonest, insincere, arbitrary, breaks promises, too clever by half	94	116	216
Weak, indecisive, hasn't courage to make hard decisions	33	12	14
Inefficient, lax, doesn't get things done	4	0	8
Could not stand up under fire	2	4	7
Too young	1	1	0
Physically unattractive	22	23	24
Manner undignified, ungracious, aggressive, big-headed, smug	140	178	212
Don't like him as a person, colourless	24	58	73
Too ambitious, just out for himself, wants office	22	36	70
Mudslinging in campaign	—	89	66
Other personal references	46	63	122
Total references to personal characteristics	469	624	850

17.7 Favourable References to Personal Characteristics of the Conservative Leaders

Nature of reference	Macmillan 1963	Home 1964	Heath 1966
Good man, well qualified, good leader, good P.M.	311	190	196
Experienced, informed, knows job	46	44	36
Intelligent, able, shrewd, wise, astute	77	59	46
Honest, sincere, fair, straightforward, keeps promises	248	298	272
Strong, decisive, courageous	58	28	32
Hard-working, dedicated, efficient, gets things done	99	51	53
Steady nerve, calm under fire	124	49	16
Age; not too old, young	8	0	19
Physical appearance – handsome, attractive	13	5	30
Manner dignified, gracious	47	77	72
Personally likeable 'I like him'	116	139	148
Education: well educated, university educated	20	21	16
Class background – upper class	82	111	16
Good speaker	77	80	145
Other personal references	54	47	63
Total references to personal characteristics	1380	1199	1160

17.8 Unfavourable References to Personal Characteristics of the Conservative Leaders

Nature of reference	Macmillan 1963	Home 1964	Heath 1966
Not a good man, not qualified, poor leader, poor P.M.	123	286	245
Inexperienced	37	15	62
Unintelligent, stupid, foolish	18	11	24
Dishonest, insincere, arbitrary, breaks promises, too clever by half	108	67	99
Weak, indecisive, hasn't courage to make hard decisions	179	260	129
Inefficient, lax, too many holidays, doesn't get things done	90	37	37
Can't stand up under fire	7	16	11
Too old	205	11	9
Physically unattractive. Dislike face, clothes	58	116	52
Manner undignified, ungracious, cold, smug, conceited, condescending	95	155	290
Don't like him as a person	57	113	174
Educational background, snobbish	29	25	25
Family and wife	22	1	—
Being a bachelor, not a family man	—	—	109
Poor speaker	56	253	146
All other personal references	68	119	88
Total references to personal characteristics	1152	1485	1500

salience. In the summer of 1963 the themes volunteered about Mr Macmillan were as frequently sympathetic as hostile. Despite the Profumo affair, then at its height, and all the other troubles that had beset Mr Macmillan's leadership, he attracted as many favourable as unfavourable mentions; his image was indeed a good deal more positive than either of his Conservative successors' was to be. References to Mr Wilson in 1963, although fewer in number, were solidly favourable by a margin of roughly two to one. But Mr Grimond, though less noticed, had the most sympathetic image of all; three comments mentioned reasons for liking him to every one containing a reason for disliking him.[5]

By the autumn of 1964 the balance of comments on Mr Wilson had become still more favourable – and the volume of comment even greater. Sir Alec Douglas-Home, who had just lost office after a year as Prime Minister, attracted rather more negative than positive mentions.[6]

In the spring of 1966 attitudes towards the Labour and Conservative leaders were just as widely divergent. Mr Wilson, at a record level of salience, attracted almost two and a half times as many favourable as unfavourable references. Mr Heath, on the other hand, was not only far less salient to the electorate; he also drew nine negative references to every seven positive ones. Figure 17.9 summarizes the direction of attitudes towards the leaders found during our surveys.

5. We were, unfortunately, not able to ask the same question about Mr Grimond in 1964 or 1966.

6. We cannot know how much the outcome of the election and the formation of a new government influenced the perceptions of Mr Wilson and Sir Alec which our respondents expressed; the interviews were in the weeks immediately after the takeover. The monthly readings of the standings of the party leaders made by Gallup and National Opinion Polls did not show any sharp discontinuities over the election periods of September to November 1964 or of February to April 1966. Moreover, neither in 1964 nor in 1966 did the report of the vote elicited from our sample show any general 'bandwagon' – or, for that matter, 'underdog' – effect when compared to the actual election returns. None the less it remains possible that the election and its aftermath did influence the way the leaders were seen by our respondents.

17.9 Direction of Attitudes towards the Leaders, 1963–66

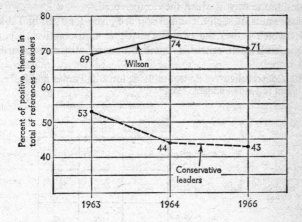

The Electoral Impact of the Leaders

What effect did the widening gap between the Conservative and Labour leaders shown in Figure 17.9 have on the electorate's decision in 1964 and 1966? The answer to such a question is complicated by the fact that attitudes towards the leaders are only a limited part of the influence on the electorate. Since an elector's party preferences can bias his perceptions of leaders we need evidence that the effect of attitudes towards the leaders is independent of the influence of attitudes towards the parties themselves.

We can help to distinguish between these effects by comparing our respondents' reactions to the leaders and to the parties. Our free-answer responses offer an index of whether the elector's attitudes were favourable or unfavourable, or were neutral or mixed, towards the Labour and Conservative parties; they also offer a similar index of attitudes towards the Labour and Conservative leaders. We can compare these indices to see how strongly each is related to the way in which the elector voted.[7]

The results of such a comparison are given for 1964 in Table 17.10 which shows the percentage voting Conservative among people with each potential combination of attitudes towards

17.10 Conservative Voting by Attitudes towards Parties and Attitudes towards Leaders, 1964[a]

		Attitudes towards leaders		
		Pro-Conservative	Balanced, Neutral	Pro-Labour
Attitudes towards parties	Pro-Conservative	97%	91%	76%
	Balanced, Neutral	86%	48%	28%
	Pro-Labour	35%	19%	6%

[a] This analysis is limited to electors who voted Conservative or Labour in 1964.

the leaders and parties. Several aspects of this table invite comment. First, it is clear that attitudes towards the parties were a better guide to voting behaviour than were attitudes towards the leaders. Such a conclusion may be drawn from the fact that the gradient of Conservative voting is much steeper within columns than within rows, that is to say, from the fact that voting varies more strongly by attitudes towards parties among those having a common attitude towards leaders than it does by attitudes towards leaders among those having a common view of the parties.[8]

7. In fact we have formed distinct indices of attitudes towards each of the major parties and towards each of the leaders; but in our presentation of results here we combine the two party indices and the two leader indices.

8. This aspect of the conditional distributions shown here coincides well with the partial regression slopes obtained by regressing voting choice on separate measures of attitude towards the two parties and the two leaders. For this purpose we have scored a Labour vote 1 and a Conservative vote 0 and have formed indices of attitude towards Labour (L), the Conservatives (C), Wilson (W) and Home (H) by taking the arithmetic difference of

Indeed, those who were pro-Conservative in terms of parties but pro-Labour in terms of leaders voted Conservative by three to one, while those who were pro-Labour in terms of parties but pro-Conservative in terms of leaders voted Labour by two to one. It is interesting to note that those who were of neutral or mixed view both towards parties and leaders divided their votes almost evenly, as if they decided by tossing a coin. But the table makes it equally clear that substantial effects on voting can be traced to attitudes towards the leaders. Although these effects were less than those of attitudes towards the parties they were none the less visible.

Table 17.11 shows the results of similar analysis of our findings

17.11 Conservative Voting by Attitudes towards Parties and Attitudes towards Leaders, 1966[a]

		Attitudes towards Leaders		
		Pro-Conservative	Balanced, Neutral	Pro-Labour
Attitudes towards parties	Pro-Conservative	99%	89%	72%
	Balanced, Neutral	76%	54%	26%
	Pro-Labour	49%	16%	6%

[a] This analysis is limited to electors who voted Conservative or Labour in 1966.

the number of favourable and unfavourable references to each given spontaneously in response to questions 9 to 12 and 14 to 17 of the 1964 questionnaire. We then expressed the probability of voting Labour as a linear function of these four indexes of attitude, choosing the values of the coefficients by the ordinary least-squares criterion:

$$P(Lab) = -0.0022 + 0.139L - 0.071C + 0.069W - 0.046H$$
$$(0.033) \quad (0.033) \quad (0.032) \quad (0.030)$$

The values of these coefficients suggest that in each case choice was more strongly related to the elector's attitudes towards the party than towards its leader, but that attitudes towards each made a distinct contribution to choice in an immediate sense.

for 1966. The correspondence with the 1964 table is remarkable. Once again attitudes towards the parties emerge as the stronger influence on voting, but attitudes towards the leaders did make a distinct contribution. Those who expressed neutral or mixed views towards the parties once more divided their votes almost evenly. The percentages in these two tables show that the chances of voting Conservative under each combination of attitude changed relatively little between the two elections.[9]

What did change between these two years were the proportions holding each of these combinations of attitude. As Table 17.12 on the next page shows, there was a strong shift towards Labour between 1964 and 1966 in terms of attitudes towards the parties and a moderate shift in terms of attitudes towards the leaders as well. The heightened salience of Mr Wilson and the esteem in which he still was held, by contrast with the weaker and less favourable response to Mr Heath, provided a further increment of votes for Labour.

That attitudes towards the leaders were in fact involved in shifts of votes between the parties is confirmed by our panel data on individual electors. We saw in Chapter 12 how much of the swing to Labour between 1964 and 1966 was due to the straight conversion of Conservatives. If we now divide 1964 Conservatives into those whose view of the party leaders in that year was consistent with their party stand and those whose view of the leaders was inconsistent with it, we find a stronger movement towards Labour between the two years among those who had valued Mr Wilson more highly than the Conservative leader, as Table 17.13 on p. 466 shows.

Complementary findings emerge when we divide 1964 Conservatives according to whether their attitudes towards the party leaders became more favourable to Labour between 1964 and 1966. Table 17.14 shows that among those whose attitudes did

9. The main exception to this is the change among those who held a pro-Conservative view of the leaders but a pro-Labour view of the parties. The equal division of support in this group in 1966 may reflect the fact that those who could form a more favourable view of Mr Heath than of Mr Wilson in that year were likely to have had long-standing attachments to the Conservative Party.

17.12 Attitudes Towards Parties by Attitudes Towards Leaders, 1964–66[a]

		1964 Attitudes Towards Leaders			
		Pro-Conservative	Balanced, Neutral	Pro-Labour	
Attitudes Towards Parties	Pro-Conservative	19	9	12	40
	Balanced, Neutral	3	5	10	18
	Pro-Labour	2	4	36	42
		24	18	58	100%

		1966 Attitudes Towards Leaders			
		Pro-Conservative	Balanced, Neutral	Pro-Labour	
Attitudes Towards Parties	Pro-Conservative	20	6	9	35
	Balanced, Neutral	2	4	8	14
	Pro-Labour	3	4	44	51
		25	14	61	100%

[a] This analysis is limited to electors who voted Conservative or Labour.

shift in this way a stronger movement to Labour occurred. Indeed, one in five of those who adopted a view of the party leaders more favourable to Labour transferred their allegiance from the Conservatives to Labour.

We conclude therefore that the party leaders have enough hold on the public's consciousness and are, by the nature of their office, sharply enough set apart by party for popular feeling towards them to have demonstrable effects on the party balance when it becomes preponderantly positive or negative. If these effects are

17.13 Conversion from Conservative to Labour Voting, 1964–66, by Attitude Towards Leaders in 1964[a]

| | Attitudes towards leaders in 1964 | |
	Pro-Labour	Pro-Conservative
Shifted vote towards Labour	14%	5%
Did not shift vote	86	95
	100% (n = 131)	100% (n = 206)

[a] This analysis is limited to electors who voted Conservative in 1964 and Conservative or Labour in 1966.

17.14 Conversion from Conservative to Labour Voting, 1964–66, by Shifts of Attitude Towards Leaders[a]

| | Attitudes towards leaders | |
	Shifted towards Labour	Did not shift
Shifted vote towards Labour	20%	10%
Did not shift vote	80	90
	100% (n = 94)	100% (n = 224)

[a] This analysis is limited to electors who voted Conservative in 1964 and Conservative or Labour in 1966.

less marked than in America they are none the less clear. In the period of our work they benefited Labour; in another period, such as Mr Macmillan's heyday at the end of the 1950s, the advantage would have been otherwise. Indeed, the difficulties that beset Mr Wilson later in the decade must have diminished his party's advantage along these lines, although the polls do suggest that changing estimates of Mr Heath had little to do with the Conservative recovery. The fact that the Conservative upsurge in

1967–8 was not linked to any increase in their leader's standing should remind us that the pull of the leaders remains but one among the factors that determine transient shifts of party strength; it is easily outweighed by other issues and events of concern to the public, including the movements of the economy which do so much to set the climate of the party battle.

18 The Economic Context

'A Government is not supported a hundredth part so much by the constant, uniform, quiet prosperity of the country as by those damned spurts which Pitt used to have just in the nick of time.' So wrote Brougham to Thomas Creevey in 1814. The fact that he could attribute the Tory hegemony in the 1790s to the same cause that was commonly given as the reason for the party's success in the 1950s shows how deeply rooted in British politics is the idea that the Government is accountable for good and bad times. Popular acceptance of this idea means that the state of the economy had loomed large in the minds of all modern Prime Ministers as they pondered on the timing of a dissolution. And in the post-Keynesian era more than one government has been tempted to seek a favourable context for an election by expanding the economy, although dissolutions are more easily timed to coincide with expansion than the other way round.

The Government's responsibility for the economy is a fundamental assumption of the contemporary dialogue between the parties and the electorate. In the 1959 Parliament economic conditions provided the dominant theme, from the 'never had it so good' euphoria of the 1959 election, through the pay pause of 1961 and the 1962 recession, to the recovery of 1963–4. In the 1964 Parliament the balance of payments crisis was by itself sufficient to keep economic questions in the forefront of politics.

On fairly uncertain evidence many observers have assumed that the state of the economy was the main cause for the Conservatives' decline in 1961–2 and for their recovery in 1963–4. In this chapter we explore the extent to which support can be found for such a theory. We also examine changes in economic perceptions during the 1964 Parliament, when a swing to the Government occurred despite the continued economic difficulties in which the country found itself. The way in which the economy shapes the electorate's behaviour is complex, and the conclusions to be drawn about the effect of the economy on party advantage in the early 1960s are sometimes surprising.

The Economy as an Issue

Of all the outputs of government, good times and bad must be among those most strongly valued by the mass of the people. The material and psychic deprivations of being out of work are vivid to those who experience them – as well as to many who only observe them in others. Similarly, the consequences of having a fatter pay packet or of being on short time or of having to contend with higher prices in the market are directly felt by those whose lives are touched. Changes of personal economic condition are overwhelmingly salient to the mass of electors and evoke in them strong and definite attitudes.

This does not, of course, mean that voters respond only to those aspects of the state of the economy that they can themselves see. Many will be responsive to the more generalized information about economic conditions that reaches them through the mass media. A rise in the unemployment figures has a clear meaning for the ordinary citizen because he can picture its consequences in personal terms and news of such a rise may create a sense of unease in millions of people who themselves are for the moment quite unaffected by it. In a similar way, news of a general price increase can give point to price changes that the voter can recall from recent shopping. Even a national deficit in the balance of payments has some meaning for ordinary people who could not trace the effects that the deficit will have on their own well-being but who know from everyday experience the unpleasant consequences of a deficit in their personal or household accounts.

We may also note that the issues of economic well-being probably come as close as any in modern politics to being pure 'valence' issues, as we have defined these.[1] If we conceive of

1. See Chapter 8, p. 236.

economic issues in dimensional terms, the electorate is not spread along a continuum of preference extending between good times and bad; its beliefs are overwhelmingly concentrated at the good times end of such a continuum. This is, of course, an empirical observation and not a logical necessity. There are in British society isolated individuals who see genuine moral values for others, or even for themselves, in a degree of severity to economic life. This view was expressed to us by an aging widow in Poole, who said, 'It's awfully good for one to have to get along on less, isn't it?' Indeed, at an élite level one can find some very conservative observers as well as some doctrinaire Socialists who view with ambivalence the rising affluence of recent years. But such views are the perquisite of a tiny minority. The goal of economic betterment enjoys overwhelming mass support and any values that may lie in economic adversity are not visible to most people.

It is of course true that the relationship between rival economic goals does offer possible dimensions of political conflict. The classic example of this in most western economies lies in the 'trade-off' between economic expansion and price stability; all too often governments can buy economic expansion only by allowing inflation, or stable prices only by limiting expansion. For a nation as dependent on international trade as Britain, there are further trade-offs between domestic expansion on the one hand, and the balance of international payments on the other. The dilemma of choosing an appropriate position on such a continuum has faced Conservative and Labour Governments alike.[2] Moreover, if an understanding of the relationships between these goals were to

2. Economists on both sides of the Atlantic have discussed the electoral implications of the relationship between unemployment and price inflation for those in power. See in particular the excellent papers by C. A. E. Goodhart and R. J. Bhansali, 'Political Economy', *Political Studies* **18** (1970) 43–106, and by Susan J. Lepper, 'Voting Behavior and Aggregative Policy Targets', New Haven, 1968 (mimeo.). If, as is generally supposed, the structure of the economy imposes an inverse correlation between unemployment and inflation, those who take economic decisions are likely to be very aware of the trade-off between the two, and their choice of an optimal combination may be deeply influenced by their judgements of the electorate's sensitivities. But this by no means implies that the structural relationship between the two is understood by the electorate itself.

reach more deeply into the public's consciousness, the dialogue between parties and the electorate on economic issues might involve genuine position dimensions, with the parties manoeuvring for the support of electors who had very different preferences between, let us say, economic expansion and stable prices. Although little is known about the reality of such dimensions to most voters, the dominant mode of popular response to economic goals seems to be one that approves at the same time of full employment, larger pay packets, stable prices, and, to the extent that they are salient for the public, a strong currency and balanced international payments – and that disapproves of the opposite of these conditions.

We may assume therefore that the economic outputs of government are very salient to the electorate, although there are some short-run variations as between different economic goals, and that opinion is overwhelmingly skewed in favour of the achievement of rising prosperity and related economic goals. It follows that the political consequences of economic issues depend almost entirely on the way in which the parties come to be linked in the public's mind with the achievement of these goals, or the failure to achieve them.

The type of connection that has dominated both academic and more popular views of the electorate's response to the economy is one under which voters reward the Government for the conditions they welcome and punish the Government for the conditions they dislike. In the simplest of all such models the electorate pays attention only to the party in power and only to conditions during its current tenure of office.[3] Such a model might be extended in either of two directions. On the one hand, we might suppose that the electorate judges the performance of the governing party to some extent against what the Opposition party might do if it were in

3. Borrowing a term from Herbert Simon, Gerald Kramer has characterized models of this kind as ones entailing 'satisficing' behaviour, since the electorate judges only whether economic conditions are satisfactory, not whether they are optimal. See his penetrating analysis of the relationship of economic to electoral series over more than half a century of American experience, 'An Empirical Analysis of Some Aggregative Hypotheses About U.S. Voting Behavior, 1896–1964', Washington, D.C., 1968 (mimeo.).

charge of affairs. In a country where politics takes the form of a regularized competition between two major parties, it is unlikely that a comparison of this kind would be entirely absent from the electorate's mind, although public reactions to economic conditions may focus much more on the Government than on the Opposition.[4] This is a question to which we shall return later.

On the other hand, the links between economic conditions and the parties might be built up in the electorate's mind over much longer periods of time. A good deal of evidence from electoral surveys suggests that this is the case. For example, Milne and Mackenzie's studies early in the postwar period suggest that the British electorate held strongly negative feelings towards the Conservatives on the basis of what it remembered of the depressed economic conditions between the wars. Despite the other dislocations of life, the Second World War had brought rapid economic expansion and increases of real incomes for millions of people. This transformation could well have put quite a different face on the long decades of economic hardship that had gone before.[5] But the austerity of Labour's policies in the late forties followed by the new expansion that became visible in the 1950s after the Conservatives had taken office may well have left the electorate of the early 1960s with a somewhat different view on how the parties are associated with good and bad times. One important factor in any such transformation over the years lies, of course, in the extent to which the electorate had been physically replaced.

In a similar way the American electorate may have drawn from the Republican prosperity under McKinley ('the full dinner pail'), following the severe depression under the Democrats in the early 1890s, an image of better times under the Republicans which

4. This possibility is not really excluded from the class of 'satisficing' models proposed by Kramer; nor is it excluded by the results of the empirical tests he applies to the economic and electoral data of the American past.

5. See R. S. Milne and H. C. Mackenzie, *Straight Fight*, London, 1954, p. 136, which records that in 1951, a dozen years after the end of mass unemployment, over half their Labour respondents in N.E. Bristol gave full employment or the fear of unemployment as a reason for voting Labour.

carried over well into the twentieth century and was reinforced by the general prosperity of the Republican twenties. But any such image was drastically transformed by the Great Depression of the 1930s, and survey evidence from twenty years later showed how strongly the Democrats were linked with good times in the public's mind, and the Republicans with economic distress.[6] The links that survive in popular consciousness over longer periods are of course modified by new experience and will occasionally be entirely overthrown, as our account suggests. The absence of a serious depression under the Republicans in the 1950s attenuated the party's association with bad times. But this change was overlaid on a substratum of belief in better times under the Democrats which probably continued to work to the Republicans' disadvantage throughout the Eisenhower years.[7]

Any tendency of the electorate to reward the parties for achieving conditions that are universally approved and to punish them for failing to achieve these conditions is consistent with our view of economic issues as 'valence' issues. Such a model of the economy's political effects can, however, be distinguished broadly from a quite different class of models under which the parties are in some way thought to hold differentiated 'positions' with respect to the economy. A possibility discussed by Kramer is that one of the parties would in general be seen as expansionist and the other not.[8] The consequence of a downturn might in such a case not necessarily be the lessening of the voters' esteem for the governing party

6. See in particular *The American Voter*, pp. 45–6.

7. Since longer-surviving beliefs about the performance of the parties in relation to the economy can be modified by new experience, their presence is not at all inconsistent with the relationships that have been found between short-term economic changes and changes of party strength. It would be a mistake, however, to conclude from the relationships found between short-term economic and political changes that the electorate's horizons are limited to the very recent past in the connections that it forms between the parties and economic conditions. This is a point on which survey and aggregative evidence need to be interpreted together.

8. Gerald Kramer, 'An Empirical Analysis of Some Aggregative Hypotheses About U.S. Voting Behavior, 1896–1964', Washington, D.C., 1968 (mimeo.) *passim*.

but rather a strengthening of their desire to have the more expansionist party in power.

Such a view of the bearing that the economy has on the strength of the parties may be much less applicable in an era when all governments are committed to using their powers, subject to the other constraints upon them, to assure high employment and economic expansion. But it may have been more plausible in an earlier day. Indeed, the American experience during the 1930s might be seen partly in these terms. The Democrats under Roosevelt were far more expansionist than their Republican predecessors under Hoover, and the contrast was vividly imprinted on the electorate's mind. As a result, the continued economic distress did not diminish support for Roosevelt, although his administration made little headway in reducing unemployment before the Second World War came at the end of the decade. It would seem that economic distress persuaded the country that it ought to keep the more expansionist party in power.

Another 'position' model of the links of economic conditions to party support is one under which the strength of the class alignment increases with economic distress. According to such a view, the consequence of hard times is not the lessening of support for the governing party generally in the country but rather an increase of support for each party in the class whose interests it represents and a decline of support for each party in the opposite class. We have already suggested in Chapter 5 that a rising level of affluence in Britain may gradually have reduced the strength of the alignment by class. It is quite possible to conceive that such a pattern would apply to shorter-term changes of the economy with the 'polarization' of party support by class rising in hard times and falling in good.[9] We shall return later in this chapter to the evidence that can be found to support such a model of the response of the British electorate to the economic conditions of the 1960s.

9. For a systematic statement of such a model see P. E. Converse, 'The Shifting Role of Class in Political Attitudes and Behavior', E. E. Maccoby and others, eds, *Readings in Social Psychology*, London and New York, 3rd edition 1966.

The State of the Economy 1959–66

The health of an economy is too complex to be charted by any single index. Several aspects of national prosperity can each have their own political effect and we can identify in the period from 1959 to 1966 economic changes which must have worked upon the electorate in different ways. One extra complication in describing the economic context of politics is that the absolute level of the various economic indices may be less important than a comparison of their present levels against past or anticipated levels. The number of unemployed may be less significant than whether the number is rising or falling – or is expected to rise or fall. In all this we must consider the electorate's perceptions as well as the objective economic realities.

Several indices suggest that it is easy to exaggerate the fluctuations of the period. The national product rose year by year (although in 1962 there was something of a plateau), and wages and salaries increased faster than prices. Indeed, if we look at the quarterly figures for total disposable personal income (seasonally adjusted) the picture presented is one of steady advance, as the dotted line in Figure 18.1 on page 476 shows. Even the figures for the sale of durable goods, also displayed in Figure 18.1, show a general rise behind a strong seasonal pattern. But there are discernible differences between years. In particular this index shows how the buying of durable goods in 1960, 1961 and 1962 fell below the boom year of 1959. Buying was again strong from late 1963 until 1965 but fell off once more in 1966.

Similar fluctuations can be seen in the employment figures. The proportion of the work force unemployed, as Figure 18.2 on page 477 shows, fell markedly in the six months before the Conservative victory in 1959 and continued low until mid-1961. But with the policies associated with the pay pause and an unusually severe winter unemployment climbed upwards to a high peak in early 1963 and then fell just before the Conservative recovery of 1963–4. Unemployment continued low under the new Labour Government until the measures taken in July 1966 began to take effect.

Parallel trends are manifest in the numbers of workers on short

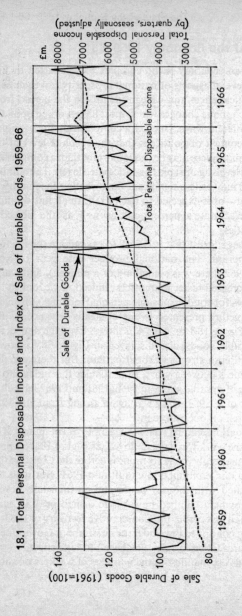

18.1 Total Personal Disposable Income and Index of Sale of Durable Goods, 1959-66

Total Personal Disposable Income
(by quarters, seasonally adjusted)

£m.

Sale of Durable Goods (1961=100)

Sale of Durable Goods

Total Personal Disposable Income

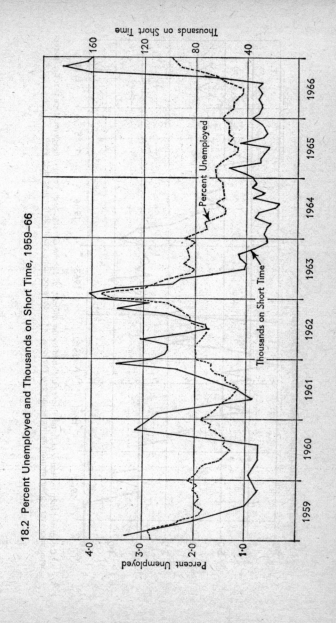

18.2 Percent Unemployed and Thousands on Short Time, 1959–66

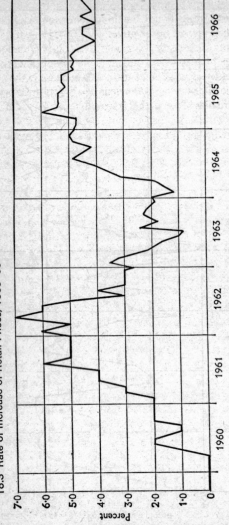

18.3 Rate of Increase of Retail Prices, 1959–66[a]

[a] Calculated from the Index of Retail Prices published by the *Ministry of Labour Gazette*. Each value is the percentage that the level of retail prices for a given month has increased over the level of the corresponding month in the preceding year.

time, a partial form of unemployment. In Figure 18.2 this series exhibits even more strikingly the improvement in employment in the months before the Conservatives' victory of 1959. It shows too the uncertainty of the early 1960s and the peak of economic distress in the winter of 1962–3, as well as the economic improvement before and after the election of 1964. The increase in the numbers on short time after the July 1966 deflation is very striking.

The upward bias of prices that is so familiar an aspect of modern economies continued almost without a break in Britain throughout this period. But the rate of increase varied substantially. There were in fact two periods of particularly rapid increase as Figure 18.3 on page 478 shows. The sharpest advance took place in the latter half of 1961 and the first half of 1962, when the Ministry of Labour's index of retail prices recorded increases of 6 and even 7 per cent over the corresponding month of the preceding year. The second period was during Labour's first year of power, when increases exceeding 5 per cent were not uncommon. By contrast, the first year after the 1959 election and the eighteen months leading up to the 1964 election were periods of relative price stability.

Somewhat more removed from the lives of ordinary people but the subject of extensive discussion in the mass media were the vicissitudes of Britain's trading position. Figure 18.4 on the next page shows the quarterly trends in the balance of visible trade. How these external constraints on Britain's economic position affected popular attitudes and behaviour is far from clear. They must of course have had great indirect influence by inducing the Government to take deflationary measures – in the extreme case, the devaluation of the pound. But the extent to which Britain's balance of trade or of international payments was of direct concern to the electorate remains problematic. The very distance of these questions from ordinary people's experience may help to explain the parties' brisk skirmishing over their responsibility for Britain's position.

Lying behind the movement of these various indicators are several of the relationships which gave structure to Britain's economic affairs. In particular, the characteristically inverse rela-

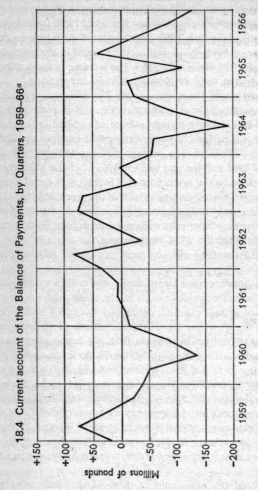

18.4 Current account of the Balance of Payments, by Quarters, 1959–66[a]

[a] Figures are positive or negative balance of trade, including invisible trade, by quarters as given by the *Monthly Digest of Statistics*.

tionship between unemployment and inflation was very evident.[10] So too was the relationship between domestic expansion and the deterioration of Britain's trading position which dogged Chancellors of both parties. From the standpoint of the broad public, however, we may identify several main phases through which the economy passed during our period. To begin with, economic conditions remained outwardly satisfactory for more than a year after the Conservative triumph in the autumn of 1959; unemployment and short time were at low levels and prices were outstandingly stable. In 1961 and 1962, however, both unemployment and short time were markedly higher, peaking sharply in the severe winter of 1962–3. Consumer buying was down, and prices rose sharply throughout most of 1961 and 1962. The recovery that preceded the 1964 election began early in 1963. Unemployment and short time fell again fairly rapidly, while the rate of the increase of prices also fell, and consumer buying rose to a level higher than that of 1959. Finally, during the 1964 Parliament the economy's performance was distinctly mixed. Unemployment and short time remained at very low levels and wages went up. But prices also rose rapidly, while Britain's difficult trading position became a principal theme of the 1964 Parliament.

Perceptions of Individual Well-Being

That these fluctuations did bear at least a rough correspondence to feelings of well-being held by the electorate is suggested by the figures from the Gallup survey each December on expectations for the year ahead. As Table 18.5 shows, the public's buoyancy at the end of 1959 was relatively high but declined steadily to the end of 1962, when almost as many said that the next year would be worse as said that it would be better. By the end of 1963, however, the feeling of recovery was strong, and the proportion who were optimistic was even higher than at the end of 1959. In December 1964 and 1965 feelings were more guardedly optimistic, consistent

10. The (product moment) correlation between the unemployment figures in Figure 18.2 and the average rate of price increases over the preceding and following six months is −0·66 over the period 1959–66.

18.5 Expectations for the Year Ahead, 1959–65

So far as you are concerned, do you think that next year will be better than this year?	Dec. 1959	Dec. 1960	Dec. 1961	Dec. 1962	Dec. 1963	Dec. 1964	Dec. 1965
Better	46%	40%	38%	34%	54%	39%	42%
Worse	6	14	18	30	7	24	21
Same	48	46	44	36	39	37	37
	100%	100%	100%	100%	100%	100%	100%
Percent optimistic less percent pessimistic	40	26	20	4	47	15	21

Source: Gallup Poll.

with the performance of the economy during Labour's early months in office.

At each of our interviews we sought to measure the respondent's sense of whether he and his family were better or worse off than at some previous time, or had remained about the same. We also probed the detailed reasons why our respondents felt that their economic condition had changed. The results suggest that the effects of broad changes of the economy are overlaid on differences linked to the individual's life cycle. In general, those who were younger were more likely to feel that their well-being had improved,[11] those who were older that their well-being had remained the same or worsened. In 1963, for example, those in the post-1951 cohort who felt better off were in a 32 per cent majority over those who felt worse off; in the 1945 cohort this majority was only 21 per

11. The detailed definitions of cohorts are set out in Chapter 3, p. 73. The full figures for perceptions of changes of economic well-being by cohort in 1963 are these:

	Pre-1918	Interwar	1945	Post-1951
Better off	19%	26%	38%	47%
About the same	50	49	45	39
Worse off	31	25	17	14
	100%	100%	100%	100%

cent; in the inter-war cohort there was no majority either way; in the pre-1918 cohort it was those feeling worse off who were 12 per cent more numerous. Moreover, variations in the reasons given for changes of economic circumstances make quite clear how often changes associated with the life cycle – marriage, child-bearing, the movement of grown children out of the home, retirement and the like – are seen as the source of changes of well-being.

Yet it is plain that our sample as a whole saw the Government as being of great significance for their economic condition. Even among those who gave personal reasons for their circumstances having improved or worsened, almost two-thirds were prepared to say that the actions of government could affect how well off they were. Among the rest of the sample this proportion stood at more than 70 per cent. Some (7 per cent) actually cited the Government's fiscal or monetary policies as the direct reason for their change in prosperity.

The electorate's sense of economic well-being differed measurably between the three periods in which we took interviews. Table 18.6 sets out the reports of recent changes given by our sample in each of these periods. The figures suggest that the electorate's judgements in the summer of 1963 were not starkly negative, although a fifth of our sample said that their condition had worsened: whatever the degree of economic difficulty in the prior winter and the years before, almost half had noticed no change.

18.6 Perceived Changes of Economic Well-Being, 1963–6

Compared with a year ago (three or four years ago) are you and your family[a]	Summer 1963	Autumn 1964	Spring 1966
Better off now	33%	21%	22%
Worse off now	21	17	23
About the same	46	62	55
	100%	100%	100%

[a] See questions 34a of the 1963 questionnaire, 37 of the 1964 questionnaire, and 39 of the 1966 questionnaire.

The reports given at the two later points of time were distinctly mixed. In the autumn of 1964 a little more than a fifth thought that their condition had improved over the prior year and a few less than a fifth thought that their condition had worsened. In the spring of 1966 the two proportions were roughly equal.

Expectations of future changes of well-being also fluctuated over the period of our studies. As Table 18.7 shows, our interviews in 1963 revealed that among those who expected their

18.7 Perceived Economic Prospects, 1963–6

Now looking ahead over the next three or four years, do you think that you will be[a]	Summer 1963	Autumn 1964	Spring 1966
Better off then	24%	30%	26%
Worse off then	9	11	19
About the same then	48	40	45
Don't know	19	19	10
	100%	100%	100%

[a] See questions 35a of the 1963 questionnaire, 39a of the 1964 questionnaire, and 40 of the 1966 questionnaire.

economic conditions to change over the next year, a clear majority expected them to improve. By the time of our second interview, in the autumn of 1964, this majority was somewhat greater. But in 1966 the mixed assessment of economic conditions was clearly reflected in the fact that those who expected their circumstances to improve were not much more numerous than those who expected them to worsen.

The extent to which such perceptions can affect support for the party in power emerges plainly from our findings. Let us consider, to begin with, how support for the Conservative Government changed between the elections of 1959 and 1964 according to whether the individual saw his economic well-being as having improved or not. We shall for this purpose consider only those who had the same perception in both the first and second of our interviews; that is to say those who, both in 1963 and 1964, thought that their economic well-being had improved, had worsened, or had stayed about the same. The remarkable contrast of the movements of support towards and away from the Conservatives in these three groups is set out in Table 18.8. Those who consistently saw their condition as worsening exhibited a much stronger

18.8 Change of Conservative Support, 1959–64 by Perceived Change of Own Economic Condition, 1963 and 1964

Among those whose report of change of their condition was consistently	Change of Conservative support 1959–64[a]
Better off now	+7%
About the same	−3%
Worse off now	−8%

[a] Each entry is the change of the Conservatives' support from 1959 to 1964 expressed as a percentage of the total number of respondents in a given group. A positive value means a swing towards the Conservatives, a negative value a swing away from the Conservatives.

than average trend away from the Conservatives, while those who found their condition unchanged moved fairly much with the national party tide. But those who consistently felt their position had improved showed a strong trend *towards* the Conservatives and *against* the general movement of the party tide between these elections.[12]

Figures such as those in Table 18.8 naturally suggest that reactions to changes of economic condition follow the lines of a 'valence' model, with the Government of the day, whichever party is in power, being rewarded for good times and being disapproved

12. An interesting aspect of these findings is that the trends that were above and the trends that were below the average for the electorate as a whole were disproportionately the result of younger electors' responding to their perceived economic conditions. Not only were younger electors more likely than older ones to see their condition as having improved, as we have noted, they were also more likely to be *moved* by such perceptions, whether they were of an improvement or worsening of their condition, as we would expect from the argument of Chapter 3.

of for bad times. Additional evidence that this is a realistic image is supplied by changes of party support over a period when there was a turnover of party control. For this purpose we may examine the movements of support between the two main parties according to three patterns of perceived well-being that the individual could have had in 1964 and 1966. We shall consider, first, those who thought that their economic well-being had improved over the last year of the 1959 Parliament but had deteriorated over the 1964 Parliament; second, those who thought that their well-being had remained roughly the same during both these periods; and third, those who thought their well-being had worsened over the final year of Conservative rule but had improved during the first year of Labour rule.

The contrast of movements of support in these three groups is very sharp, as Table 18.9 shows. Among those who thought their

18.9 Increases of Support for Labour, 1964–6 by Perceived Changes of Economic Well-Being 1963–4 and 1965–6

Perceived Changes of Economic Well-Being, 1963–4 and 1965–6	Change of Support for Labour, 1964–6[a]
Thought well-being improved in 1963–4 and worsened in 1965–6	0%
Thought well-being remained unchanged in both 1963–4 and 1965–6	+3%
Thought well-being worsened in 1963–4 and improved in 1965–6	+13%

[a] Entries are increases in percentage Labour between the elections of 1964 and 1966.

position was improved at the end of the Conservatives' years in power but worsened under Labour, there was almost no movement of opinion during a period when the country as a whole swung markedly towards Labour. Among those who thought their position had remained unchanged under both parties the swing to Labour was about average. But among those who thought their well-being had changed from one of decline to one of improvement, the swing towards Labour was fully 13 per cent, far beyond that recorded in the electorate as a whole.

The strong confirmation for a valence model of the impact of perception of economic change on party support which these patterns of swing provide finds reinforcement when we disaggregate our evidence for the electorate as a whole and examine the support for the governing party within the middle and working class. Let us make such a comparison for the summer of 1963, when the Conservatives held power. Figure 18.10 shows the

18.10 Conservative Support Within Middle and Working Class by Perceived Change of Economic Well-Being, 1963[a]

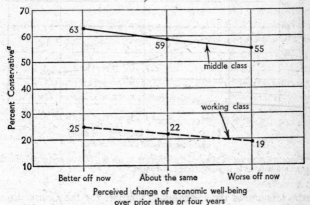

[a] Percent Conservative of support for three main parties. Middle and working class groups are defined in terms of class self-images.

proportion supporting the Conservatives by class according to whether the respondent felt that his well-being had improved or worsened or stayed the same over the preceding three or four years. The slope of the curve downward to the right within each class shows the lessening of support for the Conservative Government among those who felt their economic well-being also makes clear once again the dominant political alignment of the two main classes.

A similar portrait of support within classes for the outgoing Conservative Government was given by the 1964 figures for those who felt that their well-being had improved or worsened or stayed about the same over the year prior to the election, as Figure 18.11 shows. The slope downward to the right within

18.11 Conservative Support Within Middle and Working Class by Perceived Change of Economic Well-Being, 1964[a]

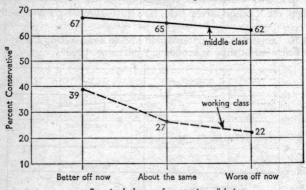

[a] Percent Conservative of support for three main parties. Middle and working class groups are defined in terms of class self-images.

each class shows the lessening of support for the Conservative Government among those who felt they had stood still or gone downhill economically. The general rise of the location of these curves in Figure 18.11, by comparison with Figure 18.10, reflects the general swing back to the Conservatives between 1963 and 1964. Figure 18.11 suggests that support for the Conservatives was remarkably strong among working class electors who thought their well-being had improved over the prior year.

Further support for a valence model of economic effects, under which the ruling party, whichever party it is, gets the credit or the blame, comes when we complete this series of figures with the pattern for 1966. Figure 18.12 shows the proportion supporting the

18.12 Conservative Support Within Middle and Working Class by Perceived Change of Economic Well-Being, 1966[a]

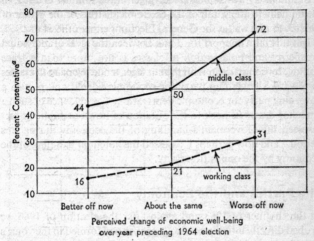

^a Percent Conservative of support for three main parties. Middle and working class groups are defined in terms of class self-images.

Conservatives within the two main classes according to whether the respondent felt that his well-being had improved or worsened or stayed about the same over the year before the 1966 election. With the Conservatives now in opposition the slope of the curves in the figure is dramatically altered. Support for the governing party still is higher among those who felt they were better off than before. But the identity of the Government had changed. The Conservatives in their new role as the opposition party received greater support from those who experienced economic stagnation or decline and this now lends the curves a slope *upward* to the right.

Although these results mainly confirm a valence model of political effects, they do also faintly suggest that economic deprivation may lead to greater polarization of class support. The figures for 1964 and 1966 show that the difference in Conservative support between the middle and working class was least among those who experienced economic improvement and greatest among those who experienced decline. Moreover, the general alignment between class and party was somewhat stronger in the summer of 1963, in the immediate aftermath of the economic distress of the winter of 1962–3, than it was at the General Elections either of 1964 or 1966.

But this faint support for a link between the level of individual prosperity and polarization of classes is not more than a trace finding, by comparison with the stronger tendency of both classes to reward a governing party for economic benefit and punish a governing party for economic deprivation. The evidence of such a tendency draws us back to the question of how the public in fact assessed the Goverment's handling of the economy during this period – and how perhaps it assessed the potential handling of the economy by the opposition party.

The Parties and the Economy

In the summer of 1963 and again after the election of 1966 we probed directly into the connections that had formed in the voter's mind between the parties and economic well-being. We did so only among those respondents, about 70 per cent of the total, who told us that they believed that the Government could affect how well off they were. Table 18.13 sets out the results of this assessment in

18.13 Perceived Bearing of Parties on Economic Well-Being, 1963

| | | Conservative government has made respondent | | |
		Better off	About same	Worse off
Labour government would make respondent	Better off	3	14	12
	About same	11	32	5
	Worse off	15	7	1

100%

the summer of 1963. It is immediately apparent that the individual elector did tend to form a contrasting view of the actual performance of the Conservatives in power and the putative performance of Labour were it to be brought to power. The largest number of respondents fell in the cell for those who said their well-being would remain unchanged under either party. But among those who felt that their well-being would change, there was a marked tendency to see one party or the other as more likely to improve their economic condition, a tendency that is shown by the greater number of respondents who fell in the cells at the lower left and upper right.

But what is mainly of interest in judging the impact of economic perceptions for party support is the way the sample was distributed in this table above and below the main diagonal running from the upper left to the lower right. Respondents below this diagonal felt that they had done relatively better under the Conservatives, while those above it felt that they would do relatively better under Labour. Opinion at this moment was not strongly skewed upon either side of this question. But it certainly could not be said that the Conservatives were at a deep disadvantage in the summer of 1963. It is difficult to know whether this reflects the degree of recovery between the prior winter and the middle of 1963 or whether it shows that the Conservatives carried over from the 1950s a fairly clear image as the party better able to handle the economy and assure prosperity. If the latter were true the electoral cost of the Conservative Government's economic difficulties in 1961–2, while real, would merely have been somewhat to reduce a strong advantage over Labour in the economic sphere which had been built up during the 1950s.

Evidence of the sort presented in Table 18.13 is of course subject to the biasing effects of party allegiance, and when we compare the perceptions of the economic performance of the parties held by those who have always been Conservative and Labour we do in fact see a marked contrast, as Table 18.14 shows.[13] But this table

13. Not all of this contrast should be laid to the biasing influence of party allegiance, however. In such cases such as those of electors whose allegiance is rooted in perceptions of class interest, ties to party may have

18.14 Economic Well-Being Under the Conservative Government as Perceived by Traditional Supporters of Main Parties, Summer 1963[a]

| | | Traditional Allegiance | |
		Conservative	Labour
Conservative government had made respondent	Better off	42%	16%
	About same	50	54
	Worse off	8	30
		100%	100%
		(n = 310)	(n = 346)

[a] Traditional Conservative and traditional Labour supporters are those who replied to questions 44a to 44v of the 1963 questionnaire by saying that they had never supported another party. Perceptions of changes of well-being under the Conservative Government were assessed in terms of replies to question 36b of the 1963 questionnaire.

also shows that traditional Conservatives were far readier in the summer of 1963 to say that they had prospered under the Conservatives than traditional Labour supporters were to say that their well-being had declined under Conservative rule. A reasonable conclusion to be drawn from these data is that the Conservatives were little disadvantaged by the links between the parties and personal well-being that were evident to the electorate at this time, although the Conservatives may well have dissipated a far greater advantage with which they had begun the 1959 Parliament.

A comparable assessment of perceptions of the parties with Labour in power is set out in Table 18.15 for the election of 1966. These figures again show a marked inverse correlation of perceptions of the two parties; the mass of the table tends to run from the lower left to the upper right. But once again neither party seemed strongly advantaged by perceptions of this sort; this is shown by the relatively equal numbers of our respondents who fell in the

been formed and preserved by very long-lasting beliefs about relative economic well-being when each party is the Government.

18.15 Perceived Bearing of Parties on Economic Well-Being, 1966

Labour government
has made respondent

		Better off	About same	Worse off
Conservative government would make respondent	Better off	1	8	11
	About same	9	39	12
	Worse off	9	9	2

100%

cells above and below the main diagonal of the table from upper left to lower right. This pattern is quite consistent with the distinctly mixed perceptions of individual well-being in the spring of 1966 which we examined before, in Tables 18.6 and 18.7.

An additional type of perception seemed, however, to work to Labour's advantage at the time of the 1966 election. In view of the recency of Labour's accession to power the question of responsibility for Britain's economic difficulties was inevitably an open one in the electorate's eyes. Our evidence suggests that Labour was in fact able to exploit this sort of uncertainty surrounding transfers of power so as to persuade the great majority of electors that the problems which beset the economy during the 1964 Parliament were mainly the work of their Conservative predecessors. The support for this conclusion is set out in Table 18.16, which shows that fewer than three electors in twenty held the Labour Government primarily responsible for these difficulties, whereas almost nine in twenty were prepared to lay the chief blame at the door of the Conservatives. We shall see in the next chapter that the electorate's willingness in 1966 to grant Labour, as a new government, a period of grace in economic affairs tied in with more general attitudes about the length of time that Labour should be allowed to prove itself in power.

18.16 Responsibility of Parties for Britain's Perceived
Economic Difficulties, 1966

Do you think that Britain's economic difficulties
are mainly the fault of the Labour Government
or of the last Conservative Government?

Labour Government	13%
Last Conservative Government	43
Both equally	30
Don't know	14
	100%

The rise of the opinion polls with their frequent readings of party strength greatly extends the opportunities for analysing the political impact of economic changes and of changing perceptions of the parties' abilities to deal with economic affairs. Indeed, the importance of the electorate's perceptions of the parties in this sphere is vividly suggested by superimposing two statistical series that may be calculated from the Gallup Poll for part of the period of our work. The first of these is the positive or negative lead which Labour enjoyed over the Conservatives in voting intentions as recorded by Gallup's monthly index. The second is the positive or negative 'lead' of Labour over the Conservatives in terms of the proportions in successive Gallup samples that said they approved or disapproved of each party's handling of economic affairs.[14]

Figure 18.17 shows the remarkable agreement of these two series over a period of nearly five years. Some divergence is evident

14. From December 1959 until August 1964 Gallup asked these questions each month: 'How strongly do you approve or disapprove of the way the Government is handling the problem of economic affairs?' and 'How do you rate the way the Labour Party Opposition is handling the problem of economic affairs in the House of Commons debates and elsewhere?' To form the index of Labour's 'lead' in these perceptions we have subtracted the proportion approving of the Government's handling of the economy from the proportion approving of Labour's handling of the economy.

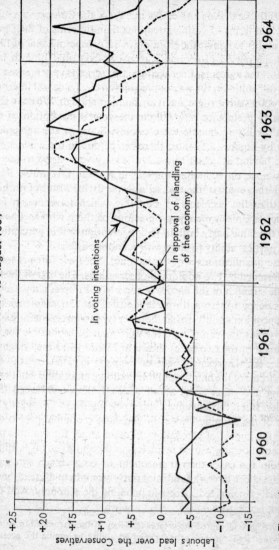

18.17 Labour's Lead Over the Conservatives in Gallup's Monthly Series on Voting Intentions and Approval of Parties' Handling of the Economy, December 1959 to August 1964[a]

[a] These series are derived from the Gallup Poll's published figures for December 1959 to August 1964. Labour's lead in voting intentions is the arithmetic difference of the proportions giving their voting intentions as Labour and Conservative. Labour's lead in approval of parties' handling of the economy is the arithmetic difference of the proportions approving the Labour Opposition's and the Conservative Government's handling of economic affairs.

towards the beginning and end of this span; the Conservatives did less well in terms of voting intentions than in terms of their perceived ability to handle the economy in the prosperous year of 1960 and in the period of economic recovery from mid-1963 to late 1964. But the agreement between the two series is very marked.

The difficulties in the way of placing too clear a causal interpretation upon such an agreement are familiar enough. We have seen that party preference may colour the voter's perception of the parties' ability to handle the economy. Some of the agreement shown by Figure 18.17 must therefore be due to the tendency of voters, having attached themselves to a given party, to see its performance on economic matters in a more favourable light. Indeed, the match of the two series is partly the result of nothing more than the accidents of sampling which have drawn into different samples different proportions of these who incline towards the same party both in voting intention and in perceptions of the parties' ability to cope with economic affairs.

These qualifications are genuine ones. Yet their force is somewhat lessened by two additional observations. The first of these is that the strength of the parties in successive samples shows much less tendency to vary with perceptions of the Government's and the Opposition's ability to handle other types of problems or issues. If party bias and sampling error were mainly responsible for the agreement of the two series shown in Figure 18.17 they ought to produce equal agreement between the party lead in terms of votes and in terms of the handling of international affairs and health and housing and other areas about which Gallup questioned their samples. But if the agreement shown by Figure 18.17 is partly the result of the genuine impact of changing economic perceptions and if the impact of perceptions in other areas, for example pensions and housing, varied much less in the short run (as is almost certainly the case) then there ought to be a closer agreement between short-term variations of party strength and variations of the parties' perceived success in handling the economy. And this, indeed, is what we find.[15]

15. We have measured the greater tendency of the party lead in votes to match the 'lead' in the parties' perceived ability to handle the economy

It should be emphasized that the fact that the party lead in votes matches best with the series showing judgements on the economic performance of the parties does not call into question the importance that the electorate's response to other problems or issues had for the division of party strength at a given moment. The closeness of the match does suggest that fluctuations in the parties' perceived ability to handle the economy have more to do with short-run fluctuations of party support. But motives of much longer duration may enter the electorate's choice of party throughout such a period. This would obviously be true, for example, of perceptions of class interest. If we were to be furnished with a monthly index of perceptions of the Government's link with the interests of a given class it is unlikely that such an index would exhibit a variation that closely matched short-run fluctuations of party support. Yet perceptions of class interest would in every month be of immense importance for the strength of British parties.

A second pattern that makes it plausible to see in the agreement of the two series in Figure 18.17 the influence of changing perceptions of the parties' handling of the economy can be seen if we disaggregate the electorate's comparative judgement of the two parties and examine separately its evaluation of government and opposition. This separation is accomplished by Figure 18.18. It is at once apparent from the contrast of these figures that perceptions of the Government's economic performance are much more variable and match more closely the movements of party strength.[16]

---

by utilizing the coefficient of agreement proposed by W. S. Robinson. See 'The Statistical Measurement of Agreement', *American Sociological Review*, **22** (February 1957), pp. 17–25. This coefficient achieved a value of $+0.56$ when applied to the movements over time of the lead in votes and the lead in the parties' perceived handling of the economy; but a value in no case higher than $+0.04$ when applied to the movements of the lead in votes and the party 'lead' in terms of each of a number of other issues, including international affairs, housing, pensions, health and education.

16. Measures of linear relationship can be misleading on this point, since a few of those who shifted to and away from the parties on the basis of rising and falling confidence in the Government's economic performance may also have adjusted their views of the opposition's ability to handle the economy. The wider variation in attitudes towards the Government's performance suggest that these played the larger role in shifting party support.

18.18 Gallup's Monthly Series on Approval of Handling of Economic Affairs by Conservative Government and Labour Opposition, December 1959 to August 1964[a]

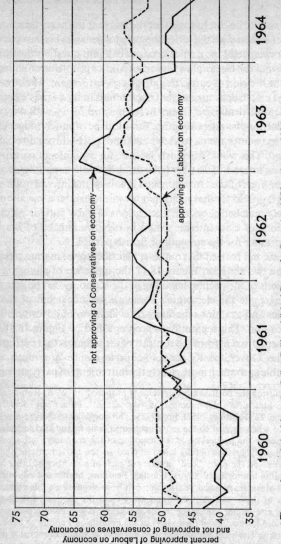

percent approving of Labour on economy and not approving of conservatives on economy

not approving of Conservatives on economy

approving of Labour on economy

[a] These series are derived from the Gallup Poll's published figures for December 1959 to August 1964.

If party bias and the accidents of sampling accounted for the agreement of the series in the earlier figure (18.17), the party lead in votes ought to provide an equally good match with each of the two series showing the changing approval of the economic performance of government and opposition. The fact that the agreement with approval of the Government is much the closer of the two is evidence that we are tapping changes which have genuine influence on party strength and is at the same time evidence that it is the Government's performance that is of greater salience for the electorate.

The most important analytical opportunity that these polling series provides is the possibility of measuring the relationship between fluctuations of party strength and fluctuations of the economy itself. Indeed, it seems likely that analyses of this sort will become a standard part of the repertory of those who wish to account for electoral change.[17] A number of factors, including the time a party has been in office, will intervene between changes of party support and changes of the economic realities that are experienced by millions of electors. But it would be very surprising if approval of the Government's economic record were not systematically tied to the performance of the economy itself.

The strong presumption that it is can be supported by plotting together the time series for unemployment and the Gallup series for the party lead during the period of our work. A marked relationship between the two is evident in Figure 18.19. Closer inspection makes it plausible that changes in the level of unemployment precede changes of party support; Goodhart and Bhansali have estimated that an average lag of four to six months separates a change of unemployment from its maximum political effect. Their investigations suggest that changes in prices as well as unemployment have yielded changes of support for the Government throughout the postwar period and that such influences have been more pronounced in the years since 1959. Although these results must be regarded as provisional, they do indicate that the movements of unemployment and price level charted in Figures 18.2

17. A pathbreaking analysis of this sort in Britain is reported by C. A. E. Goodhart and R. J. Bhansali in their paper 'Political Economy', *passim.*

18.19 Gallup Poll's Monthly Series on Labour's Lead Over Conservatives and Monthly Series on Thousands of Unemployed, Seasonally Adjusted, 1959–64

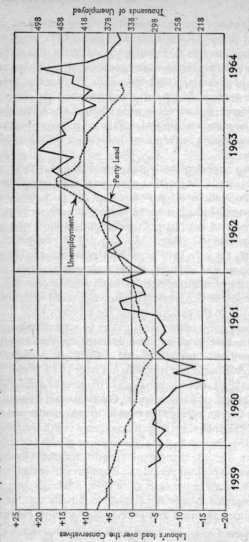

a The series for Labour's lead over the Conservatives is taken from the Gallup Poll's published figures for 1959 to 1964. The series for wholly unemployed, seasonally adjusted, is taken from the *Ministry of Labour Gazette*. That source gives a seasonally adjusted series only from June 1963. For the earlier period the figures given for actual number of wholly unemployed, excluding school leavers, were adjusted for seasonal variation by applying a constant seasonal adjustment factor computed as the mean of the adjustment factors used by the Ministry of Labour for the years 1964–7.

and 18.3 exerted a marked influence on the support of the parties during the period of our work.[18] In particular, the decline of Conservative support between 1959 and 1963 and the partial Conservative recovery between 1963 and 1964 owed a good deal to changes of price and unemployment levels in 1961–2 and 1963–4.

In a broader sense these findings argue how important these two aspects of the country's economic well-being are in the electorate's choice at the polling-station. But they certainly do not lead to any simple and sovereign economic theory of electoral outcomes. We should emphasize once again that short-term movements of party support due to changes in the economy are overlaid on more gradual changes due to factors, such as perceptions of class interest, which are of immense importance for the electorate's choice in any election during a given period. Much more than economic well-being alone will bear on the country's final choice of a government.

18. Goodhart and Bhansali, 'Political Economy', *passim*. These investigators were unable to find evidence that changes of Britain's trading position influenced public support for the Government. This and other results of their illuminating analysis must be regarded as provisional, as they are at pains to say, owing to the error attaching to various economic indicators, the range of indicators from which to choose, and the influence on their findings of the treatment given various 'dummy' variables commissioned inductively to stand for such things as post-election 'euphoria' for the winning party, the 'normal' loss of support by the Government during the life of a Parliament, and the 'swing back' to the Government as an election approaches. Moreover, since unemployment and inflation are themselves related by the structure of the economy, identification of their separate effects on party support would require the simultaneous estimation of a full model of their relationship to each other and to the strength of the parties.

19 The Final Choice of Government

All the pressures towards an electoral decision culminate in Britain in a three-week campaign that ends with the actual casting of votes and the change or continuation of the Government in power. If the foregoing pages have any theme it is that the voter's choice is not normally a sudden thing, but the product of months or years or even generations. Even those who change their votes are often reverting to some past pattern or reflecting some long-established attitude rather than reacting to the specific stimulus of the campaign. Those whose behaviour is influenced by a topical issue may have formed their attitude far more over the length of the preceding Parliament than in the few short weeks of final argument. Over the last thirty years one of the primary contributions of studies of opinion change during campaigns has been to revise traditional judgements of the impact of campaigns. Time and again it has been shown that relatively few votes are changed and that these are largely in mutually cancelling directions.[1]

Two elementary yet fundamental points should warn us, however, against discounting the campaign too far. The first of these is that judgements of the campaign's importance can be very different according to whether the test is victory for one party or the other or simply net changes in party strength. If the parties are closely matched, as they often are, a modest change due to the campaign can be decisive even though the shift of the party balance has been quite small. In three of the last six British elec-

1. See in particular P. F. Lazarsfeld, B. Berelson and H. Gaudet, *The People's Choice*, New York, 1944; B. Berelson, P. F. Lazarsfeld and W. N. McPhee, *Voting*, Chicago, 1954; M. Benney, R. H. Pear and A. P. Gray, *How People Vote*, London, 1956; R. S. Milne and H. C. Mackenzie, *Straight Fight*, London, 1954, and *Marginal Seat*, London, 1958.

tions the margin of victory has certainly been narrow enough to have been at the mercy of last-minute changes.

The second point to bear in mind is that the parties' actual success in campaigning for votes must be distinguished from what might have happened in a different sort of campaign – or in the absence of any campaign at all. The evidence that campaigns matter little is, after all, drawn from elections in which both sides campaigned actively. It would take a convinced sceptic to say that nothing would have changed if one of the parties had unilaterally abandoned all efforts to persuade the undecided and rally the faithful. The recollection of Thomas Dewey's defeat by President Truman after he had waged almost a non-campaign stands as a warning to any political manager tempted to read voting studies with too literal an eye.

Moreover, our interest in campaigns is partly that they are in some ways distinct from the long periods in between. The campaign and election do provide the moment when the parties sum up the arguments they want to address to the great public, and when the public itself is exposed to specific stimuli, especially at the local level, which are distinctive to the campaign. Our consideration of the forces which can modify partisan dispositions ought not to close without some attention to these distinctive influences.

The Several Campaigns

To compress into a single phrase 'the election campaign', all the diverse activities of the pre-election weeks is to falsify the reality. There are at least three types of formal campaign being conducted simultaneously. First, there is the campaign engaged in by local party workers: canvassing, distributing literature and getting the faithful to the polls. Next, there is a campaign fought at the constituency level by the individual candidates making their round of public meetings, talking to the press, shaking hands and being 'seen' throughout the area. Lastly, there is the campaign of the party leaders waged through election broadcasts, press conferences and platform speeches.

These three campaigns have different audiences and different aims. A casual viewer of television hardly has the same reactions as someone who has bothered to go out to a public meeting. The types of persuasion open to a canvasser are different from those exercised by a party leader. Some campaigning is aimed directly at the voter but some is aimed more to the party activist or functionary for him to pass on, directly or indirectly, to the voter. It is not only the immediacy of the approach that varies but also the goal – is it to achieve conversions or merely to get the faithful to the polling-station? Some electioneering activities may indeed be directed not at the current contest but at staking out positions that may help in later struggles between or within the parties.

There is also a fourth type of campaign – a completely unorganized one. Ordinary people going about their daily business inevitably engage in political persuasion as they argue with their family and friends and urge them to vote or to vote in a given way. More votes are probably changed by domestic discussion than by all the official campaigning. In 1964 only 3 per cent of our sample claimed to have done any party work during the campaign but 12 per cent said they had tried to persuade someone how to vote and 59 per cent said they had discussed the campaign. Such activities may be largely self-cancelling – for every Labour husband who argues his wife into voting with him there may be an equally compelling Conservative. But it is certainly possible that spontaneous talk does, on balance, advantage one of the parties more than the other. As we showed earlier, some groups of people are exposed to situations in which political discussion carries some pressure to conform to a majority view. The measurement of such effects lies largely outside the scope of our research. Yet as we discuss the impact of more direct campaigning we must always remember that any stimulus given to an individual elector may always have repeated and multiplied effects through his subsequent conversations.

The Campaign of the Party Activists

Only a small fraction of the British population takes any formal part in electioneering. But though a mere 3 per cent claimed to have done so in 1964, 3 per cent represent a million people – an impressive army giving up hours of their time in efforts to maximize their party's vote. The rough figures in Table 19.1 suggest that some half-million Conservatives, 300,000 Labour supporters and

19.1 Proportion Participating Actively in 1964 Campaign

All Voters	Con. Voters	Lab. Voters	Lib. Voters	All Party Members	All Con. Members	All Lab. Members	All Lib. Members
3%	4%	3%	5%	14%	13%	11%	42%

175,000 Liberals may have lent a hand to their parties. Over a third of them were not even party members. The more conscious effort involved in joining a minority party is perhaps reflected in the much greater zeal of Liberal activists suggested by these figures.

Local campaign activity goes largely into distributing literature – mainly the candidate's traditional 'election address' – and into canvassing in order to get a fully marked-up register so that supporters can be checked off and rounded up on polling day. Sixty-four per cent of our respondents claimed that they had seen some party literature and 34 per cent claimed that someone had canvassed at their door.

When we divide those who remembered being canvassed according to the party they remembered as having called, sharp differences emerge. Table 19.2 shows these for voters who remember being

19.2 1964 Vote of People Canvassed by One Party by Party of Canvasser

| | Voter Canvassed By: | | |
	Conservatives Only	Labour Only	Liberals Only
Conservatives	58	31	39
Labour	35	63	25
Liberal	7	6	36
	100% ($n = 167$)	100% ($n = 102$)	100% ($n = 63$)

canvassed only by a single party in 1964. There seems little doubt that some portion of these differences is to be explained by the fact that those disposed to vote a given way are somewhat more likely to remember the canvassing done by their own party. But, more important, parties naturally focus their canvassing on favourable areas and known supporters; canvassing is aimed at activation, not conversion, and experienced party workers are careful not to stir up opponents gratuitously.

Much of the ambiguity in these data vanishes when we look at the evidence on the link between canvassing and partisan change. We may reasonably assume that the likelihood of a given voter's being contacted by a given party has more to do with long-term factors in partisanship – especially social class – than with the factors which yield more transient changes. On this assumption, changes of party preference, when they coincide with the experience of being canvassed, are a truer reflection of the partisan effect of canvassing.

We examine this effect, first of all, in terms of canvassing by the two major parties. Table 19.3 draws from the sample interviewed in both the summer of 1963 and the autumn of 1964 those who in the 1964 General Election were canvassed only by the Conservatives, by neither party, and only by Labour, and examines within

19.3 Change of Conservative Lead 1963–4 by Major Party Canvassing in 1964

	Canvassed by Conservative Only	Canvassed by Neither Party	Canvassed by Labour Only
Net change in Conservative lead, 1963–4	+4·4%	+1·3%	+1·0%

each of these three groups the net change of party preference towards, or away from, the Conservatives. The difference of these three change figures is nothing like so sharp as the difference of Conservative support in Table 19.2. Moreover, some part of the differences shown in Table 19.3 can also be due to voters being more likely to recall the persuasions of the party to which they currently incline. None the less, these differences leave open the possibility that the major parties do achieve some slight effect through canvassing.

A stronger influence of canvassing is, however, upon Liberals. We saw in Chapters 12 and 14 how very high was the turnover of Liberal support: of those who were Liberal at any point of time many inclined to some other party shortly before and many changed again soon after. To a remarkable extent the Liberal vote is a 'pick-up' vote, one that must constantly be renewed. The wide variation in the Liberal vote in adjacent and socially similar constituencies is indeed largely a reflection of differing levels of Liberal activity.

Our evidence that canvassing is an important means of renewal is given by Table 19.4, which divides our 1963–4 panel respondents from constituencies fought by the Liberals in 1964 into those who were and were not Liberal in 1963, and, within these groups, into

19.4 Liberal Support in Seats the Liberals fought in 1964 by 1963 Preference and Liberal Canvassing 1964

| | 1963 Preference | | | |
| | For Liberals | | Other than Liberals | |
	Canvassed by Lib.	Not Canvassed by Lib.	Canvassed by Lib.	Not Canvassed by Lib.
Voted Liberal 1964	72	45	12	9
Voted Other than Liberal 1964	28	55	88	91
	100% ($n = 32$)	100% ($n = 99$)	100% ($n = 85$)	100% ($n = 488$)

those who were and were not canvassed by the Liberals in 1964. The comparison of Liberal support in the first two of these columns suggests the more rapid draining away of Liberal strength among those the party failed to reach through canvassing in 1964. The comparison of the second two columns suggests, on the other hand, the greater headway the Liberals made with electors whom they did reach on the doorstep during the campaign.

As we saw in Chapter 14 the Liberals enjoy a degree of favour with the electorate which reaches well beyond their explicit supporters. We have argued that the gap between favour and behaviour, between inclination and actual vote, is explained by two kinds of constraint: first, that there are many seats left unfought by the Liberals, depriving potential supporters of a candidate and, second, that many voters see no prospect of Liberal victory, nationally or locally.

Each of these constraints can be eroded by vigorous canvassing. Doorstep contacts will not, of course, produce a candidate where none is standing, but where one is standing they can do much to publicize the fact. Our evidence suggests that there were some potential Liberal voters in 1964 who were unaware that they had a Liberal candidate to vote for. But even more, doorstep contact can heighten the sense that the local challenge is a credible one, that the seat will be vigorously fought, and that the Liberals have a chance of victory. Table 19.5 shows the greater optimism over the Liberals'

19.5 Perception of Liberal Chances of Electing Local Member by Whether Canvassed by Liberals in 1964

Estimate of Liberal Chance of Winning in Local Constituency	Canvassed by Liberals	Not canvassed by Liberals
Very Good	43%	24%
Fairly good	25	21
Not very good	32	55
	100%	100%
	($n = 142$)	($n = 773$)

chances expressed by respondents in seats fought by the Liberals in 1964 if they had been canvassed by the party. From the contrast of these columns it is reasonable to suppose that the incidence of canvassing holds an appreciable part of the explanation for the uneven distribution of Liberal success.

The Constituency Campaign

Electors may decide their allegiance in terms of national parties and leaders and issues. But they can record their allegiance only by putting a cross beside the name of one of their constituency candidates. Since party designations did not appear on the ballot during this period, a momentary identification of the candidate representing their side was essential to taking an effective part in the national choice.

The M.P. does not loom very large in the elector's consciousness. In the summer of 1963, only 51 per cent of our respondents could name their M.P. Even among those who were supporters of his party the proportion was not much higher. But the onset of an election made a vast difference. Local campaigns inevitably focus on making the candidate's name known and associating it with the party label. When we interviewed people a few weeks after polling day, the great majority knew who their candidates had been.

Yet our evidence even from the weeks following the election suggests how fugitive such information is for part of the electorate. Figure 19.6 illustrates graphically the decay of popular memory of the candidates' names in terms of five curves – two for M.P.s and three for defeated candidates, separated according to party. These curves indicate how much more durable is knowledge of the M.P., although our data from the summer of 1963 suggest how low the public's knowledge of the member's name can have sunk by the time a Parliament is several years old. Figure 19.6 shows that knowledge both of successful and unsuccessful candidates begins at a high level in the aftermath of a General Election campaign. It would be found to be higher still if we were to confine our figures to a candidate's own supporters, the only people who *must* know his name, however briefly, if they are to record their preference at the polls. Indeed, if we extend these decay curves back to election day, it is reasonable to suppose that there was almost no confusion on

19.6 Post-Election Recall of Candidates' Names, 1964, by Lapse of Time Between Election and Interview

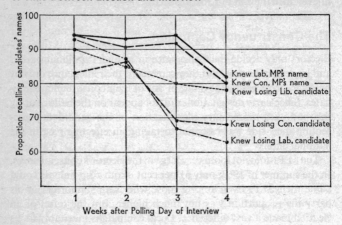

the subject at the polls, although we did encounter one or two respondents who confessed that they had in the end wasted their vote by forgetting their candidate's name when in the polling-booth.[2]

The election campaign adds to the public's knowledge of the M.P. in many ways. In the summer of 1963 a fifth of electors were ignorant even of the party to which their M.P. belonged. After the 1964 election the number had fallen to a twentieth, while the fraction having some knowledge of the M.P. beyond name and party more than doubled between 1963 and 1964 (from 30 per cent to 66 per cent). There seems reason to believe that the increased

2. The very ill-fortune of many Independent candidates suggests, however, that this sort of confusion is slight. Since we would expect 'blind' votes to be distributed fairly randomly between candidates, the fact that there have been contests in which Independents have received less than 0·2 per cent of the total vote implies that very few people mark their ballots mistakenly. The six words of self-description allowed to parliamentary candidates under the 1969 Act do not appear to be needed to cure any very widespread confusion.

diffusion of information about the M.P. at election time comes largely from the local press, local party propaganda and informal political conversation. Despite the diligence with which M.P.s cultivate their constituencies during campaigns, the proportion of electors reporting that they had actually seen their M.P. was exactly the same (35 per cent) in the wake of the 1964 election campaign as it was in the summer of 1963. Of course, 35 per cent of electors represents 13 million people and such exposure by M.P.s reflects thousands of hours of devoted constituency work. But the absence of difference between the campaign and the inter-election period suggest that the people to whom the member is exposed in the weeks before the poll are primarily people who have seen him before. Candidates who were not elected were seen by fewer than one elector in seven.

It is not surprising that candidates seem to influence results so little; our evidence makes plain that only a very meagre image of the M.P., let alone of the other candidates, gets through before or during the campaign. Despite all the efforts that some M.P.s make to communicate their personal stand on issues, very little seems to reach down to their constituents. After the 1966 General Election the proportions of our respondents who had heard anything about their M.P.s' stand on four leading issues was very small, as Table 19.7 shows. Furthermore, despite the lengths to which many M.P.s

19.7 Awareness of M.P.'s Stand on Issues, 1966

		Proportion Aware of M.P.'s Stand
Issues	Nationalization of Industry	26%
	Common Market	16%
	Capital Punishment	16%
	Nuclear Weapons	12%

go in identifying themselves with local problems or interests, only one elector in seven could think of anything his M.P. had done for the people of the constituency.

The fact that the public's impression of the M.P.s' stands is so faint does not of course prevent the elector from connecting his vote with policy choices. We have seen that knowledge of the candidate's party is close to universal, and we have seen in Chapters 8 and 15 that the public has a very sharp image of party positions on various issues. Hence the elector's support of a candidate may involve a calculus of policy choices. But it is a calculus to which the parliamentary candidate adds little beyond his adherence to party.

It would also be a mistake to suppose that because the public's knowledge of the candidates is so limited, it must necessarily have little effect. In the vastly different constitutional setting of the United States, the Congressman is on average even less known to his constituents than is the British M.P., but the limited information that does reach American constituents can have very marked influence on their voting, allowing entrenched Congressmen to build up a formidable incumbent's advantage over a period of years.[3]

The National Campaign

Whatever the relative importance of the several levels of campaign for inducing changes at the individual level, it is the national campaign which is much the most likely to produce a net alteration in party strength. The individual changes induced by candidate and constituency activities may add up to a net gain for one party or the other, but most changes from such sources are likely to be self-cancelling, and the sum of these effects will tend to be much less in net term, than the effect of the national campaign, which can exert a parallel force on the whole electorate at once.

In fact, the campaign carried on by the national party leaders, fully covered by the press and, since 1959, by television and radio

3. Evidence on this point is presented in D. E. Stokes and W. E. Miller, 'Party Government and the Saliency of Congress', *Public Opinion Quarterly*, **26** (1962) 531–46; reprinted in *Elections and the Political Order*, pp. 194–211. See also M. Cummings, *Congressmen and the Electorate*, New York, 1966. For a revisionist British view see P. M. Williams, 'Two notes on the British Electoral System', *Parliamentary Affairs*, **17**, (1966), 13–30.

as well, seems to attract far more hours of attention and to reach directly to far more people than anything done on the local level. It is certainly the main cause for the vast increase in the audience for politics that comes with the campaign. The number of people paying no attention to politics in any of the mass media fell from 32 per cent in the summer of 1963 to 8 per cent after the campaign in the autumn of 1964. The fact that 92 per cent of our sample claimed to have followed the campaign is an impressive tribute to the pervasiveness of the mass media and the political socialization of the mass British public.[4]

This attention to the campaign is not, however, matched by dramatic shifts of voting intention. Anyone who retains an idealized picture of the campaign at a moment when people listen to the arguments and make up their minds afresh must be discouraged by the electorate's own account of when it reaches a judgement. The great majority of electors say that they had made up their minds before the campaign began. As Table 19.8 shows, only the Liberals won over a substantial part of their support during the actual

19.8 Proportion Deciding During Campaign by Party

	Conservative Voters	Labour Voters	Liberal Voters	All Voters
1964	8%	10%	34%	11%
1966	10%	9%	34%	11%

campaign, a fact which emphasizes again the 'pick-up' quality of the Liberal vote. Table 19.8 also shows that the numbers who said they came to the choice in the last few weeks before the poll was no higher in the tense situation of 1964 than it was in face of the foregone conclusion of 1966.

Opinion polls during the elections of 1964 and 1966 lend support to the view that few votes change during the campaign. In both years National Opinion Polls based their pre-election forecast

4. See Chapter 10 for a fuller discussion of the campaign impact of the mass media.

upon re-interviews with people contacted earlier in the campaign. This 'panel' yielded a kind of average portrait of change over the last few weeks by allowing eve-of-poll intentions to be compared with intentions expressed by the same electors at varying lengths of time before. The turnover of intentions recorded during the 1964 campaign is given by Table 19.9, which conveys most of all a

19.9 Turnover of Opinion During the 1964 Campaign

Final Pre-Election Survey

	Con.	Lab.	Lib.	Other	Wouldn't Vote	Still Un-decided	
Con.	37·0	2·7	1·6	0·1	0·5	0·3	42·2
Lab.	2·0	38·0	2·0	0·1	0·9	1·0	44·0
Lib.	1·3	2·2	5·5	0·0	0·0	0·0	9·0
Other	0·0	0·1	0·1	0·1	0·0	0·0	0·3
Wouldn't Vote	0·1	0·2	0·1	0·0	1·4	0·0	1·8
Undecided	0·7	1·2	0·4	0·0	0·0	0·4	2·7
	41·1	44·4	9·7	0·3	2·8	1·7	100·0

(Con. 42·2, Lab. 44·0 bracketed as 1·8 on the right)

(41·1, 44·4 bracketed as 3·3 below)

Earlier Pre-Election Survey (row axis label)

Source: National Opinion Polls

sense of stability of choice during the campaign period. Labour's net lead changed by less than 2 per cent during these weeks and the proportion of the whole panel lying on the main diagonal of the table is high; the proportion off the main diagonal is in fact nicely consistent with the proportion who (Table 19.8) told our own interviewers that they decided during the campaign. True to form, the Liberal vote is much the most volatile: of those who were Liberal at the first survey, more than a third were Conservative or Labour a few weeks later; and of those who were Liberal at the eve of poll, more than a third had been Conservative or Labour a few weeks before.

Of course, given the evenness of the parties at the campaign's outset, even a very modest net shift could be decisive. In this case the N.O.P. panel data, arranged in the manner of Table 19.9, show a net increase of 1·5 per cent in Labour's lead during the campaign. If we break this shift down into its component pathways of change, on the same lines as in Chapter 12, the straight conversion of Conservatives to Labour proves to have been the main source of Labour's increase:

Straight conversion	+ 1·4%
Circulation of Liberals	+ 0·5%
Circulation of Others, Undecided and intending non-voters	− 0·4%
Net change in Labour's lead	+ 1·5%

These types of circulation brought substantially more former Liberals and former 'non-voters' and undecideds to Labour than to the Conservatives, but the advantage was offset by Labour's losing more of its own supporters to Liberalism or to non-voting and indecision than did the Conservatives.

The comparable N.O.P. figures for the 1966 campaign again convey a sense of the stability of opinion during the campaign but present in detail some interesting contrasts with 1964. As Table 19.10 shows it was the Conservatives who drew a slight net advantage from change during the campaign period. This appreciation of Conservative strength came neither from a favourable balance of straight conversions nor from the circulation of Liberals but rather from a consolidation of Conservative opinion among the undecideds:

Straight conversion	− 0·2%
Circulation of Liberals	− 0·2%
Circulation of others, including non-voters, and undecideds	− 1·5%
Net change of Labour's lead	− 1·9%

19.10 Turnover of Opinion During the 1966 Campaign

Final Pre-Election Survey

Earlier Pre-Election Survey	Con.	Lab.	Lib.	Other	Wouldn't Vote	Still Un-decided		
Con.	34·2	1·9	0·4	0·0	0·4	0·2	37·1	⎫ 12·4
Lab.	2·0	45·3	0·9	0·0	0·5	0·8	49·5	⎭
Lib.	1·1	1·4	5·2	0·0	0·1	0·0	7·8	
Other	0·0	0·1	0·0	0·3	0·0	0·0	0·4	
Wouldn't Vote	0·2	0·2	0·1	0·0	0·9	0·2	1·6	
Undecided	1·6	0·7	0·5	0·1	0·0	0·7	3·6	
	39·1	49·6	7·1	0·4	1·9	1·9	100·0	

10·5

Source: National Opinion Polls

What the N.O.P. evidence plainly suggests is that, for the second election running, the campaign changes benefited the opposition rather than the Government. It is worth recalling that in the 1950s the regular pre-election recovery of successive governments in terms of by-elections and opinion polls began to establish the idea that campaigns could normally be expected to improve the position of the party in power.

The Alternation of Governments

Whether voters are more likely, as polling day draws near, to move towards or away from those who hold the reins of government, there is no doubt that the idea of the reins changing hands is widely appreciated. The possibility of alternation in office is central to understanding the way that party leaders think about British politics. This possibility sustains the 'out' party, shaping both its recruitment of parliamentary talent and its style of conducting the business of opposition. The desirability of such transfers of power is in fact overwhelmingly accepted by the leaders of both the main parties, and is a standard argument available to the opposition in pressing its case before the mass electorate.

How much influence has this belief on the electorate itself? Our studies embraced a period in which one government was very old, indeed the oldest in a century, and its successor very new. We have therefore an unusual opportunity to test whether the public held quite general beliefs about the transfer of power which affected the choices it reached in these years.

Some familiar problems of opinion analysis stand in the way of any simple assessment of the importance of such beliefs. In particular, two sorts of responses can overlay real convictions as to the desirability of the alternation of governments. On the one hand, party allegiance may bias the elector's response to the idea that the parties should alternate in power: those whose party is for the moment out of office will be more likely to endorse such a view than those whose party provides the government. On the other hand, some of the responses given to the idea of alternation in power will be the uncertain and transient views of those who do not hold a genuine belief on the matter. Here, as in so many other places, we must be alert to the way that response uncertainty can blur our measurement of well-rooted attitudes.

The fact that power was actually transferred in the midst of our research provides, however, the means of separating party bias and response uncertainty from genuine belief. Let us first of all consider the detection of the biasing effect of party allegiance. It would be reasonable to suppose that Conservatives whose allegiance remained fixed throughout 1963 to 1966 would become more receptive to the desirability of alternation once Labour was in power and that constant Labour supporters would be more enthusiastic about the idea while their party was still in opposition. Our evidence shows this to have been the case. The responses to a question about the desirability of alternating governments given in 1963 and 1966 by those who were steadfastly Conservative or Labour throughout the period make it plain that opinion shifted markedly according to whose ox would be gored; Table 19.11 shows that perceptible, and opposite, shifts took place among these

19.11 Belief in Turnover of Party Control Among Stable Conservative and Labour Partisans, 1963–6[a]

| | Beliefs Held by Those Who Were Consistently | | | |
| | Conservative | | Labour | |
	1963	1966	1963	1966
Control of the Government should pass from one party to another every so often	43%	53%	64%	51%
It's all right for one party to have control for a long time	46	38	26	40
Don't know	11	9	10	9
	100%	100%	100%	100%
	(n = 334)		(n = 410)	

[a] This analysis is limited to those whose partisan self-image was consistently Conservative or consistently Labour in 1963, 1964 and 1966. Beliefs as to the desirability of turnover of party control are based on the replies to question 63a in the 1963 questionnaire and question 52 in the 1966 questionnaire.

two groups of party stalwarts at the time when a Labour Government replaced a Conservative one. It is interesting to note that Labour partisans were more united in their belief in the virtues of party turnover in 1963 than were the Conservatives in 1966. This may reflect the fact that in 1963 the Conservative Government was very old, while in 1966 the Labour Government was still quite young. But it may also reflect the fact that Conservatives are more used to seeing their party in power. A general belief in the virtues of alternation is more likely to spring up in those who are accustomed to their party's being in opposition.

The detailed shifts of individual belief over the period of the transfer of power give insight into the presence of pure uncertainty of response. Table 19.12 shows the turnover among constant Conservative and Labour supporters between a period when their party was in power and a period when it was not. The percentages

19.12 Changes of Belief in Turnover of Party Control Among Stable Conservative and Labour Partisans, 1963–6[a]

		Report When Own Party Held Government			
		Should Be Turnover	Long Control All Right	Don't Know	
Report When Opposite Party Held Government	Should Be Turnover	30	21	7	58
	Long Control All Right	13	17	3	33
	Don't Know	4	4	1	9
		47	42	11	100% (n = 744)

[a] This analysis is limited to those who remained supporters of the Conservative or of the Labour Party during three interviews from 1963 to 1966. Conservatives are classified by columns according to their answers in 1963 and by rows according to their answers in 1966. Labour supporters are classified by rows according to their answers in 1963 and by columns according to their answers in 1966.

set at the row and column margins of this table show once again the greater attractiveness of the idea of alternation when one's own party is out of power, and this change of marginal percentages is reflected in the relative size of the figures in the interior cells of the table that lie above and below the main diagonal of constant opinion from upper left to lower right. But the figures in the cells below this diagonal show that there were substantial movements of opinion in a direction *opposite* to the trend that party bias would suggest. It is reasonable to conclude that these contrary movements reflect pure uncertainty of response, the tendency of respondents to give more or less random answers in successive interviews in the absence of any true belief.

In view of the actual turnover of party control midway in our work, each of these forms of 'false' report implies a change of the respondent's position between successive interviews.[5] We can therefore examine the effects which generalized attitudes towards the turnover of party control may have on party choice by selecting from our panel sample those who remained constant in their views at all three interviews, either endorsing the idea of turnover or saying that the long retention of power was quite all right.

The evidence provided by these two groups makes clear that generalized beliefs about the desirability of periodic transfers of control do play a role in the behaviour of the mass electorate and that they had a decisive effect in this period on the fortunes of a Conservative Government that had been in power since the early 1950s. Evidence of this is set out in Table 19.13, which contrasts the stability of Conservative preferences between 1959 and 1964

19.13 Support for Conservatives in 1964 Among 1959 Conservative Voters By Beliefs About Desirability of Turnover of Party Control[a]

	Control of government should pass from one party to another every so often	It's all right for one party to have control of government for a long time
Voted Conservative in 1964	63%	89%
Did not vote Conservative in 1964	37	11
	100% ($n = 93$)	100% ($n = 42$)

[a] This analysis is limited to respondents within our panel who endorsed the same position about the desirability of circulation of governments at all three interviews and reported that they had voted Conservative at the 1959 General Election.

among those who held a generalized belief in the desirability of

5. We must once again allow for the fact that someone who gave a completely random reply at each interview can have given the same reply by chance at all three interviews. But these will constitute only a small element of those in our panel who remained constant in their views in three successive interviews. See Chapter 9, pp. 242–7.

the circulation of governments and those who did not hold such a belief. The erosion of Conservative strength was substantially greater among the first of these groups. Moreover, this finding is consistent with those for each category of 1959 voters. The movement of prior Labour supporters towards the Conservatives was much weaker among those who expressed a generalized belief in the turnover of party control. Furthermore, Labour's relative share of support in 1964 from those who had been Liberal or who had not voted or who had been too young to vote in 1959 was substantially larger among those who thought the circulation of governments desirable. Given the closeness of the result in 1964 the numbers involved in these differences were quite enough to show that general beliefs in favour of alternation in power supplied the last margin needed to dismiss from office the aging Conservative Government.[6]

Our argument here is based on movements over the whole of the 1959 Parliament, the greater part of which occurred prior to our first interview in 1963. Those of our respondents who expressed a belief in the circulation of governments were not, however, merely justifying a shift from the Conservatives they had already made. The tendency seen in Table 19.13 is also evident in shifts away from the Conservatives between 1963 and 1964, after we had taken one measurement of the voter's belief in turnover in power. Of supporters of the Conservatives in 1963, the proportion shifting away from the party in the next seventeen months was considerably greater among those who believed in turnover of control than it was among those who thought the long control of a single party acceptable. This is one of those nice cases where repeated interviews enable us, with the wisdom of hindsight, to select a characteristic that foreshadows an increased likelihood of change among seemingly constant voters.

Acceptance of the norm of turnover in office has its counterpart in the tendency of the electorate to accord a new government a

6. The swing to Labour between 1959 and 1964 among all those who held stable beliefs as to the desirability of the circulation of governments was 6·1 per cent, whereas those who accepted the idea of the long tenure of a single party actually recorded a swing of 3·6 per cent to the Conservatives.

period of grace in which to establish itself and deal with the country's problems. If a government long in office is unusually suspect, one new to office is unusually easily forgiven. Part of this tendency is due, as we have said, to the rough processes of causal reasoning by which the electorate establishes the responsibility of governments. The bulk of the public probably underestimates the lag of time that separates an observed effect from its ministerial or departmental cause; but it does have some sense of these delays, and the conditions found under a new government may well be thought to be the work of its predecessor. We observed in Chapter 18 how spectacularly Labour benefited from the tendency of the electorate in 1966 to see the country's economic difficulties as a legacy of Conservative rule.

Apparently this sort of allowance was extended Labour in 1966 on a much broader front. We asked our sample the question, 'Did you feel, before this election, that the Labour Government had been in office long enough to have had a fair trial?' Only 26 per cent said that they did, whereas fully 71 per cent said that they did not. The remaining 3 per cent, a remarkably small percentage, were unable to answer. The one-sidedness of these replies makes it unlikely that they reflect simple party bias or uncertain response. It seems more reasonable to think that we have touched on another aspect of the norms of party control which is of wide influence on the electorate. At this moment of electoral history it worked powerfully to Labour's advantage.

The norms of party control held by the electorate, especially the wide acceptance of the desirability of turnover in office, help to explain why actual transfers of power are so easily accepted. The votes cast in 1964 threw one party from power after thirteen years in office and put another in its place. The tranquil acceptance of such abrupt changes of authority is one of the more remarkable features of the older democracies. The good grace with which partisans at both the élite and the mass level accept loss of office is the more noteworthy in view of how small are the transfers of votes which cause governments to change hands. The election which produced the new Labour administration in 1964 gave the parties almost equal votes and seats. In 1951 the Conservatives took power on a swing of little more than 1 per cent in popular support and actually with fewer votes than the Labour Government they were replacing.

Of course the small scale of the party swings is somewhat deceptive, and the magnitude of the political tides probably goes a good deal beyond the limited arithmetic of votes. This is not just a matter of the way the single-member constituency causes the composition of the House of Commons to fluctuate more widely than does the popular vote. It is more a matter of the way electors who themselves stay loyal to a long-standing party allegiance may nevertheless feel the pull of the issues and leaders that have caused others of less fixed allegiance to change sides. When a party is driven from power an appreciation of the reasons for its defeat will not be limited to those whose votes produced it.

In this sense, those who change act as surrogates for those who, although they do not change, recognize in themselves the reactions which have moved the less committed. Such an interpretation indeed puts a new face on the evidence that it is the less interested and informed voter who contributes most to electoral change. The less involved are a disproportionate element of electoral tides; but this need not mean they have produced changes that contradict the mood of those who are more interested and informed. In most cases they simply are more easily swayed by forces which are felt quite generally across the electorate. The very generality of these forces prepares a wider acceptance of the transfers of authority.

Yet it would be difficult not to see the generalized belief in the value of party turnover as one of the influences in the acceptance of such transfers. This is an important element of the British political culture, as it is of the political culture of other liberal democracies. Many of those who supported the Conservatives in 1964 were ready to concede, as we have seen, that a turnover of party control from time to time is good in itself. For such people the result is easier to accept. Just as the electoral forces which move the country are felt by many who do not themselves change, the displacement of one party by another is supported by a general belief in the value of change that is held by many who have remained loyal to the displaced Government.

Conclusion

20 Analytic Perspectives

The sheer complexity of the processes by which the parties' strength changes is underlined again and again throughout this book. Indeed, the variety of the factors at work is perhaps the dominant theme of our discussion of the physical replacement of the electorate, of fundamental shifts of party alignment and of more transient variations of electoral strength. Any catalogue of the factors involved in these processes must include some that are to be found in the voter's mind, some in the circumstances that govern his chances of being born and of surviving to any given age, some in his interaction with his family and with his neighbours and workmates, some in the structure and operations of the communications media, some in the behaviour of political leaders and party organizations and some in the trends of the economy or in world events – and even this list is far from exhaustive.

The complexity of change naturally inspires a diversity of approach. We have brought to these manifold problems a wide variety of analytic frameworks rather than any one approach. Only by cutting away huge segments of political reality would it be possible to apply a single, elegant model of change that was parsimonious in its terms. It may sometimes be desirable to attempt this and to treat change as a property of a very simple 'closed' system. For example, we might follow some theorists in supposing that voters respond to governments in terms of movements of prices and employment and that governments seek support by choosing a position along the melancholy continuum of modern economics that lies between full employment and inflation on the one hand and unemployment and price stability on the other. Or we might suppose that electoral change results from movement of voters along a dimension between left and right on which the parties seek maximum support and voters choose the party closest to themselves. When each of these quite widely held conceptions of the sources of political change is captured in a suitable model, it is found to imply patterns of change that provide new insights into the behaviour of actual party systems. But the value of such models lies partly in showing that the systems they represent are too closed to be real. The party systems in which change actually occurs need to be seen in more complex and open terms.

We have shunned the adoption of any single model of change, trying instead to distinguish in the system we are studying some persistent processes that give partial clues to change. An understanding of these processes can be of considerable explanatory or predictive value. Yet the explanations and predictions are conditional ones. The parts of the system represented by our analytic frameworks are open in the sense that although the frameworks connect consequence with cause they do not account for the occurrence of the cause itself.

This simple point is well illustrated by our analysis of the rise of Labour support in this century. Accepting as given certain basic conditions involving the institutional framework of the electoral system, the split of the Liberals, and the presence of a new party specifically aligned with working class interests, we have examined how the processes of the socialization of new electoral cohorts can account both for the form of Labour's growth – rapid in earlier decades, levelling off in later ones – and for the pattern that is found in today's electorate of greater Conservative support among manual workers in the older cohorts. But such explanations are only conditional and accept as given the conditions that set the stage for Labour's growth.

In a similar way the predictions to which these frameworks lead are conditional ones. No part of our analysis illustrates this more clearly than the projected effects of selective death set out at the end of Chapter 11. Given an initial distribution of political attitudes by cohort we can say how the balance of party strength will change as these cohorts move out of the electorate through death. We may refine such an analysis by substituting other initial distributions of party support and by varying the future rates of death. But this does not lessen the essentially conditional nature of our projections. Since we do not account within such a framework either for the future mortality of these cohorts or for changes of their political attitudes other than from selective death it would be quite wrong to read these projections as unconditional forecasts of future political change.

The conditional nature of our explanations is especially evident in relation to the transient forces of politics. In Chapter 8 we identified the conditions required for a political issue to move the division of opinion strongly towards one party or the other. This will happen when an issue evokes strong attitudes in much of the electorate, when the distribution of attitudes towards it is strongly skewed (as is true of all the great 'valence' issues of modern politics), and when the parties are clearly differentiated in relation to it in the public's mind. In Chapters 15 to 18 these conditions provide the framework for analysing the probable effects of the transient influences which produced the political tremors of the 1960s. Such conditional explanations of short-term political movements are quite useful ones, even if this sort of framework does not seek to account for the processes which would explain why these conditions were fulfilled or not. The student of politics, like the seismologist, is better able to account for past tremors than to predict future ones.

It will be clear from the stress we have laid on the conditional nature of our explanations that we certainly do not see electoral behaviour or change in any narrowly deterministic way. No one who undertakes a study of this kind can suppose he has penetrated the dynamics of electoral politics very far. If by a wild fancy we imagine our frameworks having been refined and extended to the point where the system they describe were 'closed' (a fancy that seems to us philosophically untenable in any case), it is plain how very much more open are the systems we have treated here. This is a realm in which the understanding of human behaviour is so incomplete that it would be grotesque to portray the electorate as playing out any fully determined role.

This point seems to us a partial antidote for exaggerated fears that politics may be nearing a day when the findings and methods of research such as ours will allow party leaders to manipulate the public at will. The role of public relations consultants and advertising agencies in promoting the electoral fortunes of parties and individuals has attracted wide attention in the United States and is increasingly discussed in Britain. There is no escaping the fact that governments and leaders do at times have immense impact on mass opinion: this is presupposed by the very concept of leadership in a democracy. In any case, this influence was there long before the rise of opinion polls and is certainly not their creation. Studies of mass opinion may give party leaders information that helps them in winning office. This information is accessible in principle to all parties and leaders, although those in power may be more able to obtain it and to act upon it. The leading example is the additional information on the mood of the country that is now available to a prime minister contemplating an election. It is indeed arguable that contemporary prime ministers are less likely to repeat the mistakes occasionally made by their predecessors who had to rely on by-election returns or any other more primitive omens. But this does not guarantee that a prime minister will always be able to choose a time when his party will win. All this indeed is a far cry from the view that governments now have a guaranteed power to manipulate consent and that political surveys are eroding the sovereignty of the people.

On the contrary, a lengthening series of electoral studies might simply give the repeated evidence of how very limited is the influence which political leaders are able to exercise over the mass electorate. Certainly it would be quite wrong to assume that the extension of this knowledge of electoral behaviour must also extend the manipulative power of the leaders who might want to exploit it. The realm of economic policy suggests how finite are the limits of a government's power. Recent studies, as we suggested in Chapter 18, have clarified the major role played by economic trends in changing the parties' standing in the country. It is possible that these findings will convey to party leaders some information they did not have before, perhaps most of all on the electorate's relative dislike of unemployment and inflation. But a government seeking to win support on economic grounds does not need surer information about the public's response to economic stimuli so much as surer information about how to provide the right economic stimuli. The constraints of international trade and the uncertainties of economic science make any suggestion that management of the economy offers governments an infallible tool for the engineering of electoral consent – an idea that is likely to win only wry smiles from prime ministers or chancellors of the exchequer for as far ahead as anyone can see.

The incompleteness of present knowledge is, however, a challenge for future work. In every part of this book the limitations of our frameworks of analysis are more than anything else a call for the extension of inquiry. Three kinds of extension seem to us to deserve special comment. The first of these lies in the extension of such studies in time. Temporal extensions have a double warrant. On the one hand, since we are dealing with processes of change, time is an essential element of our subject matter, and many of the processes examined here extend over very much longer periods than the span of our studies. The difficulties that this puts in the way of analysis may be illustrated by the problem of examining conversions over the later stages of the individual's life cycle. By contrasting the attitudes of those at different stages of the cycle and by probing the recollections which our respondents held of their earlier attitudes and behaviour we have reached some tentative judgements about the importance of senescent conservatism (conversion to the party of the right) as against political immunization (strengthening of existing party ties through repeated exposures to politics). But our conclusions are much less certain than those we should be able to draw if we could observe these processes over a longer period, ideally over many years.[1]

Extending this work through time has also the warrant of revealing more about the political contest of change. Indeed, this belief has already shaped our design in a fundamental way: the

1. This is an admonition we intend ourselves to heed. By a further approach to our samples at the end of the 1966 Parliament we shall extend our observations of change over a much longer period than the thirty-four months which elapsed between the first and last of the interviews on which this book is largely based.

changeover of party control in the middle of our studies and the two mild reversals of political tide that we were able to observe directly gave us the opportunity to dispose of questions that would have remained unanswered if our evidence came only from a single moment. None the less our interviews were all conducted during three years that happened to coincide with Labour's zenith during the 1950s and 1960s. With observations that extended to quite different periods we would be able to see how the processes we have tried to analyse operated under contrasting circumstances. We may indeed think of this extension as a kind of natural sampling of additional varieties of political experience. Consider, for example, the framework we set out in Chapters 8 and 15 for the analysis of issues. Several of the regions of this framework were sparsely represented in the issues of the middle 1960s, and some were not represented at all. Passing to the issues of a different period would help to fill out these gaps and allow some much more confident conclusions about the role of issues in political change.

Lengthening the historical perspective of research must inevitably widen the reach of its analytical frameworks. In the short run many of the broadest determinants of social and political processes – such things as the structure of communications, the nature of the educational system, the norms of the world community – must be treated as fixed. Hence, it is only when the observer takes a much longer view that he is likely to ask himself what would be the consequence of change in some of the basic determinants of the processes he has analysed in the short run. We may illustrate this point in terms of mass communications. The findings of Chapter 10 demonstrate how strongly the flows of partisan information from the national press magnetize the parties for their readers. These findings raise a series of fascinating questions about the consequences that the rise of the partisan press earlier in the century had for mass political attitudes. The analyst is in effect invited to extend his framework and to treat as variable some fixed determinants of the processes he has examined in the contemporary setting. The indication in Chapter 13 that those who get their information from the national media are more likely to respond in common to national forces suggests how powerful the rise of the morning press may have been in nationalizing the swings of support between the parties. But the press is not an immutable institution; certainly there is evidence that its political role shifted markedly with the growth of political coverage on radio and television. As the span of these studies lengthens it seems likely that investigators will increasingly pursue questions about the evolution of the role of some of the most enduring structures of society and politics.

A similar logic argues for a second and quite different extension of this work – to the politics of other nations. This is a book about British politics and is written in terms that are directed largely to British problems. Yet comparison of British experience with that of other countries can extend our understanding of British politics and lead to still more general formulations of the process of change. Each of these purposes was indeed among the motives prompting the present endeavour, and our work fits into a family of comparative studies that now encompasses the United States, France, Norway, Japan, Canada, Sweden, India and Australia. The justification for a comparative approach is closely linked to the one which we have given for extending our work through time: just as the variation in the circumstances of different periods allows us to see more clearly the role of factors that remain fixed in the short run, so the varied experience of different countries allows us to see more clearly the role of factors that remain fixed within any one of them. The experience of a single country, even over a fairly long interval, will vary little in terms of factors that are present in a number of our analytical frameworks. In Britain, for example, the electoral system has survived remarkably unchanged since the coming of universal adult suffrage. There is no doubt that the election of single members by simple majority has had a major influence within British politics. But this influence is most clearly revealed when the British experience is set against that of countries with differing electoral institutions. For this reason we set out in Chapter 2 a comparative analysis of the generality of the electors' allegiance to party in Britain and America, a comparison which suggests the pervasive influence in the two countries of the form of the ballot and the extent of mixing of elections for different offices. Although this book focuses on a single country, we are committed to an increasingly vigorous tradition of comparative studies.

A third type of extension of the approaches of this book lies in a more intensive examination of the interplay between party leaders and the mass electorate.[2] This interplay is fundamental to many of the analyses we have attempted. We have emphasized the importance of events at the élite level in the decline of the Liberals and the rise of the Labour Party. But we have also asserted the importance of the actions and identities of political leaders in the weakening that has begun to be apparent in the class alignment. The possible reasons for erosion of the class alignment are complex and much is due to the passing of an era when class hatred could feed on severe economic deprivation in much of the working class. Yet some part of the weakening of this cleavage may be due to Labour's having turned to a more middle class leadership and having presented the country in power with policies that strongly converged towards those of the Conservatives, especially, perhaps, in asserting national interests against those of the Trade Unions.

An interest in interactional frameworks, in the mutual impact of leaders and led, has rightly provided a major element in recent theoretical and empirical work on political change. This aspect is fundamental to the models which Downs and others have abstracted from economic theory, and the refinement of spatial models of political competition offers a further instance of how an interactional emphasis can extend what we know of political change. We have seen in Chapter 9 that no single dimension of left

2. Empirical investigation of the interplay between leaders and led inevitably calls for data beyond those which are the centrepiece of this book. Indeed, each of the collaborators in this volume has been engaged in systematic contacts with British political leaders – one through the interviewing that is a continuing part of the Nuffield election studies, the other by extending to Britain the interviews of Members of Parliament and national party leaders that have matched the interviews of the mass electorate in studies undertaken in several national settings. We have not drawn on these additional materials in the findings set out here. But they will be an indispensable part of this extension of our work which this book so clearly foreshadows.

and right organized the attitudes of the British electorate in the early 1960s. But this is far from saying that the Labour Government did not give evidence of the sort of convergent behaviour that models of this kind would under many circumstances predict. During the 1964–6 Parliament electoral considerations undoubtedly entered into the Wilson government's attempts to assume the Tories' clothes on nuclear weapons, the control of immigration and the defence of sterling (and even on a British presence east of Suez before the party reverted to a more traditional attitude when the costs of such a presence proved high). Only on the issue of nationalizing the steel industry did the Labour Party stake out a position that was strongly discrepant from that of the Conservatives – and the calculations that actuated the Labour Cabinet certainly had more to do with placating left-wing M.P.s at Westminster rather than with winning votes in the country.

Although voting by secret ballot is so remarkably diffused across the world the public's intervention in the affairs of government through popular elections is far from a settled matter. Indeed, in the liberal democracies themselves the institutions of regular elections are under sharper attack than at any time since the rise of the fascist challenge between the wars. The alienation of people from the forms of parliamentary democracy or popular government is a familiar theme of current political commentary.

The focus of this book has been analytic rather than evaluative or reformative. It has not sought to describe how the system of popular involvement in government ought in ideal circumstances to work or how it ought to be changed. We have sought primarily to develop and apply to British politics a series of frameworks for the analysis of political change. But that does not mean that we are uninterested in the evaluation of electoral institutions. Indeed, we believe that the descriptive and analytic content of these pages is of direct relevance to the assembling of the empirical evidence on which any informed judgements of the system would be based.

Appendix

Background. This book has depended largely on information derived from three interview surveys of people selected to represent the adult population of England, Wales and Scotland. Northern Ireland was left out partly because, having its own parliament at Stormont, it is deliberately under-represented at Westminster, but mainly because it lies outside the mainstream of British party competition. A separate and special questionnaire would have been needed. Moreover, unless we had increased our sampling fraction in Northern Ireland, the three dozen interviews we might have expected there would have been too few for reliable statistical analysis.

Our first round of interviews took place between 24 May and 13 August 1963, with 90 per cent of a total of 2009 interviews completed by the end of June. The second round took place between 18 October and 4 December 1964, with 95 per cent of a total of 1830 interviews completed by 7 November. The third round took place between 4 April and 4 June 1966, with 90 per cent of a total of 2086 interviews completed by 2 May. The interviews were undertaken by the field staff of the British Market Research Bureau Ltd. At each of the first two rounds they averaged a little more than an hour in length, at the third round a little less than an hour. The response rates are discussed below and the questionnaires are set out in summary form. The replies were coded by a team of graduates in Oxford and punched into Hollerith cards from which the data files necessary for the subsequent analysis were organized. Each respondent who was interviewed three times provided more than 1200 distinct items of information ranging from attributes such as sex or age to complex beliefs as to the relationship of class to party or the extent to which British politics conformed to a model of responsible party government.

Sample design. Our initial sample was a self-weighting, multi-stage, stratified sample of the adult population of England, Wales and Scotland living in private households or institutions. Parliamentary constituencies served as the primary sampling units. The 618 constituencies of Great Britain were arrayed into 40 strata (80 half-strata) on the basis of region, relative Conservative and Labour strength in 1959, the presence of a Liberal candidate in 1959 and of a prospective Liberal candidate in the forthcoming election, urban or rural character, and level of unemployment. Two constituencies were chosen within each stratum (one within each half-stratum) with probability proportionate to size of electorate.

The sample design within each of the eighty chosen constituencies depended on the density of population.

1. Within forty-three borough constituencies and three geographically compact county constituencies a systematic sample was taken from a random start without further clustering.

2. Within sixteen county constituencies in which an urban core contained at least 40 per cent of the population the core was represented by a systematic sample selected from a random start without clustering; the rest of the constituency was represented by a systematic sample selected from a random start within a single polling district that was chosen with probability proportionate to size of electorate.

3. Within eighteen county constituencies of low population density the polling districts were arrayed into two strata on the basis of relative proportions of jurors.[1] Within each such stratum a systematic sample was selected from a random start within a single polling district chosen with probability proportionate to size of electorate.

1. All electors qualified for jury service are marked with a J in the electoral register. The J-index (the ratio of J's to the electorate) therefore provides a rough means of stratifying polling districts in economic terms since the qualifications for jury service involve basically the paying of local taxes on property valued at more than £10 per annum. Although this figure is low enough to include the great majority of dwellings, it is common in cheaper rented property for the landlord rather than the tenant to pay the rates.

By these procedures thirty-two names were selected from the electoral register of each sample constituency at the first round of interviews – 2560 names in all. For two reasons, however, we chose to regard this sample partly as a sample of households rather than as a sample of individuals. In the first place, by May of 1963 the register which had been compiled in October of 1962 and which had come into force in February of 1963 was already seven months out of date. By re-enumerating the sample households we could impose a sampling frame closer to the register that was to be compiled in October of 1963, and upon which a 1964 General Election would be fought. In the second place, the register compiled in October of 1962 had excluded some 4 per cent or so of the adult population which escapes being registered in a given year[2] and the twenty-year-olds coming of age between 2 June 1963 and 2 June 1964, who would be included either as Y voters[3] or as full electors on the register in force at the time of a 1964 General Election.

Interviewers were therefore instructed to enumerate the persons over 20 living in the sample households and if this enumeration disclosed names not included on the electoral register to select an additional respondent for interview by a predetermined random procedure. In every case an interview was also sought with the originally selected sample elector if he still lived at the sample address. No effort was made, however, to follow electors who had moved away from these addresses prior to the first round.[4]

2. See P. Gray and T. Corlett, *The Electoral Register as a Sampling Frame*, Central Office of Information, 1950, and P. Gray and F. A. Gee, *Electoral Registration for Parliamentary Elections*, H.M.S.O., London 1967.

3. Under the electoral law then in force, twenty-year-olds who came of age between 10 October, the date of compilation of the register, and 2 June were entered on the register with a Y against their names and were entitled to vote in any election after the following 2 October.

4. Under these procedures the probability of our selecting a given 'new' respondent varied about the probability of selection of those whose names were drawn from the electoral register as the ratio of the number of electors who had been registered at the address to the number of unregistered adults which the interviewer found to be living at the address. The inverse of this ratio is therefore an appropriate 'weight' which might be applied to the information gathered from such a new respondent. We have found, however, that the application of such weights has negligible effects.

This sample of households remained our essential device for representing the qualified electorate at the second and third rounds of interviews seventeen and thirty-four months later. To keep the group of households representative of all households in Britain a fresh sample of names was drawn from the electoral register in force at the time of each of these later rounds and the addresses associated with these names were cancelled against the register in force at the time of the prior round to give a sample of 'new' households. To keep our sample of respondents representative of all adults living in these households we also examined the electoral registers in force at each of the later rounds to see what 'new' names had appeared at existing sample addresses. Within each household in which one or more new names had appeared an additional respondent was selected for interview by a procedure analogous to that used for the supplementary selections at the first round. Respondents from prior rounds who were no longer registered at sample addresses in effect dropped out of our sample of the current electorate, although they were still sought for interview in order to keep our panels as near to full strength as possible.

Over three rounds of interviews this design yielded seven overlapping but analytically distinct samples:

1. A sample of the adult population in the early summer of 1963.

2. A sample of the electorate qualified to vote in the General Election of 1964.

3. A sample of the electorate qualified to vote in the General Election of 1966.

4. A panel of respondents originally interviewed in 1963 and re-interviewed in 1964.

5. A panel of respondents originally interviewed in 1963 and re-interviewed in 1966.

6. A panel of respondents originally interviewed in 1964 and re-interviewed in 1966.

7. A panel of respondents originally interviewed in 1963 and re-interviewed both in 1964 and 1966.

Response rates. No survey of a large national population ever achieves an interview with each of the people with whom it is wished to make contact. This fact matters little if the fraction of the sample which escapes interview is small. But as the fraction increases the possibility of serious bias must always be considered. If the persons who have not granted an interview differ from those who have, and if they constitute a substantial part of the whole, the findings obtained from the part of the sample interviewed will not be fully representative.

We therefore took steps to ensure as high a rate of response as was reasonably possible. The original interviewer was instructed to call at a sample address at least three times before accepting a failure to contact a respondent. Many interviews were in fact successfully made at a fourth or subsequent call. In addition, after an appreciable lapse of time, new interviewers were sent into areas in which non-response, either from refusal or non-contact, was relatively high. On the first round of interviews alone, this supplementary technique yielded more than one hundred and fifty respondents who had previously refused or who had not yet been contacted.

Table A.1 gives the proportion of our initial sample [1] which was interviewed in 1963, or interviewed for the first time in 1964 or 1966, as well as the proportion not interviewed in 1963, distributed across the several possible reasons for non-response. For a non-governmental survey of a nationwide random sample involving interviews of an hour's length this rate of response is extraordinarily high. Indeed, the eventual response rate was only slightly below 90 per cent, although part of this total represents respondents who were originally selected in 1963 but not successfully interviewed until 1964 or 1966.

Substantially lower rates of response were achieved with the samples of the electorate qualified to vote in 1964 and 1966 [2 and 3], owing in part to the complexities of our longitudinal design. Presumably the bias which this lessened response may have introduced was partially offset, however, by introduction of weights to eliminate in the panel element of these electorate samples the

A.1 Rate of Response with Original Sample

Names issued in May 1963		2560
Dead by May 1963	30	
Premises empty or demolished	54	
Had moved away before contacted	165	249
Interviews attempted with electors whose names had been issued		2311
Interviews attempted with persons selected by enumeration process		218
Total interviews attempted		2529	100·0%

Reasons for non-response in 1963			
Temporarily away	126		
Out or no reply	133		
Refused	217		
Too old or ill	33		
Other	11	520	
Total interviews obtained in 1963		2009	79·4%
Additional first interviews obtained in 1964		207	
Additional first interviews obtained in 1966		47	
Total interviews obtained		2263	89·5%

known effects of panel mortality. The basis and construction of these weights are explained below. The relative rates of response in our three electorate samples are shown in Table A.2:

A.2 Rates of Response with Electorate Samples

	1963	1964	1966
Total interviews attempted	2529	2590[a]	2682[a]
Total interviews obtained	2009	1769	1874
Proportion obtained	79·4%	68·3%	69·9%

[a] These totals include some potential respondents with whom interviews were not in fact sought for reasons of ill health or prior record of refusal.

Our panel samples [4, 5, 6 and 7] were subject to an additional source of non-response, the drop-out of respondents who could not be re-interviewed. No longitudinal study of a dispersed and mobile population escapes losses of this kind. By the standards of other national studies which have extended over comparable periods ours were not excessive. A nationwide re-interview study undertaken by the Oxford University Institute of Statistics in 1953–4 reported a panel survival rate of 66·1 per cent after a year's time, although that study made less effort than ours to trace people who had moved more than a short distance from their original addresses.[5] A national re-interview study of American electoral behaviour undertaken by the Survey Research Center of the University of Michigan achieved a survival rate of 70 per cent after twenty-six months and of 61 per cent after fifty months. A study of consumer behaviour undertaken by the Survey Research Center achieved a survival rate of 61 per cent after twenty-one months.[6]

The survival rates of the four interlocking panels of our own study are shown by Table A.3. Since anyone who drops out of a panel has given at least one interview we are able to study the bias due to this source by comparing the information given by the surviving panel and the full sample when the drop-outs were still in the project. In the case of our own panels, the results of such a comparison are distinctly reassuring. Over a wide range of characteristics the full sample interviewed in 1963 looked remarkably like the sub-sample of respondents who would survive three rounds of interviews. For example, the proportion of men was 44·6 per cent in the full 1963 sample and 46·4 per cent in the three-interview panel; the proportion who had left school at age fifteen

5. See P. Vandome, 'Aspects of the Dynamics of Consumer Behaviour', *Bulletin of the Oxford Institute of Statistics*, **20**, (1958), 65–105 and T. P. Hill, L. R. Klein, and K. H. Straw, 'The Savings Survey 1953: Response Rates and Reliability of Data', ibid., **17**, (1955), 89–126.

6. See Philip E. Converse, Angus Campbell, Warren E. Miller and Donald E. Stokes, 'Stability and Change in 1960: A Reinstating Election', *American Political Science Review*, **55**, (1961), 269–80, and Marion Sobol, 'Panel Mortality, Panel Bias', *Journal of the American Statistical Association*, **54**, (1959), 52–68.

A.3 Survival Rates of Panels

	Original Sample[a]	Surviving Panel	Percent Surviving
1963–4 Panel	1982	1481	74·7%
1963–6 Panel	1945	1282	65·9%
1963–4–6 Panel	1945	1154	59·3%
1964–6 Panel	1769	1360	76·9%

[a] These base figures have been reduced by the number of initial respondents who were known to have died before the time of re-interview since this type of shrinkage affects population and sample alike and introduces no bias.

or earlier was 81·9 per cent in the full sample and 80·8 per cent in the panel; the proportion intending to vote Labour at the forthcoming general election was 43·6 per cent in the full sample and 44·1 per cent in the panel. The clearest tendency towards bias appeared in the possession of political information. For example, the proportion who knew the name of their M.P. in the summer of 1963 was 50·9 per cent in the full sample but 56·3 per cent among those who were to survive in the panel.

This sort of diagnosis also supplies a partial cure. If we know how a panel differed from a full sample at some initial time we can apply weights to remove these known differences and, with them, many of the unknown but correlated differences which would appear at later interviews if the drop-outs remained in the study. Three initial differences are the basis of the weights we have applied. In the first place, we have taken account of the difference of survival rate between those who did and those who did not know at least three items of information in 1963 which seemed to form a cumulative scale in Guttman's sense. Next, we took account of the difference of survival rate between those who did and did not answer 'Don't know' to at least one of the issue questions which we put to our respondents in 1963. Finally, we took account of a very slight remaining difference of survival rate between men and women within the classes formed by crossing the first and second of these dimensions.

These differences of survival are summarized in Table A.4. The bias due to the factors which have defined the cells of the table can

A.4 Proportion of Original Sample Surviving by Characteristics in 1963

| | Knowledge of items of information | | | |
| | Knew three or more | | Knew less than three | |
	Replied to all questions on issues	Said don't know to at least one issue	Replied to all questions on issues	Said don't know to at least one issue
Men	70%	62%	61%	51%
Women	69%	64%	58%	50%

be removed by applying to the panel respondents a set of weights that is proportional to the inverse of these rates of survival. For this purpose we set the weight for men of high information and high attitude formation equal to 1·0 and have set the weight for each of the other groups proportionately higher. The weight for women of low information and low attitude formation, for example, was set at 1·5 since the proportion of this group surviving three interviews was only five-sevenths that of men with both high information and high attitude formation.

Table A.5 compares our three-interview panel with the full original sample before and after the application of these weights. The first two columns of the table make clear how remarkably little bias across a wide range of characteristics was introduced by the removal of 40 per cent of our initial respondents from the surviving panel. The third column shows the effect of the application of our weights in bringing the panel more nearly in line with the original sample. A weighting procedure exactly analogous to this was applied to each of our four interlocking panels, with comparable results.

The weights calculated to reduce bias due to panel drop-out were allowed to influence the analysis of the 1964 and 1966 electorate samples as well. Since these electorate samples heavily overlapped the 1963–4 and 1964–6 panels, part of the non-response of

A.5 Comparison of Characteristics of Original Sample with Unweighted and Weighted 1963-4-6 Panel

Characteristics in 1963	Original Sample[a]	Unweighted Panel	Weighted Panel
Social grades I–III	27·7%	28·2%	27·5%
Social grades IV–VI	69·7	69·3	70·2
Men	44·6	46·4	44·9
Left school before age 16	81·9	80·8	81·4
Follows politics very or fairly closely	47·8	50·5	48·2
Knows M.P.'s name	50·9	56·3	51·2
Read or heard about M.P.	30·0	33·0	30·0
Favours entry into Common Market	31·8	33·6	32·3
Favours more nationalization	24·2	25·3	24·7
Voted in 1959	78·6	80·6	79·6
Intending to vote Conservative	32·4	34·8	34·2
Intending to vote Labour	43·6	44·1	44·7
Labour 'lead' over Conservative	11·2	9·3	10·5

[a] Original sample reduced by removal of respondents who had died before 1966.

these samples was comprised of people whom we had interviewed before. By applying the appropriate panel weights to the surviving panel element of these samples we could in effect weight those whom we did interview in the later year to represent those whom we did not. This is the sense in which we noted above that the somewhat higher non-response of the 1964 and 1966 electorate samples had been partially offset.

Repeated interviewing of the same respondents raises the possibility of 'contamination' of the panel, as well as of bias due to panel drop-out. The evidence on this sort of learning in comparable studies has, however, been generally negative.[7] Our design did not permit a conclusive judgement to be made on this possibility, but

7. The most elaborate study of possible contamination in a political survey, one whose findings were also negative, is P. F. Lazarsfeld, B. Berelson and H. Gaudet, *The People's Choice*, New York, 1944.

our impressions were again strongly negative. None of the several indicators of the degree of the respondent's political interest or involvement showed a tendency to rise over the full thirty-four months, once the effects of panel mortality were removed; indeed, the trend between the second and third interviews was if anything in the reverse direction. How large the experience of being interviewed looms in the life of the average respondent is easily exaggerated. Many vignettes from what our respondents said illustrate how trifling an element of three years of life three hours of casual conversation with one of our interviewers constituted.

Sampling error. A sample survey is liable to many errors which have nothing to do with sampling. Errors which arise from the failure to contact all potential respondents or from misleading answers being given to certain questions may indeed be far more serious than those which arise from choosing a sample to represent the population from which it is drawn. None the less, those who report sample estimates owe their readers the means of judging the reliability of these estimates in a sampling sense. Explicit sample designs are meant not only to minimize sampling error; they are meant to furnish explicit estimates of its probable magnitude as well.

Unfortunately the estimation of sampling error is greatly complicated by modern developments of sample design. If we had drawn a simple random sample of the British electorate any reader acquainted with the formulas of an elementary statistics text could calculate the probable error of many of the figures reported in this book. But we should have paid dearly for such a simplification, since a simple random sample of the same cost would have to be much smaller in size and would yield sampling errors much larger than those of the multistage stratified design that we actually employed. The effects of the 'clustering' of respondents under such a design are mildly paradoxical. On the one hand, the sampling errors of a clustered design will in general be larger than those of a simple random sample of equal size.[8] But, on the other hand, the sampling errors of a clustered design will in general be smaller than

8. See Leslie Kish, 'Confidence Intervals for Clustered Samples', *American Sociological Review*, **22**, (1957), 154–65.

those of a simple random sample of equal cost. The reason this is true is of course that an appropriate clustered design for sampling a large and dispersed population vastly reduces the unit cost of interviewing, yielding a larger sample and smaller sampling error for the same outlay of resources.

The formulas for sampling error under complex sample designs are, however, unfamiliar and difficult to apply. We therefore have set out in Tables A.6 and A.7 some average values of the sampling errors of percentages and differences of percentages calculated from the exact formulas appropriate to our design. Table A.6 gives the average value of the sampling error associated with percentages according to the magnitude of the percentage and the size of the sample on which it is based, since the sampling error varies with

A.6 Approximate Sampling Error of Percentages[a] (expressed in percentages)

Reported Percentages	Number of Interviews									
	2000	1500	1000	700	500	400	300	200	100	50
50	3·0	3·3	3·8	4·4	5·1	5·6	6·4	7·7	11	15
30 or 70	2·7	3·0	3·5	4·0	4·6	5·1	5·8	7·1	9·8	14
20 or 80	2·4	2·6	3·0	3·5	4·0	4·5	5·1	6·2	8·6	12
10 or 90	1·8	1·9	2·3	2·6	3·0	3·3	3·8	4·6	6·4	9·1
5 or 95	1·3	1·4	1·6	1·9	2·2	2·4	2·8	3·4	4·7	6·6

[a] The figures in this table represent *two* standard errors. Hence, for most items the chances are 95 out of 100 that the value being estimated lies within a range equal to the reported percentages, plus or minus the sampling error.

both of these things. Under the assumption that the sample estimates are normally distributed, an assumption that is quite appropriate with samples of this size, an interval the width of the sampling error (two standard errors) on each side of the sample estimate has a chance of 19 in 20 of including the true value in the underlying population. Let us suppose that 50 per cent of 1000 newspaper readers within the sample are found to be 'very much' interested in politics and that we wish to know how much their sample estimate may vary around the percentage of newspaper readers who would be found to be very much interested in politics if we were able to interview all readers in Britain rather than a sample of 1000. By inspecting the row of Table A.6 for percentages of 50 and the column for samples of 1000 we find that the average sampling error associated with this combination is 3·8 per cent. Therefore, we may say that the interval from 46·2 to 53·8 has a chance of 19 in 20 of including the percentage of newspaper readers in the underlying population that would be found to be very much interested in politics.

Table A.7 gives the average value of the sampling error associated with a difference of two percentages according to the magnitude of the percentages and the size of the samples on which each percentage is based, since the sampling error varies with each of these things. Under the assumption that our sample estimates of these differences are normally distributed, an observed difference that is as large as the given value of the sampling error (two standard errors) has a chance of at least 19 in 20 of reflecting a real difference in the underlying populations rather than being a reflection of nothing more than the accidents of sampling. Let us suppose that we are interested in the difference between the 50 per cent of 1000 newspaper readers who are very much interested in politics and the 35 per cent of 500 non-readers who are very much interested. By inspecting the part of Table A.7 that gives the sampling errors for the difference of two percentages that are in the 35–65 per cent range we find that the value in the row for one group of 1000 and the column for a second group of 500 is 6·3 per cent. Since the observed difference of 15 per cent is larger than this we may say that the chance is at least 19 in 20 that the observed difference reflects a greater interest on the part of readers that we would find if we interviewed all readers and non-readers rather than drawing a sample of 1000 of one and of 500 of the other.

We also give in Figure A.8 a graph of the relationship between the ratio of the sampling errors obtained from our actual sample and those from a simple random sample of equal size according to the size of the groups on which sample estimates are based. It will be observed that the magnitude of this ratio increases with the size of the group; the practical significance of the clustering of our

A.7 Approximate Sampling Error of Differences[a] (in percentages)

	2000	1500	1000	700	500	400	300	200	100	50
For Percentages from 35% to 65%										
2000	4·2	4·4	4·8	5·3	5·9	6·3	7·0	8·3	11	16
1500		4·6	5·0	5·4	6·0	6·5	7·1	8·4	11	16
1000			5·3	5·8	6·3	6·7	7·4	8·6	11	16
700				6·2	6·7	7·1	7·7	8·9	12	16
500					7·1	7·5	8·1	9·2	12	16
400						7·9	8·5	9·5	12	16
300							9·0	10	12	17
200								11	13	17
100									15	19
50										22
For Percentages around 20% and 80%										
2000	3·3	3·5	3·8	4·2	4·7	5·0	5·6	6·6	8·9	12
1500		3·7	4·0	4·3	4·8	5·2	5·7	6·7	9·0	12
1000			4·3	4·6	5·0	5·4	5·9	6·9	9·1	13
700				4·9	5·3	5·7	6·2	7·1	9·3	13
500					5·7	6·0	6·5	7·4	9·5	13
400						6·3	6·8	7·6	9·7	13
300							7·2	8·0	10	13
200								8·7	11	14
100									12	15
50										17

	2000	1500	1000	700	500	400	300	200	100	50
				For Percentages around 10% and 90%						
2000	2·5	2·6	2·9	3·2	3·5	3·8	4·2	4·9	6·7	9·3
1500		2·7	3·0	3·3	3·6	3·9	4·3	5·0	6·7	9·4
1000			3·2	3·5	3·8	4·0	4·4	5·1	6·8	9·4
700				3·7	4·0	4·2	4·6	5·3	7·0	9·5
500					4·3	4·5	4·9	5·5	7·1	9·6
400						4·7	5·1	5·7	7·3	9·7
300							5·4	6·0	7·5	9·9
200								6·5	7·9	10
100									9·1	11
50										13

	2000	1500	1000	700	500	400	300	200	100	50
				For Percentages around 5% and 95%						
2000	1·8	1·9	2·1	2·3	2·5	2·8	3·1	3·6	4·9	6·8
1500		2·0	2·2	2·4	2·6	2·8	3·1	3·6	4·9	6·8
1000			2·3	2·6	2·7	2·9	3·2	3·7	5·0	6·9
700				2·7	2·9	3·1	3·3	3·8	5·1	6·9
500					3·1	3·3	3·5	4·0	5·2	7·0
400						3·4	3·7	4·1	5·3	7·1
300							3·9	4·4	5·4	7·2
200								4·7	5·8	7·4
100									6·6	8·1
50										9·3

[a] The values shown are the differences required for significance (two standard errors) in comparisons of percentages derived from two *different* subgroups of the population.

A.8 Ratio of Actual Mean Sampling Errors to Sampling Errors under Simple Random Sampling by Size of Groups on Which Estimates Based

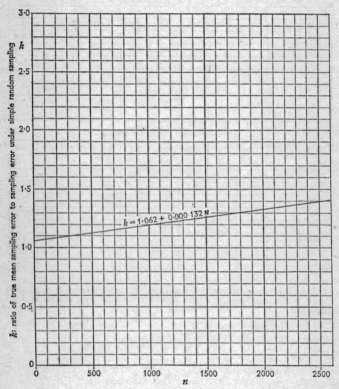

k: ratio of true mean sampling error under simple random sampling

$$k = 1.062 + 0.000\ 132\ n$$

n: Size of group on which sample estimate based

observations becomes greater as the number of observations per cluster is greater.[9] The relationship between the value k of this ratio and the magnitude n of the group on which the sample estimate is based is fitted best in a least-squares sense by the line whose equation is

$$k = 1 \cdot 062 + 0 \cdot 000132n. \tag{1}$$

This relationship provides a basis for interpolating sampling errors for cases which are intermediate between the values given by Tables A.6 and A.7. For a single percentage p based on a group of size n the mean sampling error of p is given by

$$2k \sqrt{\frac{p(1-p)}{n-1}} \tag{2}$$

Similarly, for a difference of two percentages p_1 and p_2 based on groups of size n_1 and n_2 the mean sampling error of $p_1 - p_2$ is given by

$$2k \sqrt{\frac{p_1(1-p_1)}{n_1-1} + \frac{p_2(1-p_2)}{n_2-1}.} \tag{3}$$

Explicit formulas are not available and new methods are only now emerging for calculating the sampling errors of more refined statistics such as correlation and regression coefficients under complex sample designs. Fortunately there is evidence that the errors of these statistics are less likely to be inflated by clustering than are the errors of ratio estimates.[10] Therefore, the reader is better able to apply the conventional formulas to the occasional values of such statistics that have entered our report, and we have in some cases given in the footnotes our own estimates of these errors.

9. This assumes that the observations of a part-sample are distributed fairly well over all primary sampling units, rather than being concentrated in a restricted subset of the primary sampling units.

10. L. Kish and M. Frankel, 'Balanced Repeated Replications for Analytical Statistics', *Proceedings of the Social Statistics Section of the American Statistical Association, 1968*, Washington D.C., pp. 2–10.

Questionnaires

We include here the texts of our questionnaires from the summer of 1963, the autumn of 1964, and the spring of 1966. For reasons of space, the format of each questionnaire has been condensed by the deletion of boxes that aided the interviewer in following certain logical contingencies and by closing up the spaces allowed for the verbatim replies to free-answer questions. The scheme by which we determined the composition of the household and certain data on the occupations and income of its members is given in summary form after each questionnaire.

The texts of the 1964 and 1966 questionnaires omit certain additional questions that were put to respondents who entered the study at these later times. Respondents interviewed for the first time in 1964 were also asked questions 21, 22, 38, 39a and b, 40, 41a and b, 42, 43a, 71a to c, 72a to c, 74a and b, 77, 79, 80a and b, 83, 84 and 85 from the 1963 questionnaire; respondents interviewed for the first time in 1966 were asked questions 38, 39a and b, 40, 41a and b, 43a and b, 74a and b, 77, 79, 80a and b, 83, 84 and 85 from the 1963 questionnaire and questions 52a and b, 76, 77, 78, 79, 80a to e and 81a to c from the 1964 questionnaire .

To detect possible effects of the order of presenting items, several questions were rotated on a random basis in the 1963 interview. In particular, the order of questions 6, 7 and 8 and of questions 11, 12 and 13 was rotated from respondent to respondent. In addition, the order of presentation of parties was randomly rotated in questions 37a and 64. Since there was not the slightest evidence that the data obtained under different rotations exhibited more than chance variation, this feature was eliminated from the 1964 and 1966 interviews.

Wherever possible we have interspersed the percentage distributions of replies in the text of the questions. Since vastly more room would be needed to give the distributions of replies coded from the 'free-answer' questions, we have limited the percentages to the replies to the 'closed' questions in each questionnaire. In each case the distribution refers to the replies given by the sample of the electorate then qualified to vote (denoted as samples 1, 2 and 3 in the sampling appendix) rather than by any of the panels. In forming the percentage distributions we have deleted all cases which could not be coded as either a specific response or as 'don't know'. The base of any percentage is the part of the sample which replied to the question: the whole sample (less those 'not ascertained') in the case of a question put to everyone, the part-sample to which the question was put in the case of questions which were asked only of those who had given a specified reply to certain prior questions.

Questionnaire, Summer 1963

I am working on some research being conducted at Oxford University, and would like you to help me by answering some questions.

1*a*. First of all do you read a morning newspaper regularly? (Yes 77%)

If Yes

    1*b*. Which newspaper is that? Are there any other morning papers you read regularly?

    First morning newspaper mentioned – Name of newspaper

    1*c*. When did you begin to read (name of newspaper) regularly?
    1*d*. Did you stop reading (name of newspaper) any time after that?

      If stopped reading newspaper at any time
      1*e*. When was that?
      1*f*. When was the last time you weren't reading (name of newspaper) regularly?

    Ask all readers
    1*g*. What do you especially like in (name of newspaper)?

1*h*. Do you follow news about politics much in (name of newspaper)? (Yes 49%)

1*i*. Do you like the way news about politics is handled in (name of newspaper), do you dislike it, or doesn't it make much difference to you?

1*j*. Do you think that (name of newspaper) tends to favour any particular party? What party is that?

If second morning newspaper mentioned – Name of newspaper

1*k*. When did you begin to read (name of newspaper) regularly?

1*l*. Did you stop reading (name of newspaper) any time after that?

  If stopped reading newspaper at any time

  1*m*. When was that?

  1*n*. When was the last time you weren't reading (name of newspaper) regularly?

Ask all readers

1*o*. What do you especially like in (name of newspaper)?

1*p*. Do you follow news about politics much in (name of newspaper)?

1*q*. Do you like the way news about politics is handled in (name of newspaper), do you dislike it, or doesn't it make much difference to you?

1*r*. Do you think that (name of newspaper) tends to favour any particular party? What party is that?

2*a*. Do you follow news about politics much in any evening or Sunday newspaper? (Yes 26%)

  If Yes

  2*b*. Which is that? Any others?

3. Do you follow news about politics much on television? (Yes 55%)

4. Do you follow news about politics much on the radio? (Yes 19%)

If follows politics by more than one medium

5. Of all the ways that you follow news about politics, which one would you say you get the most information from?

Now I would like to ask you what you think the good and bad points about the political parties are.

6a. Is there anything in particular that you like about the Conservative Party? What is that? Anything else?

6b. Is there anything in particular that you don't like about the Conservative Party? What is that? Anything else?

7a. Is there anything in particular that you like about the Labour Party? What is that? Anything else?

7b. Is there anything in particular that you don't like about the Labour Party? What is that? Anything else?

8a. Is there anything in particular that you like about the Liberal Party? What is that? Anything else?

8b. Is there anything in particular that you don't like about the Liberal Party? What is that? Anything else?

9. Considering everything the parties stand for, would you say that there is a good deal of difference between the parties (36%), some difference (20%), or not much difference (34%)? (Don't know 10%)

10a. Do you think there once was a time when there was more of a difference between the parties than there is now? (Yes 48%, No 27%, DK 25%)

If thinks there was more of a difference than now
10b. When was that?
10c. And when do you think the parties came closer together?

Now I would like to ask you about the good and pad points of the party leaders.

11a. Is there anything in particular that you like about Harold Macmillan? What is that? Anything else?

11b. Is there anything in particular that you don't like about Macmillan? What is that? Anything else?

12a. Is there anything in particular that you like about Harold Wilson? What is that? Anything else?

12b. Is there anything in particular that you don't like about Wilson? What is that? Anything else?

13a. Is there anything in particular that you like about Jo Grimond? What is that? Anything else?

13b. Is there anything in particular that you don't like about Grimond?
What is that? Anything else?

14. Apart from Macmillan, how do you feel about the other Conservative leaders? Do you generally like them (21%), dislike them (11%), or don't you have much feeling about them (59%)? (DK 9%)

15. Apart from Wilson, how do you feel about the other Labour leaders? Do you generally like them (23%), dislike them (13%), or don't you have much feeling about them (55%)? (DK 9%)

government ——self feel are the most important problems the
———— about? Anything else?

First problem mentioned

16b. What would you like to see the government do about that?
16c. Which party would be the most likely to do what you want on this, the Conservatives, Labour, the Liberals, or wouldn't it make much difference?

Second problem mentioned

16d. What would you like to see the government do about that?
16e. Which party would be the most likely to do what you want on this, the Conservatives, Labour, the Liberals, or wouldn't it make much difference?

Third problem mentioned

16f. What would you like to see the government do about that?
16g. Which party would be the most likely to do what you want on this, the Conservatives, Labour, the Liberals, or wouldn't it make much difference?

17. Were you generally glad (30%) or sorry (26%) that Britain didn't go into the Common Market, or don't you have an opinion on that (44%)?

18. If the question of going into the Common Market comes up again, do you think that Britain should go in (32%) or stay out (29%), or don't you have an opinion on that (39%)?

19. There's a lot of talk these days about nuclear weapons. Which of these three statements comes closest to what you yourself feel should be done? If you don't have an opinion about this, just say so.

a. Britain should keep her own nuclear weapons, independent of other countries. (34%)
b. Britain should have nuclear weapons only as a part of a western defence system. (42%)
c. Britain should have nothing to do with nuclear weapons under any circumstances. (15%)
d. No opinion/Don't know. (9%)

20. There's also a lot of talk about nationalizing industry. Which of these statements comes closest to what you yourself feel should be done? If you don't have an opinion about this, just say so.

a. A lot more industries should be nationalized. (10%)
b. Only a few more industries, such as steel, should be nationalized. (14%)
c. No more industries should be nationalized, but the industries that are nationalized now should stay nationalized. (36%)
d. Some of the industries that are nationalized now should be de-nationalized. (22%)
e. No opinion/Don't know. (18%)

21. How close do you feel Britain's ties with America should be? (Very close 36%, fairly close 38%, not very close 19%, DK 7%)

22. Would you like to see the death penalty kept (71%) or abolished (20%)? (DK 9%)

23. Do you think that big business has too much power in this country (59%), or do you think that it doesn't have too much power (25%)? (DK 16%)

24. How important do you yourself feel the Queen and royal family are to Britain? (Very important 63%, fairly important 22%, not very important 14%, DK 1%)

25. Do you think that too many (83%) immigrants have been let into the country or not (12%)? (DK 5%)

26. Do you think that the trade unions have too much power (53%) or not (31%)? (DK 16%)

27. Do you generally like to see things modern and up-to-date (67%) or do you think that well-tried, traditional things (22%) are generally better? (Half and half 3%, DK 8%)

28. If the government had a choice between reducing taxes (52%) and spending more on social services (41%), which should it do? (DK 7%)

29. Do you think that Britain gave up her empire too fast (41%) or not (38%)? (DK 21%)

30a. Have you heard anything about Dr Beeching's proposals for changing the railways? (Yes 91%)

   If has heard proposals
   30b. Do you think these changes should be made in the railways (52%) or not (39%)? (Mixed 3%, DK 6%)
   30c. Why is that?

31. How much interest do you generally have in what's going on in politics – a good deal (16%), some (37%), or not much (47%)?

32a. Do you talk much about politics to other people? (Yes 27%)

   If Yes
   32b. Who do you talk to about politics? Anyone else?

33a. Do you ever think of yourself as being to the left, the centre, or the right in politics (25%), or don't you think of yourself that way (69%)? (DK 6%)

   If Yes
   33b. Where would you say you are? (Left 33%, Centre 33%, Right 33%, Other 1%)

34a. We are also interested in how well off people are these days. How about you? Compared with three or four years ago, are you and your family better off now (33%), worse off (21%), or have you stayed about the same (45%)? (DK 1%)

If better or worse off now

34b. Why is that?

35a. Now looking ahead over the next three or four years, do you think that you will be better off (24%), worse off (9%), or will you stay about the same (48%)? (DK 19%)

If better or worse off than now

35b. Why is that?

36a. Do you think that what the government does makes any difference to how well off you are? (Yes 62%, No 28%, DK 10%)

If government does make a difference

36b. Well, has the Conservative Government made you better (27%) or worse off (17%), or hasn't it made much difference (51%)? (DK 5%)

36c. If a Labour Government comes in would you be better (22%) or worse off (18%), or wouldn't it make much difference (36%)? (DK 24%)

Now I would like to ask you a little more about the political parties.

37a. Generally speaking, do you usually think of yourself as Conservative (36%), Labour (44%) or Liberal (10%)? (None 8%, DK 2%)

Only for those with party affiliation

37b. Well, how strongly (chosen party) do you generally feel – very strongly (36%), fairly strongly (43%), or not very strongly (21%)?

37c. Was there ever a time when you thought of yourself as (first party not chosen) or (second party not chosen) rather than (chosen party)? Which was that?

If reports previous affiliation

37*d*. When did you change from (former party) to (present party)?

37*e*. What was the main thing that made you change from (former party) to (present party)?

Only for those without party affiliation

37*f*. Well, do you generally feel a little closer to one of the parties than the others? (Yes 49%) Which party is that? (Con. 36%, Lab. 42%, Lib. 22%)

If feels closer to a party

37*g*. Was there ever a time when you felt closer to (first party not chosen) or (second party not chosen) rather than to (chosen party)? Which was that?

If reports former affiliation

37*h*. When did you change?

37*i*. What was the main thing that made you change?

If does not feel closer to a party

37*j*. Was there ever a time when you did feel a little closer to one of the parties than the others? Which party was that?

If used to feel closer

37*k*. When was that?

37*l*. What made you move farther away from (party mentioned)?

38. Do you remember when you were young whether your father was very much interested in politics (30%), somewhat interested (28%), or didn't he pay much attention to it (26%)? (DK 16%)

39*a*. Did he have any particular preference for one of the parties when you were young? Which party was that? (Con. 27%, Lab. 31%, Lib. 13%, Other 1%, None 7%, DK 21%)

If father did have preference

39*b*. What was the main reason he felt that way?

40. How about your mother? When you were young, was she very

much interested in politics (8%), somewhat interested (22%), or didn't she pay much attention to it (56%)? (DK 14%)

41a. Did she have any particular preference for one of the parties when you were young? Which party was that? (Con. 25%, Lab. 21%, Lib. 8%, None 21%, DK 25%)

If mother did have preference

41b. What was the main reason she felt that way?

42. About how old were you when you first began to hear anything about politics?

43a. About how old were you when you first began to have likes and dislikes about the parties?

43b. Which party did you like best then? (Con. 38%, Lab. 46%, Lib. 9%, Other 1%, DK 6%)

44a. Do you remember which was the first general election you voted in? Well, did you start voting before or after the Second World War? (1959 7%, 1955 7%, other election after war 46%, before war 28%, never voted 5%, too young to have voted 6%, DK 1%)

If first voted in 1959; Macmillan vs. Gaitskell

44b. Which party did you vote for in that election? (Con. 43%, Lab. 49%, Lib. 7%, DK 1%)

If first voted in 1955; Eden vs. Attlee

44c. Which party did you vote for in that election? (Con. 48%, Lab. 46%, Lib. 2%, DK 4%)

44d. Now think of the last general election, the one four years ago in the autumn of 1959, when the Conservatives were led by Macmillan and Labour by Gaitskell. Do you remember for certain whether you voted then? (Sure voted 76%, fairly sure voted 6%, did not vote 15%, DK 3%)

If did vote

44e. Which party did you vote for then? (Con. 50%, Lab. 42%, Lib. 5%, DK 3%)

If did not vote

44*f*. Do you remember whether you would have preferred one of
the parties to the others? (Yes 82%) Which party was that?
(Con. 44%, Lab. 56%)

*If first voted in other postwar election (1945, 1950 or 1951); Churchill
vs. Attlee*

44*g*. Which party did you vote for in that election? (Con. 35%,
Lab. 60%, Lib. 2%, DK 3%)

44*h*. Now think of the last general election, the one four years ago in the
autumn of 1959, when the Conservatives were led by Macmillan
and Labour by Gaitskell. Do you remember for certain whether
you voted then? (Sure voted 83%, fairly sure voted 4%, did not
vote 12%, DK 1%)

If did vote

44*i*. Which party did you vote for? (Con. 40%, Lab. 55%, Lib. 4%,
DK 1%)

If did not vote

44*j*. Do you remember whether you would have preferred one of the
parties to the others? (Yes 79%) Which party was that? (Con.
36%, Lab. 56%, Lib. 6%, Other 2%)

44*k*. In the general elections since you have been old enough to vote,
have you always voted for the same party (83%) or have you voted
for different parties (16%)? (DK 1%)

If voted for same party

44*l*. Which party is that? (Con. 38%, Lab. 60%, Lib. 2%)

If voted for different parties

44*m*. Which parties were they?

If first voted before the war

44*n*. Which party did you vote for in that election? (Con. 42%, Lab.
43%, Lib. 10%, DK 5%)

44*o*. Now think of the last general election, the one four years ago in
the autumn of 1959, when the Conservatives were led by
Macmillan and Labour by Gaitskell. Do you remember for certain
whether you voted then? (Sure voted 83%, fairly sure voted 5%,
did not vote 11%, DK 1%)

If did vote

44p. Which party did you vote for? (Con. 49%, Lab. 45%, Lib. 5%, DK 1%)

If did not vote

44q. Do you remember whether you would have preferred one of the parties to the others? (Yes 73%) Which party was that? (Con. 40%, Lab. 39%, Lib. 21%)

44r. In the general elections since you have been old enough to vote, have you always voted for the same party (79%) or have you voted for different parties (20%)? (DK 1%)

  If voted for same party

  44s. Which party is that? (Con. 47%, Lab. 49%, Lib. 4%)

  If voted for different parties

  44t. Which parties were they?

  44u. Taking just the general elections since the end of the Second World War, have you voted for the same party (55%) or for different parties (41%)? (DK 4%)

    If same party

    44v. Which party is that? (Con. 52%, Lab. 43%, Lib. 5%)

45a. Talking to people around the country, we've found that a great many people weren't able to vote in the local elections early this May. How about you? Did you vote in the local elections this year (49%) or did something prevent you from voting (51%)?

If did vote

45b. How did you vote? What party is that? (Con. 34%, Lab. 48%, Lib. 11%, Indep. 5%, Other 2%)

45c. Do you always vote that way in local elections? (Yes 80%)

45d. Were there any issues in the local elections this year that were especially important to you? (Yes 20%)

  If Yes

  45e. What were they?

46. There will be a general election sometime this year or next. How likely would you say it is that you will vote in that election – quite certain (71%), very likely (14%), fairly likely (7%), or not very likely (6%)? (DK 2%)

47a. If the general election were held tomorrow, which party would you vote for? (Con. 33%, Lab. 44%, Lib. 12%, wouldn't vote 3%, DK 8%)

If vote Conservative or Labour

47b. Would you prefer (chosen party) very strongly (60%), fairly strongly (32%), or not very strongly (8%)?

47c. If the (chosen party) wasn't successful, would you rather see a (first party not chosen) or a (second party not chosen) government? (Con. 15%, Lab. 9%, Lib. 60%, DK 16%)

If vote Liberal

47d. Would you prefer the Liberals very strongly (51%), fairly strongly (42%), or not very strongly (7%)?

47e. If you thought the Liberals had a chance of winning in this constituency but not in the country as a whole, how would you vote? (Con. 5%, Lab. 3%, Lib. 88%, wouldn't vote 1%, DK 3%)

If would still prefer Liberals

47f. And if you thought that the Liberals hadn't much chance of winning in this constituency either, how would you vote? (Con. 7%, Lab. 4%, Lib. 81%, other 1%, wouldn't vote 5%, DK 2%)

If would still prefer Liberals

47g. Suppose there were a straight fight between the Conservatives and Labour in this constituency, how would you vote? (Con. 36%, Lab. 31%, wouldn't vote 25%, DK 8%)

If don't know which party to vote for

47h. Well, are you leaning towards one of the parties? Which party is that? (Con. 20%, Lab. 12%, Lib. 16%, No 40%, DK 12%)

48a. Regardless of your own preference, which party do you think has the best chance of winning the next general election? (Con. 20%, Lab. 63%, Lib. 1%, DK 16%)

If Conservative or Labour

48*b*. Do you feel very sure of this (36%), fairly sure (49%), or are you not very sure (15%)?

48*c*. How close do you think the Liberals could come to winning? (Could win 1%, fairly close 28%, not very close 64%, DK 7%)

If Liberals

48*d*. Do you feel very sure of this, fairly sure, or are you not very sure?

48*e*. Have you changed your mind about this during the past year or so?

49*a*. How about here in (name of constituency)? Which party has the best chance of winning in this constituency? (Con. 35%, Lab. 49%, Lib. 2%, DK 14%)

If Conservative or Labour

49*b*. How good a chance do you think the Liberals have of winning here in this constituency? (Very good 3%, fairly good 17%, not very good 26%, no chance 38%, don't stand here 7%, DK 9%)

If says Liberals don't stand here

49*c*. How good a chance would they have if they did stand here? (Very good 5%, fairly good 20%, not very good 35%, no chance 34%, DK 6%)

50. Would you say that you usually care a good deal which party wins a general election (65%) or that you don't care very much which party wins (33%)? (DK 2%)

51. How much attention do you generally pay to what's going on in politics when there isn't an election? Would you say you generally follow politics very closely (11%), fairly closely (37%), or not much at all (52%)?

52*a*. Have you paid a subscription to any political party in the last year? (Yes 12%)

If Yes

52*b*. Which party was that? (Con. 45%, Lab. 49%, Lib. 5%, Other 1%)

  If Labour

  52*c*. Was that as a member of the local party (40%) or through a trade union (59%)? (DK 1%)

52*d*. Do you take an active part in party work? (Yes 17%)

  If Yes

  52*e*. What is that?

53*a*. Have you attended any public political meetings during the past year? (Yes 4%)

If Yes

53*b*. What meetings were those?

54*a*. Do you ever think of the parties as being to the left, the centre, or to the right in politics (21%), or don't you think of the parties that way (74%)? (DK 5%)

If thinks of parties this way

54*b*. Which party would you say is the farthest to the left? (Con. 2%, Lab. 95%, Lib. 2%, DK 1%)

54*c*. And which party is the farthest to the right? (Con. 95%, Lab. 3%, Lib. 1%, DK 1%)

  If respondent has now named two parties

  54*d*. And where would you put the (party not yet named)?

    If 'in between' and not already clear

    54*e*. Would you say that the (party mentioned in 54*d*) is closer to the (party mentioned in 54*b*) or to the (party mentioned in 54*c*)?

Ask all who said yes to 54a

54*f*. What do you have in mind when you say that a party is to the left or to the right?

55. Now I would like to ask you some questions about the Member of

Parliament from this constituency. Do you happen to remember your M.P'.s name? What is that? (Remembers correctly 55%)

If doesn't know name

Of course, names aren't too important, but his/her name is ———.

56. Do you happen to remember which party he/she belongs to? Which party is that? (Remembers correctly 79%)

57a. Have you read or heard anything about (name of M.P.)? (Yes 30%)

If has read or heard something

57b. Can you tell me anything in particular about what (name of M.P. has done in Parliament? Anything else?

57c. Do you know if (name of M.P.) has held any special position in parliament or in the government? What is that?

57d. Do you know of any problems facing the government that (name of M.P.) has taken a stand on? What is that?

If necessary

57e. Do you know what stand (name of M.P.) has taken on that?

57f. Have you heard anything about (name of M.P.)'s opinion on the Common Market?

If Yes

57g. What is that?

If not already clear

57h. Do you think he/she favours Britain going into the Common Market or not?

57i. Have you heard anything about (name of M.P.)'s opinion on defence, disarmament or nuclear weapons?

If Yes

57j. What is that?

If not already clear

57k. Do you think he/she favours Britain having her own nuclear weapons or not?

57*l*. Have you heard anything about (name of M.P.)'s opinion on public ownership or nationalizing industry?

If Yes
57*m*. What is that?

    If not already clear
    57*n*. Do you think he/she favours nationalizing more industry or not?

57*o*. Do you happen to remember anything that (name of M.P.) has done for the people of this constituency?

If remembers anything
57*p*. What is that?

57*q*. Has he/she ever done anything for you or your family personally?

If he/she has done something
57*r*. What is that?

57*s*. Can you tell me what sort of person he/she is?
57*t*. Would you say that he/she is upper class, middle class, or working class?
57*u*. Do you know if he/she has any business or trade union connection or any other connection of that kind? What sort of connection is that?
57*v*. On the whole, do you feel that (name of M.P.) is doing a good job as a Member of Parliament, a fair job, or only a poor job?

57*w*. Why do you feel that way?

58. Have you ever seen (name of M.P.) in person? (Yes 35%)

59*a*. Now I would like to ask your opinion on some questions about the way the government works. First of all, over the years how much do you feel the government pays attention to what the people think when it decides what to do? (Good deal 8%, some 20%, not much 50%, DK 22%)

59b. Why is that?

60a. How much do you feel that having political parties makes the government pay attention to what the people think? (Good deal 21%, some 29%, not much 16%, DK 34%)

60b. Why is that?

61a. And how much do you think that having elections makes the government pay attention to what the people think? (Good deal 46%, some 26%, not much 9%, DK 19%)

61b. Why is that?

62a. How much attention do you think most M.P.'s pay to the people who elect them when they decide what to do in Parliament? (Good deal 14%, some 27%, not much 32%, DK 27%)

62b. Why is that?

63a. Do you think that in a country like this control of the government should pass from one party to another every so often (54%), or that it's all right for one party to have control for a long time (32%)? (Depends 1%, coalition 1%, DK 12%)

If choice made

63b. How strongly do you feel about this? (Very strongly 45%, fairly strongly 43%, not very strongly 12%)

Question 64 was asked of a random half-sample

64. Here is a list of twelve pairs of words and phrases you might use to describe political parties, and between each pair is a measuring stick of seven squares. Taking the first pair of words – i.e., 'Out of date/Modern' – as an example, the square on the extreme left would mean that the party concerned is very out of date, the next square would mean it was fairly out of date, and so on. The words at the top of your card will help you to choose the square you think is appropriate.

Now will you tell me which square you would use to describe the (Conservative Party) (Labour Party) (Liberal Party)?

	Very	Fairly	Slightly	Neither	Slightly	Fairly	Very	
Out of date	☐	☐	☐	☐	☐	☐	☐	Modern
Expert	☐	☐	☐	☐	☐	☐	☐	Clumsy
Powerful	☐	☐	☐	☐	☐	☐	☐	Weak
Foolish	☐	☐	☐	☐	☐	☐	☐	Wise
Middle Class	☐	☐	☐	☐	☐	☐	☐	Working Class
United	☐	☐	☐	☐	☐	☐	☐	Split
Bad	☐	☐	☐	☐	☐	☐	☐	Good
Left Wing	☐	☐	☐	☐	☐	☐	☐	Right Wing
Weak-minded	☐	☐	☐	☐	☐	☐	☐	Strong-minded
Honest	☐	☐	☐	☐	☐	☐	☐	Dishonest
Dull	☐	☐	☐	☐	☐	☐	☐	Exciting
Young	☐	☐	☐	☐	☐	☐	☐	Old

65*a*. There's quite a bit of talk these days about different social classes. Most people say they belong to either the middle class or to the working class. Do you ever think of yourself as being in one of these classes? (Yes 66%)

If thinks of self in these terms

65*b*. Which class is that? (Middle 27%, Working 73%)

If does not think of self in these terms

65*c*. Well, if you had to make a choice, would you call yourself middle class (29%) or working class (54%)? (DK 17%)

If class chosen on Q.65b or 65c

65*d*. Would you say that you are about average (chosen class) or that you are in the upper or lower part of the (chosen class)?

66. What would you say your family was when you were young, middle class (23%) or working class (74%)? (DK 3%)

67*a*. What sort of people would you say belong to the middle class?

67*b*. What sort of people would you say belong to the working class?

If not already clear what jobs

67*c*. What sort of jobs do middle class people have?

67*d*. What sort of jobs do working class people have?

68*a*. How difficult would you say it is for people to move from one class to another? (Very difficult 24%, fairly difficult 22%, not very difficult 33%, DK 21%)

68*b*. Why is that?

69. Some people feel they have a lot in common with other people of their own class, but others don't feel this way so much. How about you? Would you say you feel pretty close to other (chosen class above) people (55%), or that you don't feel much closer to them than you do people in other classes (37%)? (DK 8%)

70. How much interest would you say you have in how (chosen class) people as a whole are getting along in this country? Do you have a good deal of interest in it (36%), some interest (40%), or not much interest at all (20%)? (DK 4%)

71a. Do you think that middle class people vote mainly for one party (37%) or are they fairly evenly divided between the parties (48%)? (DK 15%)

   If mainly for one
   71b. Which party is that? (Con. 94%, Lab. 2%, Lib. 3%, DK 1%)
   71c. Why do you think they vote mainly for that party?

72a. And how about working class people? Do they vote mainly for one party (62%) or are they fairly evenly divided between the parties (31%)? (DK 7%)

   If mainly for one
   72b. Which party is that? (Con. 1%, Lab. 99%)
   72c. Why do you think they vote mainly for that party?

73. On the whole, do you think that there is bound to be some conflict between different social classes (34%) or do you think they can get along together without any conflict (57%)? (DK 9%)

74a. Can you tell me how old you were when you left school?

   If went to school
   74b. And what kind of school was that?

75a. Did you have any full-time or part-time education after leaving school? (Yes 32%)

   75b. What was that?

76*a*. Does anyone in this household belong to a trade union? (Yes 41%)

If Yes

76*b*. Who is it that belongs?

76*c*. What trade union is that?

76*d*. About how long has (member) belonged to this trade union?

76*e*. Some members of trade unions feel they have a lot in common
with other members: but others don't feel this way so much.
How about (member)? Would you say that (member) feels pretty
close to trade union members in general (37%) or that (member)
doesn't feel much closer to them than to other kinds of people
(49%)? (DK 14%)

76*f*. How much interest would you say (member) has in how trade
union people are getting along in this country. Does (member)
have a good deal of interest in it (33%), some interest (34%), or
not much interest (33%)?

76*g*. Do you think that trade union members vote mainly for one
party (54%) or are they fairly evenly divided between the parties
(46%)?

If mainly for one

76*h*. Which party is that? (Con. 1%, Lab. 98%, DK 1%)

76*i*. Why do you think they vote mainly for that party?

76*j*. Do you think the trade unions should have close ties to the
Labour Party (25%) or do you think the trade unions should
stay out of politics (60%)? (DK 15%)

77. Can you tell me where your parents were living when you were
born? (i.e., town/village and county)

78*a*. Were your parents brought up there or did they come from somewhere else?

If either parent from somewhere else

78*b*. Where exactly did they come from?

79. Where did you live during your childhood? (i.e., particular town/
village and county)

80*a*. And where have you lived since then? (i.e., particular town/village
and county) Anywhere else?

Unless always lived in area

80*b*. How long have you lived in this area?

81. How long have you lived in your present home?

82. Do you or your family rent (private 25%, council 29%), or own your own home (43%)? (Other 3%)

83. What is your religion?

84. When you were young, what was your parents' religion?

Unless 'no religion' in Q.83

85. How often do you attend Church? (For Jews: Synagogue)

___

Household Composition and Occupational Details (In Summary Form)
  – Can you tell me who else there is in your household living here besides yourself? (list showing relationship to respondent, sex, age, whether in a job, marital status)

  – Which member of your family living here actually is the owner/is responsible for the rent?

  – What type of firm or organization does (householder) work for?
    (If in public services) What is his/her rank or grade?
    (If other) Does he/she hold any particular position in the organization?
    (If proprietor or manager) How many employees are there?

  – Has (householder) any qualification? (e.g., apprenticeship or degree)

  – Would you mind telling me which of these income groups he/she falls into? (Show card)

(If respondent is not householder, repeat occupation questions for him/her)
  – What was your father's occupation when you were a child? What job did he actually do?

Questionnaire, Autumn 1964

This is part of some research being conducted at Oxford University. For this study we need the answers to a few questions which we are asking people all over the country.

1*a*. First of all, did you follow the election campaign on television? (Yes 75%)

> *If Yes*
>
> 1*b*. Were there any programmes about the election campaign which you found especially interesting? Which were they?

2*a*. Do you read a morning newspaper regularly? (Yes 81%)

> *If Yes*
>
> 2*b*. Which newspaper is that? Are there any other morning newspapers you read regularly?
>
> *List name of first morning newspaper mentioned*
>
> 2*c*. Did you follow the election campaign in (first newspaper)? (Yes 72%)
>
> 2*d*. Did you think that (first newspaper) tended to favour any particular party? Which party was that?

3*a*. Did you follow the election campaign in any other newspaper? (Yes 27%)

> *If Yes*
>
> 3*b*. Which newspaper was that?

4. Did you follow the election campaign on the radio? (Yes 24%)

If has followed campaign by more than one medium

5. Of all the ways that you followed the election campaign, which one would you say you got the most information from?

Ask all

6*a*. Did you talk to other people about the election campaign? (Yes 59%)

If Yes

6b. Who did you talk to about the campaign? Anyone else? (State relationship or type of person)

6c. Do you feel that you found out more about the campaign from talking to other people or from newspapers and TV?

7. How much interest did you have in the campaign – a good deal (34%), some (36%), or not much (30%)?

8a. Did you suggest to anyone how they should vote? (Yes 12%)

If Yes

8b. Who was that? Anyone else? (State relationship or type of person)

Now I would like to ask you what you think the good and bad points about the political parties are.

9. Is there anything in particular you like about the Conservative Party? What is that? Anything else?

10. Is there anything in particular that you don't like about the Conservative Party? What is that? Anything else?

11. Is there anything in particular that you like about the Labour Party? What is that? Anything else?

12. Is there anything in particular that you don't like about the Labour Party? What is that? Anything else?

13. Considering everything the parties stand for, would you say that there is a good deal of difference between the parties (46%), some difference (23%), or not much difference (26%)? (DK 5%)

Now I would like to ask you about the good and bad points of the party leaders.

14. Is there anything in particular that you like about Sir Alec Douglas-Home? What is that? Anything else?

15. Is there anything in particular that you don't like about Home? What is that? Anything else?

16. Is there anything in particular that you like about Harold Wilson? What is that? Anything else?

17. Is there anything in particular that you don't like about Wilson? What is that? Anything else?

18. Apart from Home, how do you feel about the other Conservative leaders. Do you generally like them (28%), dislike them (10%), or don't you have much feeling about them (54%)? (DK 8%)

19. Apart from Wilson, how do you feel about the other Labour leaders. Do you generally like them (27%), dislike them (16%), or don't you have much feeling about them (47%)? (DK 10%)

20. Which party would be better able to handle foreign affairs, the Conservatives (46%) or Labour (16%), or wouldn't there be any difference between them on this (20%)? (DK 18%)

21. Which party would be better able to handle problems here at home, the Conservatives (27%) or Labour (44%), or wouldn't there be any difference between them on this (17%)? (DK 12%)

22*a*. There's a lot of talk these days about nuclear weapons. Which of these statements comes closest to what you yourself feel should be done? If you don't have an opinion, just say so.

   a. Britain should keep her own nuclear weapons, independent of other countries. (40%)
   b. Britain should have nuclear weapons only as a part of a western defence system. (42%)
   c. Britain should have nothing to do with nuclear weapons under any circumstances. (10%)
   d. No opinion/Don't know. (8%)

   If has opinion
   22*b*. Which party would be more likely to keep nuclear weapons for Britain, the Conservatives (72%) or Labour (8%), or wouldn't there be any difference between them on this (13%)? (DK 7%)

23*a*. There's also a lot of talking about nationalizing industry. Which

of these statements comes closest to what you yourself feel should
be done? If you don't have an opinion about this, just say so.

a. A lot more industries should be nationalized. (8%)

b. Only a few more industries, such as steel, should be nationalized. (17%)

c. No more industries should be nationalized, but the industries that
are nationalized now should stay nationalized. (45%)

d. Some of the industries that are nationalized now should be de-
nationalized. (18%)

e. No opinion/Don't know. (12%)

If has opinion

23*b.* Which party would be more likely to nationalize some more
industry, the Conservatives (6%) or Labour (90%), or wouldn't
there be any difference between them on this (2%)? (DK 2%)

24. Do you think that the Trade Unions have too much power (54%)
or not (32%)? (DK 14%)

25*a.* Do you feel that the government should spend more on pensions
and social services (77%), or do you feel that spending for social
services should stay about as it is now (20%)? (DK 3%)

If has opinion

25*b.* Which party would be more likely to spend more on pensions
and social services, the Conservatives (8%) or Labour (69%), or
wouldn't there be any difference between them on this (16%)?
(DK 7%)

26. Do you think that big business has too much power in this country
(54%) or not (29%)? (DK 17%)

27*a.* If the question of going into the Common Market comes up again,
do you think that Britain should go in (33%) or stay out (32%), or
don't you have an opinion on that (35%)?

If has opinion

27*b.* Which party would be more likely to take Britain into the
Common Market if the question comes up again, the Con-

servatives (44%) or Labour (22%), or wouldn't there be any difference between them on this (21%)? (DK 13%)

28. Do you think the trade unions should have close ties to the Labour Party (19%) or do you think the trade unions should stay out of politics (69%)? (DK 12%)

29. How important do you yourself feel the Queen and royal family are to Britain – very important (61%), fairly important (25%), or not very important (13%)? (DK 1%)

30. How serious a problem do you think strikes are – very serious (78%), fairly serious (14%), or not very serious (6%)? (DK 2%)

31. When you hear of a strike, are your sympathies generally for (13%) or against (47%) the strikers? (Depends 24%, DK 16%)

32. Which party do you think has the better approach to strikes, the Conservatives (10%) or Labour (32%), or don't you think there is much difference between them on this (43%)? (DK 15%)

Ask if respondent is not coloured

33a. Do you think that too many immigrants have been let into this country (81%) or not (13%)? (DK 6%)

If yes too many

33b. How strongly do you feel about this – very strongly (52%), fairly strongly (34%), or not very strongly (14%)?

33c. Is it a problem around this neighbourhood? (Yes 14%, No 85%, DK 1%)

33d. Which party is more likely to keep immigrants out, the Conservatives (26%) or Labour (19%), or don't you feel there is much difference between them on this (41%)? (DK 14%)

34a. Do you ever think of yourself as being to the left, the centre, or the right in politics (28%), or don't you think of yourself that way (65%)? (DK 7%)

If Yes

34b. Where would you say you are? (Left 32%, Centre 40%, Right 28%)

34*c*. Do you think you have moved further left or right recently (33%), or don't you think of yourself as having moved (67%)?

If has moved
34*d*. How would you say you have moved?

35*a*. Over the years, how much do you think that having elections makes the government pay attention to what people think? (Good deal 35%, some 18%, not much 22%, DK 25%)

Unless don't know
35*b*. Why do you think it works that way?

36*a*. In between elections, how much does having political parties make the government pay attention to what the people think? (Good deal 17%, some 16%, not much 28%, DK 39%)

Unless don't know
36*b*. Why do you think it works that way?

37. We are also interested in how well off people are these days. How about you? Compared with a year ago, are you and your family better off now (21%), worse off now (17%), or have you stayed about the same (62%)?

38. Now looking ahead over the next three or four years, do you think that you will be better off (30%), worse off (11%), or will you stay about the same (40%)? (DK 19%)

39*a*. Do you think that the fact that Labour won the election will make any difference to how well off you are? (Yes 37%, No 48%, DK 15%)

If Yes
39*b*. Why is that?

40*a*. We find many people around the country who have good reasons for not voting. How about you? Did you vote in the General Election this year (89%), or did something prevent you from voting (11%)?

If voted

40*b*. Did you vote in person (99%) or by post (1%)?

  If in person

  40*c*. At what hour did you vote?

  40*d*. And which party did you vote for? (Con. 41%, Lab. 46%, Lib. 11%, Other 1%; Refused 1%)

If voted Conservative

40*e*. How long ago did you decide to vote that way?

40*f*. What would you say is the main reason you voted Conservative?

40*g*. Would you say that you preferred the Conservatives very strongly (52%), fairly strongly (40%), or not very strongly (8%)?

40*h*. Did you think of voting for any other party? (Yes 24%) Which party was that? (Lab. 18%, Lib. 79%, Other 3%)

40*i*. Suppose you had thought the Conservatives couldn't win. Would you rather have seen Labour (19%) or the Liberals (67%) form the new government? (Neither 6%, DK 8%)

  Ask if no Liberal stood

  40*j*. Would you have voted Liberal if a Liberal candidate had stood in this constituency? (Yes 19%, might have 9%, No 71%, DK 1%)

If voted Labour

40*k*. How long ago did you decide to vote that way?

40*l*. What would you say is the main reason you voted Labour?

40*m*.Would you say that you preferred Labour very strongly (54%), fairly strongly (35%), or not very strongly (11%)?

40*n*. Did you think of voting for any other party? (Yes 22%) Which party was that? (Con. 24%, Lib. 69%, Other 7%)

40*o*. Suppose you had thought that Labour couldn't win. Would you rather have seen the Conservatives (24%) or the Liberals (62%) form the new government? (Neither 7%, DK 7%)

  Ask if no Liberal stood

  40*p*. Would you have voted Liberal if a Liberal candidate had stood in this constituency? (Yes 16%, Might have 11%, No 70%, DK 3%)

If voted Liberal

40*q*. How long ago did you decide to vote that way?

40*r*. What would you say is the main reason you voted Liberal?

40*s*. Would you say that you preferred the Liberals very strongly (40%), fairly strongly (41%), or not very strongly (19%)?

40*t*. Did you think of voting for any other party? (Yes 39%) Which party was that? (Con. 55%, Lab. 40%, Other 5%)

40*u*. Would you have voted for another party if you had felt that the Liberal candidate hadn't much chance of winning in this constituency? (Yes – Con. 11%, Lab. 8%, Other 2%, No 77%, DK 2%)

If would still have voted Liberal

40*v*. Would you rather have seen the Conservatives (48%) or Labour (35%) win the election? (Neither 6%, DK 11%)

If did not vote

40*w*. What would you say is the main reason you didn't vote?

40*x*. If you had voted, which party would you probably have voted for? (Con. 40%, Lab. 41%, Lib. 9%, Other 2%, wouldn't have voted 1%, DK 7%)

If don't know

40*y*. Were you a little more inclined to one of the parties than the others? (Yes 39%) Which party is that? (Con. 60%, Lab. 40%)

41*a*. Did you attend any political meetings during the campaign? (Yes 8%)

If Yes

41*b*. Were those indoor (83%) or outdoor meetings (13%)? (Both 4%)

41*c*. Which party was that?

42*a*. Did you do any party work during the election campaign? (Yes 3%)

If Yes

42*b*. What was that? Which party was that?

43*a*. Did you read any party leaflets or election addresses during the election campaign? (Yes 64%)

If Yes

43*b*. What were those? Which party was that?

44*a*. Have you paid a subscription to any political party in the last year? (Yes 14%)

If Yes

44*b*. Which party was that? (Con. 53%, Lab. 40%, Lib. 6%, Other 1%)

If Labour

44*c*. Was that as a member of the local party (33%) or through a trade union (59%)? (Both 8%)

45*a*. Did any of the parties canvass at your home during the election campaign? (Yes 33%, No 63%, DK 4%)

If Yes

45*b*. Which parties called?

46. Regardless of your own preference, which party did you think would win the election? (Con. 33%, Lab. 56%, DK 11%)

Unless Liberals

47*a* How about here in this constituency? Which party did you think would win here? (Con. 47%, Lab. 47%, Lib. 2%, DK 4%)

47*b*. How close did you think the Liberals would come to winning in this constituency – fairly close (21%), not very close (21%), or not at all close (52%)? (DK 6%)

48. Would you say that you cared a good deal which party won the election (69%) or that you didn't care very much which party won (31%)?

49*a*. Generally speaking, do you usually think of yourself as Conservative (39%), Labour (42%), Liberal (12%), or what? (None 5%, DK 2%)

If accepts party affiliation

49b. How strongly (chosen party) do you generally feel – very strongly
(47%), fairly strongly (41%), or not very strongly (12%)?

49c. Was there ever a time when you thought of yourself as (first
party not chosen) or (second party not chosen) rather than
(chosen party)? Which was that?

If reports previous affiliation

49d. When did you change from (former party) to (present party)?

49e. What was the main thing that made you change from (former
party) to (present party)?

If does not accept party affiliation

49f. Well, do you generally think of yourself as a little closer to one
of the parties than the others? (Yes 44%) Which party is that?
(Con. 36%, Lab. 37%, Lib. 27%)

If feels closer

49g. Was there ever a time when you thought of yourself as closer
to (first party not chosen) or (second party not chosen) rather
than (chosen party)? Which party was that?

If reports previous affiliation

49h. When did you change from (former party) to (present
party)?

49i. What was the main thing that made you change from
(former party) to (present party)?

If does not feel closer

49j. Was there ever a time when you did think of yourself as closer
to one of the parties than the others? Which was that?

If Yes

49k. When did you move away from (former party)?

49l. What was the main thing that made you move away from
(former party)?

50a. Do you ever think of the parties as being to the left, the centre, or
to the right in politics (19%), or don't you think of the parties that
way (76%)? (DK 5%)

If does think of parties in this way

50*b*. Do you think of any party as having moved left or right recently (48%), or don't you think of any party as having moved in this way (50%)? (DK 2%)

   If party has moved

   50*c*. Which party is that? How has it moved?

   50*d*. Do you think of any other party as having moved in this way? Which party is that? How has it moved?

50*e*. What is it about a party that would make you think of it as to the left or right?

51*a*. Now think of the General Election five years ago in the autumn of 1959, when the Conservatives were led by Macmillan and Labour by Gaitskell. Do you remember for certain whether you voted then? (Yes 76%, fairly certain 2%, No 19%, DK 3%)

If sure or fairly sure voted

51*b*. Which party did you vote for then? (Con. 48%, Lab. 45%, Lib. 6%, DK 1%)

If did not vote or don't know

51*c*. Do you remember whether you preferred one of the parties to the others then? (Yes 66%) Which party was that? (Con. 49%, Lab. 43%, Lib. 8%)

52*a*. What was the first General Election you voted in?

Unless has never voted

52*b*. Which party did you vote for in that election?

53. Can you tell me which General Elections seem to you to have been especially important? Any others? Did you vote in that election? Which party did you vote for in that election?

54*a*. Talking to people around the country, we find a great many people weren't able to vote in the local council elections earlier this spring. How about you? Did you vote in the local elections this year (62%) or did something prevent you from voting (38%)?

If did vote

54b. How did you vote? Which party is that?

55. Do you happen to remember the name of the candidate who was elected to Parliament for this constituency? (Remembers correctly, 85%)

56. Do you happen to know which party he/she is? (Remembers correctly 94%)

Interviewer completes respondent's information by saying, for example: 'Sometimes it's hard to remember these things, but his name is . . . and he is . . .'

57. Have you read or heard anything about (MP)? (Yes 66%)

58. Have you ever seen him/her in person? (Yes 35%)

59. Do you happen to know whether he/she was in Parliament before the election?

60. Do you remember the names of any other candidate standing for Parliament from this constituency? And which party is he/she?

Interviewer completes or corrects information by saying, for example: 'Names aren't too important, but the Conservative candidate is . . ., the Labour candidate is . . .'

61. Now take (name of Conservative), the Conservative candidate. Have you read or heard anything about him/her?

62. Have you ever seen him/her in person?

63. How about (name of Labour candidate), the Labour candidate. Have you read or heard anything about him/her?

64. Have you ever seen him/her in person?

Ask if Liberal has stood

65. And how about (name of Liberal), the Liberal candidate. Have you read or heard anything about him/her?

66. Have you ever seen him/her in person?

67*a*. Over the years, do you think that control of the government should pass from one party to another every so often (58%), or do you think that it's all right for one party to have control for a long time (30%)? (DK 12%)

   If control should change
   67*b*. Why do you think a change of parties is a good thing?

   If one party all right
   67*c*. Why would you like to see one party have control of the government for a long time?

   Question 68 was asked of a random half-sample.

68. Here is a list of twelve pairs of words and phrases you might use to describe political parties, and between each pair of words is a measuring stick of seven squares. Taking the first pair of words – that is, 'Out of date/Modern' – as an example, the square on the left-hand side of the card would mean that party is very out of date, the next square would mean it was fairly out of date, and so on. The words at the top of your card will help you to choose the square you think is appropriate.

   Now will you tell me which square you would use to describe the Conservative Party ... the Labour Party ... and then Liberal Party. (*See Question 64 of 1963 Questionnaire.*)

   Questions 69a to 69g were asked of a random half-sample.

69*a*. Do you ever think of yourself as belonging to a particular social class? (Yes 50%)

   If Yes
   69*b*. Which class is that? (Upper 2%, Middle 28%, Working 68% Other 2%)

   If has said middle or working class
   69*c*. Would you say that you are about average (chosen class) or that you are in the upper or lower part of the (chosen class)?

If has used other class description

69d. Most people say they belong either to the middle class or to the
working class. If you had to make a choice, would you call
yourself middle class or working class?

Unless don't know

69e. Would you say that you are average (chosen class) or that
you are in the upper or lower part of (chosen class)?

If No

69f. Most people say they belong either to the middle class or to
the working class. If you had to make a choice, would you call
yourself middle class (30%) or working class (63%)? (DK 7%)

Unless don't know

69g. Would you say that you are about average (chosen class) or
that you are in the upper or lower part of the (chosen class)?

Questions 69a* to 69d* were asked of the remaining half-sample.

69a*. There's quite a bit of talk these days about different social classes.
Most people say they belong to either the middle class or the
working class. Do you ever think of yourself as being in one of
these class? (Yes 60%)

If Yes

69b*. Which class is that? (Middle 27%, Working 73%)

If No

69c*. If you had to make a choice, would you call yourself middle
class (30%) or working class (57%)? (DK 13%)

69d*. Would you say that you are about average (chosen class) or
that you are in the upper or lower part of the (chosen class)?

70. How often would you say people move from one class to another –
very often (4%), fairly often (16%), or not very often (61%)? (Not
at all 7%, DK 12%)

71. Under what circumstances do you think a person could move
from the working class to the middle class?

72. On the whole, do you think that there is bound to be some conflict between different social classes (42%) or do you think they can get along together without any conflict (52%)? (DK 6%)

73a. Do you currently have a job? (Yes 60%)

If Yes has a job

73b. Are you a member of a trade union? (Yes 40%)

If Yes is a member

73c. Which trade union is that?

73d. At your place of work how many people who are doing your kind of job are members of a trade union – all of them (58%), most of them (30%), or only some of them (11%)? (DK 1%)

If all or most

73e. At your place of work do you have to be a trade union member to do your job? (Yes 50%)

73f. Do you see any trade union magazines or journals? (Yes 65%)

If Yes

73g. What is it that you see?

73h. How much attention do you pay to it – a good deal (31%), some (33%), or not much (36%)?

73i. Do you recall seeing any articles or discussions on political questions? (Yes 30%)

If Yes

73j. What was that?

73k. Did a shop steward or any other trade union representative approach you during the election campaign and ask you to vote? (Yes 2%)

If Yes

73l. Who was that? What position did he have?

If No, not a member

73m. At your place of work, are any of the people who are doing your kind of job members of a trade union? (Yes 18%, No 74%, DK 8%)

If Yes

73n. How many of them are members of a trade union – most of them (39%), some of them (24%), or only a few of them (31%)? (DK 6%)

73o. Have you been asked to join a trade union since you have been at your present place of work? (Yes 13%, No 87%)

If Yes

73p. Can you tell me why you didn't join?

If No

73q. Would you join if asked? (Yes 24%, No 53%, DK 23%)

73r. Why is that?

If No, do not have a job

73s. Does anyone in this household belong to a trade union? (Yes 32%, No 64%, DK 4%)

If Yes

73t. Who is it that belongs?

73u. Which trade union is that?

74. How long have you lived in your present home?

75. Do you or your family rent (private 22%, council 28%) or own your own home (46%)? (Other 4%)

76. Can you tell me where your father was brought up? What town or village and what county was that?

77. And can you tell me where your mother was brought up? Town or village and county.

78. What was your father's occupation when you were a child? What sort of job did he actually do?

79. Did he have any qualification (such as apprenticeships, professional qualifications, university degrees, diplomas, etc.)? What was that?

80a. What type of firm or organization did he work for?

If in civil service, forces, police, etc.

80*b*. What was his rank or grade when you were a child?

If in other type of organization

80*c*. Did he hold any particular position in this organization when you were a child?

If Yes

80*d*. What was that?

If proprietor or manager

80*e*. About how big an organization was that? For instance roughly how many people worked there?

81*a*. Were you ever in the forces? (Yes 61 % of men)

If Yes

81*b*. When was that?
81*c*. Did you serve overseas?

Household Composition and Occupation Details (In Summary Form)

– Can you tell me who else there is in your household besides yourself? (List, showing relationship to respondent, sex, age, marital status)

– Which member of your family living here actually is the owner/is responsible for the rent?

– What type of firm or organization does (householder) work for?

– What job does (householder) actually do? Does he/she hold any particular position in the organization?

(If in public service) What is his/her rank or grade?

(If proprietor or manager) How many employees?

– Has (householder) any qualification? (e.g., apprenticeship or degree).

– Would you mind telling me which of these income groups (house-holder) belongs to?

(If respondent is not householder) Do you have a paid job?

(If yes, repeat householder's occupational questions.)

Questionnaire, Spring 1966

This is part of some research being conducted at Oxford University. For this study we need the answers to some questions which we are asking people all over the country.

1a. First of all, did you follow the election campaign on television? (Yes 72%)

If Yes
1b. Were there any programmes about the election campaign which you found especially interesting? Which were they?

2a. Do you read a morning newspaper regularly? (Yes 78%)

If Yes
2b. Which newspaper is that? Are there any other morning news-papers you read regularly?

List name of first morning newspaper mentioned
2c. Did you follow the election campaign in (first newspaper)? (Yes 64%)

3a. Did you follow the election campaign in any other newspaper? (Yes 28%)

If Yes
3b. Which newspaper was that?

4. Did you follow the election campaign on the radio? (Yes 20%)

5. Did you talk to other people about the election campaign? (Yes 63%)

6. How much interest did you have in the campaign – a good deal (31%), some (36%), or not much (33%)?

Now I would like to ask you what you think the good and bad points about the political parties are.

7. Is there anything in particular that you like about the Conservative Party? What is that? Anything else?

8. Is there anything in particular that you don't like about the Conservative Party? What is that? Anything else?

9. Is there anything in particular that you like about the Labour Party? What is that? Anything else?

10. Is there anything in particular that you don't like about the Labour Party? What is that? Anything else?

11. Considering everything the parties stand for, would you say that there is a good deal of difference between the parties (42%), some difference (26%), or not much difference (29%)? (DK 3%)

Now I would like to ask you about the good and bad points of the party leaders.

12. Is there anything in particular that you like about Edward Heath? What is that? Anything else?

13. Is there anything in particular that you don't like about Heath? What is that? Anything else?

14. Is there anything in particular that you like about Harold Wilson? What is that? Anything else?

15. Is there anything in particular that you don't like about Wilson? What is that? Anything else?

16. What issues did you yourself feel were most important in this election?

17. Which party would be better able to handle foreign affairs, the Conservatives (38%) or Labour (22%), or wouldn't there be any difference between them on this (29%)? (DK 11%)

18. Which party would be better able to handle problems here at home, the Conservatives (24%) or Labour (46%), or wouldn't there be any difference between them on this (24%)? (DK 6%)

19a. There's a lot of talk these days about nuclear weapons. Which of these statements comes closest to what you yourself feel should be done? If you don't have an opinion, just say so.

   a. Britain should keep her own nuclear weapons, independent of other countries. (33%)
   b. Britain should have nuclear weapons only as a part of a western defence system. (46%)
   c. Britain should have nothing to do with nuclear weapons under any circumstances. (14%)
   d. No opinion/Don't know. (7%)

If has opinion

19b. Which party would be more likely to keep nuclear weapons for Britain, the Conservatives (42%) or Labour (10%), or wouldn't there be any difference between them on this (36%)? (DK 12%)

20a. There's also a lot of talk about nationalizing industry. Which of these statements comes closest to what you yourself feel should be done? If you don't have an opinion about this, just say so.

   a. A lot more industries should be nationalized. (8%)
   b. Only a few more industries, such as steel, should be nationalized. (17%)
   c. No more industries should be nationalized, but the industries that are nationalized now should stay nationalized. (42%)
   d. Some of the industries that are nationalized now should be de-nationalized. (19%)
   e. No opinion/Don't know. (14%)

If has opinion

20*b*. Which party would be more likely to nationalize some more industry, the Conservatives (4%) or Labour (90%), or wouldn't there be any difference between them on this (4%)? (DK 2%)

21. Do you think that the Trade Unions have too much power (64%) or not (25%)? (DK 11%)

22*a*. Do you feel that the government should spend more on pensions and social services (55%) or do you feel that spending for social services should stay about as it is now (41%)? (DK 4%)

If has opinion

22*b*. Which party would be more likely to spend more on pensions and social services, the Conservative (7%) or Labour (64%), or wouldn't there be any difference between them on this (23%)? (DK 6%)

23. If the Government had a choice between reducing taxes (55%) and spending more on social services (36%), which should it do? (DK 9%)

24. Do you think that Britain gave up her empire too fast (43%) or not (38%)? (DK 19%)

25. Do you think that big business has too much power in this country (55%) or not (32%)? (DK 13%)

26*a*. If the question of going into the Common Market comes up again, do you think that Britain should go in (54%) or stay out (17%), or don't you have an opinion on that (29%)?

If has opinion

26*b*. Which party would be more likely to take Britain into the Common Market if the question comes up again, the Conservatives (57%) or Labour (16%), or wouldn't there be any difference between them on this (23%)? (DK 4%)

27. Did you want to see the death penalty kept (77%) or abolished (17%)? (DK 6%)

28. Do you think the trade unions should have close ties to the Labour Party (16%), or do you think the trade unions should stay out of politics (74%)? (DK 10%)

29. How important do you yourself feel the Queen and royal family are to Britain – very important (58%), fairly important (26%), or not very important (16%)?

30a. Which of these statements comes closest to what you yourself feel should be done about Rhodesia? If you don't have an opinion, just say so.

   a. Grant independence on the terms Ian Smith wants. (5%)
   b. Negotiate a settlement with Smith's government. (40%)
   c. Go on using economic sanctions until Smith gives in. (29%)
   d. Use force against Smith's government. (8%)
   e. No opinion/Don't know. (18%)

   If has opinion
   30b. Which of these statements do you think comes closest to the Labour Party's position?
   30c. And which of these statements comes closest to the Conservative Party's position?

31. How close do you feel Britain's ties with America should be? (Very close 38%, fairly close 47%, not very close 12%, DK 3%)

32. How serious a problem do you think strikes are – very serious (77%), fairly serious (16%), or not very serious (6%)? (DK 1%)

33. When you hear of a strike, are your sympathies generally for (15%) or against (60%) the strikers? (Depends 9%, DK 16%)

34. Which party do you think has the better approach to strikes, the Conservatives (11%) or Labour (31%), or don't you think there is much difference between them on this (51%)? (DK 7%)

Ask if respondent is not coloured
35a. Do you think that too many immigrants have been let into this country (81%) or not (14%)? (DK 5%)

If yes too many

35b. How strongly do you feel about this – very strongly (54%), fairly
strongly (33%), or not very strongly (13%)?

35c. Is it a problem around this neighbourhood? (Yes 13%)

35d. Which party is more likely to keep immigrants out, the Conservatives (26%) or Labour (13%), or don't you feel there is any
difference between them on this (53%)? (DK 8%)

36a. Do you ever think of yourself as being to the left, the centre, or the
right in politics (27%) or don't you think of yourself that way
(66%)? (DK 7%)

If yes

36b. Where would you say you are? (Left 29%, Centre 44%, Right
26%, Other 1%)

36c. Do you think you have moved to the left or right recently (21%),
or don't you think of yourself as having moved (79%)?

If has moved

36d. How would you say you have moved?

37. Over the years, how much do you think that having elections makes
the government pay attention to what the people think? (Good
deal 42%, some 24%, not much 26%, DK 8%)

38. In between elections, how much does having political parties
make the government pay attention to what the people think?
(Good deal 19%, some 30%, not much 40%, DK 11%)

39. We are also interested in how well off people are these days. How
about you? Compared with a year ago, are you and your family
better off now (22%), worse off now (23%), or have you stayed
about the same (55%)?

40. Now looking ahead over the next three or four years, do you think
that you will be better off (26%), worse off (19%), or will you stay
about the same (45%)? (DK 10%)

41a. Do you think that what the government does makes any difference
to how well off you are? (Yes 70%, No 26%, DK 4%)

If government does make a difference

41*b*. Has the Labour Government made you better (18%) or worse off (24%), or hasn't it made much difference (56%)? (DK 2%)

41*c*. Looking ahead, do you think that the Labour Government will make you better (30%) or worse off (29%), or won't it make much difference (30%)? (DK 11%)

41*d*. If a Conservative Government had come in, would it have made you better (18%) or worse off (18%), or wouldn't it have made much difference (53%)? (DK 11%)

42. Speaking more generally, how satisfied are you with the government's handling of Britain's economic affairs? (Satisfied 50%, neutral/mixed 14%, dissatisfied 22%, DK 14%)

43. Do you think that Britain's economic difficulties are mainly the fault of the Labour Government (13%) or of the last Conservative Government (43%)? (Both equally 30%, DK 14%)

44*a*. We find many people around the country who have good reasons for not voting. How about you? Did you vote in the General Election this year? (Yes 84%)

If voted

44*b*. Did you vote in person (98%) or by post (2%)?

44*c*. And which party did you vote for? (Con. 38%, Lab. 53%, Lib. 8%, DK 1%)

If voted Conservative

44*d*. How long ago did you decide to vote that way?

44*e*. What would you say is the main reason you voted Conservative?

44*f*. Would you say that you preferred the Conservatives very strongly (50%), fairly strongly (39%), or not very strongly (11%)?

44*g*. Did you think of voting for any other party? (Yes 22%) Which party is that? (Lab. 22%, Lib. 73%, Other 5%)

44*h*. Suppose you had thought the Conservatives couldn't win. Would you rather have seen Labour (20%) or the Liberals (63%) form the new government? (Neither 10%, DK 7%)

Ask if no Liberal stood

44*i*. Would you have voted Liberal if a Liberal candidate had stood in this constituency? (Yes 18%, might have 8%, no 74%)

If voted Labour

44*j*. How long ago did you decide to vote that way?

44*k*. What would you say is the main reason you voted Labour?

44*l*. Would you say that you preferred Labour very strongly (55%), fairly strongly (37%), or not very strongly (8%)?

44*m*. Did you think of voting for any other party? (Yes 21%) Which party is that? (Con. 18%, Lib. 71%, Other 11%)

44*n*. Suppose you had thought that Labour couldn't win. Would you rather have seen the Conservatives (22%) or the Liberals (64%) form the new government? (Neither 8%, DK 6%)

Ask if no Liberal stood

44*o*. Would you have voted Liberal if a Liberal candidate had stood in this constituency? (Yes 14%, might have 8%, no 78%)

If voted Liberal

44*p*. How long ago did you decide to vote that way?

44*q*. What would you say is the main reason you voted Liberal?

44*r*. Would you say that you preferred the Liberals very strongly (30%), fairly strongly (48%), or not very strongly (22%)?

44*s*. Did you think of voting for any other party? (Yes 36%) Which party is that? (Con. 43%, Lab. 54%, Other 3%)

44*t*. Would you have voted for another party if you had felt that the Liberal candidate hadn't much chance of winning in this constituency? (Yes – Con. 8%, Lab. 18%, Other 1%, No 71%, DK 2%)

If would still have voted Liberal

44*u*. Would you rather have seen the Conservatives (38%) or Labour (49%) win the election? (Neither 10%, DK 3%)

If did not vote

44*v*. What would you say is the main reason you didn't vote?

44*w*. If you had voted, which party would you probably have voted for? (Con. 34%, Lab. 42%, Lib. 8%, Other 1%, wouldn't have voted 6%, DK 9%)

If don't know

44x. Were you a little more inclined to one of the parties than the others? (Yes 60%) Which party is that? (Con. 36%, Lab. 55%, Lib. 9%)

45. Regardless of your own preference, which party did you think would win the election? (Con. 12%, Lab. 85%, DK 3%)

46a. How about here in this constituency? Which party did you think would win here? (Con. 43%, Lab. 52%, Lib. 1%, DK 4%)

If Liberals not mentioned and Liberal stood

46b. How close did you think the Liberals would come to winning in this constituency – fairly close (17%), not very close (21%), or not at all close (56%)? (DK 6%)

47. Would you say that you cared a good deal which party won the election (71%) or that you didn't care very much which party won (28%)? (DK 1%)

48a. Generally speaking, do you usually think of yourself as Conservative (35%), Labour (46%), Liberal (10%), or what? (Other 1%, None 7%, DK 1%)

If accepts party affiliation

48b. How strongly (chosen party) do you generally feel – very strongly (48%), fairly strongly (42%), or not very strongly (10%)?

48c. Was there ever a time when you thought of yourself as (first party not chosen) or (second party not chosen) rather than (chosen party)? Which was that?

If reports previous affiliation

48d. When did you change from (former party) to (present party)?

48e. What was the main thing that made you change from (former party) to (present party)?

If does not accept party affiliation

48f. Do you generally think of yourself as a little closer to one of the parties than the others? (Yes 45%) Which party is that? (Con. 51%, Lab. 19%, Lib. 30%)

If feels closer

48*g*. Was there ever a time when you thought of yourself as closer to (first party not chosen) or (second party not chosen) rather than (chosen party)? Which party was that?

If reports previous affiliation

48*h*. When did you change from (former party) to (present party)?

48*i*. What was the main thing that made you change from (former party) to (present party)?

If does not feel closer

48*j*. Was there ever a time when you did think of yourself as closer to one of the parties than the others? (Yes 44%) Which was that? (Con. 36%, Lab. 51%, Lib. 13%)

If Yes

48*k*. When did you move away from (former party)?

48*l*. What was the main thing that made you move away from (former party)?

49*a*. Do you ever think of the parties as being to the left, the centre, or to the right in politics (21%), or don't you think of the parties that way (72%)? (DK 7%)

If does think of parties in this way

49*b*. Do you think of any party as having moved to the left or right recently (55%), or don't you think of any party as having moved in this way (42%)? (DK 3%)

If party has moved

49*c*. Which party is that?

49*d*. How has it moved?

49*e*. When would you say it moved?

49*f*. Do you think of any other party as having moved to the left or right recently? Which party is that? How has it moved? When would you say it moved?

50*a*. Now think of the General Election a year and a half ago in the autumn of 1964, when the Conservatives were led by Home and Labour by Wilson. Do you remember for certain whether you voted then? (Voted 86%, didn't vote 9%, too young 4%, DK 15%)

If sure, or fairly sure voted

50b. Which party did you vote for then? (Con. 40%, Lab. 50%, Lib. 8%, Other 1%, DK 1%)

If did not vote or don't know

50c. Do you remember whether you preferred one of the parties to the others then? (Yes 68%) Which party was that? (Con. 36%, Lab. 55%, Lib. 9%)

51a. How about the General Election of 1959, when the Conservatives were led by Macmillan and Labour by Gaitskell. Do you remember for certain whether you voted then? (Voted 76%, didn't vote 9%, too young 12%, DK 3%)

If sure or fairly sure

51b. Which party did you vote for then? (Con. 46%, Lab. 47%, Lib. 6%, DK 1%)

52. Over the years, do you think that control of the government should pass from one party to another every so often (54%), or do you think that it's all right for one party to have control for a long time (36%)? (DK 10%)

53. Did you feel, before this election, that the Labour Government had been in office long enough to have had a fair trial? (Yes 26% No 71%, DK 3%)

54. Do you happen to remember who was the member of Parliament for this constituency before the election? (Remembers correctly 79%)

55. Do you happen to remember his/her party? (Remembers correctly 91%)

Interviewer completes respondent's information by saying, for example: 'Sometimes it's hard to remember these things but his/her name is . . . and he/she is . . .'

56. Have you read or heard anything about (name of M.P. before election)? (Yes 47%)

57. Have you ever seen him/her in person? (Yes 37%)

58. Do you happen to know whether he/she stood for Parliament again in this election?

59. Do you remember the names of any (other) candidates standing for Parliament from this constituency? And which party is he/she?

Interviewer completes or corrects information by saying, for example: 'Names aren't too important, but the Conservative candidate is . . ., the Labour candidate is . . .'

60. Now take (name of Conservative), the Conservative candidate. Have you read or heard anything about him/her?

61. Have you ever seen him/her in person?

62. How about (name of Labour candidate), the Labour candidate. Have you read or heard anything about him/her?

63. Have you ever seen him/her in person?

Ask if Liberal is standing

64. And how about (name of Liberal), the Liberal candidate. Have you read or heard anything about him/her?

65. Have you ever seen him/her in person?

Question 66 was asked of a random half-sample.

66. Here is a list of twelve pairs of words and phrases you might use to describe political parties, and between each pair is a measuring stick of seven squares. Taking the first pair of words – i.e., 'Out of date/Modern' – as an example, the square on the extreme left would mean that the party concerned is very out of date, the next square would mean it was fairly out of date, and so on. The words at the top of your card will help you to choose the square you think is appropriate.

Now will you tell me which square you would use to describe the Conservative Party ... the Labour Party ... and the Liberal Party. (*See Question 64 of 1963 Questionnaire.*)

Questions 67a to 67g were asked of a random half-sample.

67a. Do you ever think of yourself as belonging to a particular social class? (Yes 46%)

If Yes

67b. Which class is that? (Middle 32%, working 68%)

  If has said middle or working class

  67c. Would you say that you are about average (chosen class) or that you are in the upper or lower part of the (chosen class)?

  If has used other class description

  67d. Most people say they belong either to the middle class or to the working class. If you had to make a choice, would you call yourself middle class or working class?

    Unless don't know

    67e. Would you say that you are average (chosen class) or that you are in the upper or lower part of (chosen class)?

If No

67f. Most people say they belong either to the middle class or to the working class. If you had to make a choice, would you call yourself middle class (28%) or working class (65%)? (DK 7%)

  Unless don't know

  67g. Would you say that you are about average (chosen class) or that you are in the upper or lower part of the (chosen class)?

Questions 67a* to 67d* were asked of the remaining half-sample.

67a*. There's quite a bit of talk these days about different social classes. Most people say they belong to either the middle class or to the working class. Do you ever think of yourself as being in one of these classes? (Yes 66%)

If Yes

67b*. Which class is that? (Middle 28%, Working 72%)

If No

67c*. If you had to make a choice, would you call yourself middle class (32%) or working class (60%)? (DK 8%)

67d*. Would you say that you are about average (chosen class) or that you are in the upper or lower part of the (chosen class)?

68. What would you say your family was when you were young, middle class (23%) or working class (75%)? (DK 2%)

69. On the whole, do you think that there is bound to be some conflict between different social classes (41%) or do you think they can get along together without any conflict (54%)? (DK 5%)

Household Composition and Occupational Details (In Summary Form)

– Can you tell me who else there is in your household besides yourself? First your family and relatives (list with relationship, sex, age and marital status).

– Which member of your family living here actually owns it/is responsible for the rent?

(If householder is not responsible, record details of householder's present or past occupation)

– Do you have a paid job now? What type of firm or organization do you work for? What do you actually do? Do you hold any particular position in the organization?

(If in public services) What is your rank or grade?

(If proprietor or manager) How many employees are there?

– Have you any qualification or degree?

– Would you mind telling me which of these income groups you belong to? (Offer card)

Sources

Apart from our own survey, discussed at length in the Appendix, we have drawn extensively on the work of others. Many of our debts are implicit in our footnotes. Here we merely acknowledge some of the principal sources on which we have drawn.

(a) *Election statistics.* Since British law makes no acknowledgement of parties, it has never been possible for official sources to publish any return of votes that makes political sense. We are much indebted to the Home Office returns, to the Registrar General's Annual Reports and to individual registration officers for statistics about the electorate. But we have naturally turned to the invaluable *Times House of Commons* for much of our data on votes; for the pre-war period successive editions of the *Constitutional Year Book* have provided our main source.

Local election returns have been far more frustrating. Nowhere are these collected centrally. Our debt to the diligence and expertise of Mr Michael Steed of Manchester University is enormous. He has assembled large bodies of returns from all kinds of sources both in connection with the local elections of our period and on a historical basis.

(b) *Opinion polls.* Anyone working in the field of recent British politics and elections must owe a lot to the data assembled over the past thirty years by Dr Henry Durant and the Gallup Poll. In all sorts of areas he has provided data where none existed before. In the last few years, his findings on the standings of parties and leaders, published since the demise of the *News Chronicle* in the *Daily Telegraph*, have had increasing impact on the politicians themselves. The voter's fever chart, published weekly or monthly, has helped to shape party strategy and election timing. But in the files of the Gallup Poll there exists more fundamental data on the composition and attitude of the electorate over time which has been a major quarry for many beside ourselves.

Since 1957 and more particularly since 1961 the findings of National Opinion Polls, published in the *Daily Mail*, have provided a rival source to Gallup. Since September/October 1963, when National Opinion

Polls switched from quota sampling to probability sampling, their findings have been of particular interest to academic students and, as has been evident, we have drawn heavily on their findings at the time of the 1964 and 1966 elections. (A summary of the election polls can be found in *The British General Election of 1964* and *The British General Election of 1966*.)

A third polling organization, Research Services, Ltd., under the guidance of Dr Mark Abrams, has done much stimulating research, some privately on behalf of the Labour Party, some published in the *Observer* and some in the *Public Opinion Quarterly* and elsewhere.

Since 1965 the Opinion Research Centre under Humphrey Taylor has provided one more very valuable source of polling data.

Our debt to all these polling organizations is a personal one and extends far beyond the figures cited in the text.

(c) *Election studies.* The pioneer survey studies of elections were in the United States and the American literature on voting research is now prodigious. Here we can only list a few major works.

P. F. Lazarsfeld, B. Berelson and H. Gaudet, *The People's Choice*, New York, 1944.

B. Berelson, P. F. Lazarsfeld and W. N. McPhee, *Voting*, Chicago, 1954.

A. Campbell, G. Gurin and W. E. Miller, *The Voter Decides*, Evanston, 1954.

A. Campbell, P. E. Converse, W. E. Miller and D. E. Stokes, *The American Voter*, New York, 1960.

A. Campbell, P. E. Converse, W. E. Miller and D. E. Stokes, *Elections and the Political Order*, New York, 1966.

In Britain, the only books involving substantial local surveys are:[1]

M. Benney, R. H. Pear and A. H. Gray, *How People Vote*, London, 1956.

R. S. Milne and H. C. Mackenzie, *Straight Fight*, London, 1954.

—— and ——, *Marginal Seat*, London, 1958.

A. H. Birch, *Small Town Politics*, Oxford, 1959.

1. Two other local surveys are reported in articles: A. H. Birch and P. Campbell, 'Voting Behaviour in a Lancashire Constituency', *British Journal of Sociology*, **1** (1950), 197–208; P. Campbell, A. H. Birch and D. Donnison, 'Voting Behaviour in Droylesden in October 1951', *Manchester School*, **20** (1952), 57–65.

F. Bealey, J. Blondel and W. J. McCann, *Constituency Politics*, London, 1965.

I. Budge and D. W. Urwin, *Scottish Political Behaviour*, London, 1966.

J. Trenaman and D. McQuail, *Television and the Political Image*, London, 1961.

J. G. Blumler and D. McQuail, *Television in Politics*, London, 1968.

Some other books which draw together a large amount of data should also be noted:

M. Abrams, R. Rose and R. Hinden, *Must Labour Lose?* London, 1960.

R. R. Alford, *Party and Society*, Chicago, 1963 and London, 1964.

A. J. Allen, *The English Voter*, London, 1964.

G. Almond and S. Verba, *The Civic Culture*, Princeton, 1963.

J. Blondel, *Voters, Parties and Leaders*, London, 1963.

J. Bonham, *The Middle Class Vote*, London, 1954.

D. E. Butler, *The British General Election of 1951*, London, 1952.

——, *The British General Election of 1955*, London, 1955.

—— and R. Rose, *The British General Election of 1959*, London, 1960.

—— and A. S. King, *The British General Election of 1964*, London, 1965.

—— and J. Freeman, *British Political Facts 1900–1968*, London, 1969.

——, *The Electoral System in Britain Since 1918*, 2nd edn., Oxford, 1963.

F. W. S. Craig, *British Parliamentary Election Statistics 1918–1968*, Glasgow, 1968.

J. H. Goldthorpe, D. Lockwood, F. Bechhofer and J. Platt, *The Affluent Worker*, Cambridge, 1968.

M. Kinnear, *The British Voter*, London, 1968.

R. L. Leonard, *Elections in Britain*, London, 1968.

R. B. McCallum and A. Readman, *The British General Election of 1945*, Oxford, 1947.

R. T. McKenzie, *British Political Parties*, 3rd edn., London, 1964.

—— and A. Silver, *Angels in Marble*, London, 1968.

B. Mitchell and K. Boehm, *British Parliamentary Election Results 1950–1964*, Cambridge, 1966.

H. G. Nicholas, *The British General Election of 1950*, London, 1951.

E. A. Nordlinger, *The Working-Class Tories*, London, 1967.

H. Pelling, *Social Geography of British Elections, 1885–1910*, London, 1967.

P. G. J. Pulzer, *Political Representation and Elections*, London, 1967.

R. Rose, *Politics in England*, London, 1965.

G. Runciman, *Relative Deprivation and Social Justice*, London and Berkeley, 1967.

Index

More about Penguins and Pelicans

Penguinews, which appears every month, contains details
of all the new books issued by Penguins as they are
published. From time to time it is supplemented by
Penguins in Print, which is a complete list of all available
books published by Penguins (There are well over three
thousand of these.)

A specimen copy of *Penguinews* will be sent to you free
on request, and you can become a subscriber for the
price of the postage. For a year's issues (including the
complete lists) please send 30p if you live in the United
Kingdom, or 60p if you live elsewhere. Just write to
Dept EP, Penguin Books Ltd, Harmondsworth,
Middlesex, enclosing a cheque or postal order,
and your name will be added to the mailing list.

Note: *Penguinews* and *Penguins in Print* are not
available in the U.S.A. or Canada

Resources for Britain's Future

Edited by Michael Chisholm

Now it is vital to consider all our resources in their relation to one another and to ourselves so that we may be in a position to make the right decisions.

Introduced by Michael Chisholm of the Department of Geography at Bristol University this book is made up of a series of articles originally published in the *Geographical Magazine*. Written by distinguished geographers from London, Edinburgh, Reading, Liverpool, Bristol and Cambridge Universities the articles cover a wide range of subjects including transport, industry, population trends, water resources, regional development, the countryside, farming, fuel, Britain and Europe, and speculations on the future society.

Voters, Parties, and Leaders
The Social Fabric of British Politics

J. Blondel

Are we witnessing the end of class-barriers in the political behaviour of the British voter? Does the businessman vote like the railway man, the white-collar worker like the unskilled labourer?

Of course they do not. But how different are their voting habits? Trade unions are Labour-inclined. but all trade unionists are not Labour men. Are these non-Labour trade unionists exceptional? And, at the other end of the scale are Labour-inclined professional people, managers, and executives rare but interesting exceptions?

These are some of the questions which the Professor of Government in the University of Essex attempts to answer in this original book. In examining the background, outlook, and interests of voters, party members, politicians, civil servants, and party leaders, and endeavouring to trace some of the subtle threads that tie certain individuals to certain organizations, he presents an anatomy of the political world. And he asks 'What is the "Establishment" we talk of? Does it exist? And if so, does it rule?'